1968
OLDSMOBILE TORONADO
(94 SERIES)

MW01387884

For service procedures and recommendations not listed within this section, refer to the appropriate section in the forward part of this manual as the service procedures are similar to the 31 through 86 series.

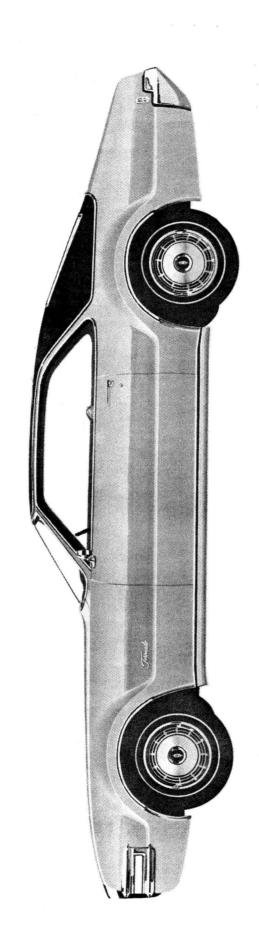

HEATER AND AIR CONDITIONER
TORONADO

CONTENTS OF SECTION 1E

HEATER

GENERAL DESCRIPTION (Fig. 1E-1)

Air enters the ventilation and heater system at the cowl vent grille, travels through the plenum chamber and into the cowl air chamber. Air can now be directed into the passenger compartment by opening the right and left side cowl doors or by opening the heater inlet door. The doors are operated by vacuum diaphragms, actuated by pushbuttons in one direction and closed by spring force in the other direction.

The ventilation and heater control pushbuttons are in a single control unit located in the instrument panel on the left side of the steering column. The control also contains the blower speed switch and the temperature control slide lever.

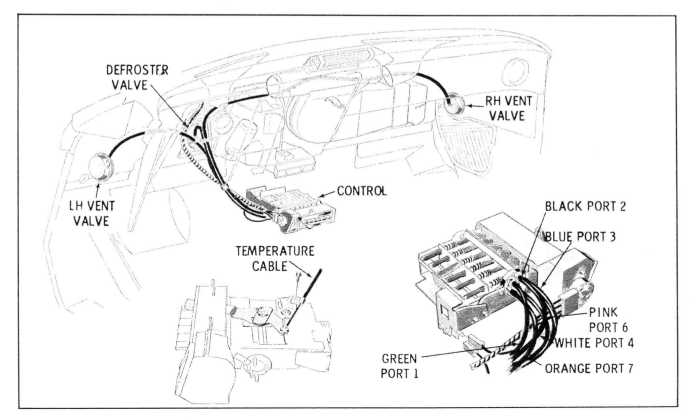

Fig. 1E-1—Heater Layout

OPERATION

Ventilation

When the MIN button is depressed the outside air and forced ventilation valve diaphragms are vented. This allows spring force to open the outside air door and move the forced ventilation valve to allow air to flow into the passenger compartment through the vent outlets in the instrument panel. Air velocity is controlled by the blower speed switch.

When the MED button is depressed, the operation is the same as when the MIN button is depressed, however the left cowl air inlet valve is also opened. Air enters the passenger compartment through the vent outlets in the instrument panel and through the left cowl air inlet.

Air velocity through the vent outlets, in the instrument panel, is controlled by the blower speed switch. Air velocity from the left cowl air inlet is controlled by forward motion of the car only.

When the MAX button is depressed, the operation is the same as when the MED button is depressed, however the right cowl inlet valve is also opened. Air enters the passenger compartment through the vent outlets in the instrument panel and through the right and left cowl air inlets.

Air velocity through the vent outlets, in the instrument panel, is controlled by the blower speed switch. Air velocity from the left and right cowl air inlets is controlled by forward motion of the car only.

Heater

When the HEAT button is depressed, vacuum is applied to the defroster and the forced ventilation valve diaphragms. This moves the defroster door to allow approximately 80% of the air to flow into the heater case and 20% to flow onto the windshield. The forced ventilation valve is moved to seal off air to the vent outlets in the instrument panel.

Outside air is drawn through the cowl air intake grille and into the heater blower and air inlet assembly. The heater blower then forces a portion of the outside air through the heater core and into the ducting system. The remaining air is forced directly into the ducting system. To obtain the desired discharge air temperature, the heater air then mixes with the unheated air in the necessary proportions.

The temperature lever operates the temperature door which controls the temperature of the discharged air by regulating the mixing of heated and unheated air. In the full left position, the flow from the heater core is completely blocked. As the lever is moved to the right, the temperature door opens, allowing more air to flow through the core and progressively decreases the amount of unheated air. In the extreme right position, the flow of unheated air is completely blocked directing all the air through the heater core, for maximum heating.

When the DEF button is depressed, the operation is the same as when the HEAT button is depressed, however the defroster diaphragm is vented and the spring moves the valve to allow approximately 80% of the air to flow onto the windshield and 20% to flow out of the heater outlets.

Rate of air flow on HEAT and DEF can be controlled by the blower speed switch.

ADJUSTMENTS

Temperature Control Cable (Fig. 1E-2)

The temperature control cable is adjusted at the heater case under the hood. To adjust hold temperature door closed at heater case and adjust turnbuckle on cable to obtain 1/8" springback of control lever from end of slot in heater control.

Air Inlet Door

Adjustment of the air inlet door and diaphragm is provided for at the diaphragm (Fig. 1E-3).

1. With the air inlet body removed, loosen set screw.

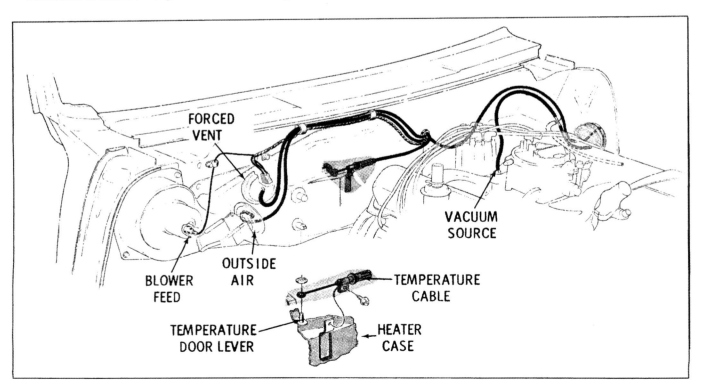

Fig. 1E-2—Temperature Control Cable Location

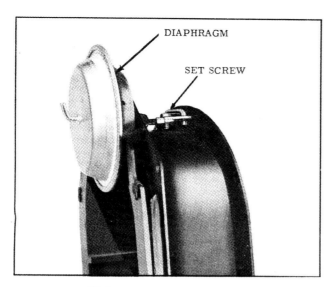

Fig. 1E-3—Air Inlet Diaphragm Adjustment

2. Pull diaphragm lever to its extreme stop, then push back 1/16".

3. While holding door closed, tighten set screw.

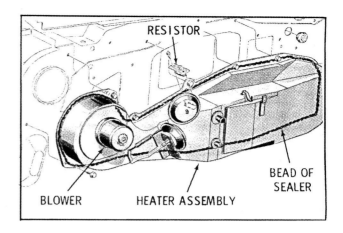

Fig. 1E-4—Heater Assembly

HEATER ASSEMBLY

Remove and Install (Fig. 1E-4)

1. Disconnect blower feed and resistor wiring.

2. Disconnect vacuum hoses from the air inlet and forced vent diaphragms.

3. Disconnect temperature cable from temperature door lever.

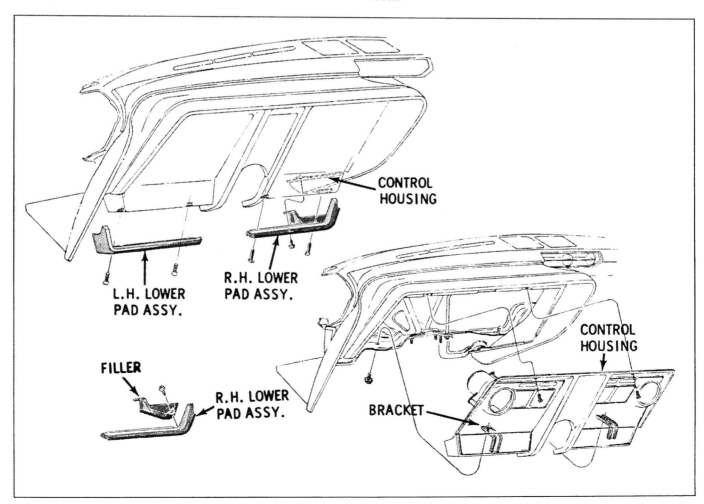

Fig. 1E-5—Trim And Filler Panel Removal

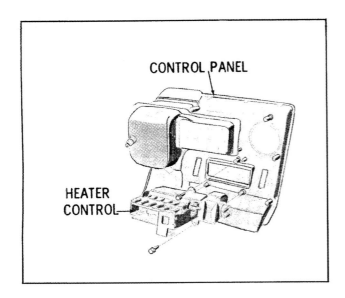

Fig. 1E-6—Control Attachment

4. Disconnect heater hoses. Keep open ends of hoses above engine coolant level to prevent loss of coolant.

5. Remove the heater assembly attaching screws.

6. Remove the heater assembly from the cowl.

7. If the heater core is to be removed, it can be removed at this time.

To install, reverse the removal procedure. Apply sealer to the mounting face of the heater assembly.

VENTILATION AND HEATER CONTROL

Remove and Install

1. Disconnect battery.

2. Remove the RH lower trim panel. (Fig. 1E-5).

3. Disconnect steering column as outlined under STEERING COLUMN, Section 9E.

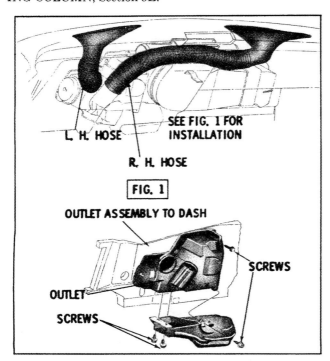

Fig. 1E-7—Heater Distributor

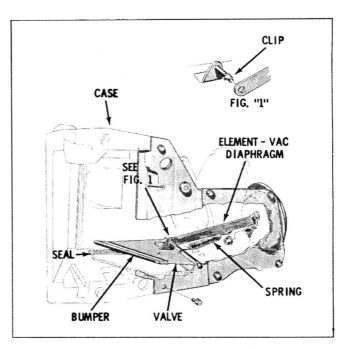

Fig. 1E-8—Heater Distributor (Rear View)

4. Loosen the two lower control panel attaching bolts and remove the two upper bolts. (Fig. 1E-5)

5. Disconnect speedometer cable from transmission. Tip control panel toward seat.

6. Disconnect the vacuum hoses, electrical connections and the temperature cable from the control.

7. Remove the three control attaching screws and remove control from control panel. (Fig. 1E-6)

To install, reverse the removal procedure.

BLOWER RESISTOR

Removal and Installation

The blower resistor is mounted on the heater case. To

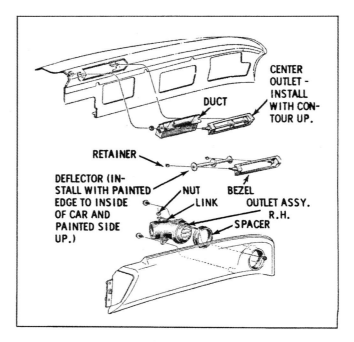

Fig. 1E-9—Vent Outlets

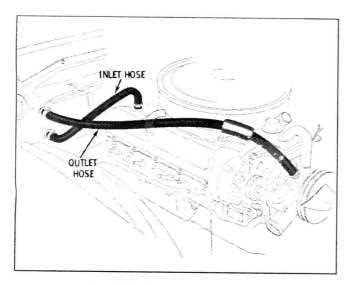

Fig. 1E-10—Heater Hose Routing

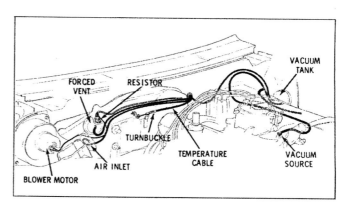

Fig. 1E-11—Electrical Connections

remove, disconnect the wiring connector and remove the attaching screws. (Fig. 1E-4)

To install, reverse removal procedure.

HEATER DISTRIBUTOR

The heater distributor, outlet and defroster hoses are installed as shown in Fig. 1E-7. Fig. 1E-8 illustrates the distributor removed from the car.

VENT DUCTS

The vent ducts are attached as shown in Fig. 1E-9. Air from the duct assembly is distributed to the vent center outlet and to the right and left side vent outlets. For removal of outlets refer to TORONADO INSTRUMENT PANEL Section 12EA.

HEATER HOSES

The heater hoses are routed as shown in Fig. 1E-10. A water valve is not used on cars equipped with a heater.

VACUUM HOSES

The routing of the vacuum hoses, electrical wiring and temperature cable is shown in Fig. 1E-11.

The vacuum hose and wiring connections and routing inside the car are shown in Fig. 1E-12.

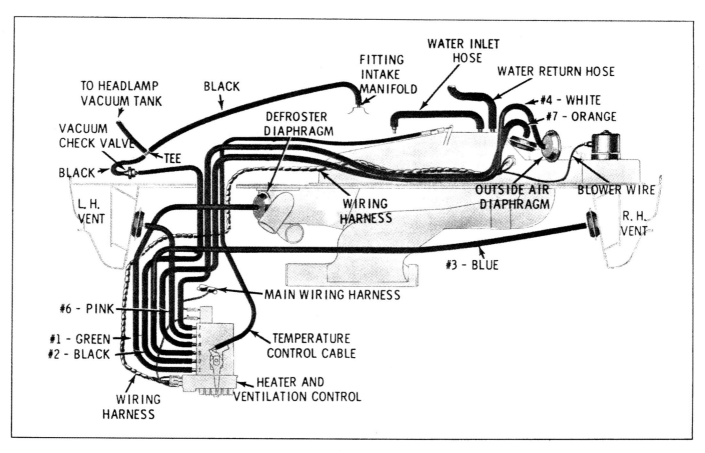

Fig. 1E-12—Vacuum Hose Connections

CUSTOM AIR CONDITIONER (MANUAL, VACUUM CONTROL)

TORONADO

GENERAL DESCRIPTION

Two types of air conditioner systems are used on the Toronado.

Custom (Manual, Vacuum Control)
Comfortron (Automatic Control)

Service information on the air conditioner systems will be covered in order as follows:

1EA Custom Air Conditioner (Manual Vacuum Control)
1EB Comfortron (Automatic Control)

For service information on General Air Conditioning items such as Compressor Servicing, Evacuating and Charging, etc., refer to GENERAL AIR CONDITIONING INFORMATION Page 1A-1.

CONTENTS OF SECTION 1EA

PERIODIC MAINTENANCE

Remove road accumulation from condenser at every engine oil change interval or as necessary.

Check and adjust compressor belt tension at each engine oil change interval.

The system should be operated for at least five minutes every two weeks.

Check refrigerant level and replenish as necessary at the start of every cooling season.

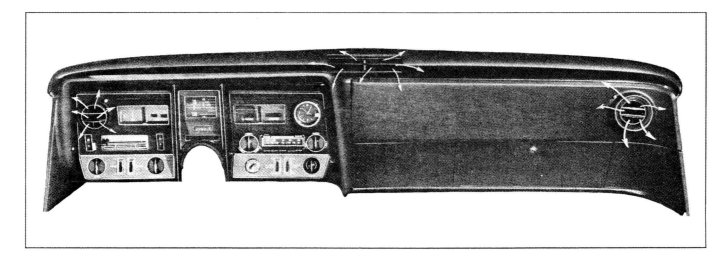

Fig. 1EA-1—Air Outlets

GENERAL DESCRIPTION

The air conditioning system provides refrigerated and dehumidified air to cool the car interior. The system uses both outside and recirculated air.

For normal cooling, A.C. control set for NORMAL, 100% outside air passes through the evaporator core. For maximum cooling, A.C. control set for RECIRC, approximately 80% recirculated air and 20% outside air is directed through the evaporator core.

AIR OUTLETS (Fig. 1EA-1)

Adjustable air outlets are located on either side of the instrument panel. The left and right air outlets may be adjusted to direct the air as desired. In addition, a center outlet is provided to allow additional upper level cooling. The sides are equipped with shut-off valves. The center outlet can be rotated to shut off air flow.

The air condition control assembly is mounted in the instrument panel. A four-speed blower switch is located in the control assembly.

FAST COOL DOWN

To rapidly cool a car which has been standing for a period of time in the sun, open the outlets, set A.C. control on NORMAL, slide temperature lever to the extreme left position and rotate blower speed switch on HI. Open car windows just long enough to expel hot air. After car has cooled, adjust temperature control lever position to suit individual comfort. Air flow can be directed by adjusting the outlets. The recommended position of the air outlets, for best over-all front and rear seat cooling, is when the side outlets are adjusted to direct the air flow along the inside roof line, and the side and center outlets are open.

DRIVING CONDITIONS

For normal driving conditions, the driver may adjust the temperature of cool air by moving the control lever to suit individual comfort. Selection of blower speeds should be regulated according to the amount of air forced into the passenger compartment by the forward motion of the car.

When driving in heavy traffic, it may be desirable to set the blower speed switch on "HI". At higher speeds, air will be forced by the forward motion of the car into the passenger compartment in greater volume, lessening the speed requirements of the blower motor. It then may be desirable to set the blower speed switch to suit individual comfort.

OPERATION

Heat Button Depressed

When HEAT button is depressed vacuum is applied to both parts of the outside air door and to the defroster door. This positions the defroster door to allow approximately 80% of the air to flow out of the heater outlet and 20% to flow onto the windshield. The outside air door is positioned to allow 100% outside air to enter the heater assembly.

When the temperature lever is moved toward the warm position, vacuum is directed to the water valve allowing engine coolant to flow through the heater core. Air flowing through the heater assembly is now warmed and flows out of the heater outlets. Temperature of heater outlet air is controlled by moving the temperature lever which is connected to the temperature door with a cable. This mixes outside air with heated air to temper the discharge air.

Air velocity is controlled by a four-speed blower switch. When the DEF button is depressed the operation is identical to HEAT except the defroster door diaphragm is vented to direct air flow to the windshield.

Vent Button Depressed

When the VENT button is depressed, vacuum is applied to both ports of the outside air door, and to the mode door. This positions the outside air door to allow 100% outside air to enter the heater assembly. With vacuum applied to the mode door, the mode door is in the A.C. position, allowing discharge air to flow out of the A.C. outlets. With the temperature lever moved to the full cool position 100% outside ambient air flows out of the A.C. outlets. When the temperature lever is moved toward the warm position, vacuum is directed to the water valve allowing engine coolant to flow through the heater core. Some of the air is now directed through the heater core by movement of the temperature door where it is warmed and mixes with the outside air to temper the discharge air from the A.C. outlets.

Air velocity is controlled by a four-speed blower switch.

Normal Button Depressed

When the NORMAL button is depressed an electrical switch is closed to start the compressor and vacuum is applied to both ports of the outside air door. This positions the outside air door to allow 100% outside air to enter the heater assembly. With vacuum applied to the mode door the door is in the A.C. position.

Air flowing through the heater assembly is cooled by the evaporator.

With the temperature lever in the full cool position all the cooled air is directed out of the A.C. outlets.

As the temperature lever is moved toward the warm position, vacuum is directed to the water valve allowing engine coolant to flow through the heater core. Some of the air is now directed through the heater core by movement of the temperature door, where it is warmed and mixes with the A.C. air to temper the discharge air from the A.C. outlets. If the temperature lever is moved to the full warm position all the air coming out of the A.C. outlets will be heated.

Air velocity is controlled by a four-speed blower switch.

Recirc Button Depressed

When the RECIRC button is depressed, an electrical switch is closed to start the compressor and vacuum is applied to one port of the outside air door. This positions the outside air door to allow 20% outside air and 80% inside air to enter the heater assembly. With vacuum applied to the mode door, the mode door is in the A.C. position.

Air flowing through the heater assembly is cooled by the evaporator.

With the temperature lever in the full cool position all the cooled air is directed out of the A.C. outlets.

As the temperature lever is moved toward the warm position vacuum is directed to the water valve allowing engine coolant to flow through the heater core. Some of the air is now directed through the heater core where it is warmed and mixes with the A.C. air to temper the discharge air from the A.C. outlets. If the temperature lever is moved to the full warm position, all the air coming out of the A.C. outlets will be heated.

Air velocity is controlled by a four-speed blower switch.

Air Outlets

The air outlets are installed as shown in Fig. 1EA-2.

SIDE OUTLETS

Adjustment

The side outlet nozzles should be free to rotate but tight enough to remain in a set position. If adjustment is required, refer to Fig. 1EA-3.

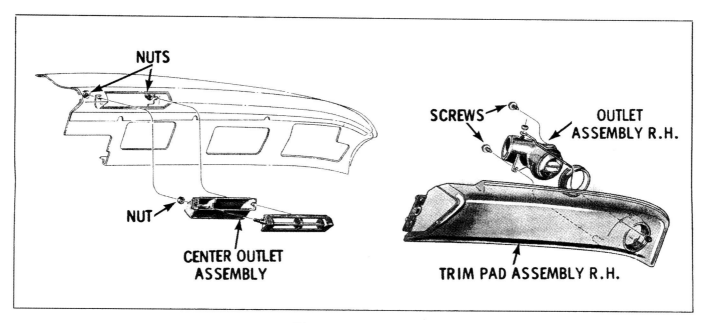

Fig. 1EA-2—Air Outlet Installation

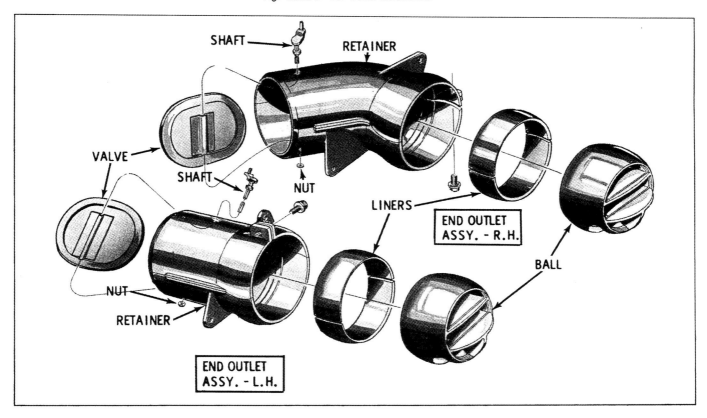

Fig. 1EA-3—Side Outlets

CONTROL

Remove and Install

1. Disconnect battery.
2. Remove the RH lower trim panel. (Fig. 1EA-4)
3. Disconnect steering column as outlined under Steering Column Section 9E.

4. Loosen the two lower control panel attaching bolts and remove the two upper bolts. (Fig. 1EA-5)
5. Tip control panel toward seat. Disconnect speedometer cable from transmission to obtain more clearance.
6. Disconnect the vacuum hoses, electrical connections and the temperature cable from the control.
7. Remove the three control attaching screws and remove control from control panel.

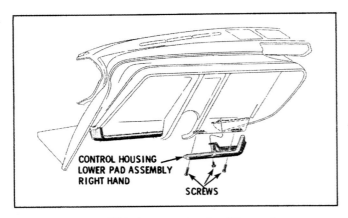

Fig. 1EA-4—Lower Trim Panel Removal

To install, reverse the removal procedure. Refer to Figs. 1EA-6 and 1EA-7 for vacuum hose and wiring connections.

BLOWER MOTOR

Remove and Install

1. Disconnect battery.
2. Disconnect wiring as necessary for accessibility.
3. Remove antenna assembly, if so equipped.
4. Remove blower motor attaching screws.
5. Rotate blower motor inside of fender and remove fan.

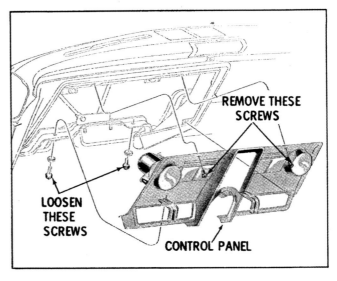

Fig. 1EA-5—Disconnecting Control Panel

6. Remove motor and blower separately, between the fender and filler plate and out through the top of the engine compartment.

To install, reverse the removal procedure.

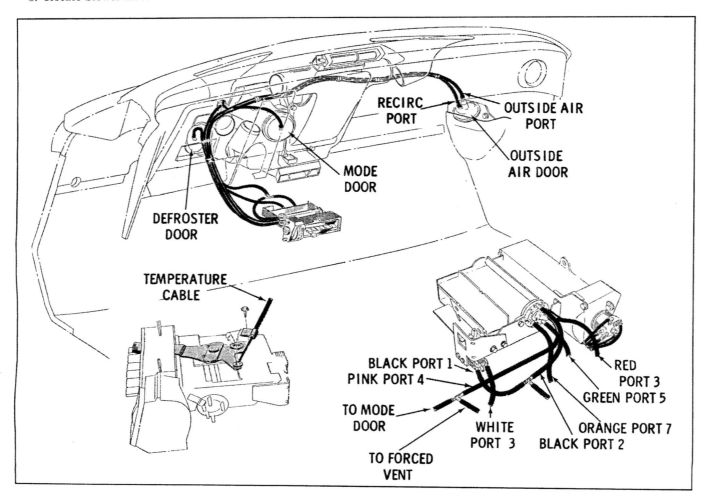

Fig. 1EA-6—Vacuum Hose Routing

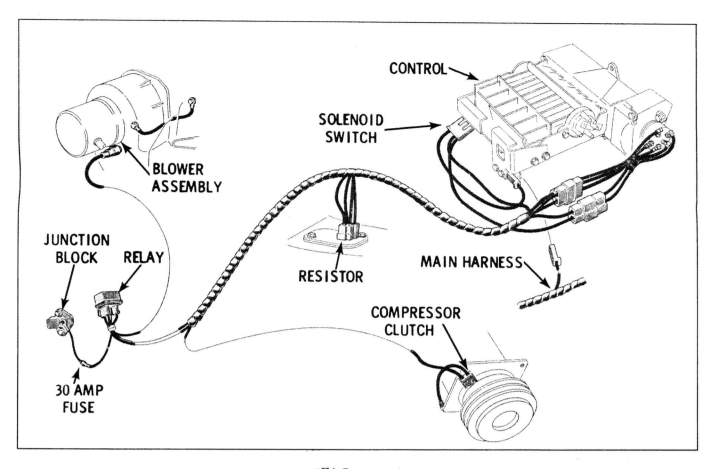

Fig. 1EA-7—Wiring Connections

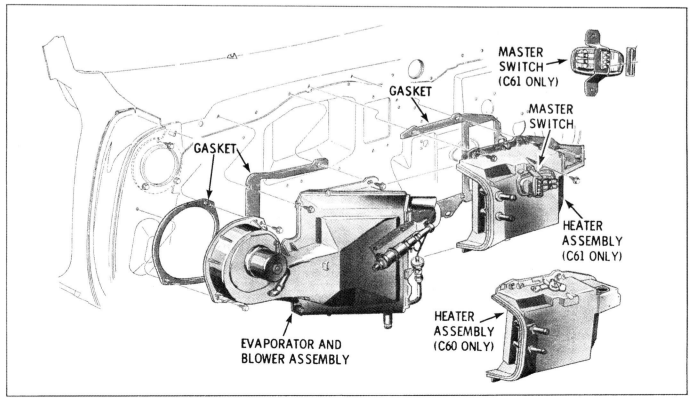

Fig. 1EA-8—Evaporator and Heater Installation

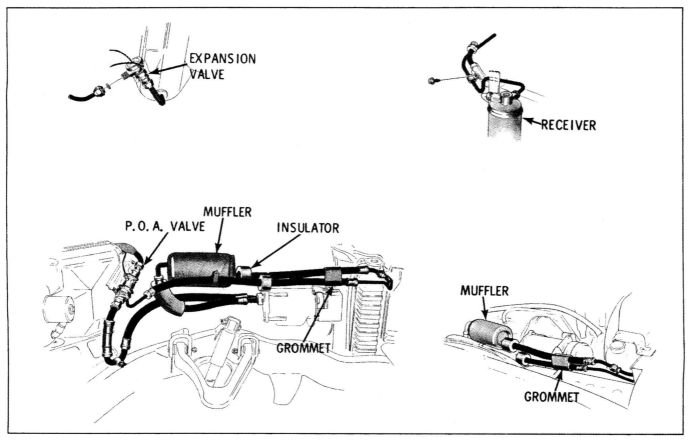

Fig. 1EA-9—Refrigerant Line Routing

HEATER CASE AND CORE

Remove and Install (Fig. 1EA-8)

1. Disconnect battery.
2. Disconnect hood from hinges and remove.
3. Disconnect vacuum hoses, electrical connections and temperature cable.
4. Remove heater hoses and suspend above engine coolant level.
5. Remove the heater case to cowl attaching screws.
6. Remove heater assembly.
7. If the heater core is to be serviced, it can be removed at this time.

To install, reverse removal procedure. Be sure all gaskets are in place. Refill radiator and check for coolant leaks.

EVAPORATOR

Remove and Install (Fig. 1EA-8)

1. Disconnect battery.
2. Disconnect hoodlight wiring.
3. Remove hood and RH hinge as an assembly.
4. Discharge system, then disconnect muffler hose at P.O.A. valve and plug fittings. (Fig. 1EA-9)
5. Disconnect vacuum hoses and wiring as necessary.
6. Remove blower motor assembly from evaporator housing and tie motor back against fender inner panel.
7. Disconnect high pressure hose at condenser and plug fittings.
8. Remove muffler clamp attaching bolt and slide muffler assembly forward out of the way.
9. Remove line at expansion valve and plug fittings.
10. Remove evaporator housing attaching bolts.
11. Loosen heater assembly attaching screws until duct can be moved to the left of elongated holes.
12. Remove top right attaching screw in heater duct.
13. Remove evaporator assembly.

To install reverse removal procedure. Evacuate and charge the system.

AIR INLET VALVE ASSEMBLY

Remove and Install

1. Remove evaporator assembly.
2. Remove the three screws holding the air inlet valve assembly to the cowl. (Fig. 1EA-8)
3. Remove cowl trim pad.
4. Remove the five screws securing the inlet valve to the cowl. (Fig. 1EA-10)
5. Remove the vacuum hoses.

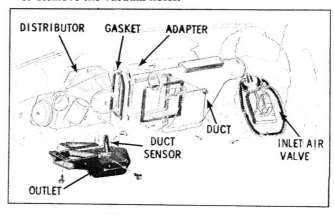

Fig. 1EA-10—Air Distribution Ducts

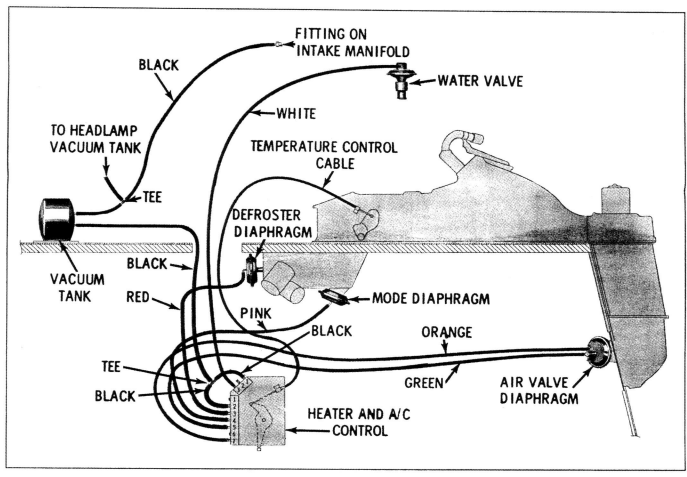

Fig. 1EA-11—Vacuum Hose Identification

6. Remove the air inlet valve assembly.

To install, reverse the removal procedure. Be sure that the alignment pin on the air inlet assembly enters the hole in the cowl. Refer to Fig. 1EA-11 for correct valve hose installation.

AIR DISTRIBUTION DUCTS

The air distribution ducts, distributor assembly and heater outlet are attached as shown in Fig. 1EA-10.

TEMPERATURE CABLE

Adjustment (Fig. 1EA-12)

The cable is connected to a cam lock device that assures positive closing of the temperature door. The cable must be adjusted so there is 1/16" to 1/8" springback with the valve fully closed (Fig. 1EA-12).

CONDENSER AND RECEIVER

The condenser is mounted in front of the radiator, and is attached as shown in Fig. 1EA-13. The condenser and receiver are serviced as an assembly.

REFRIGERANT LINES

The refrigerant lines are attached and routed as shown in Fig. 1EA-9.

The suction line, high pressure line, and high pressure muffler are of one piece construction and are serviced as an assembly.

COMPRESSOR

Belt Adjustment (Fig. 1EA-14)

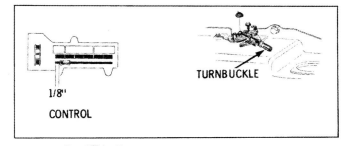

Fig. 1EA-12 — Temperature Cable Adjustment

Tool 33-70M is used to check the compressor belt tension. If belts require adjustment:

1. At rear of compressor, loosen link to compressor bolt.

2. At front of compressor, loosen link to compressor strut bolts.

3. Loosen compressor upper pivot bolts.

4. Pivot the compressor evenly at the front and rear until correct belt tension is obtained.

Check belt alignment and torque all bolts loosened.

Bolt Size	Torque Ft. Lbs.
5/16"	26
3/8"	35
7/16"	50

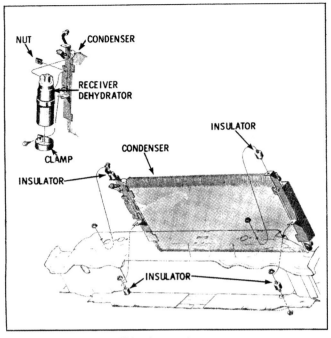

Fig. 1EA-13—Condenser Mounting

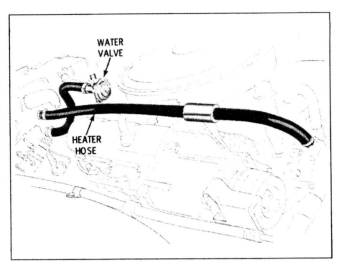

Fig. 1EA-15—Water Valve and Heater Hose Installation

Removal

1. Discharge the refrigerant system.
2. Disconnect compressor clutch wire at compressor connector.
3. Remove belt from compressor pulley.

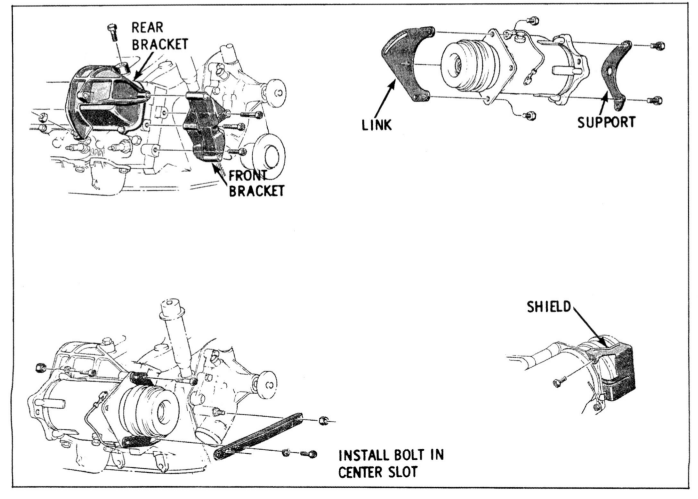

Fig. 1EA-14—Compressor Mounting Brackets

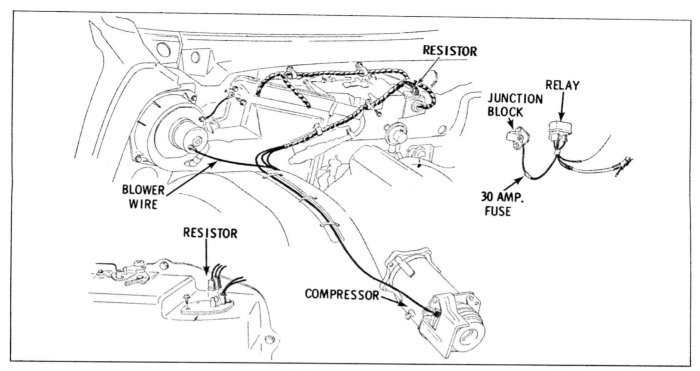

Fig. 1EA-16—Electrical Wire Routing

4. Remove the bolt holding the fittings connector to the compressor, then remove the assembly from the compressor. Tape lines and fittings to prevent entry of dirt and moisture.

5. Remove the compressor to bracket bolts, then remove the compressor assembly.

Installation

1. Position the compressor on the mounting bracket, then install and tighten the compressor to bracket bolts.

2. Connect compressor clutch wire.

3. Install two new "O" rings on the valve port openings and position the fittings connector on the compressor. Install the mounting bolts and tighten to 22 ft. lbs. torque.

4. Install belt and adjust tension using Tool 33-70M.

5. If compressor was removed for some internal malfunction and foreign material has circulated throughout the system, proceed as follows:

    a. Install a charging line to the compressor discharge Schrader valve and to a drum of refrigerant 12.

    b. Disconnect the liquid line from the dehydrator receiver assembly on the inlet side, and cap the dehydrator receiver immediately.

    c. Open the refrigerant drum valve and turn the drum upside down to allow liquid refrigerant to flush through the condenser and out the line. Use approximately 2 lbs. of refrigerant for this operation.

    d. Close the drum valve and connect the dehydrator receiver assembly.

    e. Remove the expansion valve screen and clean or replace as necessary.

    f. Remove the charging line from the compressor, install the gauge set, and evacuate the entire system.

    g. Recharge the system.

HEATER HOSE

The heater hose and water valve installation is shown in Fig. 1EA-15.

BLOWER RESISTOR

The blower resistor is installed in the heater assembly and

can be removed by disconnecting the electrical connections and removing the two attaching screws. (Fig. 1EA-16)

WIRING

For wiring location and routing in the engine compartment, refer to Fig. 1EA-16. For wiring connections at individual air conditioner components, refer to Fig. 1EA-17.

AIR CONDITIONING DIAGNOSIS

If a car is in for service with a complaint of high outlet temperatures on the road but appears to operate normally during tests, a quick check to determine which unit is at fault can be made using the following procedure.

VISUAL CHECKS

1. Check temperature door to make sure that it seals in the cool position. Adjust if necessary.

2. Check air hoses and ducts for proper connection.

3. Check vacuum hoses for correct routing and connection.

A leaking engine water valve could cause a slight rise in outlet temperature.

4. Check sight glass for "clear" condition.

5. Check compressor clutch to make sure that it engages.

6. Check compressor belt, adjust if necessary.

OPERATIONAL TEST

Install air conditioning gauge set, operate the engine at 1500 rpm in Neutral. Set control on Recirculate with blower at low speed.

1. Check evaporator pressure. If pressure is 30 psi or less and outlet air temperature is too warm, check to see that the expansion valve is clamped tightly to the evaporator outlet pipe and that the insulation is in place.

If the feeler bulb installation and insulation are satisfactory, a leak in the bulb is indicated and the expansion valve should be replaced.

2. If the evaporator pressure is above 30 psi, even with

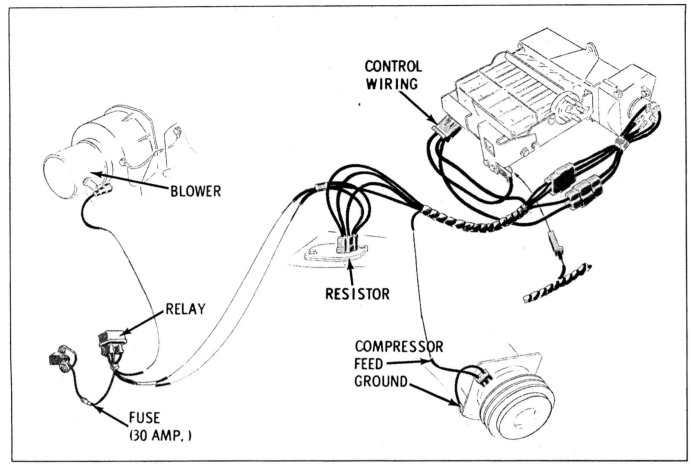

CONTROL
WIRING

BLOWER

RESISTOR

RELAY

COMPRESSOR
FEED
GROUND

FUSE
(30 AMP.)

Fig. 1EA-17—Electrical Connections

blower motor wire disconnected, replace the P.O.A. valve.

3. If evaporator pressure is 29 psi ± 1 psi and the outlet air temperature is normal, partially cover the condenser to obtain head pressure of 300 psi. If evaporator pressure rises above 30 psi, replace the expansion valve. If evaporator pressure remains at 29 psi during test, there is a possibility of water or moisture in the system which could freeze under certain conditions, and a new receiver dehydrator may be required.

PERFORMANCE TEST

The Performance Test should be made with the car doors open, the temperature control lever fully to the left, A/C control set at NORMAL, blower speed switch on "HI", all air outlets open, an auxiliary fan in front of the radiator, and the car hood partially down.

1. Remove Schrader valve fitting cap at the suction throttling valve.

2. Install Adapter J-5420 on the low pressure gauge hose, and connect the adapter to the Schrader valve fitting on the suction throttling valve, then momentarily open low pressure gauge valve to purge gauge hose.

3. Remove the high pressure Schrader valve protective cap from the back side of the high pressure muffler and install high pressure gauge hose with Adapter J-5420. Be sure high pressure gauge valve is closed.

4. Momentarily open high pressure gauge to purge the gauge and hose.

5. With transmission in PARK or NEUTRAL and parking brake applied, adjust engine speed to 2000 rpm.

6. After temperature and humidity have been determined, compare test results with the PERFORMANCE CHART.

7. When test is completed, disconnect gauge hoses, and install protective caps.

8. Install Schrader valve fitting cap at the suction throttling valve, and high pressure muffler.

PERFORMANCE CHART
TORONADO

In Front of Condenser		Evaporator Pressure At Suction Throttling Valve ± 1 psi	Engine rpm	Discharge Air Temp. R.H. Nozzle ± 2°F.	Pressure High (Discharge) ± 20 psi
Relative Humidity	Air Temp. °F.				
20	70 80 90 100 110	29 29 29 29 32	2000	39 39 41 42.5 46	170 197 242 298 357
30	70 80 90 100 110	29 29 29 30 37	2000	39 41 45 47.5 57.5	177 205 265 316 377
40	70 80 90 100 110	29 29 29.5 33 42	2000	40 42.5 47.5 54 63	183 213 277 335 390
50	70 80 90 100 110	29 29.5 30 38 47	2000	40 44 50 60 75	190 222 292 354 420
60	70 80 90 100	29 30 32 42	2000	40.5 45 52.5 65	198 230 305 373
70	70 80 90 100	29.5 30 33 47	2000	41 46 55 70	205 240 319 392
80	70 80 90 100	30 31 35 51	2000	42 47.5 57.5 75	212 248 332 405
90	70 80 90 100	30 33 36 55	2000	42 48 60 78	220 256 344 420

DIAGNOSIS OF PERFORMANCE TEST RESULTS

CONDITION AND CAUSE	CORRECTION
EVAPORATOR PRESSURE TOO HIGH A. Defective suction throttle valve. B. Loose compressor drive belt. C. Defective clutch or coil. D. Defective expansion valve. E. Expansion valve capillary tube not tight to evaporator suction line. F. Clutch slippage.	A. Replace. B. Adjust as outlined. C. Check or replace as necessary. D. Replace as necessary. E. Check clamp for tightness. F. Refer to CLUTCH SLIPPAGE.
HIGH PRESSURE SIDE OF SYSTEM TOO HIGH A. Restricted air flow through condenser. B. Air in system or overcharge of refrigerant. C. Restriction in condenser, dehydrator receiver assembly, discharge or liquid line.	A. Remove foreign material from engine radiator and condenser. B. Momentarily discharge system on discharge side with engine not running; then, operate system and recheck pressure. Repeat as necessary. Check sight glass with system under load. C. Remove parts, inspect for restricted passage, and clean or replace.
NOZZLE DISCHARGE AIR TOO WARM (With other readings OK) A. Low refrigerant charge. B. Poor seal-Evaporator to cowl. C. Temperature Control Cable misadjusted.	A. Check and add refrigerant as necessary. B. Correct sealing. C. Adjust.
CLUTCH SLIPPAGE A. Head pressure too high. B. Pulley wobbles.	A. Discharge system until bubbles appear in sight glass and then add one pound of refrigerant. B. Check and replace, if necessary, the pulley bearing. If pulley has been worn by bearing, replace pulley.
EVAPORATOR PRESSURE TOO LOW A. Insufficient Refrigerant charge. B. Defective suction throttling valve. C. Defective expansion valve.	A. Add refrigerant. B. Replace. C. Replace.
VELOCITY OF AIR AT DISCHARGE NOZZLES TOO LOW A. Restricted evaporator core in evaporator assembly. B. Restricted air hoses. C. Defective blower motor. D. Defective switches, relay or resistor. E. Poor wiring connection (Low voltage at blower.) Poor ground at blower.	A. Wash evaporator core. Restricted evaporator core caused by freezing. Adjust suction throttling valve. B. Inspect and replace if necessary. C. Check and replace if necessary. D. Check and replace if necessary. E. Correct wiring.
WATER BLOWING OUT AIR DISCHARGE NOZZLE A. Plugged or kinked evaporator drain hose.	A. Clean or align as necessary.
INOPERATIVE CONTROLS A. Inadequate vacuum. B. Temperature cable improperly adjusted.	A. Check vacuum. All controls should move with 10" Hg. Check hoses. B. Adjust cable.

COMFORTRON AIR CONDITIONING
(AUTOMATIC CONTROL)

CONTENTS OF SECTION 1EB

INTRODUCTION

The Comfortron air conditioning uses an automatic temperature control system which allows the driver to preset a desired temperature, between 65 and 85 degrees, which is then automatically maintained regardless of changes in ambient air temperatures.

Outside of the automatic control system, which is covered in this section, the basic air conditioning components are similar to the procedures outlined in Custom Air Conditioning Section 1EA. Service procedures pertaining only to the Comfortron system are covered in this section.

GENERAL DESCRIPTION

The Comfortron system consists of four major components:
1. Temperature Sensors
   a. In-car
   b. Ambient
   c. Duct
2. Control Panel
3. Transducer
4. Power Servo

In addition to the four major components, an electrical and vacuum system is used to control the complete system.

Sensors

The sensors consist of a special type of resistor (Thermistor) which varies inversely to temperature change. As the temperature rises, the resistance decreases; as the temperature falls, the resistance increases. The three sensors are connected in series.

The in-car sensor, located at the bottom of the control, Fig. 1EB-1 is positioned so that it senses the temperature of the interior of the car.

The ambient sensor, Fig. 1EB-2, mounted in the blower inlet duct senses the temperature of the air entering the system.

The duct sensor, mounted on the air outlet, Fig. 1EB-3, is positioned so that it senses discharge air temperature for the full range from heating to air conditioning.

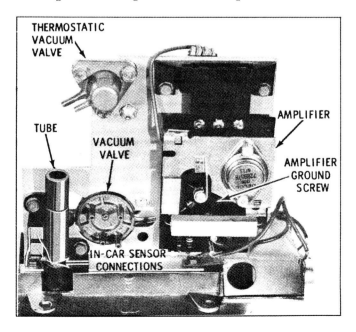

Fig. 1EB-1—In-Car Sensor Location

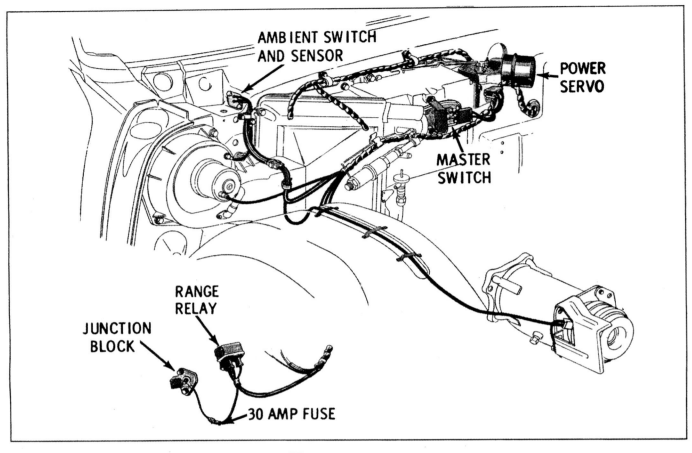

Fig. 1EB-2—Ambient Sensor Location

Control Panel (Fig. 1EB-4)

The control panel located in the instrument panel contains the Amplifier, Temperature Dial and In Car Sensor.

The amplifier is a two stage DC amplifier which provides a voltage output proportional to the input signal from the sensors to control the transducer.

The amplifier is serviced only as an assembly.

The temperature dial is graduated in 5° divisions between 65° and 85° allowing the driver to select any desired temperature within this range.

The temperature dial operates a rheostat. Setting the dial sets the resistance valve of the rheostat. This resistance, in series with the resistances of the three sensors, forms a voltage divider network supplying a voltage signal to the amplifier. If any of the sensors detect a change in temperature, or the driver changes the temperature dial rheostat setting, the resultant resistance change causes the voltage signal to the amplifier to vary accordingly.

Transducer (Fig. 1EB-5)

The transducer, mounted on the lower center of the cowl, below the instrument panel, is an electro-mechanical device that converts the DC voltage signal from the amplifier to a proportionate vacuum output that controls the power servo unit.

The transducer is constructed of four major parts; the vacuum regulator valve, wire element, production adjusting

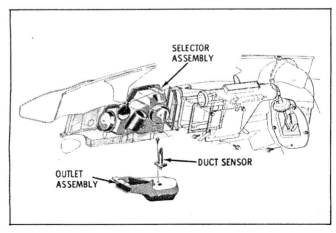

Fig. 1EB-3—Duct Sensor Location

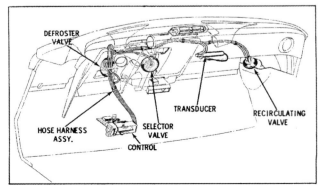

Fig. 1EB-4—Control Panel

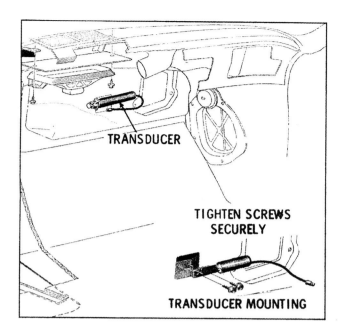

Fig. 1EB-5—Transducer

mechanism, and housing. The valve is a force actuated type where the output is proportioned to the force applied by the wire element. The wire element is enclosed in a steel tube housing that provides rigidity as well as protection from air currents.

During periods when the amplifier is supplying a weak, or no electrical signal, the wire element contracts, allowing a large amount of vacuum flow to the power servo unit. When the amplifier emits a stronger signal, the wire element is heated and expands, thereby diminishing the vacuum flow to the power servo unit. No attempt should be made to adjust the transducer during any service operation.

Power Servo (Fig. 1EB-6)

The power servo is mounted on the left top side of the heater case assembly in the engine compartment. It is composed of four basic parts; a vacuum diaphragm assembly, an electrical circuit board (blower speed switch), a rotary vacuum valve and a door link attached to the temperature door.

The vacuum diaphragm is connected to a pivot arm, and positions the pivot arm in response to the regulated vacuum output from the transducer. The pivot arm actuates the temperature door, the rotary vacuum valve and the blower speed switch.

The temperature door controls the proportions of cooled and heated air that are mixed to provide the proper discharge air temperature.

The rotary vacuum valve provides the necessary control for the operation of the mode door and the outside air door diaphragm.

The electrical circuit board controls the blower speeds through the use of resistors.

The following components are also used to operate the Comfortron system.

Thermostatic Vacuum Valve (Engine Compartment)

A valve mounted on the water valve which prevents the system from operating until the engine coolant reaches 120°F.

Thermostatic Vacuum Valve (Inside Car)

A valve mounted on the control panel which allows vacuum to pass through it whenever the in-car temperature is above 70°F.

Vacuum Master Switch

This switch located on the heater assembly turns on the blower motor whenever vacuum is applied to it.

Ambient Switch

The ambient switch located in the blower inlet duct, energizes the compressor clutch whenever the ambient temperature rises above approximately 35°F. The ambient switch and the ambient sensor are assembled as one unit.

Range Relay

The range relay is located in the engine compartment on the right fender filler plate. When the sliding lever on the instrument panel control is moved to HI, a switch on the control is closed and energizes the range relay. The range relay allows voltage from the junction block to by-pass a fixed resistor permitting the blower to operate in one of the five high range speeds.

Vacuum Relay

The vacuum relay located in the engine compartment, allows vacuum to pass from the transducer to the Power Servo

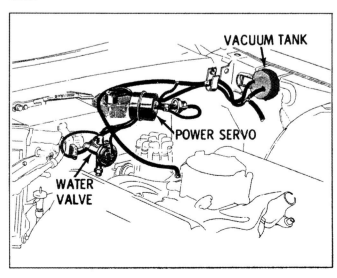

Fig. 1EB-6—Power Servo

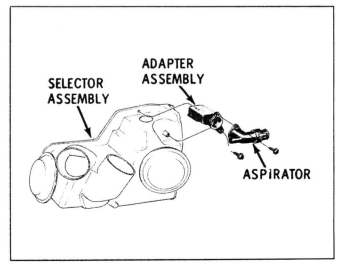

Fig. 1EB-7—Aspirator

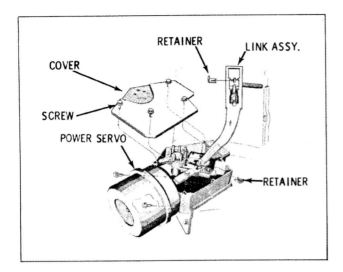

Fig. 1EB-8—Power Servo Removal

as long as vacuum is present from the engine. If engine vacuum drops, the vacuum relay closes, sealing off the vacuum line to the Power Servo, locking it in position.

Vacuum Tank

The vacuum tank, located in the engine compartment below the left front fender, is used to store engine vacuum so that the system can continue to operate even though engine vacuum is low.

Vacuum Check Valve

The vacuum check valve is an integral part of the tank and prevents loss of vacuum stored in the vacuum tank whenever engine vacuum drops.

ASPIRATOR (Fig. 1EB-7)

The aspirator is attached to the top of the selector assembly. Air is passing through the aspirator whenever the blower motor is operating. When air passes through the aspirator, it causes a low pressure area on the inside tube of the aspirator. A hose connects the aspirator to the in-car sensor tube. Due to low pressure in the tube, the in-car air is drawn over the in-car sensor through the grille on the front of the control panel.

Mode Door

A door in the distributor assembly that directs air flow either out of the air conditioning or heater ducts.

Temperature Door

A door in the heater assembly, controlled by the Power Servo, that controls the temperature of the air that comes out of the air outlets.

Defroster Door

A door in the selector assembly that directs air onto the windshield whenever the sliding lever is moved to DEFROST or DE-ICE. The door is controlled by a vacuum diaphragm.

OPERATION

While Comfortron is regulating, warm air can come from the A/C outlets (approx. 95°). This will occur just before the system changes from A/C mode to heat mode.

The operation of the Comfortron A.C. system is controlled at the control panel. The sliding lever can be positioned in five positions.

OFF-With the sliding lever in the OFF position, vacuum is shut off from the system and the system is inoperative. Voltage to the temperature control system remains on until the ignition key is turned off.

HI-With sliding lever in the HI position, engine coolant above 120°F., inside car temperature above 70°F., vacuum is supplied to the system. Movement of the sliding lever activates a switch on the control which energizes the range relay. With the range relay energized, the fixed resistor is by-passed and the blower operates in one of the five speeds in high range. The system is on automatic control.

LO-With the sliding lever in the LO position, engine coolant above 120°F., inside car temperature above 70°F., vacuum is supplied by the system. Current to the blower motor must pass through a fixed resistor and blower operates in one of the five speeds in low range. The system is on automatic control.

DEFROST

With the sliding lever in the DEFROST position, operation of the system is identical to the HI position except that approximately 80% of the air is directed to the windshield. The other 20% flows out of the heater outlets. The temperature of the air coming out of the defroster outlets can be either warm or cold as the system is on automatic control. The defroster air temperature is dependent on the temperature dial setting on the control, the temperature inside the car and outside temperature.

DE-ICE

With the sliding lever in the DE-ICE position, the thermal and temperature vacuum valves are by-passed. Vacuum is supplied to the system regardless of in-car or engine coolant temperature. The sensors are by-passed so the system is no longer on automatic control. Movement of the temperature dial has no effect on the system.

In the DE-ICE position, the defroster door directs the air to the windshield. The system is in maximum heat and maximum blower speed position, however temperature of DE-ICE air will be dependent on engine coolant temperature.

SERVICE PROCEDURES

Service procedures listed in this section pertain to the Comfortron system only. For procedures not listed refer to Section 1EA.

ASPIRATOR (Fig. 1EB-7)

Remove and Install

1. Remove aspirator hose from aspirator.
2. Remove screw holding aspirator to adapter.
To install, reverse removal procedure.

POWER SERVO

Remove and Install

1. Open hood, disconnect battery.
2. Disconnect vacuum hose and wiring connector from power servo.
3. Remove the four cover attaching screws, then remove cover. (Fig. 1EB-8)
4. Remove the retainer then disconnect link assembly from power servo.
5. Remove the power servo to heater case attaching screws then remove power servo.
To install, reverse removal procedure, making sure that the vacuum and electrical connectors are installed tightly.

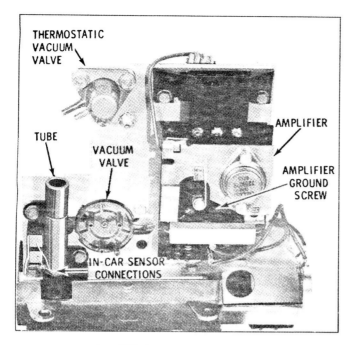

Fig. 1EB-9—In Car Sensor Removal

IN-CAR SENSOR

Remove and Install

1. Remove Comfortron control from instrument panel. (Refer to Section 1EA)

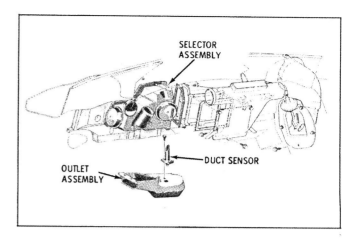

Fig. 1EB-10—Duct Sensor

2. Remove two sensor to control attaching screws. (Fig. 1EB-9)

To install, reverse removal procedure.

DUCT SENSOR

Remove and Install

1. Disconnect wiring connector from duct sensor.

2. Remove the heater outlet from the selector assembly. (Fig. 1EB-10)

3. Remove the sensor from the heater outlet.

To install, reverse the removal procedure, making sure the electrical connector is installed securely.

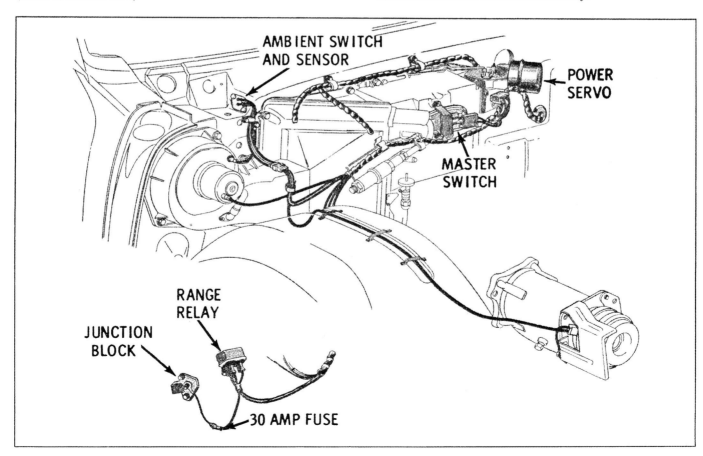

Fig. 1EB-11—Ambient Sensor and Switch

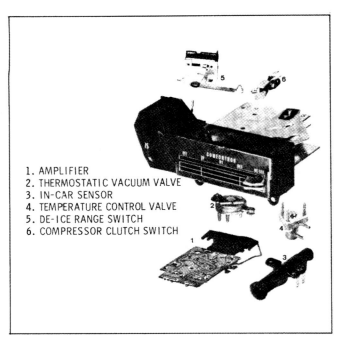

1. AMPLIFIER
2. THERMOSTATIC VACUUM VALVE
3. IN-CAR SENSOR
4. TEMPERATURE CONTROL VALVE
5. DE-ICE RANGE SWITCH
6. COMPRESSOR CLUTCH SWITCH

Fig. 1EB-12—Control Components

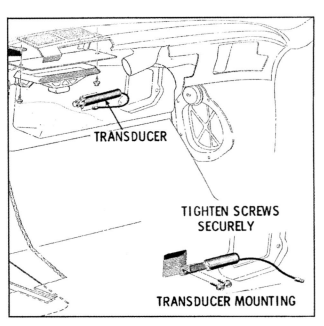

Fig. 1EB-14—Transducer Mounting

AMBIENT SENSOR AND SWITCH

The ambient sensor and switch assembly, located in the blower inlet duct can be removed by disconnecting the electrical connector, then removing the two attaching screws. (Fig. 1EB-11)

MASTER SWITCH

Remove and Install

1. Disconnect vacuum hoses and electrical connector.
2. Remove the two master switch attaching screws and remove master switch from the heater. (Fig. 1EB-11)

To install, reverse removal procedure. Vacuum hoses can be reinstalled on any connector.

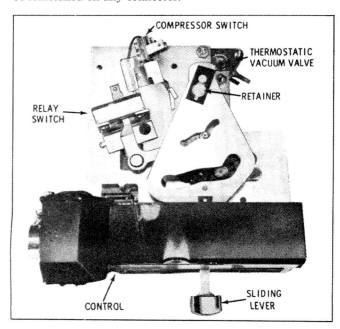

Fig. 1EB-13—Control Components

COMFORTRON CONTROL (Fig. 1EB-12)

The amplifier, range switch, temperature vacuum valve, vacuum control valve, rheostat and compressor switch can be serviced after removing the control from the instrument panel, then removing the control cover. To remove control refer to Control Remove and Install - Section 1EA.

If component parts of the control are to be serviced they can be replaced as follows: (Fig. 1EB-12 and 1EB-13)

AMPLIFIER

The amplifier is attached with three screws. Connections to the amplifier are of the plug-in type.

RANGE SWITCH

The range switch can be removed by removing the attaching screw and disconnecting the actuating arm from the sliding lever.

THERMOSTATIC VACUUM VALVE

The thermostatic vacuum valve is attached with two screws.

COMPRESSOR SWITCH

The compressor switch is attached with one screw. When replacing the compressor switch, it must be adjusted so it will be off when the sliding lever is in the "OFF" position. With the sliding lever in any of the other positions, the compressor switch must be on.

VACUUM CONTROL VALVE

The vacuum control valve can be removed by removing the attaching screw and the push-on spring nut, then disconnecting the valve from the sliding lever.

RHEOSTAT AND TEMPERATURE DIAL

The rheostat and temperature dial can be removed by disconnecting the electrical wires and removing the attaching screws.

TRANSDUCER

Remove

1. Disconnect electrical connector. (Fig. 1EB-14)

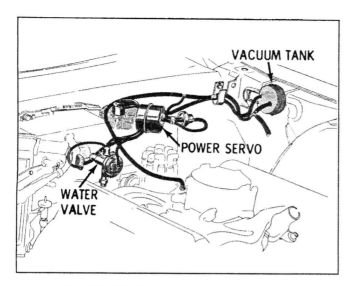

Fig. 1EB-15—Vacuum Hose and Tank Location

2. Remove the transducer attaching screws.
3. Lower transducer and remove the two vacuum hoses.

Install

1. Install vacuum hoses on the transducer. Note that the hoses and connectors are of different size and must be installed in proper order.

2. Install the attaching screws.

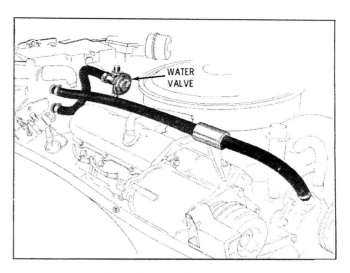

Fig. 1EB-16—Water Valve Installation

The transducer attaching screws must be tightened securely as proper operation of the complete system is dependent on a good ground at the transducer.

VACUUM TANK

The vacuum tank is installed as shown in Fig. 1EB-15.

WATER VALVE

The water valve and thermostatic vacuum switch is in-

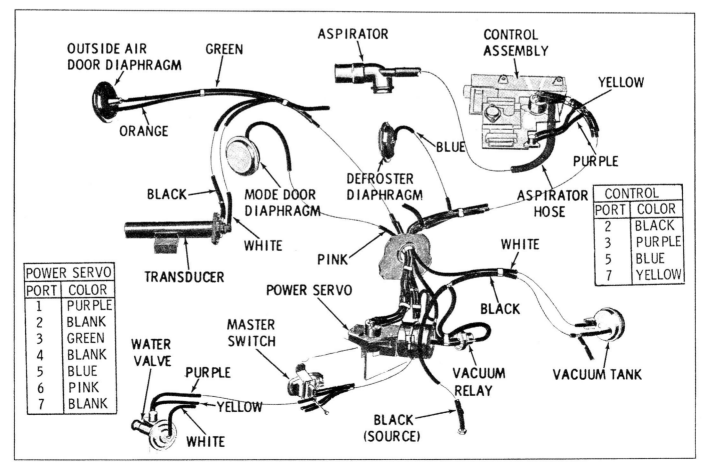

POWER SERVO	
PORT	COLOR
1	PURPLE
2	BLANK
3	GREEN
4	BLANK
5	BLUE
6	PINK
7	BLANK

CONTROL	
PORT	COLOR
2	BLACK
3	PURPLE
5	BLUE
7	YELLOW

Fig. 1EB-17—Vacuum Hose Routing

stalled in the heater inlet hose. The valve installation and heater hose routing is shown in Fig. 1EB-16.

VACUUM HOSES

Vacuum hoses used in the Comfortron system are color coded to assist in correct routing of the hoses.

Whenever any of the vacuum hoses or connections are disconnected be sure the hoses and connectors are installed securely. Vacuum hose routing is shown in Fig. 1EB-17.

A restrictor is used in the end of the purple hose that attaches to the water valve. When replacing the vacuum hose harness, the restrictor must be removed from the old harness and placed in the new harness.

WIRING

Wiring used on the Comfortron system is shown in Figs. 1EB-18 and 1EB-19. Whenever wiring connectors are removed, be sure that the connectors are fully seated on their terminals and that the terminals are clean and fit tightly. Due to the low current used in some of the circuits, a poor connection could cause a malfunction in the Comfortron system.

REFRIGERATION SYSTEM

The refrigeration system used with the Comfortron system is basically the same as used on the custom air conditioning. For repairs to the refrigeration system or components, refer to Section 1A and 1B. When making a performance test on comfortron equipped cars, the sliding lever should be on high blower speed and the vacuum line must be disconnected from the power servo and plugged.

CHARGING THE SYSTEM

The system can be charged by the refrigerant drum, disposable can or charging station method only after being evacuated as outlined in Section 1A. When charging the Comfortron System, follow the procedures as outlined in Section 1A. However, the control must be set on automatic.

CHECKING COMFORTRON SYSTEM

Before checking the Comfortron system, it is essential that the function and operation of each unit in the system is understood and that the engine is running and the coolant is warm, it is important to remember that at the transducer, the lower the voltage, the higher the vacuum, the higher the voltage, the lower the vacuum. If Tester J-22368 is not available, many of the FUNCTION CHECKS, Pages 1EB-12 through 1EB-18 can still be made without the use of the tester.

Tester J-22368 (Fig. 1EB-21) is available to assist in locating malfunctions in the system. Operating instructions are attached to the back of the tester.

When using Tester J-22368, Step 2 of the operating instructions states, "Disconnect large vacuum hose from transducer and insert tester tee in vacuum line". However, on 54 through 86 Series cars, remove the vacuum hose from the power servo and insert tester tee in this vacuum line as it is more easily accessible. Under Step 4 of the tester instructions, the only correction listed is a defective transducer. If the diaphragm in the vacuum relay is ruptured, the same problem will be encountered as a defective transducer. To determine which unit is defective, pinch the vacuum hose between the tester and the vacuum relay. If tester still indicates a defective

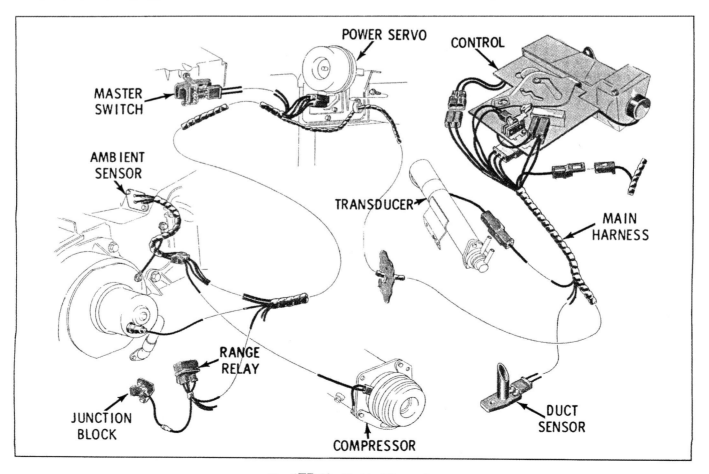

Fig. 1EB-18—Electrical Connections

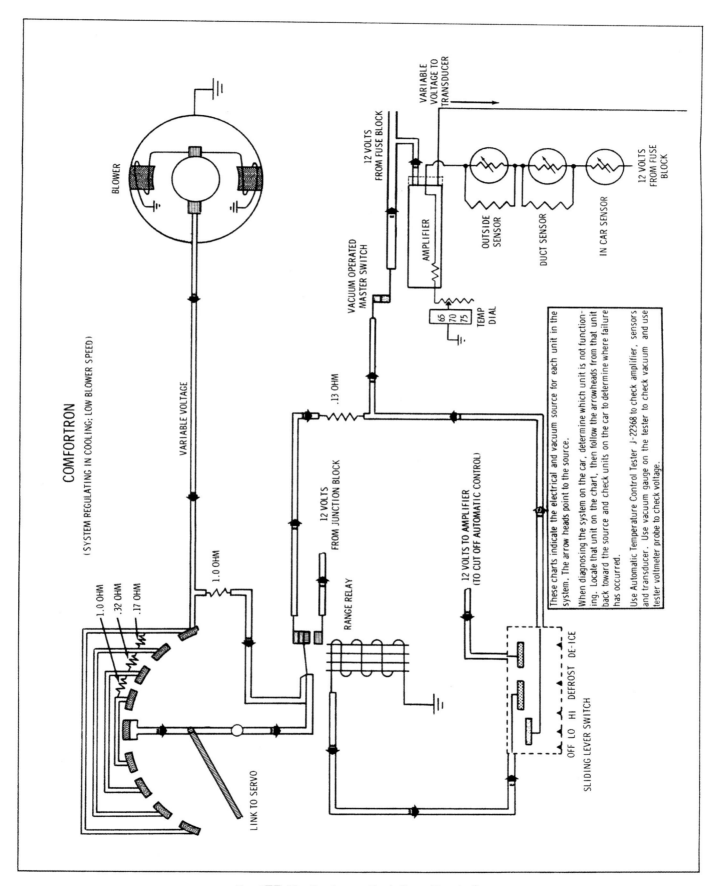

Fig. 1EB-19—Comfortron Check Chart (Electrical)

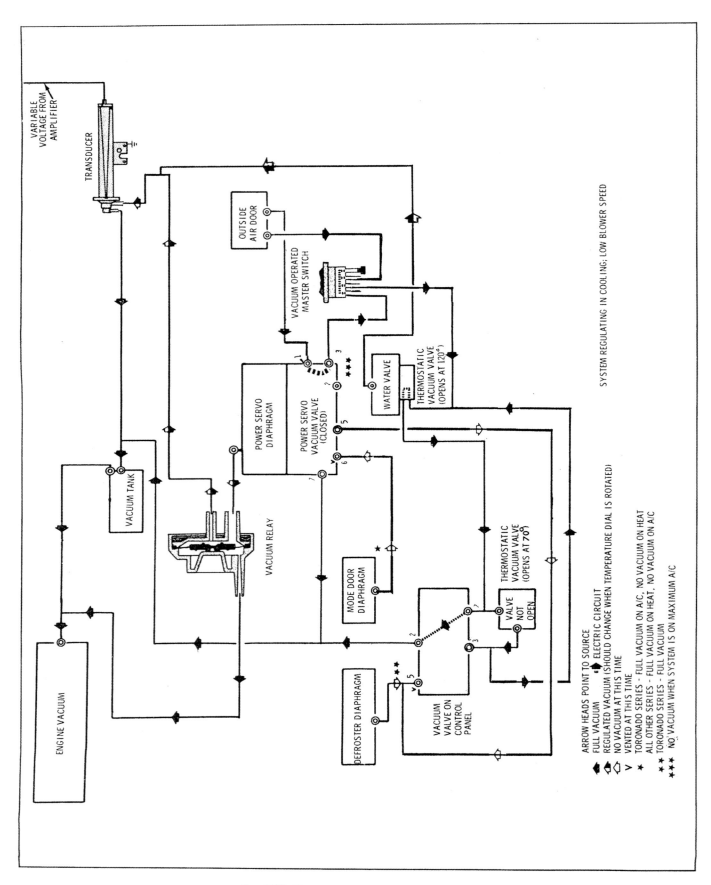

Fig. 1EB-20—Comfortron Check Chart (Vacuum)

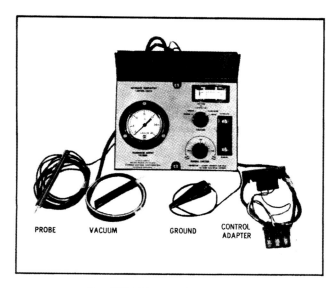

Fig. 1EB-21—Comfortron Tester

transducer, then replace it. If problem is now cured, then replace vacuum relay.

CHECKING SENSOR CIRCUIT FOR A SHORT

1. First indication of a shorted sensor in the Comfortron will be delivery of cold air (max. Air Conditioning) in the "Lo", "High" or "Defrost" position, regardless of temperature dial setting.

   a. Check sensor visually for indication of a short.

   b. Substitute known good sensor in wiring harness to check each sensor individually.

CHECKING SENSOR CIRCUIT FOR AN OPEN

1. Use Tester J-22368 voltmeter probe. Position voltage knob in the probe position. Attach tester ground clip to car. Disconnect amplifier connector.

2. With ignition switch in the ACC position, test for battery voltage at both terminals on all three connectors.

   a. Obtaining a voltage reading at both terminals indicates a good sensor.

   b. Obtaining a voltage reading at one connection only indicates an open circuit in the sensor. Replace sensor.

   c. No voltage at either connection on a sensor indicates the open circuit is at one of the other sensors or the battery feed wire to the sensor circuit is open.

AMPLIFIER AND TEMPERATURE DIAL TEST

(Step 3 on Tester J-22368)

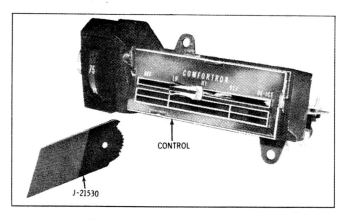

Fig. 1EB-22—Adjusting Temperature Control Dial

1. With tester connected and set as in Step 3, disconnect both wires from amplifier. Voltage should go to 8 to 9 volts minimum and should go to zero when connecting the two terminals on amplifier together with a jumper wire or screwdriver.

2. If voltage is as indicated in Step 1, replace temperature dial and rheostat assembly.

3. If voltage did not change in Step 1, replace amplifier.

TEMPERATURE CONTROL DIAL ADJUSTMENT

1. Connect Tester J-22368 to Comfortron amplifier as outlined by instructions on back of Tester.

2. Follow step 5A of Instructions, setting Manual Control on Tester as follows:

            Toronado   150

3. Insert available Tool J-21530 or a 6" steel scale to the left of temperature dial. (Fig. 1EB-20)

4. While holding temperature dial on 75°, rotate Tool J-21530 or 6" steel scale until voltmeter on Tester J-22368 reads 6.5 volts.

Tool J-21530 must contact teeth on side of temperature dial.

FUNCTION CHECK

Normal Operating System

Check to be made with engine operating and coolant warm.

1. Set control lever in OFF position. Rotate temperature dial to max. heat position.

   a. No air flow from any outlets.

2. Move control lever to NORMAL HI position.

   a. Blower speed and air flow increases.

3. Move control lever to NORMAL LO position.

   a. Blower comes on high speed.

   b. Hot air comes chiefly from heater outlet with some air from defroster outlets.

4. Rotate temperature dial to max. cold position. (65°)

   a. Cold air comes from air conditioning outlets.

   b. Blower speed goes from high down through low and up to high.

5. Move control lever to DEFROST position.

   a. Cold air comes chiefly from defroster outlets, with some air from heater outlets.

6. Move control lever to DE-ICE position.

   a. Hot air comes chiefly from defroster outlets, with some air from heater outlet.

   b. Blower operating on high speed.

FUNCTIONAL TEST ITEM 1-A

AIR SHOULD NOT FLOW FROM ANY OUTLET
BUT
AIR DOES FLOW FROM OUTLETS

TEST CONDITIONS:

1. SET CONTROL LEVER IN "OFF" POSITION.
2. SET TEMPERATURE DIAL TO MAX. WARM POSITION (85 OR HIGHER).
3. ENGINE OPERATING AND COOLANT WARM.
4. TESTER IS USED AS A VOLTMETER.

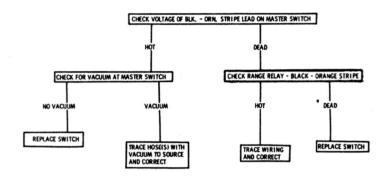

FUNCTIONAL TEST ITEM 2-A

BLOWER SHOULD COME ON HIGH SPEED
BUT
BLOWER DOES NOT COME ON HIGH SPEED

TEST CONDITIONS:

1. SET CONTROL LEVER IN NORMAL "LOW" POSITION.
2. ROTATE TEMPERATURE DIAL TO MAX. WARM POSITION (85° F. OR HIGHER).
3. ENGINE OPERATING AND COOLANT WARM.
4. TESTER USED AS VOLTMETER.

NOTE: IF AMBIENT TEMPERATURE IS HIGH OR THE IN-CAR TEMPERATURE IS HIGH (85° F. OR HIGHER), THE BLOWER WILL NOT STAY ON "HI". TO RUN THIS PROCEDURE UNDER HIGH TEMPERATURE CONDITIONS, REMOVE POWER CYLINDER HOSE FROM POWER SERVO AND SEAL THE HOSE. APPLY 12" HG. OF VACUUM ON THE POWER SERVO SO THAT THE POWER SERVO ARM GOES TO FULL WARM POSITION (DOOR LINK FULL RETRACTED).

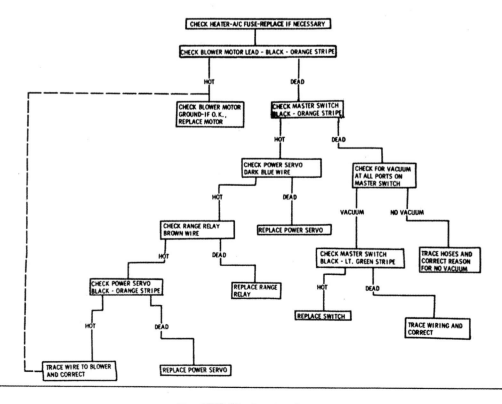

Fig. 1EB-23—Functional Test

FUNCTIONAL TEST ITEM 2-B

HOT AIR SHOULD COME CHIEFLY FROM HEATER OUTLET
BUT
HOT AIR DOES NOT COME FROM HEATER OUTLET

TEST CONDITIONS:

1. SET CONTROL LEVER IN NORMAL "LOW" POSITION.
2. ROTATE TEMPERATURE DIAL TO MAX. WARM POSITION (85° F. OR HIGHER).
3. ENGINE OPERATING AND COOLANT WARM.
4. TESTER TO BE USED AT THE AMPLIFIER CONNECTOR.

NOTE: IF AMBIENT TEMPERATURE IS HIGH OR IN-CAR TEMPERATURE IS HIGH (ABOVE 85° F.), SYSTEM
WILL NOT PUT OUT MAXIMUM HEAT AND MAY EVEN GO INTO A/C BECAUSE SYSTEM WILL TRY TO
MAINTAIN 85° F. INSIDE CAR. THE ONLY WAY TO CHECK THE SYSTEM AS A UNIT WOULD BE TO
HAVE THE CAR AMBIENT AT 75° F. AND THE ENGINE SHOULD NOT BE SO HOT THAT EXTREMELY
HOT AIR WOULD BE HITTING THE AMBIENT SENSOR.

COLD AIR COMES FROM HEATER OUTLET

CHECK FOR VACUUM AT WATER VALVE - WHITE HOSE

VACUUM → TRACE HOSE-CORRECT SOURCE OF VACUUM

NO VACUUM → CHECK IF HOSE FROM WATER VALVE TO HEATER IS WARM

COLD → REPLACE WATER VALVE

WARM → CHECK TRANSDUCER OUTPUT VACUUM USING TESTER VAC. GAGE-LARGE BLACK HOSE ON POWER SERVO

AIR COMES FROM OTHER THAN HEATER OUTLET

CHECK AMPLIFIER OUTPUT VOLTAGE USING TESTER J-22368
ROCKER SWITCH - AUTOMATIC
VOLTAGE SWITCH - AMP. OR CONTROL CALIBRATION

LESS THAN 5.9 VOLTS

MORE THAN 5.9 VOLTS → CHECK SENSOR STRING AND AMPLIFIER USING TESTER J-22368

LOW-LESS THAN 7" HG → CHECK TRANSDUCER INPUT VACUUM-WHITE HOSE

LOW → CHECK & REPAIR TRANSDUCER VACUUM SUPPLY

O.K. → REPLACE TRANSDUCER

HIGH-MORE THAN 7" HG → OBSERVE POSITION OF DOOR LINK

RETRACTED → CHECK THAT POWER SERVO IS MOVING DOOR TO MAX. HEAT POSITION

EXTENDED → CHECK FOR BINDING LINKAGE-IF O.K., REPLACE POWER SERVO

DOOR IN FULL HEAT POSITION → CHECK FOR VACUUM AT MODE DOOR DIAPHRAGM - PINK HOSE

DOOR NOT IN FULL HEAT POSITION → REPAIR AND ADJUST TEMPERATURE DOOR AND DOOR LINK AS NECESSARY

NO VACUUM → CHECK FOR BINDING DEFECTIVE MODE DOOR LINKAGE

VACUUM → TRACE AND CORRECT SOURCE OF VACUUM ON MODE DOOR DIAPHRAGM

Fig. 1EB-24—Functional Test

FUNCTIONAL TEST ITEM 3-A

BLOWER SPEED AND AIR FLOW SHOULD INCREASE
BUT
BLOWER SPEED AND AIR FLOW DOES NOT INCREASE

TEST CONDITIONS:

1. SET CONTROL LEVER IN NORMAL "HIGH" POSITION.
2. ROTATE TEMPERATURE DIAL TO MAX. WARM POSITION (85 OR HIGHER).
3. ENGINE OPERATING AND COOLANT WARM.
4. TESTER USED AS A VOLTMETER.

NOTE: AT HIGH AMBIENT TEMPERATURES, IT MAY BE NECESSARY TO SET THE
TEMPERATURE DIAL IN MAX. COLD POSITION (65 OR LESS) TO MAINTAIN
HIGH SPEED BLOWER OPERATION.

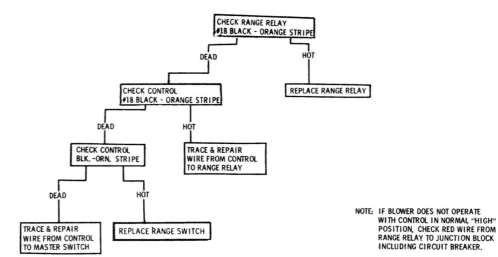

NOTE: IF BLOWER DOES NOT OPERATE
WITH CONTROL IN NORMAL "HIGH"
POSITION, CHECK RED WIRE FROM
RANGE RELAY TO JUNCTION BLOCK
INCLUDING CIRCUIT BREAKER.

VACUUM OPERATION

CONTROL						
			FUNCTION			
			AUTOMATIC			
PORT	CONNECTION	OFF	LOW-HI	DEFROST	DE-ICE
2	INPUT	SEAL	FEED	FEED	FEED
3	DE-ICE OVERRIDE	VENT	SEAL	SEAL	VAC
5	DEFROST DOOR	SEAL	VAC	VENT	VENT
7	THERMAL VAC. VALVES	VENT	VAC	VAC	VAC

POWER SERVO			
		FUNCTION	
PORT	CONNECTION	MAX. A/C	MAX. HEAT
4	BLOCKED	--	--
1	MASTER SWITCH (VAC. INPUT)	SEAL	CONNECT TO #2 & #3
3	OUTSIDE AIR DOOR	REG. VAC./VENT	CONNECT TO #1 & #2
2	BLOCKED		
5	MODE OVERRIDE (VAC. INPUT)	VAC.	SEAL
6	MODE DOOR	VAC.	VENT
7	BLOCKED	--	--

Fig. 1EB-25—Functional Test

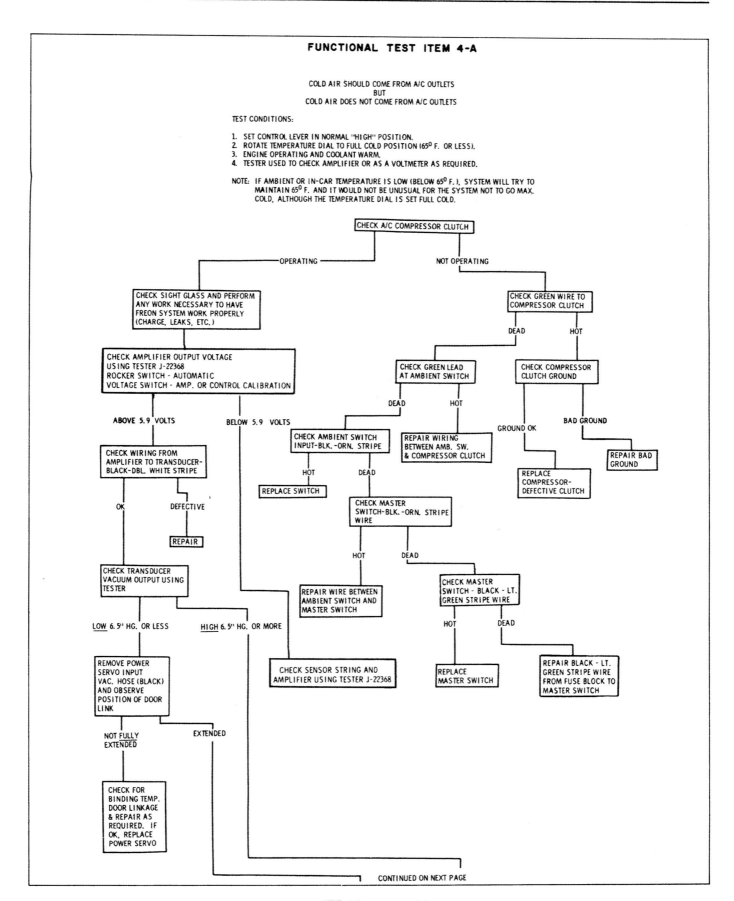

Fig. 1EB-26—Functional Test

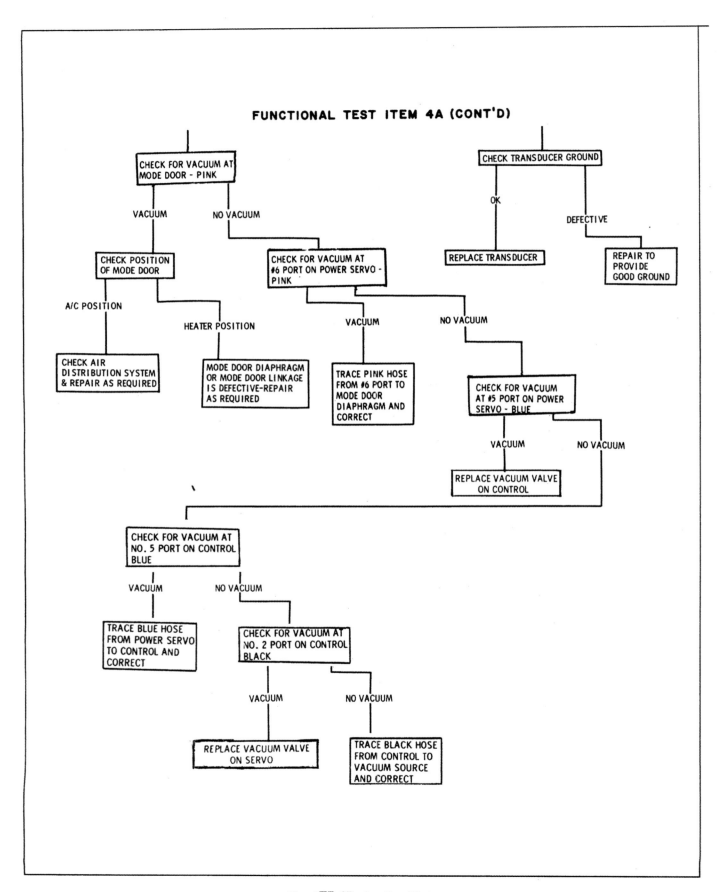

Fig. 1EB-27—Functional Test

FUNCTIONAL TEST ITEM 4-B

BLOWER SPEED SHOULD GO FROM HIGH DOWN THROUGH LOW AND UP TO HIGH
BUT
BLOWER SPEED DOES NOT GO FROM HIGH DOWN THROUGH LOW AND UP TO HIGH

TEST CONDITIONS:

1. SET CONTROL LEVER IN NORMAL "HIGH" POSITION.
2. SET TEMPERATURE DIAL IN MAX. WARM POSITION (85 OR HIGHER) - FUNCTION TEST IS TO ROTATE DIAL FROM FULL WARM TO FULL COLD.
3. ENGINE OPERATING AND COOLANT WARM.

NOTE: HIGH-LOW-HIGH BLOWER CHANGES ARE ONLY TRANSIENT AS THE POWER SERVO GOES FROM MAXIMUM HEAT TO MAXIMUM COLD IN THE FUNCTION TEST.

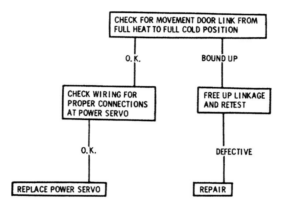

FUNCTIONAL TEST ITEM 5-A

COLD AIR SHOULD COME FROM DEFROSTER OUTLETS
BUT
COLD AIR DOES NOT COME FROM DEFROSTER OUTLETS

TEST CONDITIONS:

1. SET CONTROL LEVER IN "DEFROST" POSITION.
2. ROTATE TEMPERATURE DIAL TO MAX. COLD POSITION (65 OR LESS).
3. ENGINE OPERATING AND COOLANT WARM.

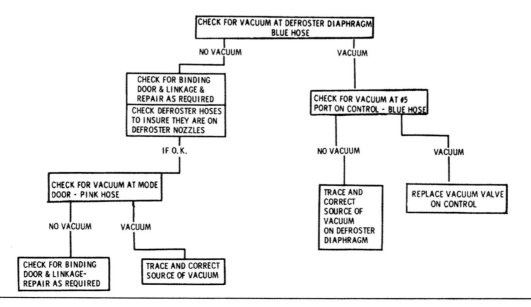

Fig. 1EB-28—Functional Test

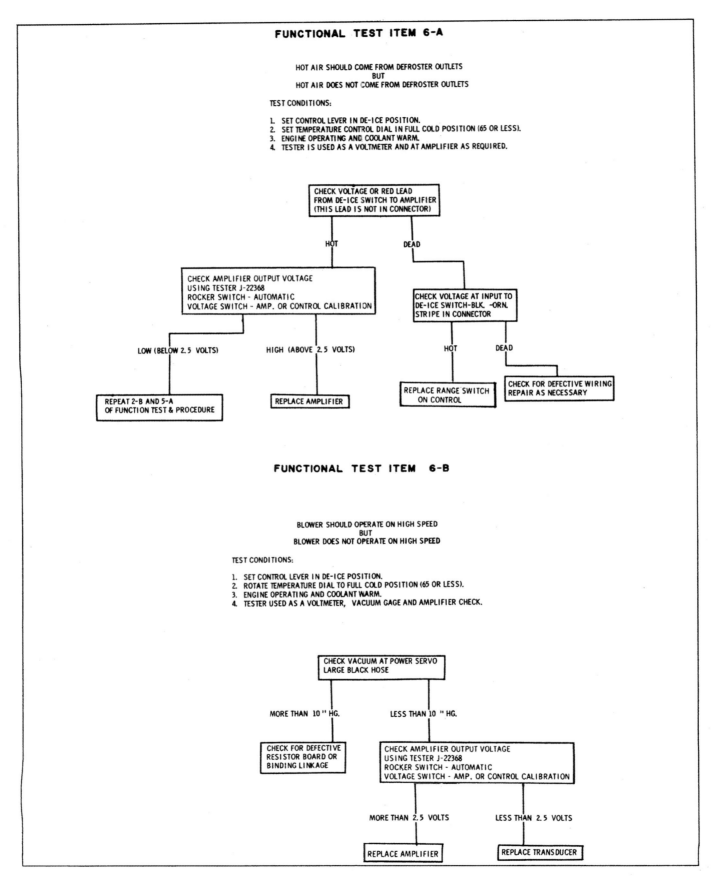

FUNCTIONAL TEST ITEM 6-A

HOT AIR SHOULD COME FROM DEFROSTER OUTLETS
BUT
HOT AIR DOES NOT COME FROM DEFROSTER OUTLETS

TEST CONDITIONS:

1. SET CONTROL LEVER IN DE-ICE POSITION.
2. SET TEMPERATURE CONTROL DIAL IN FULL COLD POSITION (65 OR LESS).
3. ENGINE OPERATING AND COOLANT WARM.
4. TESTER IS USED AS A VOLTMETER AND AT AMPLIFIER AS REQUIRED.

CHECK VOLTAGE OR RED LEAD
FROM DE-ICE SWITCH TO AMPLIFIER
(THIS LEAD IS NOT IN CONNECTOR)

HOT

DEAD

CHECK AMPLIFIER OUTPUT VOLTAGE
USING TESTER J-22368
ROCKER SWITCH - AUTOMATIC
VOLTAGE SWITCH - AMP. OR CONTROL CALIBRATION

CHECK VOLTAGE AT INPUT TO
DE-ICE SWITCH-BLK. -ORN.
STRIPE IN CONNECTOR

LOW (BELOW 2.5 VOLTS)

HIGH (ABOVE 2.5 VOLTS)

HOT

DEAD

REPEAT 2-B AND 5-A
OF FUNCTION TEST & PROCEDURE

REPLACE AMPLIFIER

REPLACE RANGE SWITCH
ON CONTROL

CHECK FOR DEFECTIVE WIRING
REPAIR AS NECESSARY

FUNCTIONAL TEST ITEM 6-B

BLOWER SHOULD OPERATE ON HIGH SPEED
BUT
BLOWER DOES NOT OPERATE ON HIGH SPEED

TEST CONDITIONS:

1. SET CONTROL LEVER IN DE-ICE POSITION.
2. ROTATE TEMPERATURE DIAL TO FULL COLD POSITION (65 OR LESS).
3. ENGINE OPERATING AND COOLANT WARM.
4. TESTER USED AS A VOLTMETER, VACUUM GAGE AND AMPLIFIER CHECK.

CHECK VACUUM AT POWER SERVO
LARGE BLACK HOSE

MORE THAN 10 '' HG.

LESS THAN 10 '' HG.

CHECK FOR DEFECTIVE
RESISTOR BOARD OR
BINDING LINKAGE

CHECK AMPLIFIER OUTPUT VOLTAGE
USING TESTER J-22368
ROCKER SWITCH - AUTOMATIC
VOLTAGE SWITCH - AMP. OR CONTROL CALIBRATION

MORE THAN 2.5 VOLTS

LESS THAN 2.5 VOLTS

REPLACE AMPLIFIER

REPLACE TRANSDUCER

Fig. 1EB-29—Functional Test

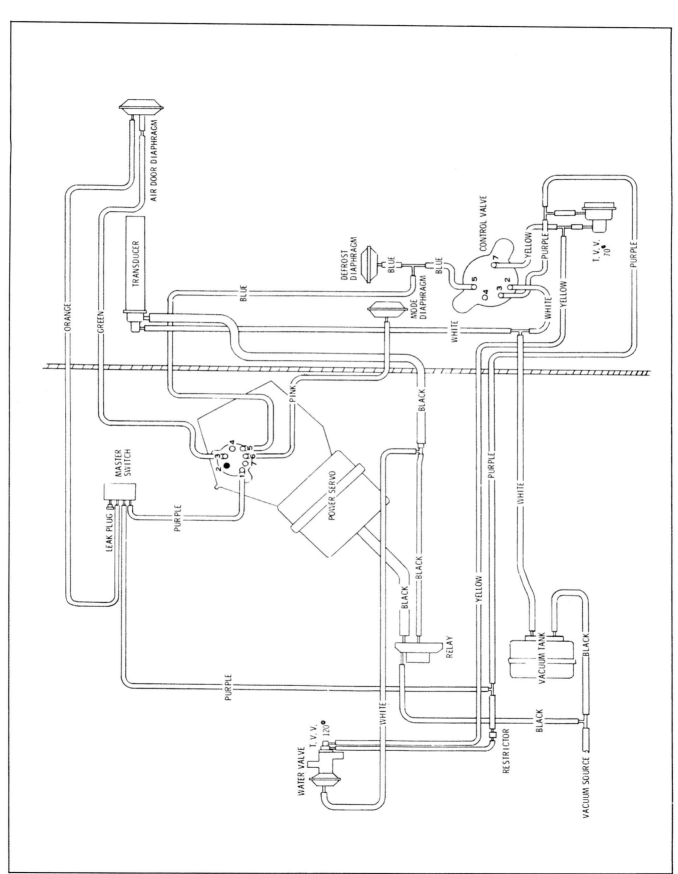

Fig. 1EB-30—Vacuum Hose Routing

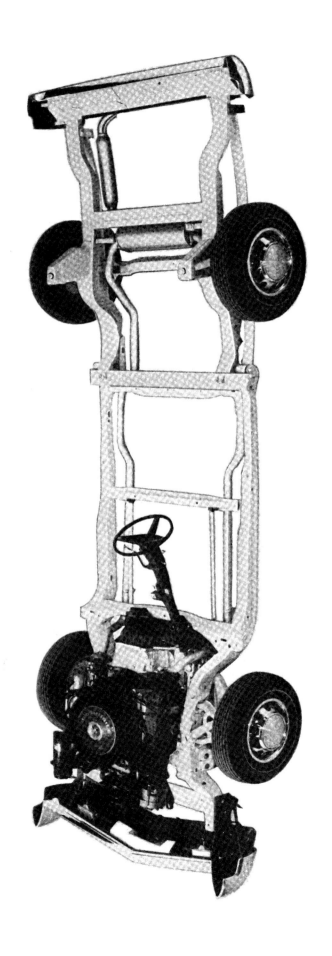

FRAME AND BODY MOUNTING
TORONADO

CONTENTS OF SECTION 2E

FRAME

When supporting car on a floor jack or floor stands, the car should be supported at the lift points only. Under no conditions should the car be supported at the extreme ends of frame, at the center of a frame side rail or on the rear crossbar.

FRAME ALIGNMENT

The diagram shown in Fig. 2E-1 can be used to check the alignment of a frame that is suspected of being damaged.

The reference points are to be checked with a tram gauge. The difference in corresponding measurements will indicate where straightening operations are necessary.

Corresponding measurements must be equal within 1/4".

1. Measure A-A. If not equal, rear end of frame or center section is misaligned.
2. Measure B-B. If not equal, then front section of frame is misaligned.

Measurement between the frame horns is given in Fig. 2E-1.

FRAME REPAIR

In case of collision, frame members can often be straightened to the required dimensions. However, some parts of the frame are service parts and can be replaced. The service parts available for the frame are the upper and lower control arm brackets, shock absorber brackets and the radiator support bar. If the front crossmember or the side rails cannot be satisfactorily straightened it will be necessary to replace the complete frame assembly.

BODY MOUNTS

To minimize vibration and noise, the body mounts must be properly torqued. Body mounts which are not tightened sufficiently will cause body "chucking" and damage to the cushions. If body mounts are tightened excessively, the cushioning effect of the cushion is impaired, resulting in squeaks and body "drumming". Torque body mount bolts to 40 ft. lbs.

For installation of body mounts, refer to Fig. 2E-2.

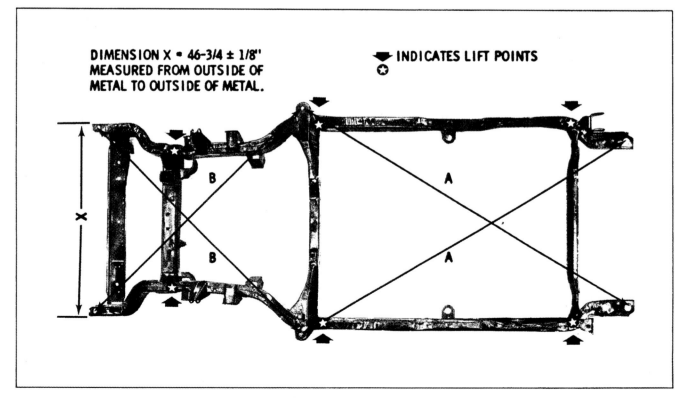

DIMENSION X • 46-3/4 ± 1/8" MEASURED FROM OUTSIDE OF METAL TO OUTSIDE OF METAL.

INDICATES LIFT POINTS

Fig. 2E-1—Frame - Toronado

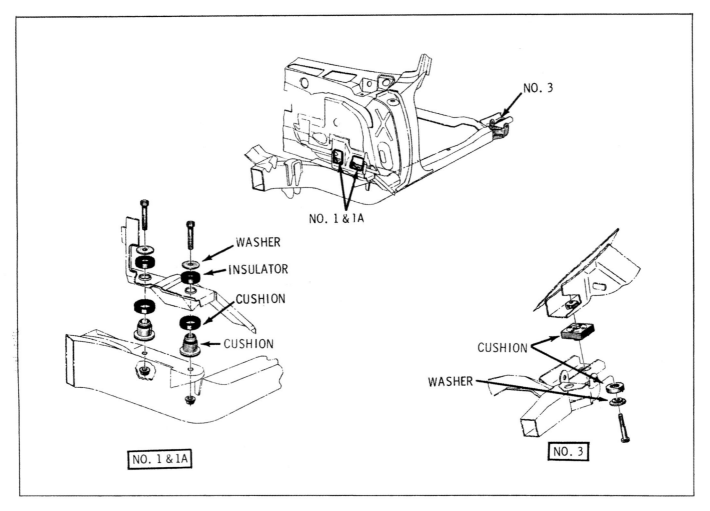

Fig. 2E-2—Body Mounting - Toronado

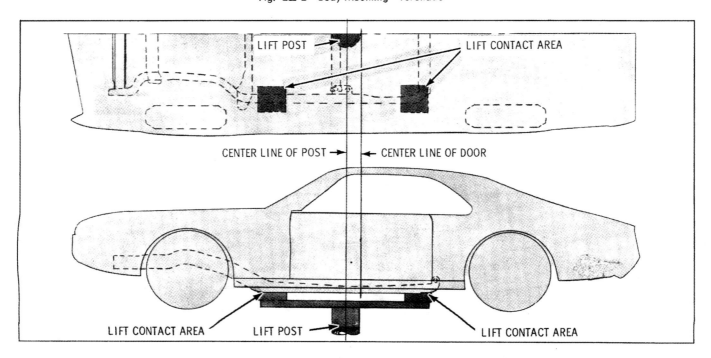

Fig. 2E-3—Lift Point Data

FRONT SUSPENSION
DRIVE AXLE
FINAL DRIVE

If equipped with disc brakes, refer to BRAKE
SECTION 5E for the removal of disc brake components in relation to front suspension.

CONTENTS OF SECTION 3EA

FRONT SUSPENSION

FRONT SUSPENSION

GENERAL DESCRIPTION

The front suspension on the Toronado consists of control
arms, stabilizer bar, shock absorbers and a right and left torsion bar. Torsion bars are used instead of the conventional
coil springs. The front end of the torsion bar is attached to
the lower control arm. The rear of the torsion bar is mounted
into an adjustable arm at the torsion bar crossmember. The
carrying height of the car is controlled by this adjustment.
(Figs. 3EA-1 and 3EA-2)

HUB ASSEMBLY (Fig. 3EA-3)

Removal (Wheel Removed)

1. Carefully pull drum from hub assembly.

It may be necessary to back off the brake shoe adjustment before drum can be removed.

2. Remove drive axle cotter pin, nut and washer.
3. Position access slot in hub assembly so each of the attaching bolts (4) can be removed. (Fig. 3EA-4) It will be necessary to push aside adjuster lever to remove one of the
bolts.
4. Position Spacer Tool J-22237 and install Tool J-21579
and Slide Hammer J-2619. (Fig. 3EA-4)
5. Remove hub assembly. It will again be necessary to
push aside adjuster lever for clearance.

If bearing is to be replaced, install Tool BT-6702 as shown
in Fig. 3EA-5 and remove bearing.

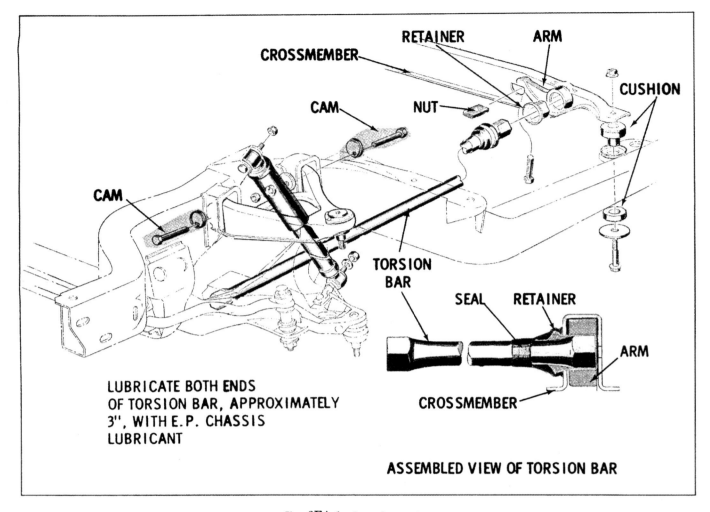

RETAINER   ARM

CROSSMEMBER

CAM   NUT   CUSHION

CAM

CAM   TORSION
                                        BAR

LUBRICATE BOTH ENDS
OF TORSION BAR, APPROXIMATELY
3", WITH E.P. CHASSIS
LUBRICANT

SEAL   RETAINER

                                    ARM

CROSSMEMBER

ASSEMBLED VIEW OF TORSION BAR

Fig. 3EA-1—Front Suspension

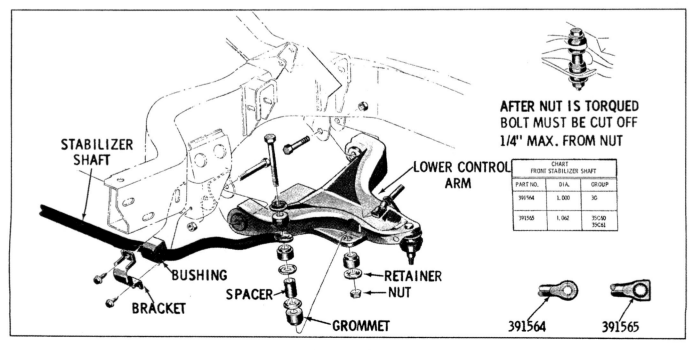

AFTER NUT IS TORQUED
BOLT MUST BE CUT OFF
1/4" MAX. FROM NUT

STABILIZER
SHAFT

LOWER CONTROL
ARM

CHART FRONT STABILIZER SHAFT		
PART NO.	DIA.	GROUP
391564	1.000	3G
391565	1.062	35C60 35C61

BUSHING

SPACER   RETAINER

BRACKET   NUT

GROMMET   391564   391565

Fig. 3EA-2—Front Suspension

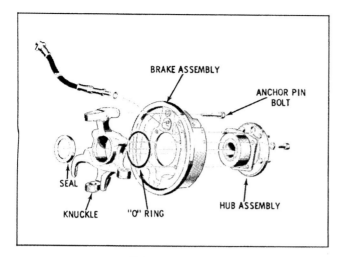

Fig. 3EA-3—Front Hub Assembly

Installation

Install bearing onto hub as shown in Fig. 3EA-6 making sure new bearing retainer is in correct position.

Reverse removal procedure.

OD of bearing must be lubricated with E.P. Chassis Lubricant.

Care must be used when installing hub assembly over drive axle splines so the splines are in correct alignment.

KNUCKLE "O" RING SEAL

Removal (Wheel Removed)

1. Remove hub and drum (refer to HUB ASSEMBLY REMOVAL.)
2. Remove upper ball joint cotter pin and nut.
3. Remove brake line hose clip from ball joint stud.

Do not loosen ball joint stud.

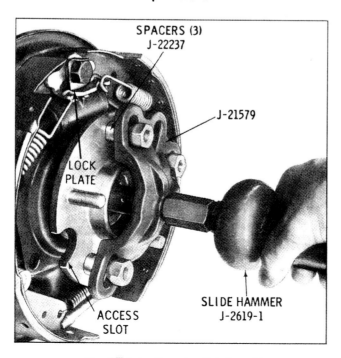

Fig. 3EA-4—Removing Hub Assembly

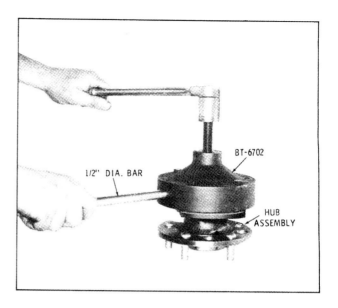

Fig. 3EA-5—Removing Hub Bearing

4. Bend lock plate on anchor bolt up and remove anchor bolt. (Fig. 3EA-4)
5. Carefully lift brake backing plate outboard over end of axle shaft and support so brake hose is not damaged. (Fig. 3EA-7)
6. Remove "O" ring seal. (Fig. 3EA-3)

Installation

To install reverse removal procedure.

KNUCKLE

Removal

1. Raise car and support lower control arm with floor stands.
2. Remove wheel and drum.
3. Remove hub assembly (refer to HUB ASSEMBLY, REMOVAL).

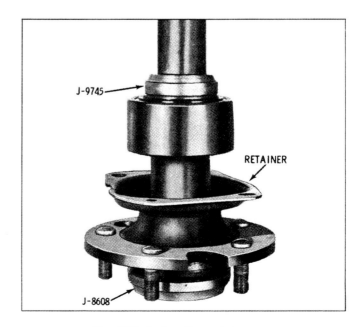

Fig. 3EA-6—Installing Hub Bearing

Fig. 3EA-7—Holding Backing Plate Assembly

4. Follow Steps 2 through 6 on KNUCKLE "O" RING, REMOVAL.

5. Place Tool J-22193 Support Block under drive axle to protect C.V. joint seal. (Fig. 3EA-8)

6. Using a brass drift and hammer, Fig. 3EA-9, loosen upper ball joint stud.

7. Remove cotter pin and nut from tie-rod end.

8. Using Brass Drift and Hammer, remove tie-rod end from knuckle. (Fig. 3EA-10)

9. Remove cotter pin and nut from lower ball joint.

10. Using Tool J-22292-3, carefully place between ball joint seal and knuckle.

11. Using Tool J-22292-1 and -2, remove lower ball joint from knuckle. (Fig. 3EA-11)

12. Remove knuckle.

13. Knuckle seal can be pried from knuckle at this time.

Fig. 3EA-8—Drive Axle Support Block

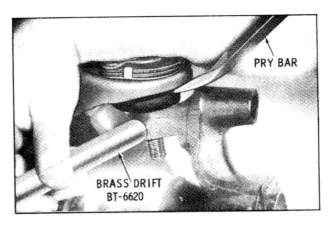

Fig. 3EA-9—Removing Upper Ball Joint

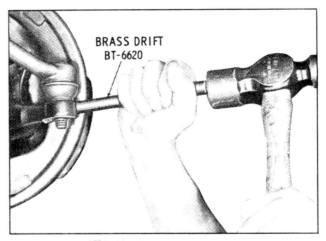

Fig. 3EA-10—Removing Tie-Rod End

Installation

1. Using Tool J-22234, install seal into knuckle. (Fig. 3EA-12)

2. Install lower ball joint stud into knuckle and attach nut. Do not torque.

3. Install tie-rod end stud into knuckle and attach nut. Do not torque.

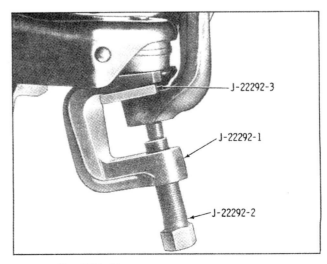

Fig. 3EA-11—Removing Lower Ball Joint

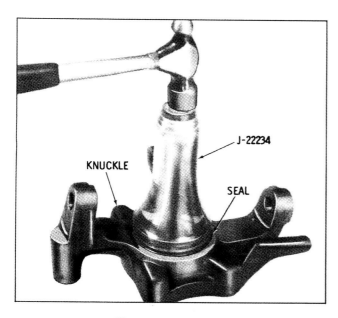

Fig. 3EA-12—Installing Knuckle Seal

4. Install upper ball joint stud into knuckle and attach nut. Do not torque.

5. Install backing plate onto knuckle with anchor bolt and lock plate. Do not torque.

6. Remove upper ball joint attaching nut and install brake line hose clip. Install nut.

7. Torque ball joint nuts to a minimum of 85 ft. lbs. Tighten to install cotter pins.

Cotter pin on upper ball joint must be bent up only to prevent interference with C.V. joint seal.

8. Torque tie-rod end to 50 ft. lbs. and install cotter pin.

9. Torque anchor bolt to 135 ft. lbs. and bend lock plate onto flat of bolt head.

10. Install hub assembly (refer to HUB ASSEMBLY INSTALLATION).

11. Install drum and wheel.

12. Remove floor stand and lower car.

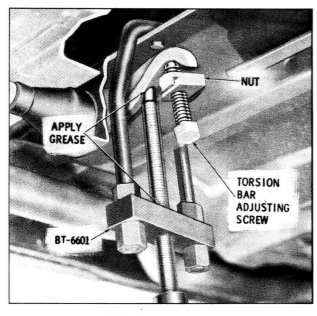

Fig. 3EA-13—Removing Torsion Bar

TORSION BAR

Torsion bar must be reused on the same side of car that it was removed. Right and left torsion bars are available for service replacement and are tagged with a sticker, which designates the front end of the torsion bar.

Removal

1. Hoist car under lower control arms.

2. Slide seal at rear of torsion bar forward.

3. Before using Tool BT-6601, remove the four nuts and center screw; then place tool over crossmember support. Align pin of tool into hole in crossmember. Install two nuts on tool and center screw; then install two remaining nuts to lock center screw. Turn center screw until seated in dimple of torsion adjusting arm. (Fig. 3EA-13)

4. Using a socket on the torsion bar adjusting bolt, turn counterclockwise, counting the number of turns necessary to remove.

The number of turns to remove the adjusting bolt will be used when installing, to obtain an initial carrying height.

5. Remove adjusting bolt and nut.

6. Turn center screw of Tool BT-6601 until torsion bar is completely relaxed.

7. Slide torsion bar forward until it bottoms in lower control arm, adjusting arm will drop out.

Do not mark, scratch or in any way damage torsion bar. Replacement will be necessary if such conditions exist.

8. Remove bolt from crossmember on the side from which torsion bar is being removed.

9. Remove center bolt assembly from Tool BT-6601.

10. Raise crossmember and twist rearward until torsion bar clears member.

11. Place floor stands under frame arms. (Fig. 3EA-22)

12. Lower hoist until the lower control arms are just free.

13. Remove lower control arm rear bushing bolt.

14. Pry lower control arm down, Fig. 3EA-15, and pull rearward on torsion bar until torsion bar is out of lower control arm. It may be necessary to force compressed air into anchor of lower control arm to relieve the vacuum caused by grease.

Inspection

1. Check rubber seal for damage. Replace if necessary.

2. Check retainer for excessive wear. Replace if necessary.

New retainer is required on replacement of torsion bar. Stake as shown in Fig. 3EA-14.

3. Check torsion bar for nicks, scratches or dents due to removal and replace if such conditions exist.

Installation

1. Lubricate both ends of torsion bar for approximately 3" with E.P. Chassis Lubricant.

2. Install torsion bar into lower control arm anchor and push forward until bar bottoms.

3. Pry crossmember back and align torsion bar with hole in crossmember.

4. Position lower control arm and install lower control arm bushing bolt and nut. Do not torque.

5. Raise hoist and remove floor stands.

6. Install torsion bar arm and pull torsion bar rearward until fully seated in arm.

7. Install crossmember bolt through rubber mounting and torque nut to 40 ft. lbs.

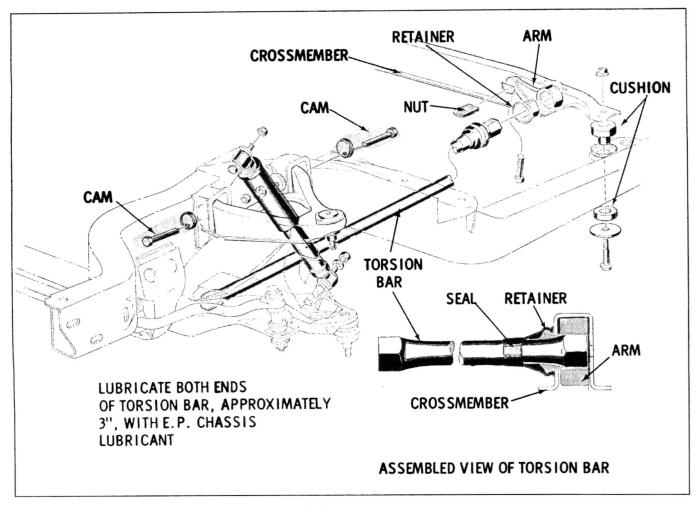

CROSSMEMBER

RETAINER   ARM

CAM

NUT

CUSHION

CAM

TORSION BAR

SEAL   RETAINER

ARM

CROSSMEMBER

LUBRICATE BOTH ENDS
OF TORSION BAR, APPROXIMATELY
3", WITH E.P. CHASSIS
LUBRICANT

ASSEMBLED VIEW OF TORSION BAR

Fig. 3EA-14—Front Suspension

8. Install Tool BT-6601 on crossmember.

9. Using Tool BT-6601, tighten torsion bar arm to install adjusting nut under arm and through crossmember.

10. Lubricate threads of torsion bar adjuster bolt with E.P. Chassis Lubricant and turn into nut the same number of turns used to remove.

11. Remove Tool BT-6601.

12. Lower car to floor.

13. Torque lower control arm bushing nut to 80 ft. lbs.

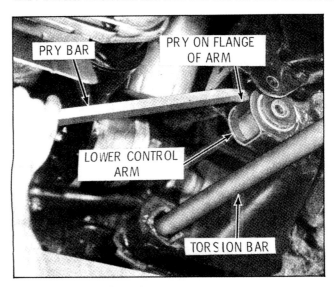

PRY BAR

PRY ON FLANGE OF ARM

LOWER CONTROL ARM

TORSION BAR

Fig. 3EA-15—Prying Lower Control Arm

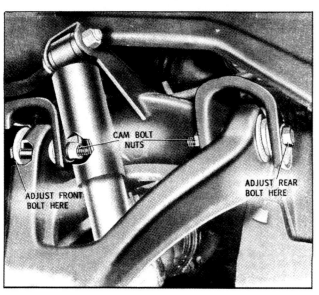

CAM BOLT NUTS

ADJUST REAR BOLT HERE

ADJUST FRONT BOLT HERE

Fig. 3EA-16—Front Wheel Alignment Cams

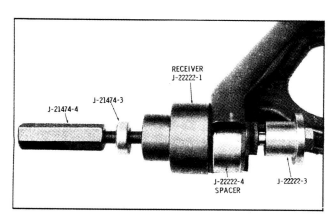

Fig. 3EA-17—Removing Upper Control Arm Bushing

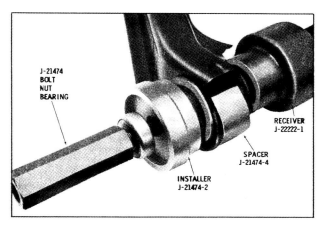

Fig. 3EA-18—Installing Upper Control Arm Bushing

UPPER CONTROL ARM

Removal

Upper control arm is serviced as an assembly less bushings.

1. Hoist car under lower control arms and remove wheel.
2. Remove upper shock attaching bolt.
3. Remove cotter pin and nut from upper ball joint.
4. Disconnect brake hose clamp from ball joint stud.

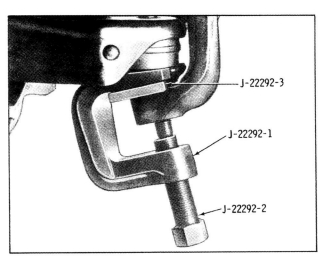

Fig. 3EA-19—Removing Lower Ball Joint

5. Using hammer and a drift, Fig. 3EA-9, drive on spindle until upper ball joint stud is disengaged.
6. Remove upper control arm cam assemblies and remove control arm from car by guiding shock absorber through access hole in arm.

Installation

1. Guide upper control arm over shock absorber and install bushing ends into frame bracket.
2. Install cam assemblies as shown in Fig. 3EA-16.

Front cam is mounted up. Rear cam is mounted down.

3. Install ball joint stud into knuckle.
4. Install brake hose clip on ball joint stud.
5. Install ball joint nut. Torque to 85 ft. lbs. Insert cotter pin and crimp.

Cotter pin must be crimped toward upper control arm to prevent interference with outer C.V. joint seal.

6. Install upper shock attaching bolt and nut. Torque nut to 80 ft. lbs.
7. Install wheel.
8. Lower hoist.
9. Check camber, caster and toe-in and adjust if necessary. Refer to FRONT END ALIGNMENT.

UPPER CONTROL ARM BUSHING (ON THE CAR)

Upper control arm bushings can be removed and installed on or off the car.

Removal

1. Hoist car under lower control arms and remove wheel.
2. Disconnect upper shock absorber attaching bolt.(Fig. 3EA-16)
3. Remove cam assemblies from control arms.
4. Move control arm out of frame brackets and attach bushing removal tools as shown in Fig. 3EA-17.

Installation

1. Install Tools as shown in Fig. 3EA-18 and press bushings into control arm.
2. Move control arm into frame brackets and install cam assemblies. The front cam is installed with the bolt in the lower position. The rear cam is installed with the bolt in the upper position.
3. Connect upper shock attaching bolt. Torque nut to 80 ft. lbs.
4. Replace wheel and lower car.
5. Align front wheels. Refer to FRONT END ALIGNMENT.

LOWER CONTROL ARM (RIGHT HAND)

Removal

1. Remove drive axle assembly. Refer to DRIVE AXLE ASSEMBLY (RIGHT HAND).
2. Hoist car and place floor stands under frame horns. (Fig. 3EA-22)
3. Position Tool BT-6601 on torsion bar. Refer to TORSION BAR REMOVAL, Items 2 through 6.
4. Remove wheel.
5. Remove shock absorber.
6. Disconnect stabilizer bar from lower control arm. Discard bolt.
7. Place Tool J-22193-1 between stabilizer bar and tie-rod.
8. Remove cotter pin and nut from lower ball joint stud.
9. Install Tool J-22292-3 Adapter under ball joint seal and install Tool J-22292-1-2 and remove ball joint stud from knuckle. (Fig. 3EA-19)

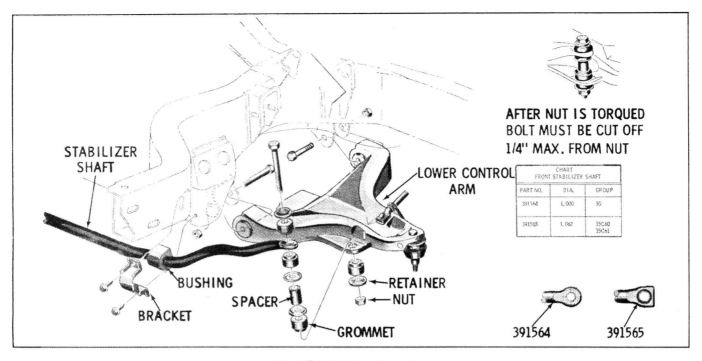

STABILIZER SHAFT

LOWER CONTROL ARM

AFTER NUT IS TORQUED BOLT MUST BE CUT OFF 1/4" MAX. FROM NUT

CHART FRONT STABILIZER SHAFT		
PART NO.	DIA.	GROUP
391564	1.000	3G
391565	1.062	35C60 35C61

BUSHING

SPACER

BRACKET

RETAINER

NUT

GROMMET

391564   391565

Fig. 3EA-20—Front Suspension

10. Remove lower control arm bushing bolts and with the aid of a helper, remove lower control arm and torsion bar as an assembly. Torsion bar arm will drop out at this time.

11. Carefully slide torsion bar from lower control arm and store in a safe, clean place.

Installation

1. Lubricate both ends of torsion bar for approximately 3" with E.P. Chassis Lubricant.

2. Install torsion bar into anchor of lower control arm.

3. With the aid of a helper, lift torsion bar and lower control arm assembled up until torsion bar will engage arm in crossmember and bushing ends of lower control arm engages frame brackets.

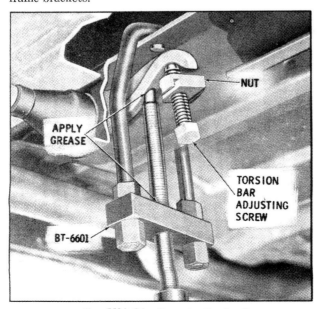

NUT

APPLY GREASE

TORSION BAR ADJUSTING SCREW

BT-6601

Fig. 3EA-21—Removing Torsion Bar

4. Install lower control arm bushing bolts and nuts. Do not torque.

5. Install lower control arm ball joint stud into knuckle. Install nut. Torque to 50 ft. lbs.

6. Remove Tool J-22193-1 from between stabilizer bar and tie-rod.

7. Using a new bolt, connect stabilizer bar to lower control arm. Refer to Fig. 3EA-20 for correct sequence of grommets, retainers and spacer. Torque nut to 14 ft. lbs. Cut bolt off 1/4" below nut.

8. Install shock absorber. Torque nuts to 80 ft. lbs.

9. Install wheel.

10. Position Tool BT-6601 over torsion bar crossmember, Fig. 3EA-21, and tighten center bolt until nut can be positioned through crossmember. Lubricate adjuster bolt with E.P. Chassis Lubricant and thread into nut the same amount of turns required to remove.

11. Raise hoist under lower control arms and remove floor stands.

12. Install drive axle assembly RH. Refer to DRIVE AXLE ASSEMBLY R.H. - Installation.

13. Torque lower control arm bushing nuts to 80 ft. lbs.

LOWER CONTROL ARM (LEFT HAND)

Removal

1. Remove drive axle assembly. Refer to DRIVE AXLE ASSEMBLY REMOVAL (LEFT HAND).

2. Place floor stands under frame horns. (Fig. 3EA-22)

3. Lower hoist slowly until floor stands are seated and hoist is still under lower control arm.

4. Remove shock absorber and bolt from stabilizer bar to lower control arm. Discard bolt.

5. Install Tool BT-6601 and completely relax torsion bar. For attachment, refer to TORSION BAR REMOVAL, Steps 2 through 6.

6. Lower front hoist to floor.

7. With the aid of a helper, remove lower control arm attaching bolts to frame and carefully lower control arm and torsion bar as an assembly. Torsion bar arm will drop out at this time.

Fig. 3EA-22—Supporting Front of Car

8. Carefully slide torsion bar from lower control arm and store in a safe, clean place.

Installation

1. Lubricate both ends of torsion bar with E.P. Chassis Lubricant for approximately 3".
2. Install torsion bar into anchor of lower control arm.
3. With the aid of a helper, lift torsion bar and lower control arm assembly up until torsion bar will engage arm in crossmember and bushing ends of lower control arm engages frame brackets.
4. Install lower control arm bushing bolts and nuts. Do not torque.
5. Position Tool BT-6601 over torsion bar crossmember, Fig. 3EA-21, and tighten center bolt until lower control arm is in a horizontal plane.
6. Install drive axle. Refer to DRIVE AXLE ASSEMBLY L.H. - INSTALLATION, Steps 1 through 9.
7. Install shock absorber. Torque nuts to 80 ft. lbs.
8. Using a new bolt, connect stabilizer bar to lower control

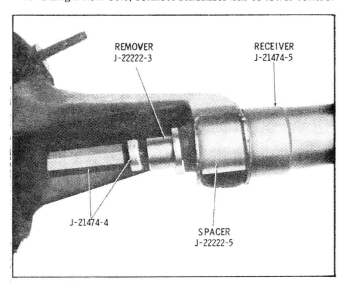

Fig. 3EA-23—Removing Lower Control Arm Rear Bushing

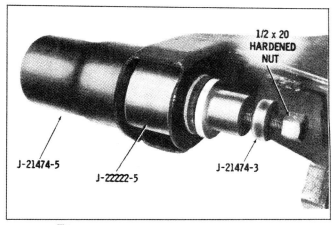

Fig. 3EA-24—Removing Lower Control Arm Front Bushing

arm. Refer to Fig. 3EA-20 for correct sequence of grommets, retainers and spacer. Torque nut to 14 ft. lbs. Cut bolt off 1/4" below nut.

9. Continue to tighten center bolt of Tool BT-6601 until nut can be positioned through crossmember. Lubricate adjuster bolt with E.P. Chassis Lubricant and thread into nut the same amount of turns required to remove.
10. Install drum and wheel.
11. Remove floor stands and lower hoist.
12. Torque lower control arm bushing nut to 80 ft. lbs.

LOWER CONTROL ARM BUSHINGS

Removal

1. Hoist car on a two post lift.
2. Remove stabilizer link bolt. Discard bolt.

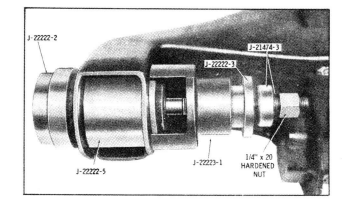

Fig. 3EA-25—Installing Lower Control Arm Rear Bushing

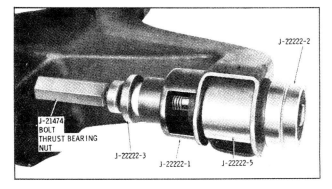

Fig. 3EA-26—Installing Lower Control Arm Front Bushing

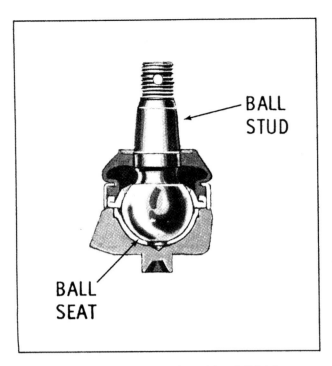

Fig. 3EA-27—Lower Control Arm Ball Joint

3. Place floor stands under frame horns, Fig. 3EA-22. Lower front lift to floor.

4. Install Tool BT-6601. Method for attaching, refer to TORSION BAR REMOVAL, Item 2 through 6.

5. Remove lower control arm bushing bolts and pull control arm down until free of frame brackets.

6. Install Tools through rear bushing and press out bushing as shown in Fig. 3EA-23.

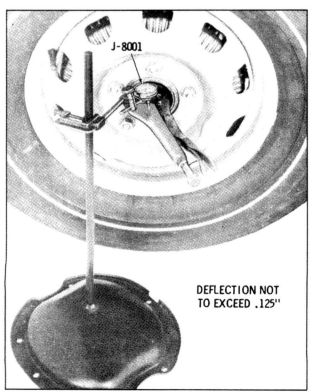

Fig. 3EA-28—Ball Joint Vertical Check

Due to the torsion bar anchor attachment to the lower control arm, it will be necessary to use a hardened 1/2" x 20 nut as shown in Fig. 3EA-24 to remove the front bushing.

Installation

1. Install Tools as shown in Fig. 3EA-25 and press rear bushing into lower control arm.

Due to the torsion bar anchor attachment to the lower control arm, it will be necessary to use a hardened 1/2" x 20 nut as shown in Fig. 3EA-26 to install the front bushing.

2. Raise lower control arm into frame brackets and install bushing bolts and nuts. Do not torque.

3. Using Tool BT-6601 turn center bolt into dimple of torsion bar arm until adjusting nut can be inserted through center frame support. Install and turn adjusting bolt clockwise the same number of turns needed to remove. Remove Tool BT-6601.

4. Raise front lift under lower control arms and remove floor stands.

5. Using a new bolt attach stabilizer link bolt to lower control arm. Torque nut to 14 ft. lbs. Cut bolt off 1/4" below nut.

6. Lower car and torque lower control arm bushing nuts to 80 ft. lbs.

Fig. 3EA-29—Pry Bar Installation

BALL JOINT

Ball Joint Lubrication

For ball joint seal inspection and lubrication interval, refer to PERIODIC MAINTENANCE Section 0E.

BALL JOINT CHECKS

Vertical Checks

1. Raise the car and position floor stands under the left and right lower control arms as near as possible to each lower ball joint. Car must be stable and should not rock on the floor stands.

2. Position dial indicator as shown in Fig. 3EA-28.

3. Place a pry bar as shown in Fig. 3EA-29 and pry down on bar. Care must be used so that drive axle seal is not damaged. Reading must not exceed .125"

Fig. 3EA-30—Ball Joint Horizontal Check

Horizontal Check

1. Place car on floor stands as outlined in Step 1 of the vertical check.

2. Position dial indicator as shown in Fig. 3EA-30.

3. Grasp front wheel as shown in Fig. 3EA-30 and push in on bottom of tire while pulling out at the top. Read gauge, then reverse the push-pull procedure. Horizontal deflection on the gauge should not exceed .125" at the wheel rim. This procedure checks both the upper and lower ball joints.

LOWER CONTROL ARM BALL JOINT (Fig. 3EA-27)

Removal

1. Remove knuckle. Refer to KNUCKLE REMOVAL.

2. Using hacksaw, saw the two side rivet heads off. Use a grinder to remove the rivet head on the top side of control arm.

3. Using a 7/32" drill bit, drill side rivets 3/16" deep. (Fig. 3EA-31)

4. Using hammer and punch, drive center rivet of joint until joint is out of control arm.

Installation

1. Install service ball joint into control arm and torque bolts and nut as shown in Fig. 3EA-32.

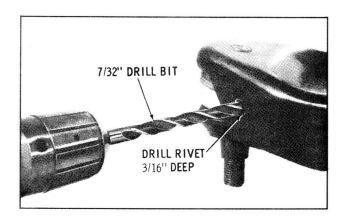

Fig. 3EA-31—Drilling Ball Joint Rivets

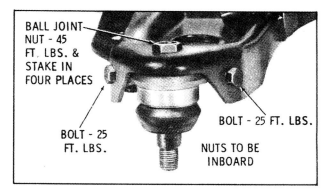

Fig. 3EA-32—Installing Service Ball Joint

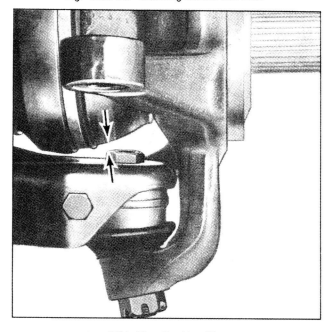

Fig. 3EA-33—Checking Clearance

2. Install knuckle - Refer to KNUCKLE INSTALLATION.

3. Check clearance from ball joint nut to drive axle outer joint as shown in Fig. 3EA-33. If no clearance is obtained, it may be necessary to grind off nut but not more than 1/16".

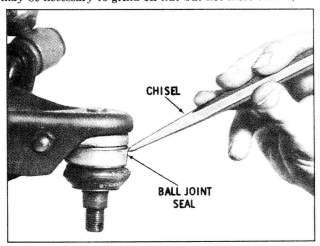

Fig. 3EA-34—Removing Ball Joint Seal

Fig. 3EA-35—Installing Ball Joint Seal

SEAL—LOWER CONTROL ARM BALL JOINT

The lower ball joint seal can be installed with lower control arm either on or off the car.

Removal

1. Remove knuckle. Refer to KNUCKLE REMOVAL, Items 1 through 12.
2. Using hammer and chisel, drive seal from ball joint. (Fig. 3EA-34)
3. Wipe grease from ball joint and stud.

Installation

1. Position new seal over ball joint stud.
2. Lubricate jaws of Tool J-5504 and carefully slide jaw between seal and retainer. (Fig. 3EA-35)
3. Tap lightly with hammer on center bolt of Tool J-5504 until retainer is fully seated.
4. Install knuckle. Refer to KNUCKLE INSTALLA-TION, Steps 2 through 12.

STABILIZER BAR

Removal

1. Remove link bolts, nuts, grommets, spacers and retainers from lower control arm. Discard bolts.
2. Remove two bolts attaching dust shield to frame (both sides).
3. Remove bracket to frame attaching bolts and remove stabilizer bar from front of car.

Installation

Reverse removal procedure.

New link nuts are torqued to 14 ft. lbs. then cut off 1/4" below nut.

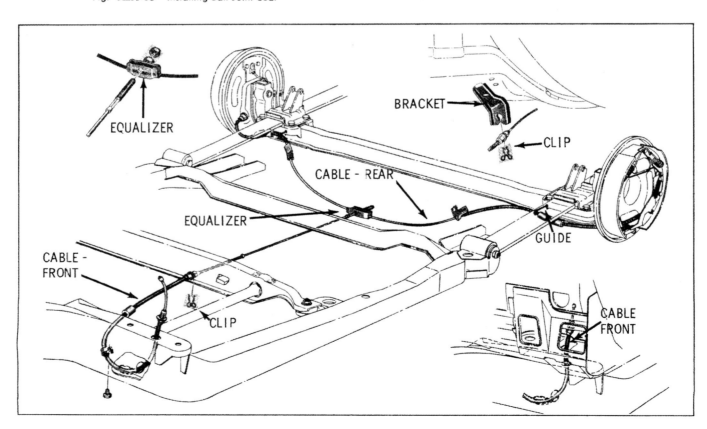

Fig. 3EA-36—Parking Brake Cable Attachment

TORSION BAR CROSSMEMBER

Removal

1. Raise car on a two post hoist and position floor stands under frame torque boxes.

It may be necessary to disconnect side battles.

2. Disconnect parking brake cable at equalizer and clip at torsion bar crossmember. Pull cable through crossmember. (Fig. 3EA-36)

3. Slide torsion bar rear seals forward.

4. Remove the four nuts and center screw from Tool BT-6601.

Position tool over crossmember installing pin of Tool into hole in crossmember. Install two nuts on Tool, install center screw assembly, then install the two remaining nuts and tighten (Fig. 3EA-37)

It may be necessary to pry up on under body and down on crossmember to install Tool.

5. Turn center screw until seated in dimple of torsion bar adjusting arm.

6. Remove torsion bar adjusting bolt and nut. Count the number of turns necessary to remove and record.

The number of turns to remove the adjusting bolt will be used when installing to obtain an initial carrying height.

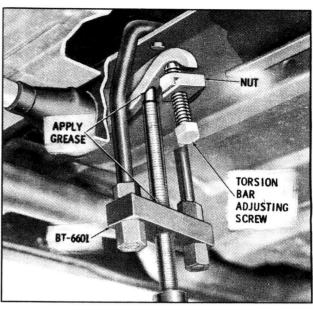

Fig. 3EA-37—Torsion Bar Remover and Installer

7. Turn center screw of Tool BT-6601 until torsion bar is completely relaxed.

8. Remove Tool BT-6601.

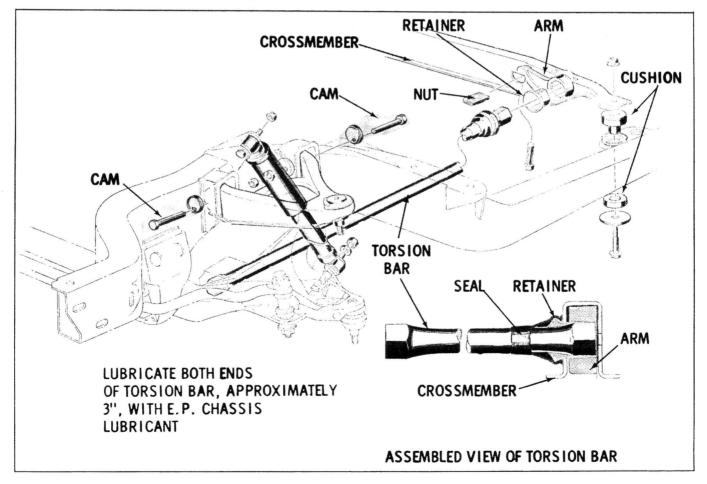

LUBRICATE BOTH ENDS OF TORSION BAR, APPROXIMATELY 3", WITH E.P. CHASSIS LUBRICANT

ASSEMBLED VIEW OF TORSION BAR

Fig. 3EA-38—Front Suspension

9. Repeat steps 4, 5, 6, 7 and 8 on opposite torsion bar.

10. Remove bolts and cushions from torsion bar crossmember at frame brackets. (Fig. 3EA-38)

11. Move crossmember rearward until torsion bars are free and adjusting arms can be removed.

It may be necessary to slide both torsion bars forward until they bottom in the lower control arm.

12. Disconnect hangers at muffler and tail pipes.

13. Move torsion bar crossmember sideways to the extreme right or left side. It may be necessary to insert a block between the body and frame, then move crossmember upward and outward until opposite end clears crossmember frame bracket. It may also be necessary to block between the intermediate exhaust pipe and the body.

Installation

To install, reverse the removal procedure.

FRONT END ALIGNMENT

Car must be on level surface, gas tank full or a compensating weight added, front seat all the way to the rear and tires, both front and rear, inflated to specifications. All doors must be closed and no passengers or additional weight should be in the car or trunk.

1. Check rocker panel molding to ground dimension. (Fig. 3EA-39)

front reading to ground	8" + 1/2"-1"
rear reading to ground	8-1/4" + 1/2"-1"
front to rear to be within	1"
side to side to be within	5/8"

If not within tolerance, adjust torsion bar.

2. Align car on wheel alignment equipment.

3. Raise up front end and check wheel runout. Set wheels at center of runout and lower car.

4. Loosen nuts on inboard side of upper control arm cam bolts.

5. Check camber, + 1/8° ± (3/8°). If necessary to adjust turn both front and rear cams in the same direction (inboard or outboard) until correct. Camber reading of the right and left wheels should be within 1/2° of each other.

6. Check caster, -2° ± (1/2°). Set caster, if necessary, in two steps as follows:

a. Adjust front cam (nearest front of car) so that the camber changes an amount equal to one-fourth of the desired caster change.

b. Adjust the rear cam (nearest rear of car) in the opposite direction so that the camber setting returns to its corrected position (Step 5).

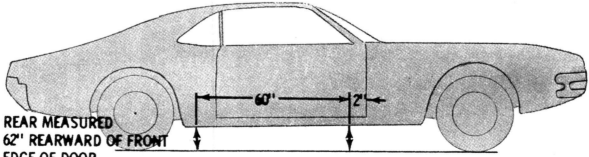

CAR ON LEVEL SURFACE
FUEL TANK FULL
TRUNK EMPTY
FRONT SEAT REARWARD
DOORS CLOSED
TIRES AT CORRECT PRESSURE

TO ADJUST FRONT CARRYING HEIGHT RAISE CAR AT FRONT CROSSMEMBER TO RELIEVE STRAIN ON ADJUSTING BOLT. LUBRICATE ADJUSTING BOLT BEFORE ATTEMPTING TO CHANGE CARRYING HEIGHT.

REAR MEASURED 62" REARWARD OF FRONT EDGE OF DOOR
SPEC. 8 1/4" + 1/2" OR - 1" ROCKER PANEL TO FLOOR.

FRONT TO REAR TO BE WITHIN 1"
SIDE TO SIDE TO BE WITHIN 5/8"

FRONT MEASURED 2" REARWARD OF FRONT EDGE OF DOOR
SPEC. 8" + 1/2" OR - 1" MEASURED FROM ROCKER PANEL TO FLOOR.

Fig. 3EA-39—Carrying Heights

EXAMPLE: Camber is set at +1/8° and caster setting is -1°. For correct setting the caster must be decreased by 1° to -2°. Therefore, first the front cam is adjusted to decrease camber by one-fourth of 1° or -1/4° to a value of -1/8°. Then the rear cam is adjusted to increase the camber reading back to the original value of +1/8°.

c. Recheck caster reading.

If a problem exists where there is insufficient cam to obtain a correct reading:

1. Turn front cam bolt so high part of cam is pointing up.
2. Turn rear cam bolt so high part of cam is pointing down.

This is a location to start from and a correct setting can be obtained with the above procedure.

Torque upper control arm cam nuts to 95 ft. lbs. Hold head or bolt securely, any movement of the cam will effect the final setting and caster camber adjustment must be rechecked.

7. Toe-in adjustment, 0 to 1/16" toe-in.

a. Center steering wheel - raise car and check wheel runout. Set wheels at center of runout.

b. Loosen tie-rod nuts and adjust to proper setting (0 to 1/16" toe-in).

c. Tighten tie-rod nuts - torque nuts to 20 ft. lbs. Position tie-rod clamps so that opening of clamp is facing up. This is a very necessary setting. Interference and a possible tie up of front end linkage could occur if clamps snag while turning.

CARRYING HEIGHTS

When checking carrying heights, the car should be parked on a known level surface, gas tank full, front seat rearward, doors closed and tire pressure at specified psi.

Measuring must be taken from lower edge of rocker panel molding to floor.

Carrying heights are controlled by the adjustment setting of the torsion bar adjusting bolt. Clockwise rotation of the bolt increases the front height. Counterclockwise decreases front height. Specifications are shown in Fig. 3EA-39.

SHOCK ABSORBER

Removal

1. Remove upper shock attaching bolt.
2. Remove lower shock attaching nut and carefully guide shock through upper control arm.

Installation

Reverse removal procedure.

SHOCK ABSORBER CODE AND USAGE			
Series	Front	Rear	
		Horizontal	Vertical
Toronado	SY	MR	SZ

Fig. 3EA-40—Shock Absorber Code Location

TORQUE SPECIFICATIONS

APPLICATION	FT. LBS.
Drive Axle Nut (Nut must be tightened to insert cotter pin)	150
Hub to Knuckle Bolts	65
Anchor Bolt to Backing Plate and Knuckle Bolt	135
Stabilizer Link Nut	14
Stabilizer Bracket to Frame Bolt	14
Torsion Bar Crossmember Nut	40
Shock Absorber	
Upper Nut	80
Lower Nut	80
Lower Control Arm Bushing Nuts	80
Upper Control Arm Bushing Nuts	95
Ball Joint (Nut must be tightened to insert cotter pin)	85
Tie-Rod to Knuckle Nut	50
Inner C.V. Joint to Output Shaft Bolts	65

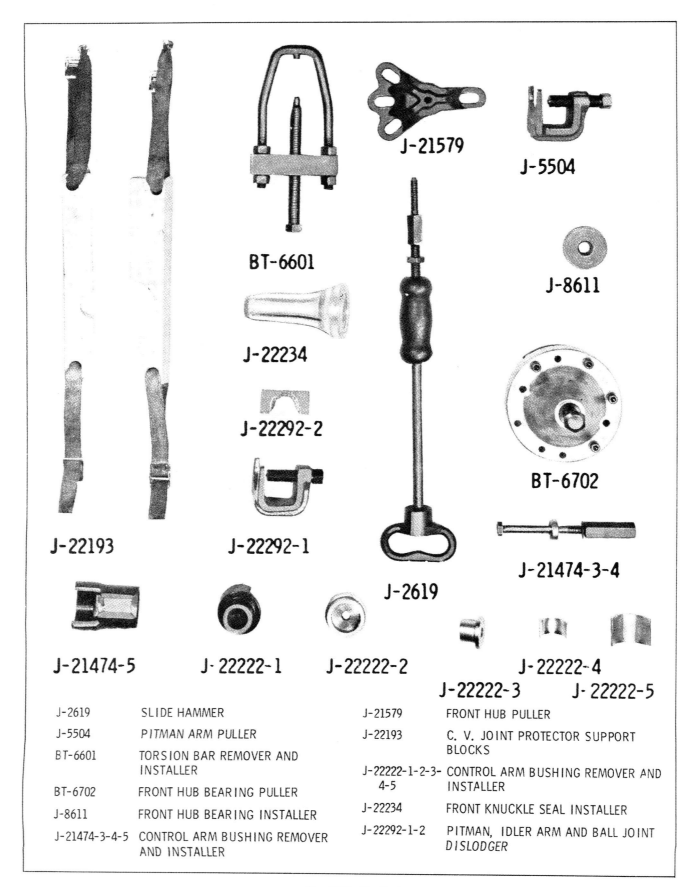

J-21579

J-5504

BT-6601

J-22234

J-8611

J-22292-2

J-22292-1

BT-6702

J-22193

J-21474-3-4

J-2619

J-21474-5   J-22222-1   J-22222-2   J-22222-4

J-22222-3   J-22222-5

J-2619	SLIDE HAMMER	J-21579	FRONT HUB PULLER
J-5504	*PITMAN ARM PULLER*	J-22193	C. V. JOINT PROTECTOR SUPPORT BLOCKS
BT-6601	TORSION BAR REMOVER AND INSTALLER	J-22222-1-2-3-4-5	CONTROL ARM BUSHING REMOVER AND INSTALLER
BT-6702	FRONT HUB BEARING PULLER		
J-8611	FRONT HUB BEARING INSTALLER	J-22234	FRONT KNUCKLE SEAL INSTALLER
J-21474-3-4-5	CONTROL ARM BUSHING REMOVER AND INSTALLER	J-22292-1-2	PITMAN, IDLER ARM AND BALL JOINT *DISLODGER*

Fig. 3EA-41—Tools

DRIVE AXLES
TORONADO

CONTENTS OF SECTION 3EB

DESCRIPTION

Drive axles on the Toronado are a complete flexible assembly and consist of an axle shaft and an inner and outer constant velocity joint. (Fig. 3EB-1) The right axle shaft has a torsional damper mounted in the center. The inner constant velocity joint has complete flexibility plus inward and outward movement. The outer constant velocity joint has complete flexibility only.

Whenever any operations call for disconnecting, connecting, removal or installation of the drive axles, care must be exercised to prevent damage to constant velocity joint seals. Seals may be wrapped with floor mat rubber or old innertube, etc. Make sure any rubber protective covers that are used are removed before car is started or driven.

DRIVE AXLE ASSEMBLY (RIGHT HAND)
(Fig. 3EB-2)

Removal

1. Hoist car under lower control arms.
2. Remove drive axle cotter pin, nut and washer. (Fig. 3EB-3)
3. Remove oil filter element.
4. Remove inner C.V. joint attaching bolts. (Fig. 3EB-3)
5. Push inner C.V. joint outward enough to disengage from R.H. final drive output shaft and move rearward.
6. Remove R.H. output shaft support bolts to engine and final drive. (Fig. 3EB-3)
7. Remove R.H. output shaft.
8. Remove drive axle assembly.

Care must be exercised so that C.V. joints do not turn to full extremes and that seals are not damaged against shock absorber or stabilizer bar.

Installation

1. Carefully place R.H. drive axle assembly into lower control arm and enter outer race splines into knuckle.
2. Lubricate final drive output shaft seal with Special Seal Lubricant, No. 1050169 or equivalent.
3. Install R.H. output shaft into final drive and attach support bolts to engine and brace.

When attaching the right hand output shaft to the engine bracket, do not let the shaft hang. Assemble bracket bolts loosely, and by moving the flange end of the shaft up and down, and back and forth, find the center location. Hold the shaft in this position and then torque the bolts to 50 ft. lbs. on support and 14 ft. lbs. on brace. Refer to Fig. 3EC-2A.

4. Move R.H. drive axle assembly toward front of car and align with R.H. output shaft. Install attaching bolts and torque to 65 ft. lbs.
5. Install oil filter element.
6. Install washer and nut on drive axle. Torque to 150 ft. lbs. Insert cotter pin and crimp.
7. Remove floor stands and lower hoist.
8. Check engine oil, add if necessary.

DRIVE AXLE ASSEMBLY (LEFT HAND)

Removal

1. Hoist car under lower control arms.
2. Remove wheel and drum.
3. Remove drive axle cotter pin, nut and washer.
4. Position access slot in hub assembly so that each of the attaching bolts (4) can be removed. (Fig. 3EB-4) It will be necessary to push aside adjuster lever to remove one of the bolts.
5. Position Spacers Tool J-22237 and install Tool J-21579 and Slide Hammer J-2619 with Adapter J-2619-1. (Fig. 3EB-4)
6. Remove hub assembly. It will again be necessary to push aside adjuster lever for clearance for hub assembly.
7. Remove tie-rod end cotter pin and nut.
8. Using hammer and brass drift, drive on knuckle until tie-rod end stud is free. (Fig. 3EB-5)
9. Remove bolts from drive axle assembly and left output shaft. Insert Tool J-22193. (Fig. 3EB-6)
10. Remove upper control arm ball joint cotter pin and nut. Remove brake hose clip from ball joint stud.
11. Using hammer and brass drift, drive on knuckle until upper ball joint stud is free. (Fig. 3EB-7)
12. Install Tool J-22292-3 carefully between lower ball

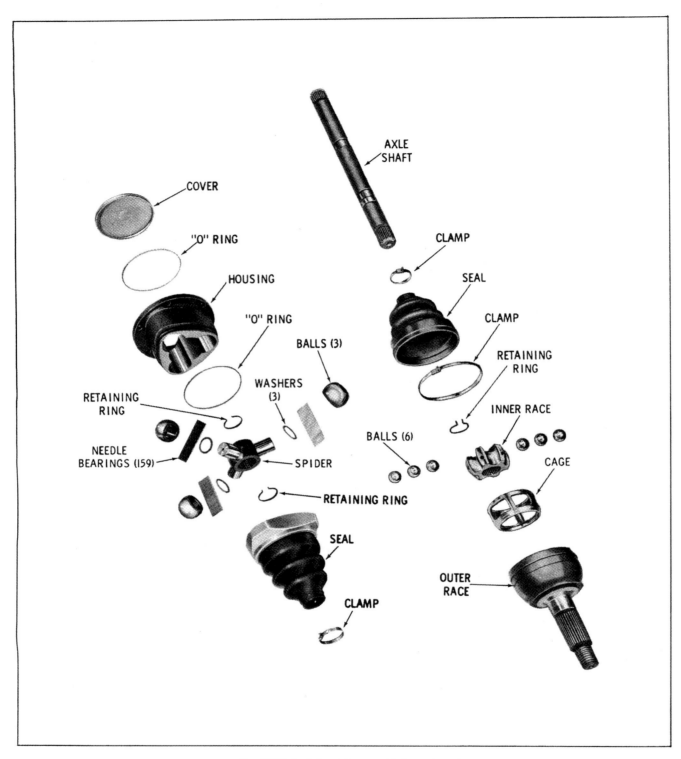

AXLE
SHAFT

COVER

"O" RING

CLAMP

HOUSING

SEAL

"O" RING

CLAMP

BALLS (3)

RETAINING
RING

WASHERS
(3)

RETAINING
RING

INNER RACE

BALLS (6)

NEEDLE
BEARINGS (159)

SPIDER

CAGE

RETAINING RING

SEAL

OUTER
RACE

CLAMP

Fig. 3EB-1—Drive Axle Assembly (L.H. Shown)

joint seal and knuckle. (Fig. 3EB-8)

13. Using Tool J-22292-1-2 (Fig. 3EB-8) remove lower ball joint from knuckle. Care must be exercised so that ball joint doesn't damage drive axle seal.

14. Remove knuckle. Support backing plate so that brake hose is not damaged.

15. Carefully guide drive axle assembly outboard.

Care must be exercised so that C.V. joints do not turn

to full extremes and that seals are not damaged against shock absorber or stabilizer bar.

Installation

1. Carefully guide L.H. drive axle assembly onto lower control arm in *position on Tool J-22193.*

2. Insert lower control ball joint stud into knuckle and attach nut. Do not torque.

3. Center L.H. drive axle assembly in opening of knuckle

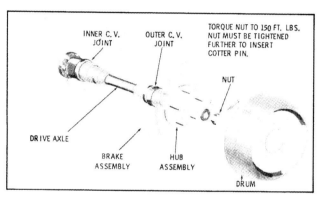

Fig. 3EB-2—Drive Axle Assembly (R.H. Shown)

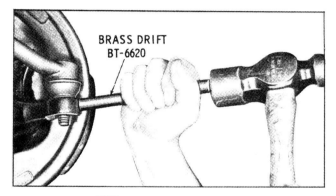

Fig. 3EB-3—Drive Axle Installed

Fig. 3EB-5—Removing Tie Rod End

and insert upper ball joint stud.

4. Place brake hose clip over upper ball joint stud and install nut. Do not torque.

5. Insert tie-rod end stud into knuckle and attach nut. Torque to 50 ft. lbs. Install cotter pin and crimp.

6. Lubricate hub assembly bearing OD with E.P. Grease and install. Torque to 65 ft. lbs.

7. Align inner C.V. joint with output shaft and install attaching bolts. Torque to 65 ft. lbs.

8. Torque upper and lower ball joint stud nuts to 85 ft. lbs. min. Tighten to align cotter pins.

Upper ball joint cotter pin must be crimped toward upper control arm to prevent interference with outer C.V. joint seal.

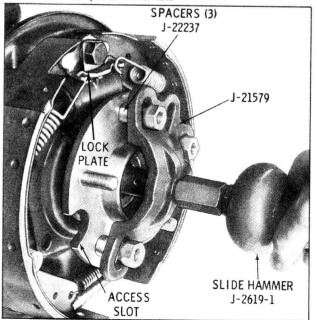

Fig. 3EB-4—Removing Hub

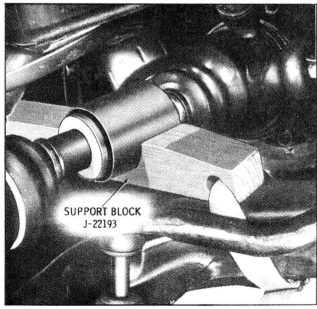

Fig. 3EB-6—Installing Support Block

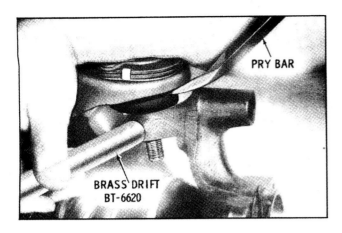

Fig. 3EB-7—Removing Upper Ball Joint

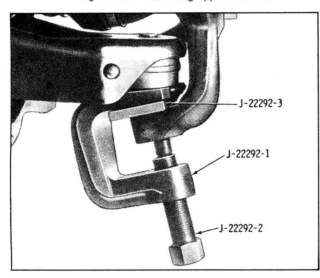

Fig. 3EB-8—Removing Lower Ball Joint

9. Install drive axle washer and nut. Torque to 150 ft. lbs. Install cotter pin and crimp.
10. Install drum and wheel.
11. Remove floor stands and lower hoist.

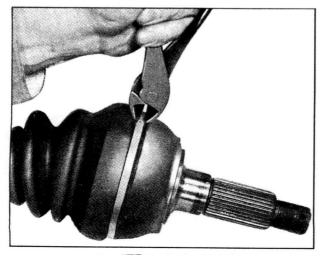

Fig. 3EB-9—Cutting Seal Clamp

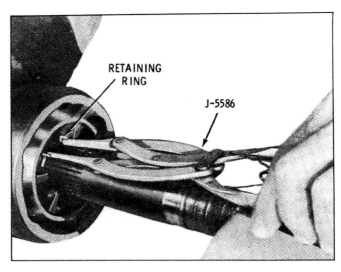

Fig. 3EB-10—Removing Retaining Ring

CONSTANT VELOCITY JOINT (C.V. JOINT OUT OF CAR)

The C.V. joints are to be replaced as a unit and are only disassembled for repacking and replacement of damaged seals.

Disassembly (Outer C.V. Joint)

1. Insert axle assembly in vise. Clamp on mid-portion of axle shaft.
2. Remove inner and outer seal clamps. (Fig. 3EB-9)
3. Slide seal down axle shaft to gain access to C.V. joint.
4. Using Tool J-5586 , spread retaining ring until C.V. joint can be removed from axle spline. (Fig. 3EB-10)
5. Remove retaining ring. (Fig. 3EB-17)
6. Slide seal from axle shaft.
7. Remove grease from C.V. joint.
8. Holding C.V. joint with one hand, tilt cage and inner race so that one ball can be removed. Continue until all (6) balls are removed. (Fig. 3EB-11)
9. Turn cage 90° and with slot in cage aligned with land in outer race lift out inner race and cage. (Fig. 3EB-12)
10. While holding cage and inner race, turn inner race 90°. Line up short land of inner race with slot in cage. Move short land through cage and turn inner race up and out of cage. (Fig. 3EB-13)

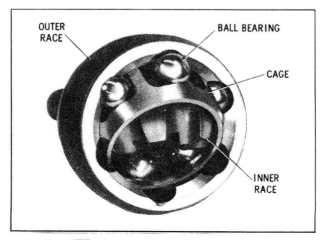

Fig. 3EB-11—Removing Balls From Outer Race

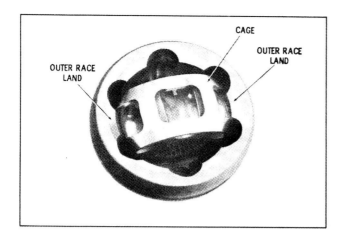

Fig. 3EB-12—Positioning Cage For Removal

CLEANING AND INSPECTION (OUTER)

Wash all metallic parts thoroughly in a cleaning solvent. Dry with compressed air. Rubber seal should be replaced whenever C.V. joint is disassembled for service.

Outer and inner race may show a definite wear pattern where the balls travel. The C.V. Joint should not be replaced for this reason. However, if this wear pattern is suspected to be the cause of a noisy or vibrating C.V. Joint, the joint should be replaced.

1. Inspect outer race for excessive wear or scoring in the ball splines. Inspect shaft splines and threads for any damage.
2. Inspect balls (six) for nicks, cracks, breaks or scores.
3. Inspect cage for cracks or breaks.
4. Inspect inner race for excessive wear, scores or breaks.
5. Inspect retaining ring for being broken.

If any of the above defects, except Item 5 are found, the C.V. joint assembly will have to be replaced as a unit. Retaining ring may be replaced separately.

Assembly

1. Insert short land of inner race into hole in cage and pivot to install in cage. (Fig. 3EB-13)
2. Align inner race and cage as shown in Fig. 3EB-12 and pivot inner race and cage 90° to align in outer race as shown in Fig. 3EB-14.
3. Insert balls into outer race one at a time until all six balls are installed. (Fig. 3EB-14) Inner race and cage will have to be tilted as shown so that each ball can be inserted.

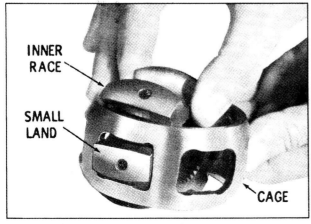

Fig. 3EB-13—Removing or Installing Inner Race From Cage

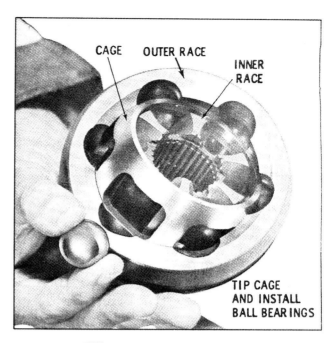

Fig. 3EB-14—Installing Balls in Outer Race

4. Pack C.V. joint full of Lubricant No. 1050530 or equivalent.
5. Pack inside of seal with Lubricant No. 1050530 or equivalent until folds of seal are full.
6. Place service clamp on axle shaft.
7. Install seal onto axle shaft.
8. Install retaining ring into inner race. (Fig. 3EB-17)
9. Insert axle shaft into splines of outer C.V. joint until retaining ring secures shaft.
10. Position seal in slot of outer race. (Fig. 3EB-15)
11. With service clamps over seal in correct position, follow procedures listed on Figs. 3EB-16A-B-C-D-E. This procedure will apply to both small clamps on axle shaft and large clamp on outer C.V. joint.

Disassembly (Inner C.V. Joint)

1. Insert axle assembly in vise. Clamp on mid-portion of axle shaft.

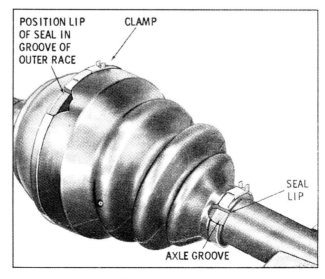

Fig. 3EB-15—Positioning Seal

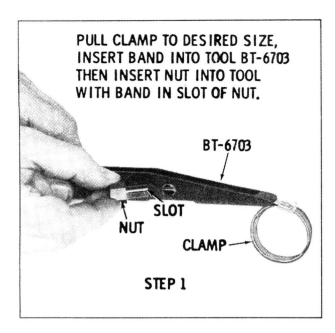

PULL CLAMP TO DESIRED SIZE,
INSERT BAND INTO TOOL BT-6703
THEN INSERT NUT INTO TOOL
WITH BAND IN SLOT OF NUT.

BT-6703

SLOT
NUT
CLAMP

STEP 1

Fig. 3EB-16A—Clamp Procedure (Step 1)

2. Remove small seal clamp.
3. Remove large end of seal from C.V. joint by prying out peened spots and driving off C.V. joint with hammer and chisel. (Fig. 3EB-18)
4. Carefully slide seal down axle shaft.
5. Carefully lift housing assembly from spider assembly (Fig. 3EB-19) and remove "O" ring from housing outer surface.

Place a rubber band over ends of spider to retain the three balls and needle bearings. Wipe all excess grease from C.V. Joint.

6. Using Tool J-5586, remove retaining ring from end of axle shaft.
7. Slide spider assembly from axle shaft. (Fig. 3EB-21)
8. Remove retaining ring (inner) from axle shaft, using Tool J-5586. (Fig. 3EB-20)

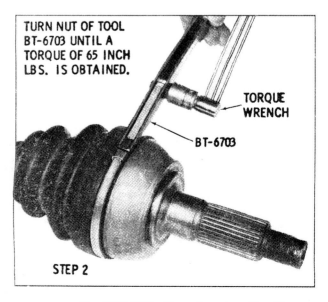

TURN NUT OF TOOL
BT-6703 UNTIL A
TORQUE OF 65 INCH
LBS. IS OBTAINED.

TORQUE
WRENCH

BT-6703

STEP 2

Fig. 3EB-16B—Clamp Procedure (Step 2)

AFTER DESIRED
TORQUE IS OBTAINED
TURN TOOL OVER TO
BEND BAND OVER LOCK
TANGS OF CLAMP.

STEP 3

Fig. 3EB-16C—Clamp Procedure (Step 3)

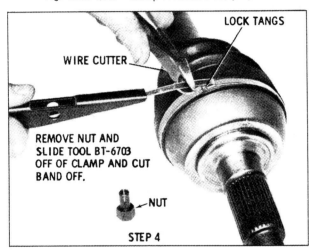

LOCK TANGS

WIRE CUTTER

REMOVE NUT AND
SLIDE TOOL BT-6703
OFF OF CLAMP AND CUT
BAND OFF.

NUT

STEP 4

Fig. 3EB-16D—Clamp Procedure (Step 4)

9. Slide seal off axle shaft.
10. Remove cover from housing as shown in Fig. 3EB-22.
11. Remove "O" ring from housing.

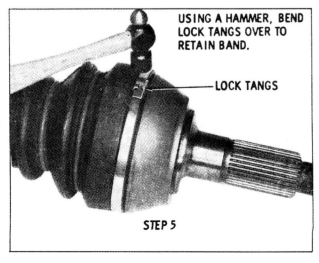

USING A HAMMER, BEND
LOCK TANGS OVER TO
RETAIN BAND.

LOCK TANGS

STEP 5

Fig. 3EB-16E—Clamp Procedure (Step 5)

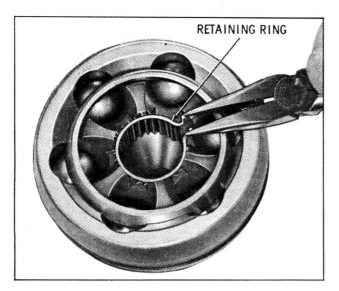

Fig. 3EB-17—Removing Or Installing Retaining Ring

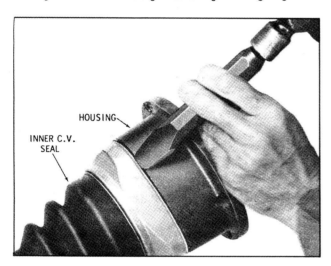

Fig. 3EB-18—Removing Inner C.V. Joint Seal

12. Remove balls (three) from spider, being careful not to lose any of the (53) needle bearings in each of the balls. (Fig. 3EB-23)

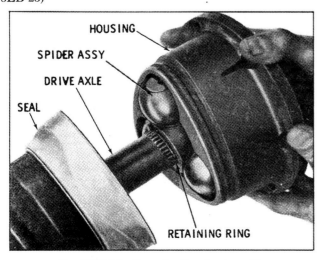

Fig. 3EB-19—Removing Housing Assembly

Fig. 3EB-20—Removing Retaining Ring

13. Remove washers from spider journals. (Fig. 3EB-24)

CLEANING AND INSPECTION

Wash all metallic parts thoroughly in a cleaning solvent. Dry with compressed air.

Rubber seal, "O" rings and clamp should be replaced whenever C.V. joint is disassembled for service.

Housing may show smooth shiny spots where balls travel; this is considered NORMAL.

A housing that has brinelling will appear as small depressions in the metal approximately .002" to 003" and can be felt, should be replaced.

1. Inspect housing for excessive wear, cracks or chips in ball grooves.
2. Inspect retaining rings for being bent or broken.
3. Inspect balls (three) for excessive wear, cracks, nicks, scores or broken.
4. Inspect needle bearings for wear, broken or bent.
5. Inspect washers for wear or bent.
6. Inspect spider for excessive wear, chips or cracks.

Assembly

1. Slide new clamp on axle shaft, to be used after seal positioning.

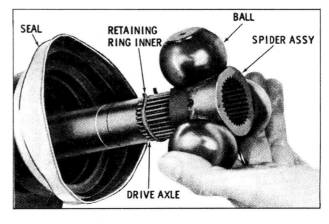

Fig. 3EB-21—Removing Spider Assembly

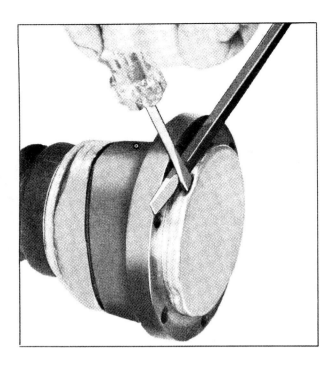

Fig. 3EB-22—Removing Cover From Housing

2. Pack new seal with Lubricant, No. 1050649 or equivalent until folds in seal are full.

3. Position retaining ring on axle shaft in the inner slot. (Fig. 3EB-25)

4. Using Lubricant, No. 1050649, or equivalent load balls (three) with the needle bearings (53 to each ball). (Fig. 3EB-26)

5. Position one washer on each of the spider journals. (Fig. 3EB-24)

Groove in washer must face toward center of spider.

6. Carefully install balls on each of the spider journals. (Fig. 3EB-23)

A rubber band may be used to retain balls in position until spider assembly is installed in housing.

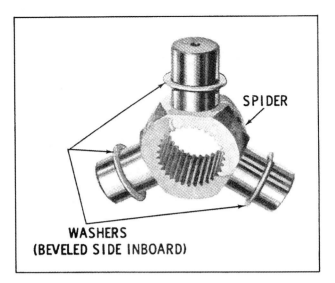

Fig. 3EB-24—Removing Or Installing Washers

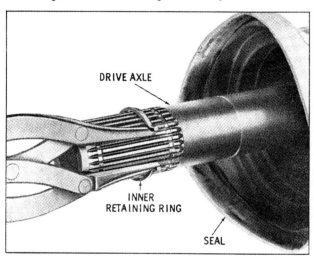

Fig. 3EB-25—Removing Or Installing Inner Retaining Ring

7. Position spider assembly on axle shaft and retain with retaining ring.

8. Install new "O" ring in outer groove in housing. (Fig. 3EB-29)

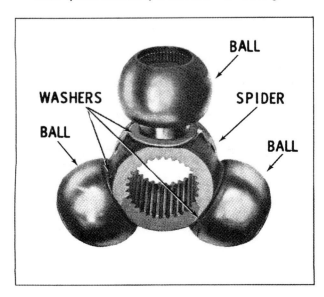

Fig. 3EB-23—Spider Assembly

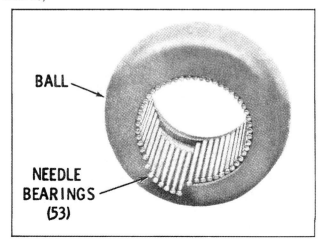

Fig. 3EB-26—Loading Ball With Needle Bearings

Fig. 3EB-27—Installing "O" Ring In Housing

9. Remove rubber band, if used, from spider assembly.

10. Position spider assembly in line with housing assembly and push into housing. (Fig. 3EB-30)

11. Lubricate housing outer groove "O" ring with Special Seal Lubricant, No. 1050169, or equivalent.

12. With housing positioned as shown in Fig. 3EB-31, slide seal into position and stake in six places, evenly spaced.

Care must be taken so that "O" ring is not cut by metal portion of seal.

13. Position seal into groove in axle shaft and install clamp following procedure listed on Figs. 3EB-16A-B-C-D-E.

14. Extend axle shaft until seal is at maximum length.

15. Using Lubricant, No. 1050649, or equivalent fill

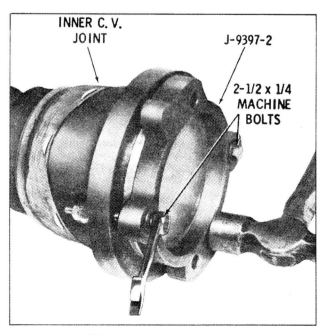

Fig. 3EB-28—Installing Cover Into Housing

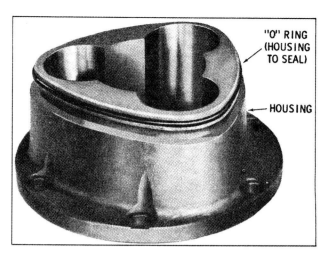

Fig. 3EB-29—Installing "O" Ring On Housing

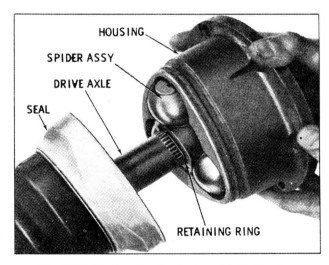

Fig. 3EB-30—Installing Spider Assembly To Housing

housing level full.

16. Install new "O" ring housing and lubricate "O" ring with Special Seal Lubricant No. 1050169 or equivalent. (Fig. 3EB-27)

17. Install cover into housing using existing A/C Tool No. J-9397-2. Attach two machine bolts (2 1/4" x 1/4") as shown in Fig. 3EB-28 and tighten bolts alternately while tapping lightly with hammer until cover bottoms.

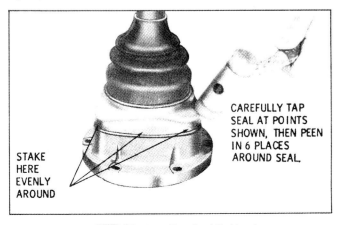

Fig. 3EB-31—Installing Seal To Housing

Fig. 3EB-32—Removing Seal Clamps

Be careful that seal is positioned correctly so that "O" ring is not cut.

DRIVE AXLE

Disassembly

1. Remove drive axle assembly. (Refer to DRIVE AXLE ASSEMBLY - R. or L. Removal).
2. Remove outer C.V. joint seal clamps. (Fig. 3EB-32)
3. Remove inner C.V. joint small clamp and pry out peened spots of seal to housing. Slide seal down shaft.
4. Slide seal inboard on shaft.
5. Remove retaining ring from inner C.V. joint. (Fig. 3EB-20)
6. Remove spider assembly.

A rubber band may be used around spider journals

to retain balls and needle bearings.

7. Remove inner retaining ring from axle shaft. (Fig. 3EB-25)
8. Remove seals from shaft.
9. Remove "O" ring from housing.

Assembly

1. Pack folds of outer seal full of Lubricant, No. 1050530 or equivalent. Inner seal with No. 1050649 or equivalent.
2. Insert new service clamp on shaft.
3. Slide new outer seal onto shaft.
4. Using Tool J-5586, spread retaining ring of outer C.V. joint until axle shaft can be inserted into outer C.V. joint.

Make sure retaining ring is in proper position.

5. Position inner seal into groove of axle and outer C.V. joint and install clamps and secure. (Fig. 3EB-16A-B-C-D-E)
6. Install new clamp on shaft.

For clamp installation procedures, follow Figs. 3EB-16A-B-C-D-E.

7. Slide new inner C.V. joint seal onto shaft.
8. Install inner retaining ring on shaft. (Fig. 3EB-33)
9. Install spider assembly on shaft and retain with retaining ring. (Fig. 3EB-30)
10. Install new "O" ring on housing and lubricate with Special Seal Lubricant, No. 1050169 or equivalent. (Fig. 3EB-31)
11. Remove rubber band, if used, from spider assembly.
12. Position spider assembly in line with housing assembly and push into housing until bottomed.
13. Using Lubricant, No. 1050649 or equivalent, fill housing level full.
14. With housing positioned as shown in Fig. 3EB-31, slide seal into position and stake in six places, evenly spaced.

Care must be taken so that "O" ring is not cut by metal portion of seal.

15. Prior to installation of the seal clamp, extend the assembly to its maximum length and equalize the pressure in the seal by lifting the lip at the axle shaft. Hold joint in extended position and install seal clamp. (Figs. 3EB-16A-B-C-D-E)
16. Install drive assembly. (Refer to DRIVE AXLE ASSEMBLY - RIGHT OR LEFT INSTALLATION.

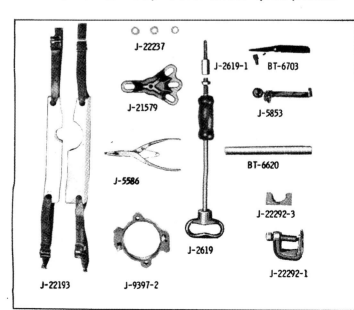

J-2619	SLIDE HAMMER
J-2619-1	ADAPTER
J-5586	SNAP RING PLIERS
J-5853	IN. LBS. TORQUE WRENCH
BT-6620	BRASS DRIFT
BT-6703	C. V. JOINT BOOT CLAMP TOOL
J-21579	AXLE AND HUB PULLER
J-22193	C. V. JOINT SUPPORT BLOCKS
J-22237	FRONT HUB PULLING SPACERS
J-9397-2	C. V. JOINT COVER INSTALLER
J-22292-1	LOWER BALL JOINT REMOVER PLATE
J-22292-3	LOWER BALL JOINT REMOVER PLATE

FINAL DRIVE

TORONADO

CONTENTS OF SECTION 3EC

FINAL DRIVE

PERIODIC MAINTENANCE

Check lubricant level at each engine oil change period. Maintain lubricant level to filler plug hole in cover. Use only Gear Lubricant, No. 1050081 or equivalent.

Always clean dirt or foreign material from around plug opening before removing filler plug.

Periodic or seasonal changes are not recommended.

RATIO CODE

Ratio codes are located as shown on Fig. 3EC-2. "T" for 3:07:1.

GENERAL DESCRIPTION (Fig. 3EC-1)

The final drive assembly, mounted and splined directly to the automatic transmission, consists of a pinion drive gear, a ring gear (bolted to the case), case assembly with two side gears and two pinion gears which are retained to the case with a pinion shaft. A lock pin is used instead of a bolt to lock the pinion shaft to the case. There are thrust washers used behind the side gears and shims behind the pinion gears the same as the conventional differential. The left side gear is different than the right side in the respect that it has a threaded retainer plate that the left output shaft bolts to. The two side bearings are the same and the pre-load shims are identical for the right and left side. The carrier is identical in external appearance and mounts to the transmission the same as in the past models.

The output shafts remain identical in external appearance as in the past. The left output shaft has the retainer bolt going through the shaft to the side gear.

RH OUTPUT SHAFT, BEARING AND SEAL

Removal

1. Disconnect battery.
2. Hoist car.
3. Remove engine oil filter element.
4. Remove attaching bolts, R.H. drive axle to R.H. output shaft. Then move drive axle rearward until free from output shaft.
5. Disconnect support from engine and brace. (Fig. 3EC-2)
6. Remove output shaft assembly.
7. If output shaft seal is to be replaced, install Seal Remover BT-6629 and BT-6229-2 into seal and drive seal out with a hammer. (Fig. 3EC-3)
8. If output shaft bearing is to be replaced, it can be removed with a press as shown in Fig. 3EC-4.

Installation

1. If output shaft bearing was removed, assemble parts as shown in Fig. 3EC-5.
2. Position assembly in a press and install bearing until seated as shown in Fig. 3EC-6.
3. Pack area between bearing and retainer with wheel bearing grease, then install slinger as shown in Fig. 3EC-7.

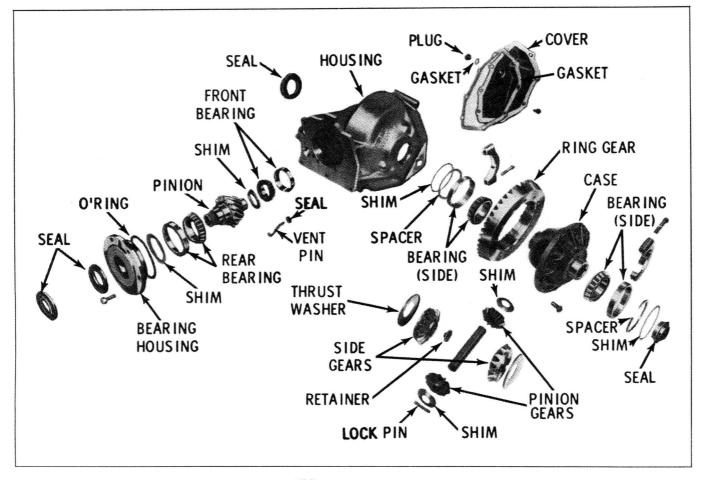

Fig. 3EC-1—Final Drive Assembly

4. If output shaft seal was removed, new seal can be installed as shown in Fig. 3EC-8.

5. Apply Special Seal Lubricant No. 1050169 or equivalent to output shaft seal, then install output shaft into final drive indexing splines of output shaft with splines in side gear.

6. Install support to engine and brace. (Fig. 3EC-2)

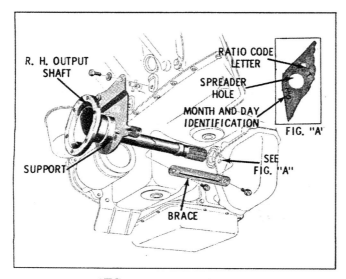

Fig. 3EC-2—R.H. Output Shaft Attachment

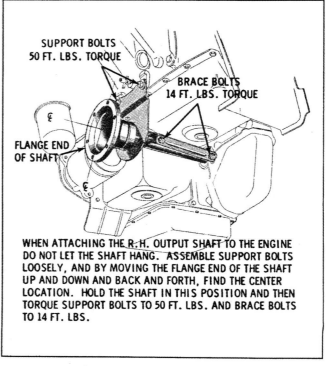

WHEN ATTACHING THE R.H. OUTPUT SHAFT TO THE ENGINE DO NOT LET THE SHAFT HANG. ASSEMBLE SUPPORT BOLTS LOOSELY, AND BY MOVING THE FLANGE END OF THE SHAFT UP AND DOWN AND BACK AND FORTH, FIND THE CENTER LOCATION. HOLD THE SHAFT IN THIS POSITION AND THEN TORQUE SUPPORT BOLTS TO 50 FT. LBS. AND BRACE BOLTS TO 14 FT. LBS.

Fig. 3EC-2A—Aligning R.H. Output Shaft

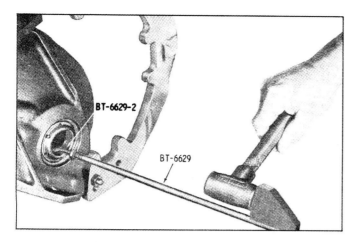

Fig. 3EC-3—Removing R.H. Output Shaft Seal

When attaching the right hand output shaft to the engine, do not let the shaft hang. Assemble support bolts loosely, and by moving the flange end of the shaft up and down, and back and forth, find the center location. Hold the shaft in this position and then torque the bolts to 50 ft. lbs. on support and 14 ft. lbs. on brace. (Fig. 3EC-2A)

7. Move drive axle forward until alignment with output shaft is obtained. Install attaching bolts. Torque to 65 ft. lbs.

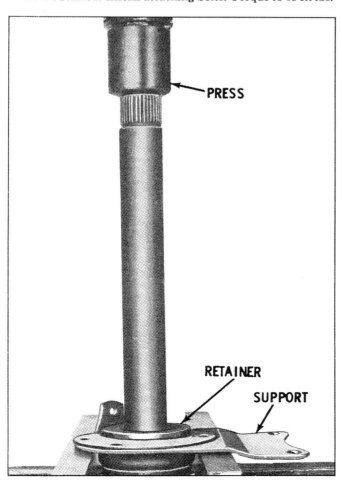

Fig. 3EC-4—Removing R.H. Output Shaft Bearing

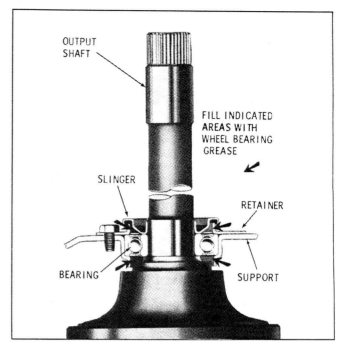

Fig. 3EC-5—R.H. Output Shaft Assembly

8. Install engine oil filter element.
9. Connect battery.
10. Check engine oil level and final drive oil level and check for oil leaks.

LH OUTPUT SHAFT AND SEAL

Removal

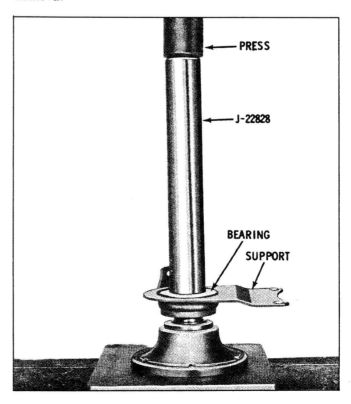

Fig. 3EC-6—Installing R.H. Output Shaft Bearing

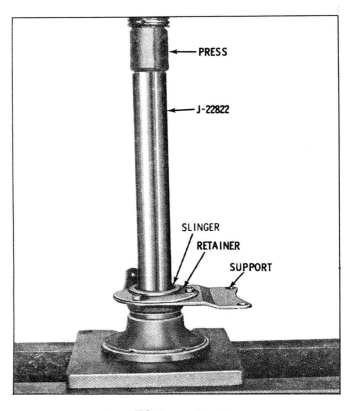

Fig. 3EC-7—Installing Slinger

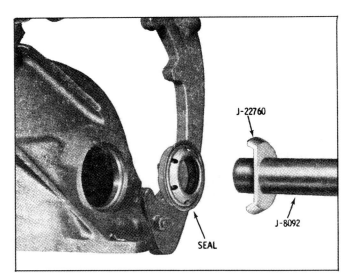

Fig. 3EC-8—Installing R.H. Output Shaft Seal

1. Remove L.H. drive axle. Refer to Section 3EB, DRIVE AXLE ASSEMBLY (LEFT HAND), Steps 1 through 15 under REMOVAL.

2. Using a 9/16" socket remove L.H. output shaft retaining bolt and remove L.H. output shaft. (Fig. 3EC-19)

If output shaft seal is to be replaced, insert Tool BT-6629 and BT-6629-3 into seal and drive out with a hammer. (Fig. 3EC-10)

Installation

1. If output shaft seal was removed, install new seal as shown in Fig. 3EC-11.

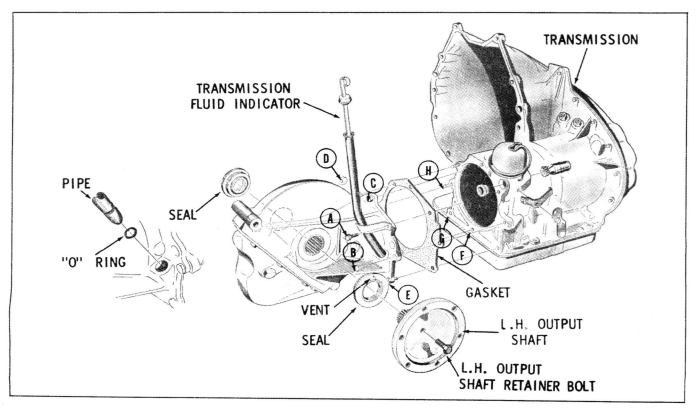

Fig. 3EC-9—Final Drive Attachment

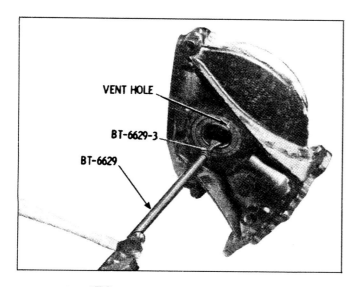

Fig. 3EC-10—Removing L.H. Output Shaft Seal

Left output shaft seal is installed with vent hole toward top of final drive housing in the in car position.

2. Apply Special Seal Lubricant No. 1050169 or equivalent to the seal; then, insert output shaft into final drive assembly, indexing splines of output shaft with splines in side gear.

3. Install L.H. output shaft retaining bolt and torque to 40 ft. lbs. (Fig. 3EC-9)

4. Install L.H. drive axle. Refer to Section 3EB, DRIVE AXLE ASSEMBLY (LEFT HAND), Steps 1 through 10 under INSTALLATION.

TRANSMISSION FILLER TUBE

Removal and Installation

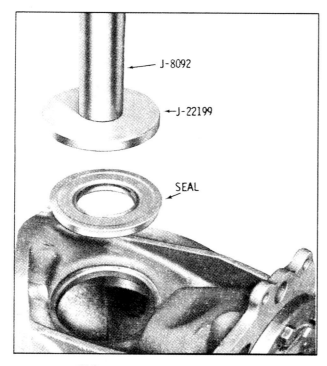

Fig. 3EC-11—Installing L.H. Output Shaft Seal

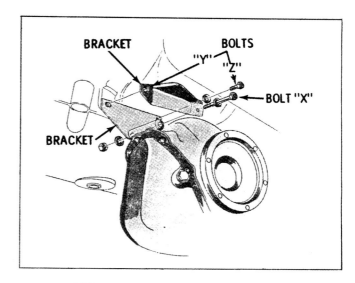

Fig. 3EC-12—Disconnecting Final Drive From Engine

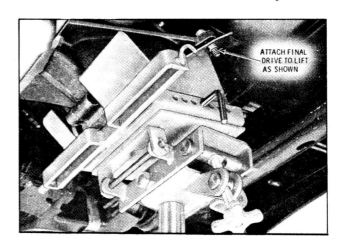

Fig. 3EC-13—Connecting Lift to Final Drive

The automatic transmission filler tube is located on the final drive. The filler tube can be removed by removing bolt "A", Fig. 3EC-9 and then pulling the filler tube out of the

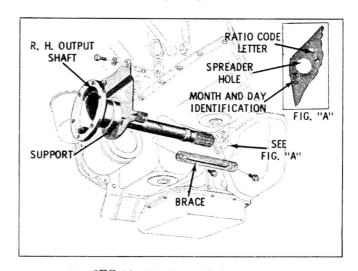

Fig. 3EC-14—R.H. Output Shaft Attachment

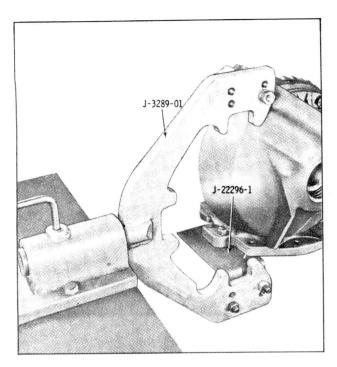

Fig. 3EC-15—Final Drive In Holding Fixture

housing. To install, position a new "O" ring seal on the filler tube. Coat seal with Special Seal Lubricant No. 1050169 or equivalent and install filler tube into housing. Install bolt "A" and torque to 25 ft. lbs.

FINAL DRIVE

Removal

1. Disconnect battery.
2. Remove bolts "A", "B", and "C" and nut "D". Nut "D" must be removed with a special wrench, such as MAC S-147. (Fig. 3EC-9)

It may be necessary to remove the transmission filler tube to obtain clearance.

3. Hoist car. If a two post hoist is used, the car must be supported with floor stands at the front frame rails and the front post lowered.
4. Disconnect right and left drive axles from the output shafts.

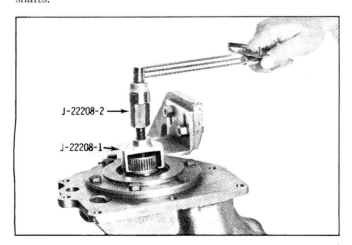

Fig. 3EC-16—Checking Pinion and Side Bearing Pre-Load

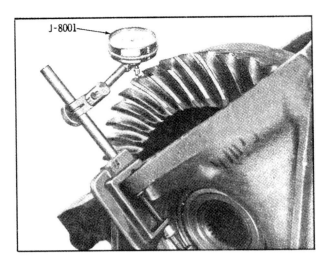

Fig. 3EC-17—Checking Ring Gear to Pinion Gear Backlash

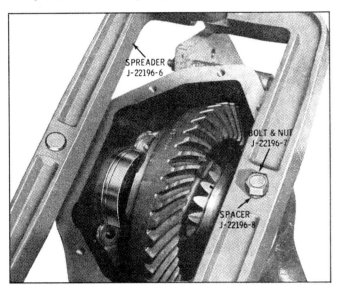

Fig. 3EC-18—Spreader Installation

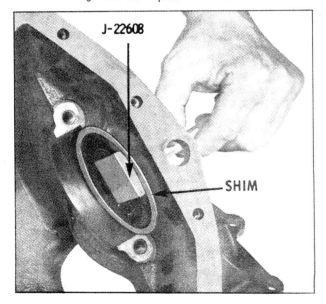

Fig. 3EC-19—Removing Shims

Fig. 3EC-20—Positioning of Tool J-22608

5. Remove engine oil filter element.

6. Disconnect brace from final drive, then disconnect R.H. output shaft support from engine. (Fig. 3EC-14)

7. Move R.H. drive axle rearward until R.H. output shaft can be removed from final drive.

8. Remove bolt "X" and loosen bolts "Y" and "Z". (Fig. 3EC-12)

9. Remove final drive cover and allow lubricant to drain.

10. Position transmission lift with adapter for final drive as shown in Fig. 3EC-13. Install an anchor bolt through final drive housing and lift pad.

11. Remove bolts "E", "F", and "G" and nut "H". (Fig. 3EC-9)

12. Move transmission lift toward front of car to disengage final drive splines from transmission.

As the final drive is disengaged from transmission, some transmission fluid will be lost. Provide a container to prevent oil from running on floor.

13. Lower transmission lift and remove final drive from lift.

14. Using a 9/16" socket remove the left output shaft retainer bolt, then pull output shaft from final drive. (Fig. 3EC-9)

15. Remove transmission to final drive gasket.

Installation

1. Apply Special Seal Lubricant No. 1050169 or equivalent to both output shaft seals.

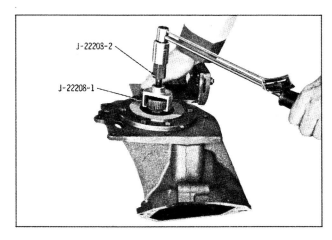

Fig. 3EC-21—Check Pinion Pre-Load

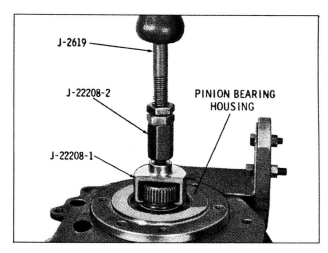

Fig. 3EC-22—Removing Pinion and Bearing Housing

2. Install the left output shaft into the final drive. Retain with bolt. Torque bolt to 40 ft. lbs. (Fig. 3EC-9)

3. Position final drive on transmission lift and install an anchor bolt through housing and lift pad. (Fig. 3EC-13)

4. Apply a thin film of Special Seal Lubricant No. 1050169 or equivalent on the transmission side of a new final drive to transmission gasket, then position gasket on transmission.

5. Raise transmission lift. Align the two bolt studs "D" and "H" on the transmission with their mating holes in the final drive. Move final drive until it mates with the transmission. (Fig. 3EC-9)

It may be necessary to rotate the left output shaft so that the splines of the final drive pinion engage the splines of the transmission output shaft. Do not allow gasket to become mispositioned while engaging splines.

6. Install bolts "E", "F" and "G" and nut "H" (Fig. 3EC-9). Install bolts "A", "B", and "C" and nut "D". (Fig. 3EC-9) Torque all final drive to transmission bolts to 25 ft. lbs. Torque nuts to an approximate 25 ft. lbs.

7. Install bolt "X" and torque to 105 ft. lbs. Tighten and torque bolts "Y" and "Z" to 50 ft. lbs. (Fig. 3EC-12)

8. Loosen and remove lift from final drive.

9. Position a new cover gasket on the final drive, then install cover. Torque cover bolts to 25 ft. lbs.

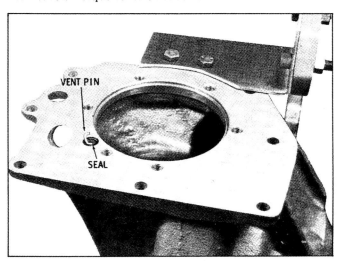

Fig. 3EC-23—Removing Vent Pin and Seal

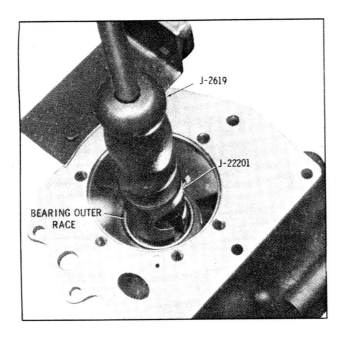

Fig. 3EC-24—Removing Front Pinion Bearing Outer Race

10. Install right output shaft into final drive indexing splines of output shaft with splines of side gear. Install support and brace bolts. (Fig. 3EC-14)

When attaching the right hand output shaft to the engine, do not let the shaft hang. Assemble support bolts loosely, and by moving the flange end of the shaft up and down, and back and forth, find the center location. Hold the shaft in this position and then torque the bolts to 50 ft. lbs. on support and 14 ft. lbs. on brace. (Fig. 3EC-2A)

11. Connect drive axles to output shafts. Torque bolts to 65 ft. lbs.

12. Install engine oil filter element.

13. Raise hoist, remove floor stands and lower car.

14. If filler tube was removed, install a new "O" ring and install filler tube.

15. Connect battery.

16. Fill final drive with 4-1/2 pints of Lubricant No. 1050081 or equivalent.

17. Check engine oil level, start engine and check transmission fluid level. Add fluid as necessary.

18. Check for any oil leaks.

FINAL DRIVE (REMOVED FROM CAR)

Disassembly

1. Install adapter J-22296-1 on Differential Holding Fixture J-3289. Mount final drive in holding fixture as shown in Fig. 3EC-15.

2. Rotate housing so that pinion is up. Install tools as shown in Fig. 3EC-16, and turn torque wrench several turns and record torque reading. This combined pinion and side bearing pre-load reading will be helpful in determining cause of final drive failure. Remove tools and rotate carrier so that pinion is down.

3. Rotate differential case several times to seat bearings, then mount dial indicator as shown in Fig. 3EC-17. Use a small button on the indicator stem so that contact can be made near heel end of tooth. Set dial indicator so that stem is in line as nearly as possible with gear rotation and perpendicular to tooth angle for accurate backlash reading.

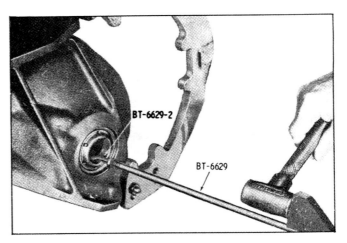

Fig. 3EC-25—Removing R.H. Output Shaft Seal

4. Check backlash at three or four points around ring gear. Lash must not vary over .002" around ring gear.

Pinion must be held stationary when checking backlash. If variation is over .002" check for burrs, uneven bolting conditions or distorted case and make corrections as necessary.

5. Remove side bearing cap bolts.

Bearing caps are of same size and must be installed in their original position. Mark right and left bearing caps to identify for reassembling. Keep the original bearing outer races with their corresponding caps.

6. Install Spreader on Housing as shown in Fig. 3EC-18.

Spreader must be modified with Tools J-22196-7-8.

7. Turn the Spreader screw to expand Spreader until the spacer and shim(s) can be removed from between the right side bearing and the housing. Retain spacers and shims for reassembly.

Spread housing only enough to relieve tension on the spacer and shims. The shims may be removed with Tool J-22608 as shown in Figs. 3EC-19 and 20.

8. Remove spreader from housing.

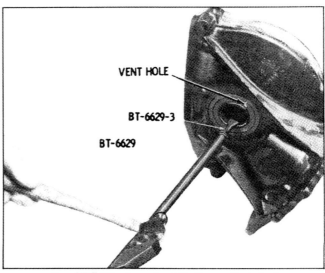

Fig. 3EC-26—Removing L.H. Output Shaft Seal

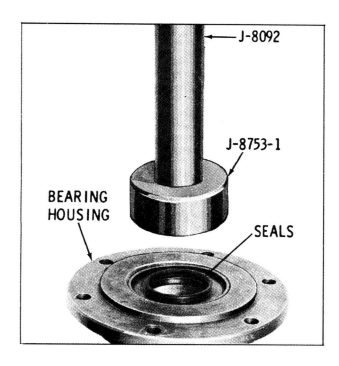

Fig. 3EC-27—Removing Oil Seals from Pinion Bearing Housing

9. Remove the spacer and shims, then slide the case assembly to the left, away from the pinion gear. Remove case assembly from housing.

10. Rotate housing so that the pinion is up. Check pinion bearing pre-load as shown in Fig. 3EC-21. Record the pinion bearing pre-load.

11. Remove the bearing housing bolts. Remove the drive pinion and housing as shown in Fig. 3EC-22. Remove housing from drive pinion. Remove "O" ring seal from bearing housing.

12. Remove seal and vent pin from housing. (Fig. 3EC-23)

13. Install Tool J-22201 on Slide Hammer J-2619. Position Tool J-22201 as shown in Fig. 3EC-24 and tighten screw. Remove pinion front bearing outer race.

14. Remove the output shaft oil seals as shown in Fig. 3EC-25 and 3EC-26.

15. Remove the two oil seals from the pinion bearing housing as shown in Fig. 3EC-27.

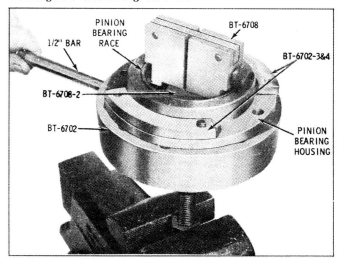

Fig. 3EC-28—Removing Rear Pinion Bearing Outer Race

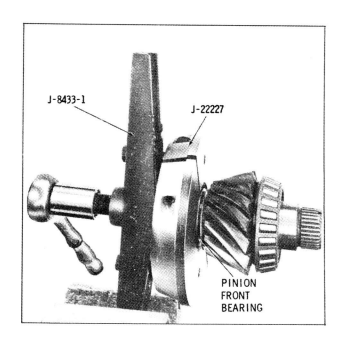

Fig. 3EC-29—Removing Pinion Front Bearing

16. If necessary to remove the pinion rear outer race, it can be removed as shown in Fig. 3EC-28.

PINION BEARINGS

Removal

1. Remove the pinion front bearing and selective shim as shown in Fig. 3EC-29. Bearing can be removed without Tool J-8433-1 if a press is available.

2. Remove the pinion rear bearing as shown in Fig. 3EC-30.

FINAL DRIVE CASE

Disassembly

1. If the side bearings are to be removed, they can be removed as shown in Fig. 3EC-31 and 3EC-32.

Fig. 3EC-30—Removing Pinion Rear Bearing

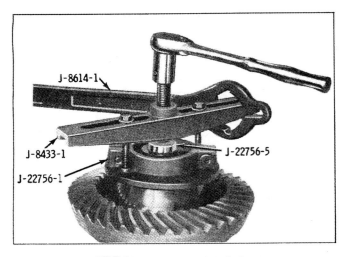

Fig. 3EC-31—Removing Left Side Bearing

2. Mark ring gear and case, then remove all but two of the case to ring gear bolts. Leave two of the bolts, 180° apart, loose.

Ring gear must be removed to remove pinion and side gears.

3. Position case as shown in Fig. 3EC-33 and tap lightly on a bench to separate the case from ring gear.

4. Remove the two remaining ring gear bolts and separate ring gear from case.

5. Drive lock pin from pinion shaft with a 3/16" punch. (Fig. 3EC-34)

6. Push pinion shaft out of case.

7. Rotate one pinion gear and shim towards access hole in case and remove.

Keep the corresponding shims and pinion gear together for correct assembly.

8. Remove the other pinion gear and shim.

9. Remove side gears keeping the same thrust washer with the side gear it is mated with. Inspect thrust washers and shims for wear and replace as necessary.

The left side gear has the threaded retainer that retains the (short) left output shaft. If threaded retainer is to be removed, use a brass drift and hammer to remove from left side gear.

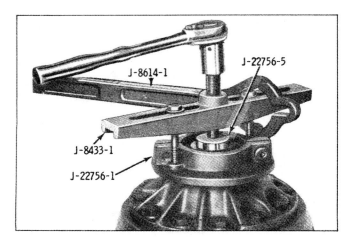

Fig. 3EC-32—Removing Right Side Bearing

Fig. 3EC-33—Separating Ring Gear From Case

CLEANING AND INSPECTION

1. Clean all bearings thoroughly in clean solvent (Do not use a brush). Examine bearings visually and by feel. All bearings should feel smooth when oiled and rotated while applying as much hand pressure as possible.

Minute scratches and pits that appear on rollers and races at low mileage are due to the initial pre-load, and bearings having these marks should not be rejected.

2. Examine the ring gear and drive pinion teeth for excessive wear and scoring. Any of these conditions will require replacement of the gear set.

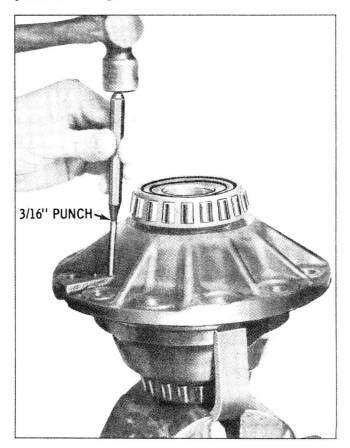

Fig. 3EC-34—Removing Lock Pin From Pinion Shaft

Fig. 3EC-35—Installing Pinion Front Bearing Outer Race

3. Examine housing bores and remove any burrs that might cause leaks around the OD of the seal.

4. Inspect the differential pinion shaft for unusual wear; also check the pinion and side gears and thrust washers.

5. Side bearings must be a tight press fit on the hub.

6. Diagnosis of a differential failure such as chipped bearings, loose (lapped-in) bearings, chipped gears etc. is a warning that some foreign material is present; therefore, the housing must be thoroughly cleaned and inspected.

CHECKING PINION DEPTH

1. Install pinion front outer race as shown in Fig. 3EC-35. Drive race until it bottoms.

2. Lubricate front bearing with final drive lubricant and install into front outer race.

3. Position Tool J-21777-10 on front bearing. Install Tool J-21579 on final drive housing and retain with two bolts. Thread screw J-21777-13 into J-21579 until tip of screw engages Tool J-21777-10. Torque screw J-21777-13 to 20 in. lbs. to pre-load bearing. (Fig. 3EC-36)

4. Remove dial indicator post from Tool J-21777-1 and install Discs J-21777-22 as shown in Fig. 3EC-37. Reinstall dial indicator post.

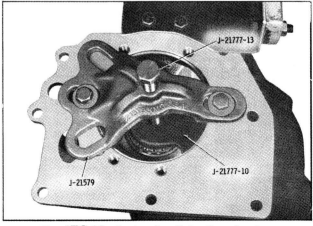

Fig. 3EC-36—Pre-Loading Pinion Front Bearing

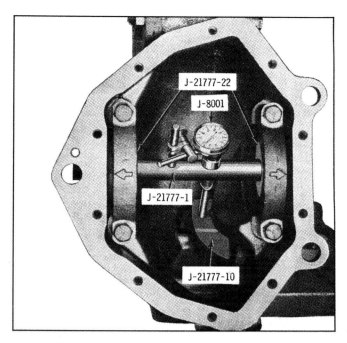

Fig. 3EC-37—Pinion Depth Gauge Installation

5. Place the gauging discs in the side bearing bores and install the side bearing caps.

6. Position the dial indicator, J-8001 on the mounting post of the gauge shaft and with the contact rod OFF the gauging area of J-21777-10. Set dial indicator on ZERO, then depress the dial indicator until the needle rotates 3/4 turn clockwise. Tighten the dial indicator in this position. RESET DIAL INDICATOR ON ZERO.

7. Position the gauge shaft assembly in the housing so that the dial indicator contact rod is directly in line with the gauging area BUT NOT ON and the discs seated fully in the side bearing bores.

8. Rotate the gauge shaft assembly until the dial indicator rod contacts the gauging area of J-21777-10. Rotate gauge shaft slowly back and forth until the dial indicator reads the greatest deflection.

9. At the point of greatest deflection, read the dial indicator directly for pinion depth.

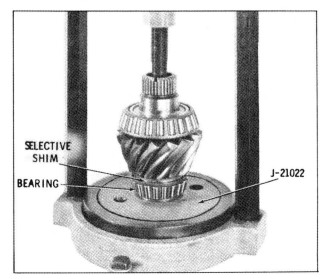

Fig. 3EC-38—Installing Pinion Front Bearing and Shim

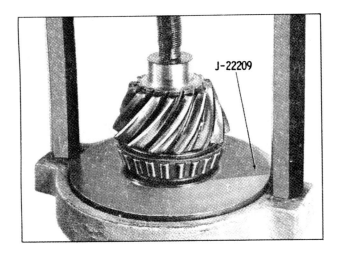

Fig. 3EC-39—Installing Pinion Rear Bearing

10. Select the correct pinion shim to be used during pinion reassembly on the following basis:

a. If a service pinion is being used, or a production pinion with no marking, the correct shim will have a thickness equal to the indicator gauge reading found in Step 9.

b. If a production pinion is being used and it is marked "+" or "-", the correct shim will be determined as follows:

Pinions marked "+" (plus) the shim thickness indicated by the dial indicator on the pinion setting gauge must be INCREASED by the amount etched on the pinion.

If the pinion is marked "-" (minus) the shim thickness indicated by the dial indicator on the pinion setting gauge must be DECREASED by the amount etched on the pinion.

11. Remove pinion depth checking tools and front bearing from housing.

12. Position correct shim on drive pinion and install the drive pinion front bearing as shown in Fig. 3EC-38.

Shims are available from .040" to .070" in increments of .002".

13. Install rear pinion bearing as shown in Fig. 3EC-39.

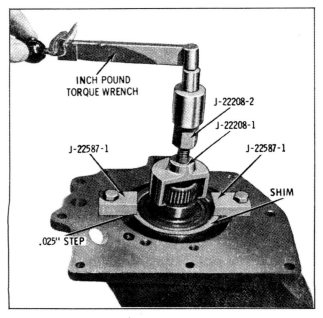

Fig. 3EC-40—Checking Shim Thickness for Pre-Load

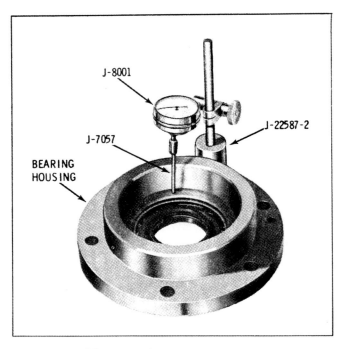

Fig. 3EC-41—Checking Inner Flange of Housing

PINION BEARING PRE-LOAD ADJUSTMENT

1. The pre-load shim will have to be changed or checked any time the following parts have been replaced:
a. Ring gear and pinion.
b. Pinion bearings (front or rear).
c. Rear bearing retainer.
d. Final drive housing.

2. Position pinion bearing race on pinion bearing and install Tool J-22587-1 as shown in Fig. 3EC-40. Using a feeler gauge check thickness between bearing race and Tool J-22587-1. Loosen bolts holding Tool J-22587-1 so that pinion bearing shim can be installed. Shims are available in sizes from .036" to .070" in increments of .002". Add shims until a pre-load of 2 to 5 in. lbs. is obtained. RECORD FINAL SHIM THICKNESS.

3. Remove Tool J-22587-1.

4. With dial indicator J-8001 and extension J-7057, attach existing dial indicator post to Tool J-22587-2. (Fig. 3EC-41). While holding contact studs (three) of Tool J-22587-2 firmly against shoulder of bearing housing, position dial indicator as shown in Fig. 3E-41 and rotate dial to ZERO.

5. Carefully lift dial indicator assembly over flange of bearing housing and position assembly as shown in Fig. 3EC-42. With the three contact studs held firmly against shoulder of bearing housing, read the dial indicator deflection. RECORD THIS DEFLECTION.

The following is an example of finding the correct pinion bearing pre-load with information obtained above.

.053"	(Shims recorded in Step 2)
+.024"	(Diff. in housing - Step 5)
.077"	
−.025"	(Built in step in Tool J-22587-1)
.052"	
−.002"	(To compensate for increase in pre-load when installing housing)
.050"	(Actual pinion bearing pre-load shim required)

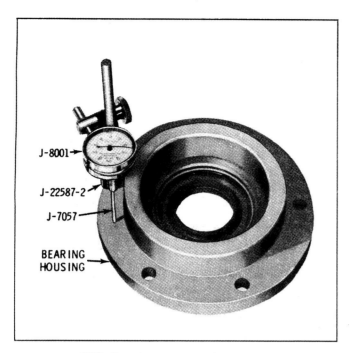

Fig. 3EC-42—Checking Outer Flange of Housing

6. Position shim into bearing housing and install pinion rear bearing outer race as shown in Fig. 3EC-43.

7. Install seals into bearing housing as shown in Fig. 3EC-44.

8. Install a new "O" ring seal on the bearing, housing.

9. Install seal and vent pin on face of housing. (Fig. 3EC-45)

10. Install seal protector J-22236 over drive pinion and install bearing housing over seal protector into position on the housing. Torque the attaching bolts to 35 ft. lbs. (Fig. 3EC-46)

11. Reinstall Tool J-22587-1 and recheck pinion pre-load. Must be within 2 to 5 in. lbs.

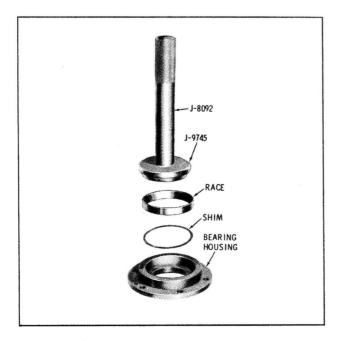

Fig. 3EC-43—Installing Rear Pinion Bearing Outer Race

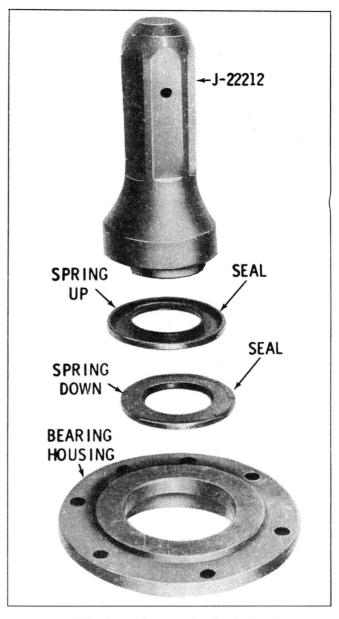

Fig. 3EC-44—Installing Seals into Bearing Housing

CASE ASSEMBLY

SIDE BEARING

Installation

1. Install the side bearings as shown in Figs. 3EC-47 and 48. Drive evenly until seated.

Do not let the bearing cock as it is being driven on. Excess metal could be wiped off the mounting surfaces and the bearing could become loose on the case.

SIDE AND PINION GEARS

Installation

Before assembling the differential case, lubricate all parts with Lubricant No. 1050081 or equivalent.

1. Place side gear thrust washers over side gear hubs and install side gears in case. If same parts are reused, install in original sides.

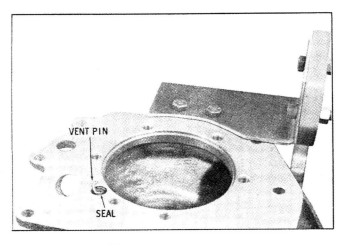

Fig. 3EC-45—Installing Seal and Vent Pin

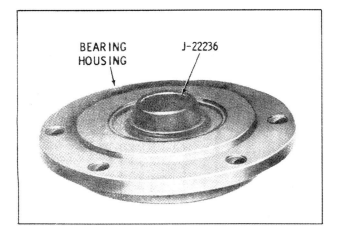

Fig. 3EC-46—Installing Bearing Housing to Housing

Fig. 3EC-47—Installing Left Side Bearing

Fig. 3EC-48—Installing Right Side Bearing

Position side gear with threaded retainer on left side of case.

2. Position one pinion (without shims) between side gears and rotate gears until pinion is directly opposite from loading opening in case. Place other pinion between side gears so that pinion shaft holes are in line; then rotate gears to make sure holes in pinions will line up with holes in case.

3. If holes line up, rotate pinions back toward loading opening just enough to permit sliding in pinion gear shims.

4. Install pinion shaft. Drive pinion shaft retaining lock pin into position. (Fig. 3EC-49)

RING GEAR

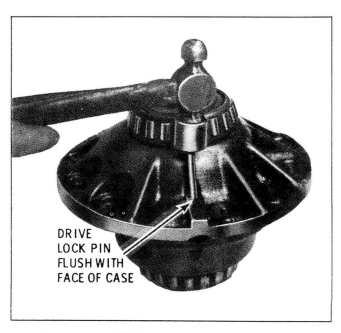

Fig. 3EC-49—Installing Lock Pin

Fig. 3EC-50—Installing Ring Gear to Case

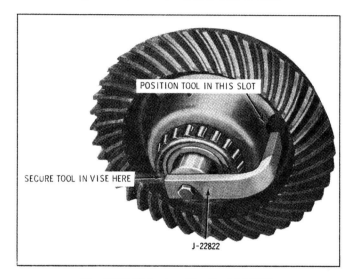

Fig. 3EC-50A—Installing Tool J-22822

Installation

1. After making certain that mating surfaces of case and ring gear are clean and free of burrs, install **Tool J-22595** as shown in Fig. 3EC-50 to correctly position ring gear.

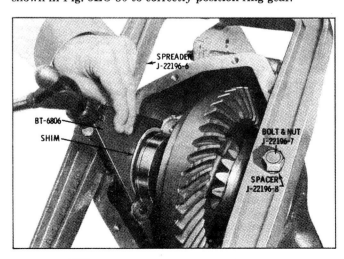

Fig. 3EC-51—Spreading Housing for Shim Installation

Fig. 3EC-52—Checking Pinion and Side Bearing Pre-Load

2. Install Tool J-22822 into a vise and place case assembly over tool as shown in Fig. 3EC-50A. Install new ring gear attaching bolts in remaining holes and then remove Tool J-22595. Install remaining three new bolts into ring gear and torque bolts alternately in progressive stages to 85 ft. lbs.

Tool J-22822 must be used to correctly torque ring gear bolts.

SIDE BEARING PRE-LOAD ADJUSTMENT

Differential side bearing pre-load is adjusted by means of shims placed between the side bearing and housing. Shims are used on both sides and 19 shims are available in increments of .002" from .038" to .074". Two spacers, .140" ± .005", are used, one on the right side and one on the left side. By adding or subtracting the same amount of shims from both sides, the ring gear to pinion backlash will not change.

1. Before installing the case assembly, make sure that side bearing surfaces in the housing are clean and free of burrs. Side bearings must be oiled with Lubricant No. 1050081 or equivalent. Turn fixture and housing so cover side is up.

2. Place differential case and bearing assemblies in position in housing.

3. Install the original spacers on left and right side. If the recorded side bearing pre-load was correct on disassembly, the original shims may be used.

Fig. 3EC-53—Checking Ring Gear to Pinion Gear Backlash

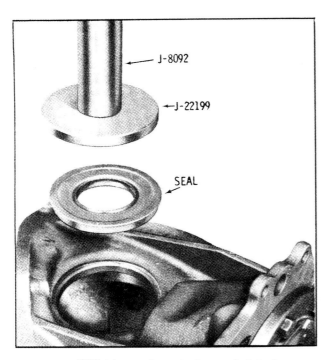

Fig. 3EC-54—Installing L.H. Output Shaft Seal

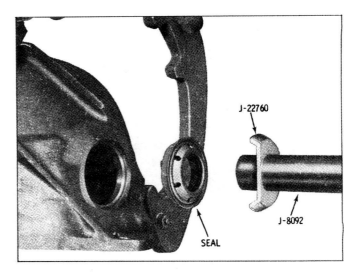

Fig. 3EC-55—Installing R.H. Output Shaft Seal

4. Install Spreader J-22196 on housing and spread housing just enough so that shim can be inserted between the spacer and the housing. (Fig. 3EC-51)

5. Release tension on spreader tool, install side bearing caps, then check pre-load as shown in Fig. 3EC-52. Pre-load should be 10 to 15 in. lbs. for new bearings, 5 to 7 in. lbs. for old bearings over the pinion bearing pre-load.

6. If pre-load is not within specifications, obtain proper combination of shims, either thicker or thinner, until side bearing pre-load is 10 to 15 in. lbs. for new bearings, 5 to 7 in. lbs. for old bearings over the pinion bearing pre-load.

BACKLASH ADJUSTMENT

1. Rotate differential case several times to seat bearings, then mount dial indicator as shown in Fig. 3EC-53. Use a small button on the indicator stem so that contact can be made near heel end of tooth. Set dial indicator so that stem is in line as nearly as possible with gear rotation and perpendicular to tooth angle for accurate backlash reading.

2. Check backlash at three or four points around ring gear. Lash must not vary over .002" around ring gear.

Pinion must be held stationary when checking backlash. If variation is over .002" check for burrs, uneven

bolting conditions or distorted case and make corrections as necessary.

3. Backlash at the point of minimum lash should be between .005" and .009" for all new gears. If original ring gear and pinion was installed, backlash should be set at the same reading obtained in Step 4 of the Final Drive Disassembly procedure, provided reading was within specifications.

4. If backlash is not within specifications, correct by increasing thickness of one differential shim and decreasing thickness of other shim the same amount. This will maintain correct differential side bearing pre-load.

For each .001" change in backlash desired, transfer .002" in shim thickness. To decrease backlash .001", decrease thickness of right shim .002" and increase thickness of left .002". To increase backlash .002" increase thickness of right shim .004" and decrease thickness of left shim .004".

5. When backlash is correctly adjusted, remove spreader. Install the bearing caps and bolts. Torque to 65 ft. lbs.

6. Install new output shaft seals as shown in Fig. 3EC-54 and 3EC-55.

Left output shaft seal is installed with vent hole toward top of final drive housing in the in car position.

7. Install new gasket on housing. Install cover, torque cover bolts to 25 ft. lbs. Fill final drive to proper level with the specified lubricant.

If final drive was removed without removing the transmission, do not install gasket, cover or lubricant until final drive has been installed in car.

TORQUE SPECIFICATIONS

APPLICATION	FT. LBS.
Final Drive Cover Bolts	25
Side Bearing Cap Bolts	65
Bearing Housing Bolts	35
Ring Gear Bolts	85
Drive Axle to Output Shaft Bolts	65
Final Drive Support Bracket to Engine Bolt	50
Final Drive to Support Bolt	105
RH Output Shaft Support to Engine Bolts	50
RH Output Shaft Brace to Final Drive and Support Bolts	14
LH Output Shaft Retainer Bolt	40
Final Drive to Transmission Bolts and Nuts	25

FINAL DRIVE SPECIFICATIONS

LUBRICATION

Capacity . . . . 4-1/2 Pints

Replenish . . . . Special Lubricant, No. 1050081
or equivalent

ADJUSTMENTS

Backlash . . . . .005" to .009"

Pinion Bearing Pre-load

New Bearings . . . . 2 to 5 in. lbs.

Old Bearings . . . . 2 to 3 in. lbs.

Side Bearing Pre-load

New Bearings . . . . 10 to 15 in. lbs. over Pinion Bearing Pre-load

Old Bearings . . . . 5 to 7 in. lbs. over Pinion Bearing Pre-load

GEAR RATIO . . . . **43:14—3.07**

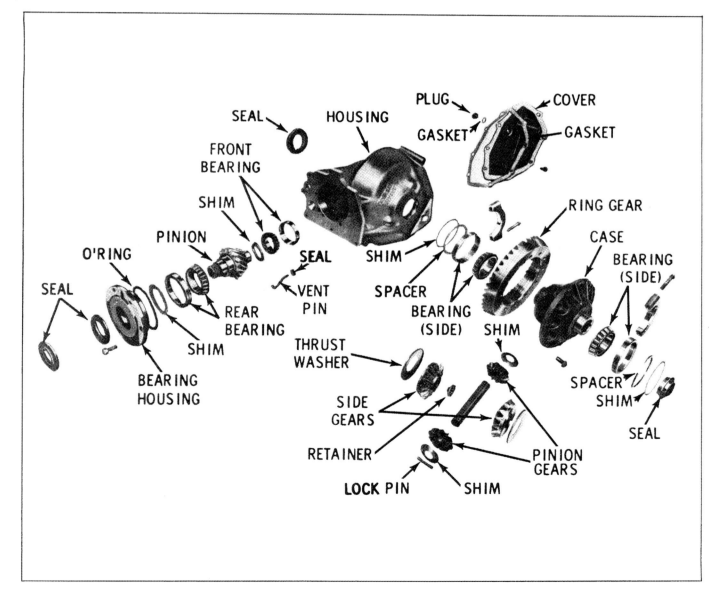

Fig. 3EC-56—Final Drive Assembly

J-2619	SLIDE HAMMER	J-22196-7-8	HOUSING SPREADER
J-3289-01	HOLDING FIXTURE	J-22199	LEFT OUTPUT SHAFT SEAL INSTALLER
BT-6629-1-2-3	SEAL REMOVER	J-22201	FRONT PINION BEARING RACE REMOVER
BT-6702	FRONT HUB BEARING PULLER SET	J-22208-1-2	ADAPTER
BT-6708-1	PINION BEARING CUP REMOVER	J-22209	PINION BEARING INST.
BT-6708-2	PINION BEARING CUP REMOVER	J-22212	PINION SEAL INST.
BT-6806	SIDE BEARING SHIM INST.	J-22227	FRONT PINION BEARING REMOVER
J-7057	EXTENSION	J-22236	PINION OIL SEAL PROTECTOR
J-8001	DIAL INDICATOR	J-22296-1	HOLDING FIXTURE ADAPTER
J-8092	DRIVER HANDLE	J-22587-1-2	PINION BEARING PRELOAD GAUGE SET
J-8433-1	PULLER	J-22595	RING GEAR INSTALLER STUDS
J-8458	RACE INSTALLER	J-22608	SIDE BEARING SHIM REMOVER
J-8614-1	COMPANION FLANGE HOLDER	J-22756-1-5	SIDE BEARING REMOVER
J-8753-1	TIMING CASE COVER SEAL INSTALLER	J-22760	R.H. OUTPUT SHAFT SEAL INST.
J-9745	RACE INSTALLER	J-22811	R.H. SIDE BEARING INST.
J-21022	FRONT PINION BEARING INSTALLER	J-22812	L.H. SIDE BEARING INST.
J-21579	PINION BEARING PRELOAD TOOL	J-22822-2	CARRIER HOLDER
J-21777-1-10-13-22	PINION SETTING TOOLS	J-22828	AXLE BRG. AND SLINGER INST.

Fig. 3EC-57—Tools

REAR SUSPENSION

TORONADO

CONTENTS OF SECTION 4E

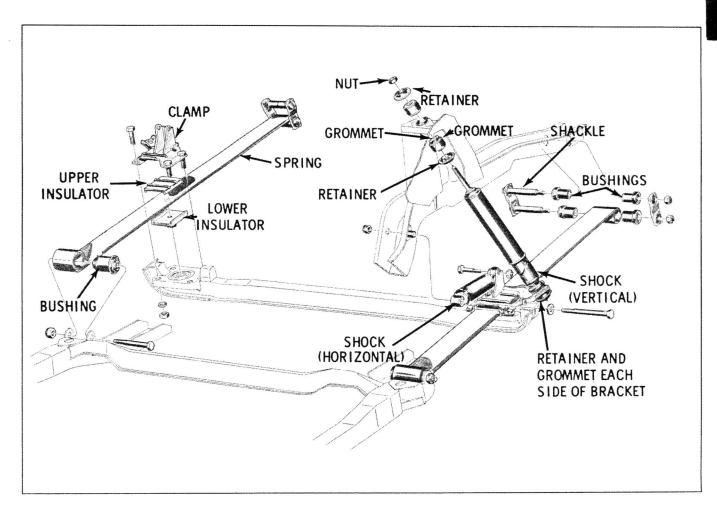

Fig. 4E-1—Rear Suspension - Toronado

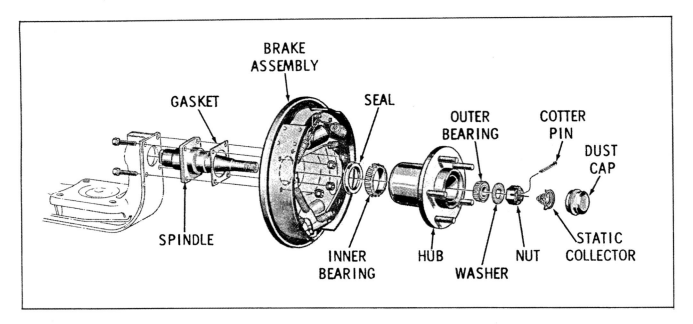

Fig. 4E-2—Rear Hub and Spindle - Toronado

REAR SUSPENSION

PERIODIC MAINTENANCE

A periodic rear wheel bearing repack is not required. However, when major brake service is being performed, it is recommended that the rear wheel bearings be cleaned and repacked with a Lithium E.P. grease.

WHEEL BEARINGS

The proper functioning of the rear suspension cannot be maintained unless the rear wheel taper roller bearings are correctly adjusted. Cones must be a slip fit on the spindle and the inside diameter of the cones should be lubricated to insure that the cones will creep. Spindle nut must be a free-running fit on threads.

Adjustment

The adjustment of the rear wheel bearings should be made WHILE REVOLVING THE WHEEL AT LEAST THREE TIMES THE SPEED OF NUT ROTATION when making the torque readings as follows:

1. Tighten adjusting nut with a torque wrench 25 to 30 ft. lbs. to insure that all parts are properly seated and threads are free.
2. Back off nut 1/2 turn. Retighten nut finger tight.
3. If unable to install cotter pin at finger tight position, back off to first securing position.

HUB AND DRUM ASSEMBLY

Removal (Wheel Removed)

1. Remove dust cap from hub.
2. Remove cotter pin, nut and washer from spindle.
3. Reinstall dust cap and carefully pull hub and drum assembly from spindle.

It may be necessary to back off the brake shoe adjustment before the hub and drum can be removed.

BEARING AND SEAL

Removal

1. Remove dust cap and remove the outer bearing inner race and the roller and separator assembly from hub.
2. Pry seal from hub; then remove inner bearing inner race and roller and separator assembly from hub.
3. If necessary to remove outer races, insert a brass drift into hub, indexing end of drift into notches in hub behind bearing outer race and tap with a hammer. Tap alternately on each side of bearing race. (Fig. 4E-4)

CLEANING AND INSPECTION

For inspection of rear drums, refer to BRAKE DRUMS, Section 5.

1. Wash all parts in clean solvent with the exception of the roller and separator assemblies and races and air dry. Roller and separator assemblies and races should be washed in gasoline.
2. Check bearings for cracked separators and worn or pitted rollers.
3. Check bearing races for cracks, scores or a brinelled condition.

BEARING AND SEAL

Installation

1. If the outer races were removed, drive or press the races into the hub as shown in Fig. 4E-6.
2. Lubricate the bores of the inner races and fully pack the roller and separator assemblies with a Lithium E.P. grease.
3. Install inner bearing roller and separator assembly into outer race; then install inner bearing into race.
4. Carefully tap seal into hub. (Fig. 4E-6)
5. Clean any traces of grease from brake lining and drum with fine sandpaper. If necessary to adjust brake linings, refer to BRAKE LINING - Adjust, Section 5.

HUB AND DRUM

Installation

1. Position hub and drum assembly over spindle.
2. Install outer bearing roller and separator into hub.
3. Install outer bearing inner race over spindle; then install the washer and spindle nut. Draw spindle nut up snug

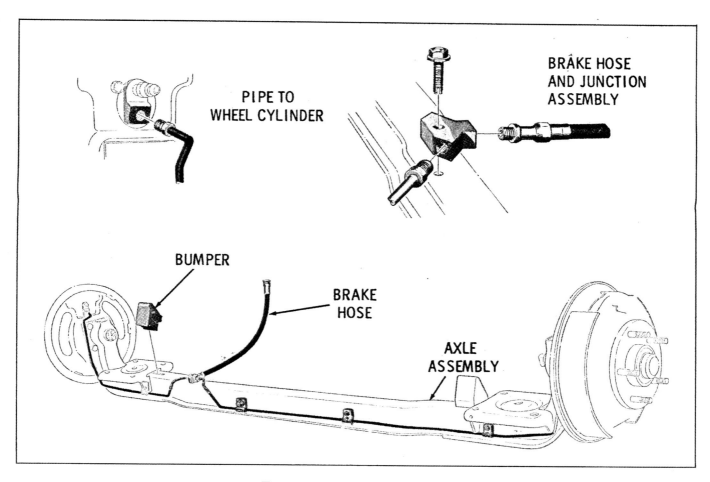

PIPE TO WHEEL CYLINDER

BRAKE HOSE AND JUNCTION ASSEMBLY

BUMPER

BRAKE HOSE

AXLE ASSEMBLY

Fig. 4E-3—Rear Axle Brake Line Routing - Toronado

and adjust bearing as outlined under WHEEL BEARING ADJUSTMENT.

HUB BOLT REPLACEMENT

1. With the hub and drum removed, drill a 5/8" hole 1/4" deep into the head of the hub bolt.

2. Support hub and drive or press hub bolt out through the front of the hub.

3. Press a new hub bolt into the hub.

4. While supporting hub bolt, peen hub bolt with the use of Peening Tool J-554-13. (Fig. 4E-5)

REAR WHEEL SPINDLE (ON THE CAR)

Removal

1. Hoist rear of car and support with floor stand under frame pad.

2. Remove wheel and drum.

3. Remove hub assembly.

4. Disconnect brake line fitting at wheel cylinder. (Fig. 4E-3)

5. Remove four attaching bolts, backing plate to spindle. (Fig. 4E-2)

6. Place backing plate out of the way.

7. Place hydraulic jack under axle.

8. Remove four attaching bolts from center spring clamp assembly. (Fig. 4E-1)

9. Remove rubber insulator from spring.

10. Lower hydraulic jack until spindle is clear of spring and spindle is accessible for removal.

11. Drive spindle out of axle, with a hammer.

Installation

1. Start new spindle, with keyway up, into axle and install the four bolts (backing plate to spindle). Tighten bolts progressively one turn each until spindle is fully seated.

2. Remove bolts.

3. Position insulators on spring. Tape if necessary to secure.

4. Raise rear axle until spring aligning pin locates into axle.

5. Replace four attaching bolts into center spring clamp assembly. Torque nuts to 30 ft. lbs.

6. Install backing plate on spindle. Torque nuts to 35 ft. lbs.

7. Connect brake line to wheel cylinder.

8. Install hub assembly. For correct torque, refer to REAR WHEEL BEARING ADJUSTMENT.

9. Install drum and wheel. Torque wheel nuts to 115 ft. lbs.

10. Bleed wheel cylinder and add fluid as necessary. Check for Leaks.

11. Remove floor stands.

VERTICAL SHOCK

Removal

1. Using Tool BT-6515, remove upper attaching nut (inside of trunk). (Fig. 4E-1)

Before removing shocks the rear axle must be supported to prevent stretching of brake hose. Raise car and remove wheel.

2. Remove lower nut, retainer and grommet, Fig. 4E-1, and remove shock.

3. Remove grommet and retainer from shock.

Installation

Reverse removal procedure. Torque upper and lower nuts to 10 ft. lbs.

HORIZONTAL SHOCK

Refer to Front Suspension, Section 3EA, for code and usage.

Removal

1. Raise car and remove wheel.
2. Remove two attaching bolts, front and rear. (Fig. 4E-1)

Installation

Reverse removal procedure. Torque nuts to 40 ft. lbs.

LEAF SPRING

Removal

1. Raise car and support with floor stand on frame pad.
2. Using hydraulic jack under axle, remove wheel.
3. Remove nut only from front of rear spring. (Fig. 4E-1)
4. Remove two attaching nuts on rear shackle (outer). (Fig. 4E-1)
5. Remove rear shackle (outer).
6. Remove four attaching bolts on center clamp assembly. (Fig. 4E-1)
7. Lift center clamp assembly up, shock will retain it in position.
8. Remove resonator bracket attaching bolts to frame and allow resonator to hang loose.
9. Lower hydraulic jack until axle is free from spring.
10. Remove shackle assembly from spring and body.
11. Remove bolt from front of rear spring and remove spring.
12. Remove bushing and replace if worn or damaged. Refer to Bushing - Front-Removal, Step 5.

Installation

1. Install rear bushings in spring and frame.

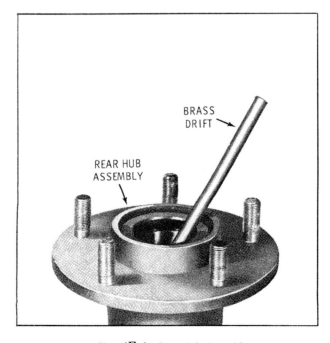

BRASS DRIFT

REAR HUB ASSEMBLY

Fig. 4E-4—Rear Hub Assembly

2. Install front bushings. Refer to Bushing - Front (Removal, Step 5 for Procedure for Expanding Spring Loop so that Bushing can be Driven into Position.)

3. Place spring into position at front attachment and install bolt and nut. Do not torque.

4. Position rear of spring so that shackle assembly can be inserted.

5. Install shackle (outer) and nuts. Do not torque.

6. Install resonator bracket attaching bolts. Torque to 10 ft. lbs.

7. Attach insulators to each side of spring, tape together if necessary.

8. Raise hydraulic jack under axle until aligning tang on spring enters hole in axle.

9. Pull center clamp assembly down towards axle until the four attaching bolts can be inserted. Torque nuts to 30 ft. lbs.

10. Install wheel. Torque nuts to 115 ft. lbs.

11. Remove floor stands and hydraulic jack.

With weight of car on the wheels, torque nuts as specified below.

Rear Shackle Nuts..........................40 ft. lbs.
Front of Spring Nut ....80 ft. lbs.

BUSHING-FRONT (IN CAR)

Removal

1. Raise car and support with floor stand on frame pad. Leave hoist under axle.

2. Disconnect vertical shock at lower attachment.

3. Remove front bushing attaching bolt.

4. Lower hoist until spring is below frame attaching bracket.

Care must be exercised when lowering hoist so that brake hose is not stretched or damaged.

5. Using small chisels or screwdrivers, wedge between edge of spring and outside of loop expanding loop so that bushing can be driven out with a hammer.

It may be necessary to block spring loop down with a block of wood to gain clearance for bushing.

Installation

To install, reverse removal procedure.

REAR AXLE

Removal

1. Lift car and use floorstands at both rear frame pads ahead of wheel opening.

2. Remove wheels, drum and hub assemblies.

3. Disconnect brake lines at wheel cylinders.

4. Disconnect parking brake cable at equalizer.

5. Remove backing plate attaching bolts and let backing plates rest on floor.

6. With hydraulic jack under center of axle, remove eight attaching bolts from center spring clamp assemblies.

7. Disconnect rubber brake hose at underbody bracket.

8. Lower jack and remove axle assembly from rear of car.

9. Remove brake line assembly and bumpers from axle.

10. Spindles can be driven from axle at this time. Brace axle end being driven to reduce bounce.

Installation

1. Insert spindle, with keyway up, into axle. (Fig. 4E-2) Using backing plate attaching bolts, progressively tighten until spindle is fully seated. Remove bolts for use later.

2. Install bumpers.

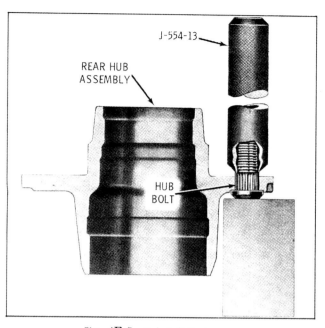

Fig. 4E-5—Hub Bolt Replacement

3. Install brake line assembly and torque junction bolt to 14 ft. lbs.

4. Place axle assembly on hydraulic jack and position axle under spring until spring aligning tangs engage. Raise jack slightly to hold axle in alignment.

5. Install center spring clamp assembly. Torque eight attaching nuts to 30 ft. lbs.

6. Install backing plates. Torque nuts to 35 ft. lbs.

7. Install brake lines to wheel cylinders.

8. Install rubber brake hose at Underbody Connector.

9. Install equalizer on parking brake cable and secure.

10. Install hub and drum assemblies. Refer to WHEEL BEARING ADJUSTMENT.

11. Bleed both wheel cylinders. Add brake fluid as necessary.

12. Install wheel. Torque wheel nuts to 115 ft. lbs.

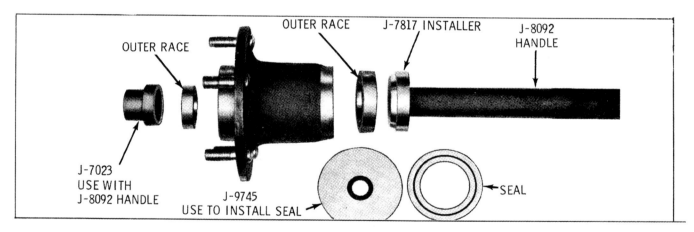

Fig. 4E-6—Installing Outer Races or Seal

TORQUE SPECIFICATIONS

Specified torque is for installation of parts only. Checking of torque during inspection may be 10% below that specified.

APPLICATION	FT. LBS.
Center Spring Clamp to Axle	30
Backing Plate to Spindle	35
Brake Line to Wheel Cylinder	14
Brake Hose Assembly to Axle	14
Wheel Nuts	115
Vertical Shock Absorber Nuts	10
Horizontal Shock Absorber Nuts	40
Resonator Bracket to Frame	14
Rear Shackle Bolts	40
Front Spring Bolt	75

BRAKES

ITEMS LISTED IN THE TABLE OF CONTENTS ARE FOR TORONADO. FOR SERVICE PROCEDURES AND RECOMMENDATIONS NOT LISTED REFER TO SECTION 5, 31-86 SERIES.

CONTENTS OF SECTION 5E

PARKING BRAKE CABLE

The rear parking brake cable can be removed as follows:

1. Disconnect the cable at the equalizer.

2. Remove the retainers which hold the conduit to the brackets.

3. Remove the rear wheels and brake drums.

4. Disconnect the cable from the operating levers.

5. Install a corbin-type hose clamp over the conduit retainer fingers as shown in Fig. 5-24, Section 5, 31-86 Series.

6. Tap the conduit lightly to remove from the backing plate.

To install, reverse the removal procedure. Adjust the parking brake.

FRONT BACKING PLATE

If the front backing plate is to be removed, proceed as follows:

1. Remove brake drum.

It may be necessary to back off the brake shoe adjustment before the brake drum can be removed. To back off the brake shoe adjustment, refer to Fig. 5E-2.

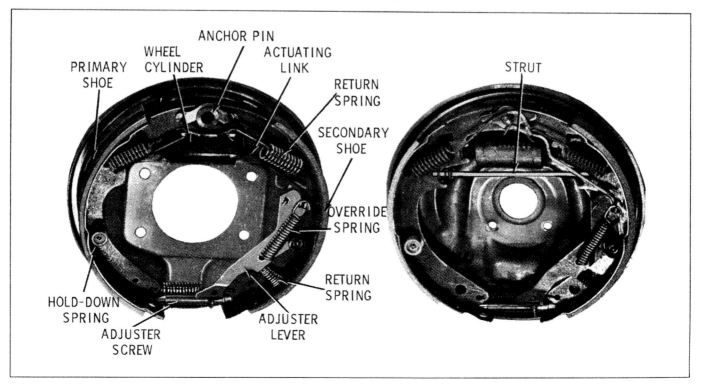

PRIMARY SHOE
WHEEL CYLINDER
ANCHOR PIN
ACTUATING LINK
RETURN SPRING
SECONDARY SHOE
OVERRIDE SPRING
RETURN SPRING
ADJUSTER LEVER
ADJUSTER SCREW
HOLD-DOWN SPRING
STRUT

Fig. 5E-1—Brake Assemblies (Toronado)

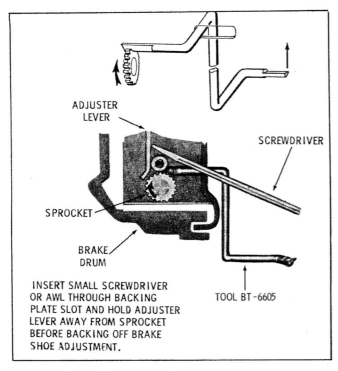

ADJUSTER
LEVER

SCREWDRIVER

SPROCKET

BRAKE
DRUM

TOOL BT-6605

INSERT SMALL SCREWDRIVER
OR AWL THROUGH BACKING
PLATE SLOT AND HOLD ADJUSTER
LEVER AWAY FROM SPROCKET
BEFORE BACKING OFF BRAKE
SHOE ADJUSTMENT.

Fig. 5E-2—Backing Off Brake Shoe Adjustment

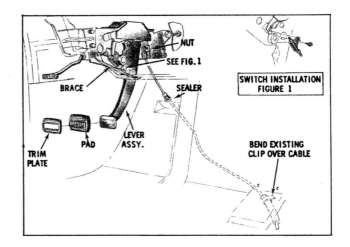

NUT

SEE FIG. 1

BRACE

SEALER

LEVER
ASSY.

TRIM
PLATE

PAD

SWITCH INSTALLATION
FIGURE 1

BEND EXISTING
CLIP OVER CABLE

Fig. 5E-3—Parking Brake

2. Remove lining as described in Section 5, 31-86 Series.

3. Loosen lock tab from anchor pin, then remove the anchor pin bolt.

4. Loosen the brake hose at the wheel cylinder.

5. Remove the wheel cylinder attaching bolts and turn cylinder off brake hose.

6. Remove the steering knuckle to hub assembly bolts and nuts. Remove axle nut. Remove hub assembly and backing plate.

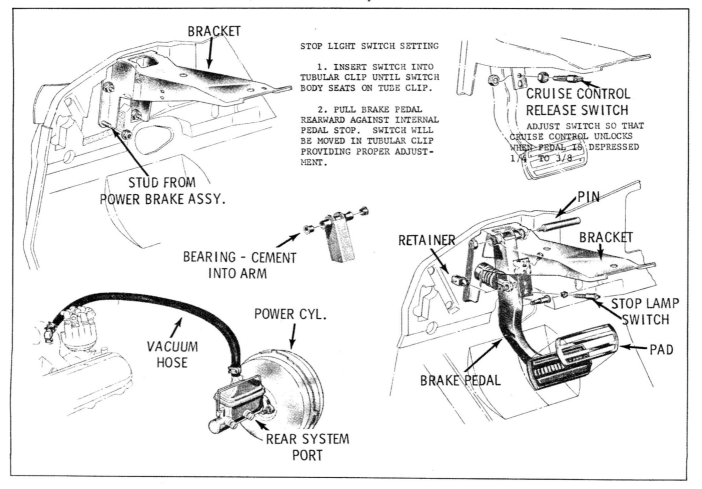

BRACKET

STOP LIGHT SWITCH SETTING

1. INSERT SWITCH INTO
TUBULAR CLIP UNTIL SWITCH
BODY SEATS ON TUBE CLIP.

2. PULL BRAKE PEDAL
REARWARD AGAINST INTERNAL
PEDAL STOP. SWITCH WILL
BE MOVED IN TUBULAR CLIP
PROVIDING PROPER ADJUST-
MENT.

CRUISE CONTROL
RELEASE SWITCH

ADJUST SWITCH SO THAT
CRUISE CONTROL UNLOCKS
WHEN PEDAL IS DEPRESSED
1/4 TO 3/8

STUD FROM
POWER BRAKE ASSY.

BEARING - CEMENT
INTO ARM

POWER CYL.

VACUUM
HOSE

REAR SYSTEM
PORT

PIN

RETAINER

BRACKET

STOP LAMP
SWITCH

PAD

BRAKE PEDAL

Fig. 5E-4—Brake Pedal Mounting

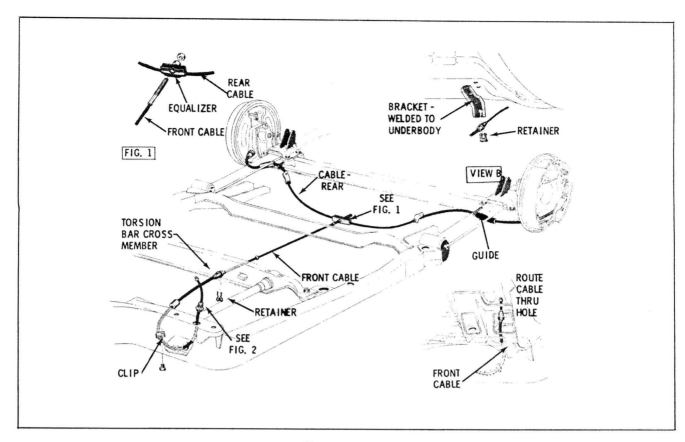

Fig. 5E-5—Parking Brake Layout

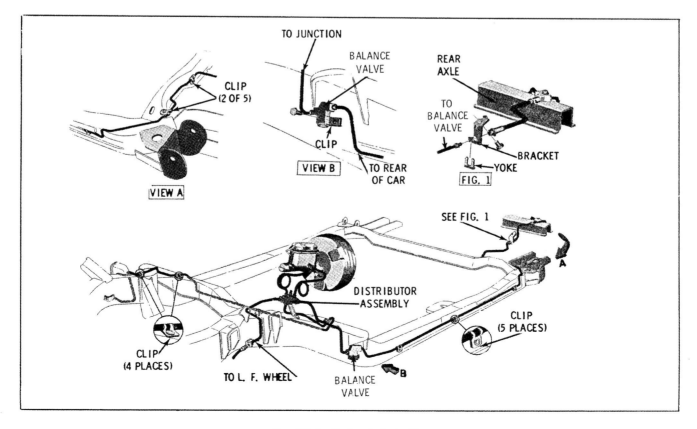

Fig. 5E-6—Hydraulic Brake Lines

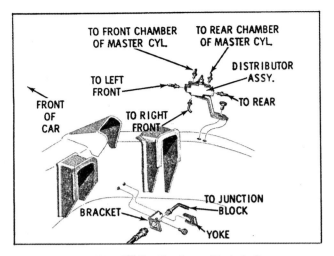

Fig. 5E-7—Distributor (Exploded)

REAR BACKING PLATE

If necessary to remove the rear backing plate, proceed as follows:

1. Remove brake drum.

It may be necessary to back off the brake shoe adjustment before the brake drum can be removed. To back off the brake shoe adjustment, refer to Fig. 5E-2

2. Remove lining as described in Section 5, 31-86 Series.

3. Remove the hub assembly and the inner bearing race from the spindle.

4. Remove brake line from wheel cylinder and remove wheel cylinder from backing plate.

5. Disconnect the parking brake cable from the backing plate.

6. Remove the backing plate.

REMOVING BRAKE SHOES (DISC BRAKE)

1. With car raised evenly on a hoist or jackstands, remove the front wheels.

2. Remove the bolts retaining the caliper splash shield, then remove the shield and anti-rattle spring assembly. (Fig. 5E-9).

3. Using two pairs of pliers, grasp the tabs on the outer ends of one of the shoes and remove the shoe and lining by pulling straight out. Repeat this operation for the second shoe. (Fig. 5E-11)

A ridge of rust may have built up on the edge of the disc surface outside of the lining contact area. If this has occurred, it will be necessary to force the pistons back slightly into their cylinders to provide clearance for the shoe removal. Do this by forcing the shoe back with a pair of water pump pliers gripped on the corner of the shoe and on the caliper housing. (Fig. 5E-12)

CLEANING AND INSPECTING THE CALIPER ASSEMBLY

1. Check the caliper seal for leaks (indicated by fluid moisture around the cavity).

2. Check for any damage to the piston dust boot.

3. Wipe the caliper cavity clean with a shop towel.

4. Check the piston dust boot for proper seating in the piston groove and on the caliper housing. If excessive fluid moisture is evident, it will be necessary to install a new piston seal and piston dust boot.

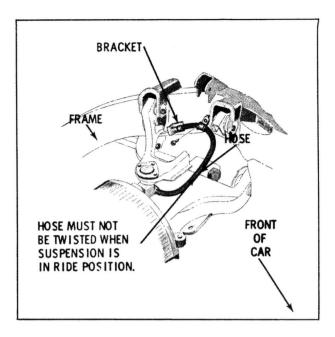

Fig. 5E-8—Front Brake Hose Installation

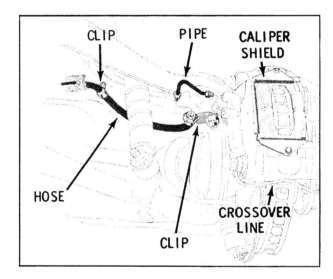

Fig. 5E-9—Caliper Shield Removal

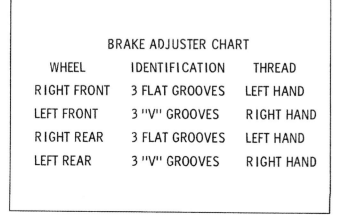

BRAKE ADJUSTER CHART

WHEEL	IDENTIFICATION	THREAD
RIGHT FRONT	3 FLAT GROOVES	LEFT HAND
LEFT FRONT	3 "V" GROOVES	RIGHT HAND
RIGHT REAR	3 FLAT GROOVES	LEFT HAND
LEFT REAR	3 "V" GROOVES	RIGHT HAND

Fig. 5E-10—Adjusting Screw Identification

Fig. 5E-11—Removing Brake Shoes

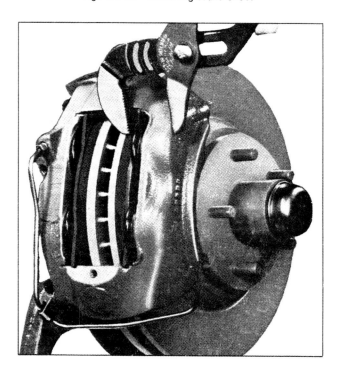

Fig. 5E-12—Forcing Pistons Back in Cylinders

INSTALLING BRAKE SHOES

1. Push all four pistons back into their cylinders until bottomed to make room for installation of new (thicker) shoes. Do this by placing a flat metal bar or tool against the piston and exerting a steady force until bottomed.

2. Slide a new shoe and lining assembly into the caliper on each side of the disc using tool BT-6717 with the ears of each shoe resting on the bridges of the caliper. Be sure the shoe is fully seated and lining is facing disc. (Fig. 5E-13)

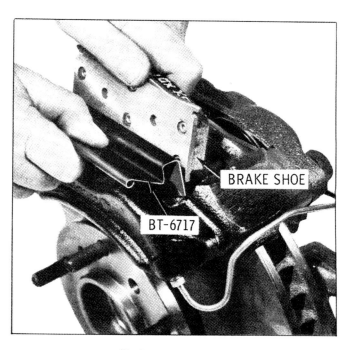

Fig. 5E-13—Installing Brake Shoes

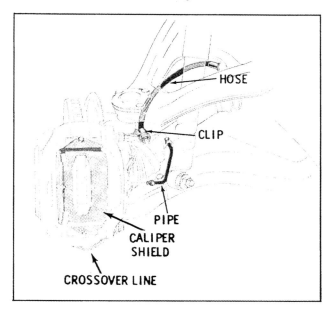

Fig. 5E-14—Disconnecting Brake Hose

3. Place the caliper splash shield and anti-rattle spring assembly in position on the caliper and install the attaching bolts. Tighten securely.

4. Repeat steps 1, 2 and 3 on the second disc brake.

5. Pump the brake several times until a firm pedal is obtained and the shoes and linings are properly seated.

6. Install the wheels.

7. Check and refill the master cylinder reservoir with brake fluid as required.

8. Road test the car and make several heavy 40 m.p.h. stops to wear off any foreign material on the brakes and to seat the shoes. The brakes may tend to "pull" if this is not done.

It should not be necessary to bleed the system if only

Fig. 5E-15—Removing Caliper

shoe and lining assemblies have been replaced.

REMOVING THE CALIPER

It is necessary to remove the caliper for installation of a new piston seal or boot. Proceed as follows:

1. Raise the car evenly on hoist or jackstands and remove the wheel, dust shield and shoes.

2. Disconnect the front brake tube at the frame mounting bracket and plug the brake tube to prevent loss of fluid. (Fig. 5E-14)

3. Remove the bolts which attach the caliper assembly to the steering knuckle.

4. Slide the caliper assembly up and away from the disc. (Fig. 5E-15)

DISASSEMBLING THE CALIPER (Fig. 5E-16)

1. Prepare a clean bench area.

2. Remove the caliper splash shield attaching bolts, then remove the splash shield and anti-rattle spring assembly, if not previously removed. (Fig. 5E-17)

3. Mount the caliper assembly in a vise equipped with padded jaws, clamping on the caliper mounting lugs. Remove the crossover line.

4. Remove the shoe and lining assemblies, if not previously removed.

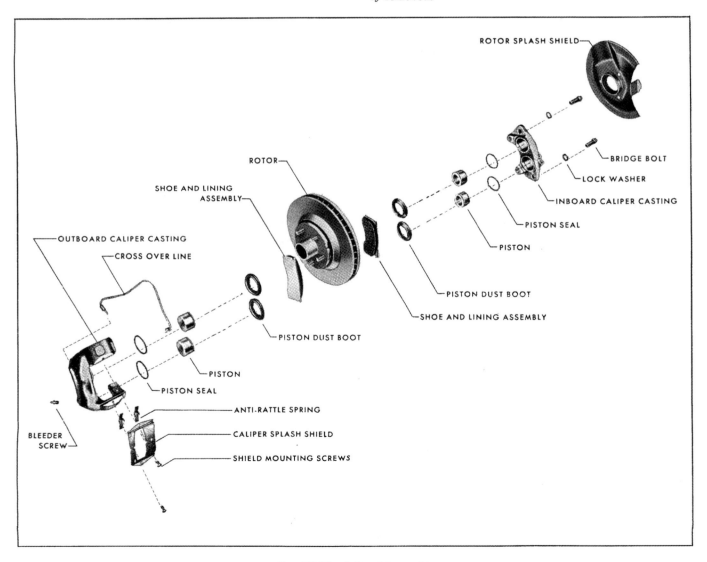

Fig. 5E-16—Caliper Disassembly

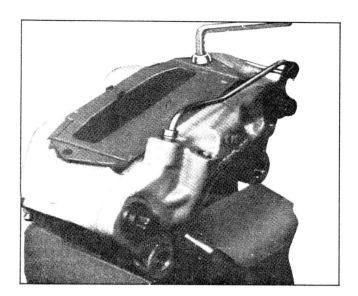

Fig. 5E-17—Removing Splash Shield

Fig. 5E-18—Removing Bridge Bolts

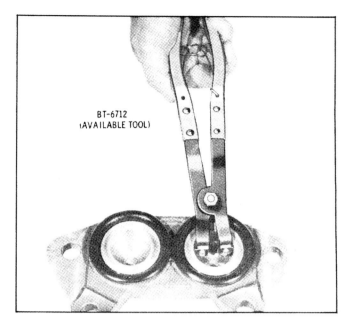

Fig. 5E-19—Removing Pistons

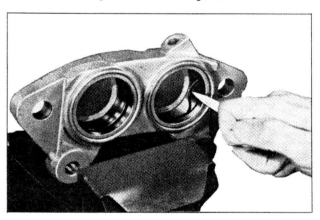

Fig. 5E-20—Removing Piston Seal

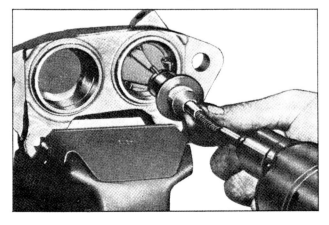

Fig. 5E-21—Honing Cylinder Bore

5. Remove the bridge bolts that hold the two halves of the caliper together. Separate the assemblies. (Fig. 5E-18)

Be sure at reassembly that these two bolts are used and tightened to the correct torque.

6. Remove each piston. Care must be used not to scratch, burr or otherwise damage the piston on its outside diameter or boot groove. Draw the piston straight out of its cylinder bore. Available tool BT-6712 may be used. (Fig. 5E-19)

7. Remove dust boot from caliper bores.

8. Using a small pointed wood or plastic tool, remove the piston seals from the grooves in the cylinder bores. Discard the old seals. Do not scratch the cylinder bores or the seal grooves. (Fig. 5E-20)

CLEANING AND INSPECTING THE CALIPER ASSEMBLY

1. Clean all parts with brake fluid and wipe dry, using a clean, lint free cloth. Using an air hose, blow out the drilled

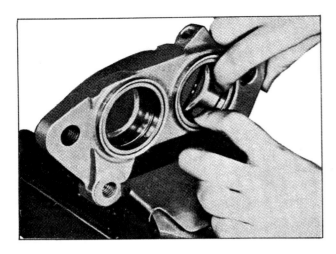

Fig. 5E-22—Installing Piston Seals

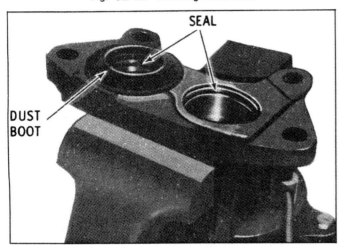

Fig. 5E-23—Installing Dust Boot

passages and bores.

2. Inspect the cylinder bores in both housing castings for scoring or pitting. Bores which show light scratches or corrosion can usually be cleaned up with crocus cloth. However, bores which have deep scratches or scoring may be honed, providing the diameter of the bore is not increased more than .002 inch. If the bore does not clean up within this specification, replace caliper housing.

Black stains on the bore wall are caused by the piston seals and will do no harm.

When using hone, be sure to install the hone baffle before honing cylinder bore. The baffle is used to protect the hone stones from damage. After honing the bore carefully, clean the seal groove with a stiff non-metallic rotary brush. (Fig. 5E-21)

3. Check each piston to see if it is pitted, scored or the chrome plating is worn off. If any of these conditions exist, discard and replace the defective piston.

Use extreme care in cleaning the caliper after honing. Remove all dust and grit by flushing the caliper with brake fluid; wipe dry with a clean lint-free cloth and then clean a second time in the same manner.

CALIPER ASSEMBLY

When reassembling caliper assembly, use only the

Fig. 5E-24—Installing Piston in Dust Boot

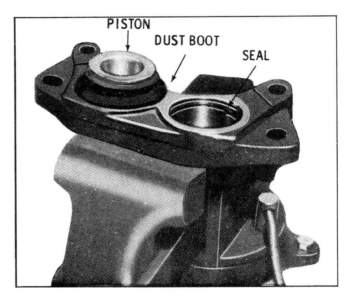

Fig. 5E-25—Piston Installed in Dust Boot

special lubricant provided in the service repair kit.

1. Clamp the inner caliper housing in a vise having brass jaws.

2. Lubricate bore in caliper housing with lubricant provided.

3. Lubricate piston seal and install in the second groove in the housing bore, being sure the seal is not twisted or rolled. (Fig. 5E-22)

4. Lubricate lips of dust boot and install dust boot in upper groove of housing bore. Make certain that dust boot is properly seated in bore groove. (Fig. 5E-23)

5. Lubricate piston and start piston inside of dust boot, working dust boot around piston until piston is installed in dust boot. (Fig. 5E-24)

6. Reposition piston as necessary. Slowly force piston into housing bore. As piston moves downward, dust boot lip will seat in groove on piston. (Fig. 5E-25)

When piston is fully seated, trapped air under dust boot may cause dust boot lip to disengage from piston groove. If this occurs, reinstall lip of dust boot in piston groove.

7. Repeat Steps 2 - 6 to install remaining pistons in hous-

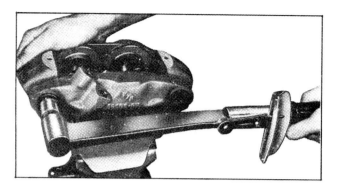

Fig. 5E-26—Tightening Bridge Bolts

Fig. 5E-27—Checking Disc Runout

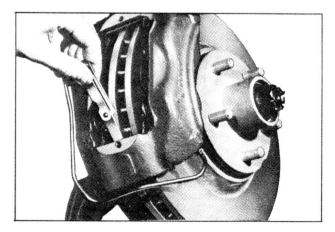

Fig. 5E-28—Checking Clearance Between Disc and Caliper

ing bore.

8. Assemble outer caliper housing to the one clamped in the vise then install the bridge bolts and tighten to 85 ft. lbs. (Fig. 5E-26)

Bridge bolts are special high tensile steel. If replacement is necessary, use only factory authorized re-

placement bolts. Do not use ordinary bolts.

9. Install the crossover line and tighten to 25 ft. lbs.

INSTALLING THE CALIPER

Before installing the caliper assembly over the brake disc, check the disc for runout. Mount a dial indicator to check lateral runout of both surfaces. Runout should not exceed .004 inch. If runout exceeds this amount, remove the disc and install a new one. Be sure the wheel bearings are adjusted to zero end play during this check. Readjust wheel bearings after check. (Fig. 5E-27)

1. Install the caliper assembly over the disc and align the mounting holes. Install the mounting bolts and tighten to 165 foot pounds. A check should be made to be sure that the disc runs squarely and centrally within the caliper opening. There should be approximately .090 to .120 inch clearance between the outside diameter of the braking disc and the caliper. There should also be a minimum of .050 inch from either disc face to the machined groove in the outboard caliper. (Fig. 5E-28)

2. Install the shoe and lining assemblies between the caliper and disc.

3. Place the caliper splash shield in position on the caliper and install the attaching bolts. Be sure that opening in caliper splash shield is centered over disc. Tighten securely, with a torque of 8 foot pounds.

4. Be sure that bleeder screw is open, then reconnect the brake line at the caliper housing. Bleed the system. Allow the caliper to fill with brake fluid. After all air bubbles have escaped, and fluid runs clear from bleeder, close the bleeder screw. Replenish the brake fluid in the master cylinder.

5. "Pump" the brake pedal several times to actuate the piston seals and position the shoe and lining assemblies.

6. Check for fluid leakage at all connections under maximum pedal pressures. Refill master cylinder reservoir as necessary.

7. Install wheel and torque wheel stud nuts to 115 ft. lb.

8. Remove jackstands or lower hoist.

Road test the car and make several heavy 40 m.p.h. stops to wear off any foreign material on the brakes and to seat the shoes. (The car may pull to one side

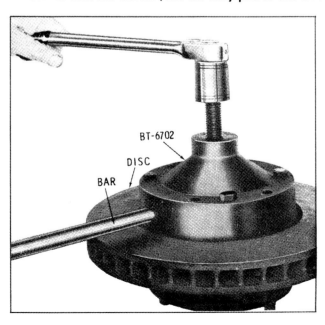

Fig. 5E-29—Removing Hub Bearing

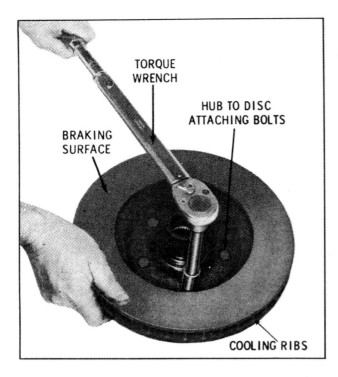

Fig. 5E-30—Installing Disc Attaching Bolts

Fig. 5E-31—Installing Hub Bearing

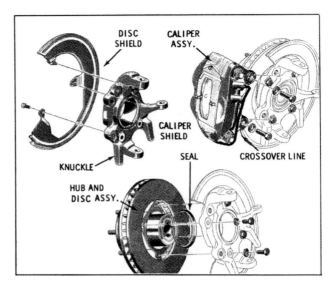

Fig. 5E-32—Disc Shield Removal

on the first application after service. This is normal until shoes are seated.)

DISC (WITH CALIPER REMOVED)

Removal

1. Remove drive axle cotter pin, nut and washer.
2. Remove bolts (four) from inboard side of knuckle from bearing retainer.
3. Position spacers, Tool J-22237 and install Tool J-21579 and slide hammer J-2619 on hub assembly and remove hub assembly. Remove tools.
4. Position Tool BT-6702 over bearing and remove bearing as shown in Fig. 5E-29.
5. Remove bolts that secure disc to hub and remove disc.

Installation

1. Install bolts through disc into hub. Torque to 70 ft. lbs. (Fig. 5E-30)
2. Position a new bearing retainer onto hub.
3. Lubricate O.D. of bearing with E.P. Chassis Lubricant and press bearing into place as shown in Fig. 5E-31.
4. Install hub assembly over drive axle splines being careful to align splines correctly.
5. Install drive axle washer and nut. Torque to 150 ft. lbs. Tighten nut to insert cotter pin.

DISC SHIELD

Disc shield can be removed only after hub and disc assy. has been removed. (Fig. 5E-32)

TORONADO GENERAL SPECIFICATIONS

LINING AREA
  Drum Brake . . . . 216 Sq. In.
  Disc Brake . . . . 124.8 Sq. In.

RATIO (Percentage of Braking Effect)
  A. Front 67%
  B. Rear 33%

DRUMS
  A. Inside Diameter . . . . 11.00"'
  B. Out-of-Round (Total Indicator Reading) Front and Rear . . . . .005"

DISC
  A. Outside Diameter . . . . 11-1/4"
  B. Lateral Runout . . . . .004"
  C. Parallelism . . . . .0005"
  D. Disc Thickness
    1. Maximum . . . . 1-1/4"
    2. Minimum . . . . 1.215"

LININGS (Drum Brake)
  A. Length - Primary (Front) . . . . 12"
  B. Length - Primary (Rear) . . . . 9"
  C. Length - Secondary (Both) . . . . 12"
  D. Width - Front . . . . 2-3/4"
  E. Width - Rear . . . . 2"

LININGS (Disc Brake)
  A. Length . . . . 6"
  B. Thickness . . . . 19/32"

WHEEL CYLINDER BORE (Disc Brake)
  A. Front . . . . 1.94"
  B. Rear . . . . .88"

MASTER CYLINDER BORE . . . . 1"

TORONADO TORQUE SPECIFICATIONS

Specified torque is for installation of parts only. Checking of torque during inspection may be 10% below that specified.

Application	Ft. Lbs.
Anchor Pin to Steering Knuckle Bolt	135
Steering Knuckle to Backing Plate Nuts	65
Backing Plate to Axle Nuts	35
Wheel Cylinder to Backing Plate Cap Screws (Front)	7
Wheel Cylinder to Backing Plate Cap Screws (Rear)	14
Wheel Nuts	115
Parking Brake Lever to Cowl	14
Parking Brake Lever to Instrument Panel Cap Screws	10
Pedal Mounting Bracket to Instrument Panel Cap Screws	6
Pedal Mounting Bracket and Master Cylinder Bolts to Cowl	24
Pedal Pivot Bolt Nut	12
Master Cylinder to Front Housing	24
Rear Housing to Cowl	24
Master Cylinder to Cowl	24
Bridge Bolts (Caliper Assembly)	85
Caliper Mounting Bolts	165
Caliper Shield Bolts	8
Splash Shield Bolts	10
Disc to Hub	70

TORONADO ENGINE – WITH W-34 OPTION

ENGINE

ITEMS LISTED IN THE TABLE OF CONTENTS ARE FOR TORONADO SERIES. FOR SERVICE PROCEDURES AND RECOMMENDATIONS NOT LISTED, REFER TO SECTION 6, 6B, V-8 ENGINE.

CONTENTS OF SECTION 6EB

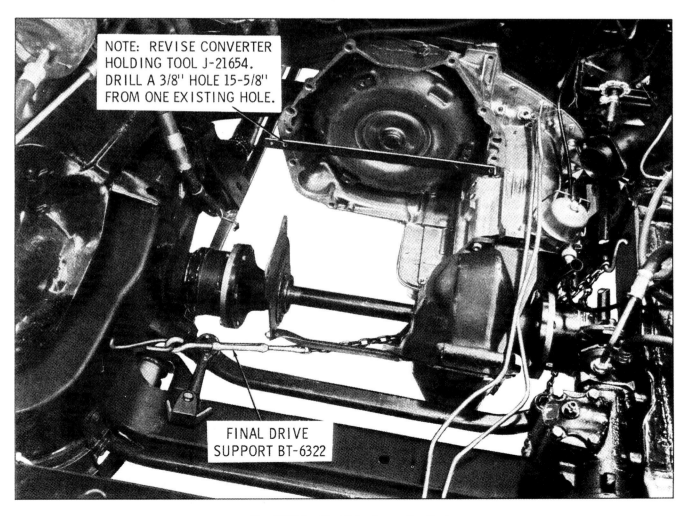

Fig. 6EB-1—Final Drive Supporting Tool

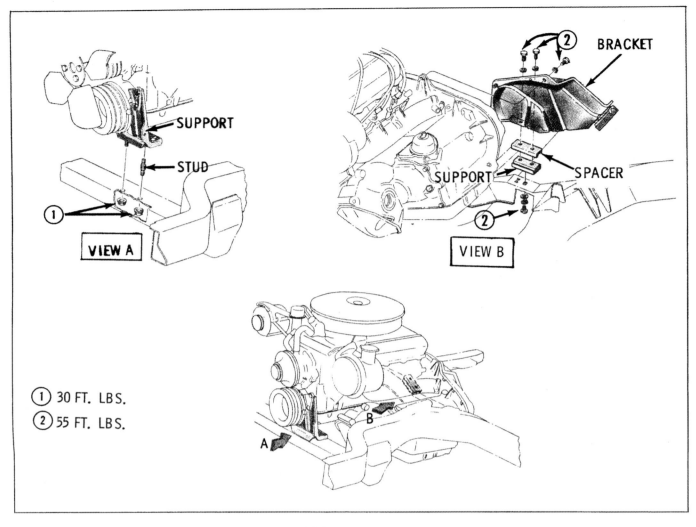

1 30 FT. LBS.
2 55 FT. LBS.

Fig. 6EB-2—Engine Mounting

ENGINE ASSEMBLY

Removal

1. Drain radiator.

2. Remove hood, marking hinge for reassembly.

3. Disconnect battery.

4. Disconnect radiator hoses and cooler lines, heater hoses, vacuum hoses, power steering pump hoses, engine to body ground strap, fuel hose from fuel lines, wiring and accelerator cable.

5. Remove coil, radiator support and radiator.

6. Raise car.

7. Disconnect exhaust pipes at manifold.

8. Disconnect wires and remove starter.

9. Remove torque converter cover and remove three bolts securing converter to flywheel.

10. Attach Tool BT-6322 supporting final drive assembly as shown in Fig. 6EB-1.

11. Remove two attaching bolts from right output shaft support bracket and one thru bolt attaching final drive to engine block, left side.

12. Remove engine mount to crossmember nuts (Fig. 6EB-2).

13. Lower car.

14. Support engine using Lift Fixture BT-6606 as shown in Fig. 6EB-3.

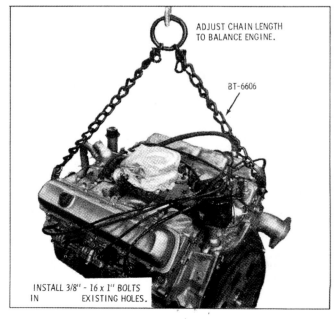

ADJUST CHAIN LENGTH TO BALANCE ENGINE.

BT-6606

INSTALL 3/8" - 16 x 1" BOLTS IN EXISTING HOLES.

Fig. 6EB-3—Engine Lift Fixture

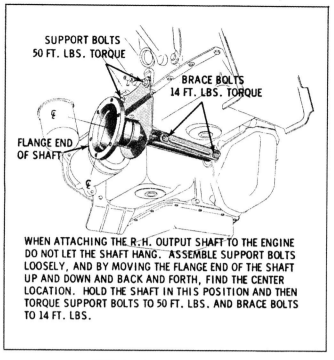

Fig. 6EB-4—Aligning R.H. Output Shaft

15. Remove six bolts, transmission to engine.
16. Using suitable lifting device, lift engine from car.

If car is to be moved install Converter Holding Tool J-21654.

Installation

1. Attach Lift Fixture BT-6606 (Fig. 6EB-3) and lower engine into position.
2. Locate engine dowels into transmission and position mount studs into front crossmember.
3. Reinstall six bolts, transmission to engine.
4. Remove Lift Fixture BT-6606 and raise car.
5. Replace torque converter to flywheel bolts.
6. Install engine mount nuts.
7. Install torque converter cover and starter.
8. When attaching the right hand output shaft to the engine support bracket, do not let the shaft hang. Assemble bracket bolts loosely, and by moving the flange end of the

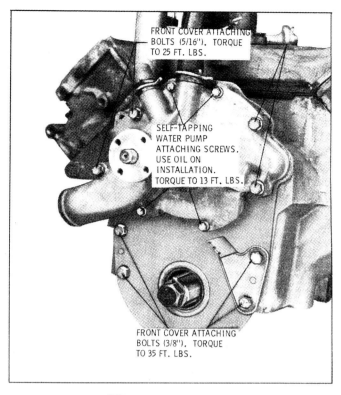

Fig. 6EB-5—Engine Front Cover Bolts

shaft up and down, and back and forth, find the center location. Hold the shaft in this position and then tighten the bolts. See Fig. 6EB-4. Reinstall the one thru bolt attaching final drive to engine block, left side.

9. Remove Tool BT-6322 supporting final drive assembly.
10. Connect exhaust pipes.
11. Lower car.
12. Install coil, radiator and radiator support.
13. Reconnect accelerator cable, wiring, fuel hoses, engine to body ground strap, power steering pump hoses, vacuum lines, heater hoses, cooler lines and radiator hoses.
14. Install and align hood (refer to Chassis Sheet Metal Section).
15. Fill radiator.
16. Connect battery.

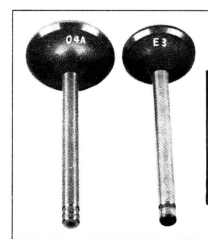

TYPE	ENGINE USAGE	PAINT CODE	FORGED LETTER	HEAD DIAMETER	LENGTH	SEAT ANGLE
INTAKE	TORONADO	RED	"04A" "S4A"	2.062	4.593	30°
EXHAUST	TORONADO	BLACK	"E3" "T3"	1.625	4.587	45°

Fig. 6EB-6—Valve Identification

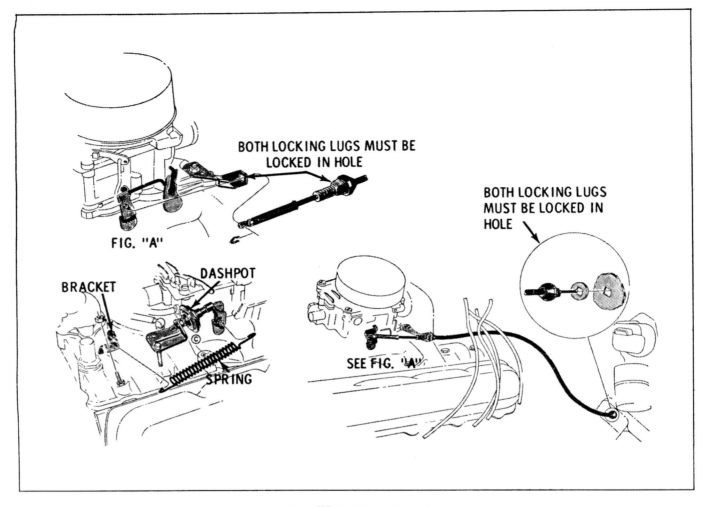

Fig. 6EB-7—Throttle Control

FRONT COVER
(With Engine and Oil Pan Removed)

Removal

1. Disconnect bypass hose from water pump.
2. Remove cover to block attaching bolts and remove cover, timing indicator and water pump assembly. (Fig. 6EB-5)

Installation

1. Install new cover gasket. Apply 1050026 Sealer or equivalent to gasket around water holes and place on block.
2. Install front cover and torque as shown in Fig. 6EB-5.

OIL PAN
Removal

1. Remove engine assembly as previously outlined.
2. Remove dip sticks.
3. Drain oil.
4. Remove mount from front cover.
5. Remove oil pan attaching bolts and remove oil pan.

Installation

1. Apply 1050026 Sealer or equivalent to both sides of pan gaskets (cork) and install on block.
2. Install front and rear seal (rubber).

3. Wipe lube 1050169 or equivalent on seal area and install pan. Torque 5/16" bolts to 15 ft. lbs. and 1/4" bolts to 10 ft. lbs.
4. Reinstall mount to front cover.
5. Reinstall engine and fill crankcase.

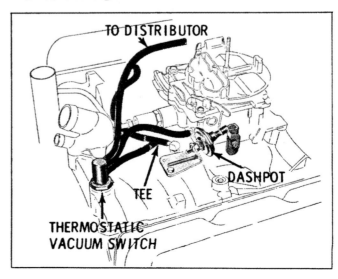

Fig. 6EB-8—Thermostatic Switch and Hoses

TORONADO ENGINE SPECIFICATIONS

CYLINDER BLOCK
Engine Type .... 90° V-Type
No. of Cylinders 8
Bore and Stroke (all) .... 4.126" x 4.250"
Piston Displacement (all) .... 455 Cu. In.
Compression Ratio 10.25:1
Firing Order 1-8-4-3-6-5-7-2
Main Bearing Bore (I.D.) .... 3.188"-3.189"

CRANKSHAFT
Diameter-Main Bearing Journal (all) .... 3.0003"-2.9993"
Width-Main Bearing Journal (with fillets)
   No. 1 .... 1.185"
   No. 2 and 4 .... 1.156"-1.166"
   No. 3 .... 1.199"-1.201"
   No. 5 .... 1.882"
Diameter-Connecting Rod Bearing Journal .... 2.4998"-2.4988"
Width-Connecting Rod Bearing (with fillets) .... 1.877"-1.880"
Length-Overall Crankshaft .... 26.470"
Diameter - Oil Holes in Crankshaft .... .201"-.209"
Clearance - Crankshaft End Thrust .... .004"-.008"

MAIN BEARINGS
Oil Clearance-Crankshaft Vertical 1, 2, 3 and 4 .... .0005"-.0021"
Oil Clearance Crankshaft Vertical 5 .... .0020"-.0034"
Width-Bearing Shell
   No. 1, 2, and 4 .... .970"-.980"
   No. 3 .... 1.193"-1.195"
   No. 5 .... 1.624"

CONNECTING RODS
Length-Center to Center .... 6.733"-6.737"
Diameter-Connecting Rod Bore .... 2.6243"-2.6250"
Diameter-Pin Bore .... .9789"-.9795"
Bearing Clearance - Crankshaft (vertical) .... .0004"-.0033"
Side Clearance - Crankshaft End .... .002"-.011"

PISTON
Diameter Nominal Outside .... 4.125"
Length Overall .... 3.490"
Top of Piston to Center of Pin .... 1.740"
Clearance at Thrust Surface (selective) .... .00075"-.00125"
Weight Less Pin and Rings (all) .... 24.057 oz.
Skirt Taper .... .0000"-.0010" Larger at Bottom
Ring Width (2 compression) .... .0798"-.0808"
        (1 oil) .... .1881"-.1891"

PISTON PINS
Diameter .... .9803"-.9807"
Length Overall .... 2.980"
Pin to Piston Clearance .... .0003"-.0005" Loose
Pin to Rod Clearance .... .0008"-.0018" Press

PISTON RINGS
No. of Compression Rings (per piston) 2
Width of Compression Rings (top and bottom) .... .0770"-.0780"
Gap Clearance Compression Rings .... .013"-.023"
Clearance in Groove Compression Rings - Upper .... .002"-.004"
                            Lower .... .002"-.004"
No. of Oil Rings (per piston) 1
Gap Clearance, Oil Ring .... .015"-.055"
Clearance in Groove - Oil Ring .... .002"-.008"

CAMSHAFT
Bearing Journal Diameters
   No. 1 .... 2.0365"-2.0357"
   No. 2 .... 2.0165"-2.0157"
   No. 3 .... 1.9965"-1.9957"
   No. 4 .... 1.9765"-1.9757"
   No. 5 .... 1.9565"-1.9557"

TORONADO ENGINE SPECIFICATIONS (Cont'd.)

CAMSHAFT (Cont'd.)
   Width (including chamfers)
      No. 1 .... .810"
      No. 2, 3, and 4 .... .761"
      No. 5 .... .788"
   Journal Clearance in Bearing (all) .... .0020"-.0058"
   End Thrust .... .011"-.077"

VALVE - INTAKE
   Diameter - Head .... 2.067"-2.077"
   Diameter - Stem .... .3425"-.3432"
   Angle - Valve .... 30°
   Angle - Valve Seat .... 30°
   Width - Valve Seat (on Cylinder Head) .... .030"-.045"
   Overall Length .... 4.703"
   Clearance in Guide .... .0010"-.0027"
   Lash .... Hydraulic

VALVE EXHAUST
   Diameter - Head .... 1.629"-1.619"
   Diameter - Stem .... .3420"-.3427"
   Angle - Valve .... 45°
   Angle - Valve Seat .... 46°
   Width - Valve Seat (on Cylinder Head) .... .037"-.075"
   Overall Length .... 4.695"
   Clearance in Guide .... .0015"-.0032"
   Lash .... Hydraulic

PUSH ROD - Length .... 9.556"

VALVE GUIDES
   Inside Diameter (intake and exhaust) .... .3442"-.3452"

VALVE SPRINGS
   Length .... 1.96"
   Diameter - Wire .... .192"
   Inside Diameter .... 1.065"-1.041"
   Load @ 1.670" .... 76-84 Lbs.
   Load @ 1.270" .... 180-194 Lbs.

VALVE LIFTERS
   Diameter - Body .... .8422"-.8427"
   Length - Overall .... 2.000"
   Clearance in Boss (selective) .... .0005"-.0020"

CAMSHAFT SPROCKET
   Width of Sprocket .... .529"-.521"
   Pitch .... .500"
   No. of Teeth 36
   Overall Width of Gear Hub .... .471"-.461"

CRANKSHAFT SPROCKET
   Width of Sprocket .... .530"-.520"
   Overall Width of Gear .... 1.001"-.991"
   Pitch .... .500"
   No. of Teeth 18

TIMING CHAIN
   Width .... .875"-Morse, .844"-Linkbelt
   No. of Links 48
   Pitch .... .500"

TURBO HYDRA-MATIC TRANSMISSION

TORONADO

CONTENTS OF SECTION 7E

PERIODIC MAINTENANCE

The fluid level should be checked at each oil change. The fluid and strainer should be replaced every 24 months. If more than 24,000 miles are driven in a 24 month period, change the fluid every 24,000 miles. Under heavy duty operating conditions or excessive stop and go driving, replace fluid and strainer every 12,000 miles.

Use only automatic transmission fluid identified with the mark DEXRON. This type fluid has been especially formulated and tested for use in automatic transmissions. Dexron fluid is available from many lubricant suppliers.

DEXRON type automatic transmission fluid is also preferred for use in all pre 1968 model GM automatic transmissions. Type A, Suffix A fluids identified by the mark "AQ-ATF" and a number followed by the suffix letter A (AQ-

ATF-XXXXA) continue to be satisfactory for use in pre 1968 GM automatic transmissions.

CHECKING AND ADDING FLUID
(Transmission at Operating Temperature)

The automatic transmission is designed to operate at the full mark on the dip stick at normal operating temperature (170°F.) and should be checked under these conditions. The normal operating temperature is obtained only after at least 15 miles of highway type driving or the equivalent of city driving.

To determine proper level, proceed as follows:
1. Apply parking brake.
2. With the selector lever in the PARK position, start engine. DO NOT RACE ENGINE. Move selector lever through each range.
3. Immediately check fluid with the selector lever in PARK, engine running at SLOW IDLE and the car on a LEVEL surface. The fluid level on the dip stick should be at the "FULL" mark.
4. If additional fluid is required, add sufficient fluid to bring it to the "FULL" mark on the dip stick.

CHECKING AND ADDING FLUID
(Transmission at Room Temperature)

If the car has not been driven sufficiently to bring the transmission to operating temperature and it becomes necessary to check the fluid level, the transmission may be checked at room temperature (80°F.) as follows:
1. With parking brake applied, selector lever in PARK position, start engine. DO NOT RACE ENGINE. Move selector lever through each range.
2. Immediately check fluid level with selector lever in park, engine running at SLOW IDLE and vehicle on a LEVEL surface. The fluid level on the dip stick should be 1" below the "FULL" mark.
3. If additional fluid is required, add sufficient fluid to bring level to 1" below the "FULL" mark on the dip stick.

If transmission fluid level is correctly established at 80°F., it will appear at the "FULL" mark on the dip stick when the transmission reaches normal operating temperature (170°F.). The fluid level is set 1" below the "FULL" mark on the dip stick to allow for expansion of the fluid which occurs as transmission temperatures rise to normal operating temperature of 170°F.

Do not overfill as foaming and loss of fluid through the vent pipe might occur as the fluid expands. If fluid is too low, especially when cold, complete loss of drive may result which can cause transmission failure.

CHECKING AND ADDING FLUID
(After Transmission Service)

If work has been performed on the transmission, add the following quantity of fluid, then check fluid as outlined in Steps 1, 2 and 3 under CHECKING AND ADDING FLUID (Transmission at Room Temperature).
1. Pan Removal - 4 quarts
2. Converter Changed - 2 quarts
3. Overhaul - 12 quarts

A point to remember when adding fluid to the transmission is that the quantity of fluid alone is not important. The important factor is the relation of the fluid level to the "FULL" mark, dependent on temperature, on the dip stick.

The end result of the checking and adding procedure is to assure that the fluid level is at the "FULL" mark when the transmission is at operating temperature.

GENERAL DESCRIPTION

The Turbo Hydra-Matic transmission used on the Toronado Series is a fully automatic transmission used for front wheel drive applications. It consists primarily of a three-element hydraulic torque converter, dual sprocket and link belt, compound planetary gear set, three multiple-disc clutches, a sprag clutch, a roller clutch, two band assemblies, and a hydraulic control system.

The three-element torque converter consists of a pump or driving member, a turbine or driven member, and a stator or reaction member.

The stator assembly is mounted on a one-way roller clutch which allows the stator to overrun when not used as a reaction member.

The torque converter couples the engine to the planetary gear set through the use of a drive sprocket, a link belt and a driven sprocket. Clockwise engine torque turns the drive sprocket clockwise. This, in turn, drives the driven sprocket in a clockwise direction. This in effect is a reverse in the direction of engine torque due to the side mounting of the gear unit. (Fig. 7E-1)

The planetary gear set provides three forward ratios and reverse. The approximate gear ratios are as follows:

First	- 2.5 gear ratio x 2. Converter stall ratio equals 5:1.
* Second	- 1.5 gear ratio.
* Third	- 1.1 gear ratio.
* Reverse	- 2.1 gear ratio x 2. Converter stall ratio equals 4:1.

* Second and third are also multiplied to a lesser degree.

The three multiple-disc clutches, the sprag and roller clutch assemblies, and the two band assemblies provide the friction elements required to obtain the desired function of the compound planetary gear set.

The hydraulic control system automatically selects the proper gear ratio depending upon vehicle load and speeds. It also provides the working pressures required to operate the friction elements of the transmission.

External control connections to the transmission are:
Engine Vacuum
12 Volt Electrical Signals
Manual Linkage Control

Engine vacuum is used to operate the vacuum modulator assembly. The vacuum modulator automatically senses any change in torque input to the transmission that the driver induces through a change in accelerator position.

The 12 volt electrical signal is used to operate the electrical detent solenoid. The detent solenoid is activated by an electrical switch in the throttle linkage. When the throttle is fully opened the switch in the throttle linkage is closed, activating the detent solenoid and causing the transmission to downshift at speeds below approximately 70 mph.

The manual linkage is used to select the desired operating ranges, reverse, neutral and park.

The selector quadrant has six positions: P, R, N, D, S, L.

P — Park position positively locks the output carrier to the transmission case by means of a locking pawl to prevent *vehicle from rolling in either direction. This* position should be selected whenever the driver leaves the vehicle. The engine may be started in Park position.

R — Reverse enables the vehicle to be operated in a Reverse direction.

N — Neutral position enables the engine to be started and run without driving the vehicle.

D — Drive range is used for all normal driving conditions and maximum economy.

Drive range has three gear ratios, from the starting ratio to direct drive. Detent downshifts are available for passing by depressing the accelerator to the floor.

S — Super range adds performance for congested traffic or hilly terrain. Super range has the same starting ratio as Drive range, but prevents the transmission from shifting above second gear to retain second gear acceleration when extra performance is desired. Super range can also be used for engine braking.

Super range can be selected at any vehicle speed, and the transmission will shift to second gear and remain in second until the vehicle speed or the throttle are changed to obtain first gear operation in the same manner as in Drive range.

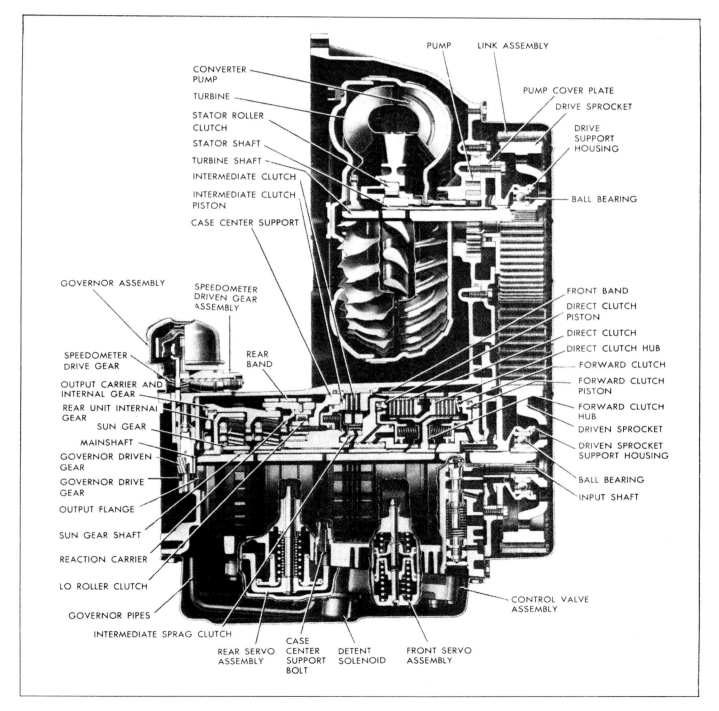

Fig. 7E-1—Turbo Hydra-Matic Transmission

L — Lo range can be selected at any vehicle speed, and the transmission will shift to second gear and remain in second until vehicle speed is reduced to approximately 40 mph, depending on axle ratio.

Lo range position prevents the transmission from shifting out of first gear. This is particularly beneficial for maintaining maximum engine braking when continuous first gear operation is desirable.

VALVES AND THEIR FUNCTIONS

The valves in the Turbo Hydra-Matic transmission used on the Toronado Series function identically to their corresponding valves in the regular Turbo Hydra-Matic transmission with the following exceptions:

1. The pressure regulator valve is located in the transmission case. The valve functions as a regulator of line pressure. The bottom pan must be removed to service this valve located in the right rear corner of the case valve body mounting pad.

2. The modulator valve has a case to valve bushing in which it operates.

3. The governor is mounted with a clip, an external stamped housing, and a square cut "O" ring seal.

POWER FLOW (Fig. 7E-2)

DRIVE RANGE - FIRST GEAR

FORWARD CLUTCH - APPLIED
ROLLER CLUTCH - EFFECTIVE

DIRECT CLUTCH - RELEASED
FRONT BAND - RELEASED
REAR BAND - RELEASED

INTERMEDIATE CLUTCH - RELEASED
INTERMEDIATE SPRAG - INEFFECTIVE

With the selector lever in "D" range, the forward clutch is applied. This delivers turbine torque to the drive sprocket, through the link belt to the driven sprocket and mainshaft and turns the rear internal gear in a counterclockwise direction. (Converter torque ratio equals approximately 2:1 at stall.)

Counterclockwise motion of the rear internal gear causes the rear pinions to turn counterclockwise to drive the sun gear clockwise. In turn, the sun gear drives the front pinions counterclockwise, turning the front internal gear, output carrier, and output flange counterclockwise in a reduction ratio of approximately 2.5:1. The reaction of the front pinions against the front internal gear is taken by the reaction carrier and roller clutch assembly to the transmission case. (Approximate stall ratio equals 5:1.)

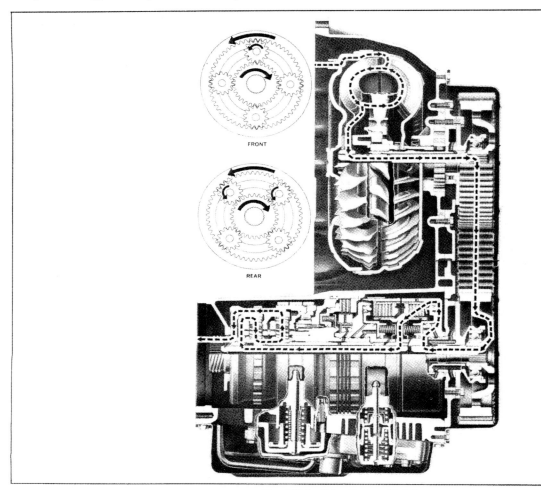

FRONT

REAR

Fig. 7E-2—Drive Range - First Gear

DRIVE RANGE - SECOND GEAR
(Fig. 7E-3)

FORWARD CLUTCH - APPLIED
ROLLER CLUTCH - INEFFECTIVE

DIRECT CLUTCH - RELEASED
FRONT BAND - RELEASED
REAR BAND - RELEASED

INTERMEDIATE CLUTCH - APPLIED
INTERMEDIATE SPRAG - EFFECTIVE

In second gear, the intermediate clutch is applied to allow the intermediate sprag to hold the sun gear against clockwise rotation. Turbine torque, through the forward clutch, is now applied through the mainshaft to the rear internal gear in a counterclockwise direction.

Counterclockwise rotation of the rear internal gear turns the rear pinions counterclockwise against the stationary sun gear. This causes the output carrier and output flange to turn counterclockwise in a reduction ratio of approximately 1.5:1.

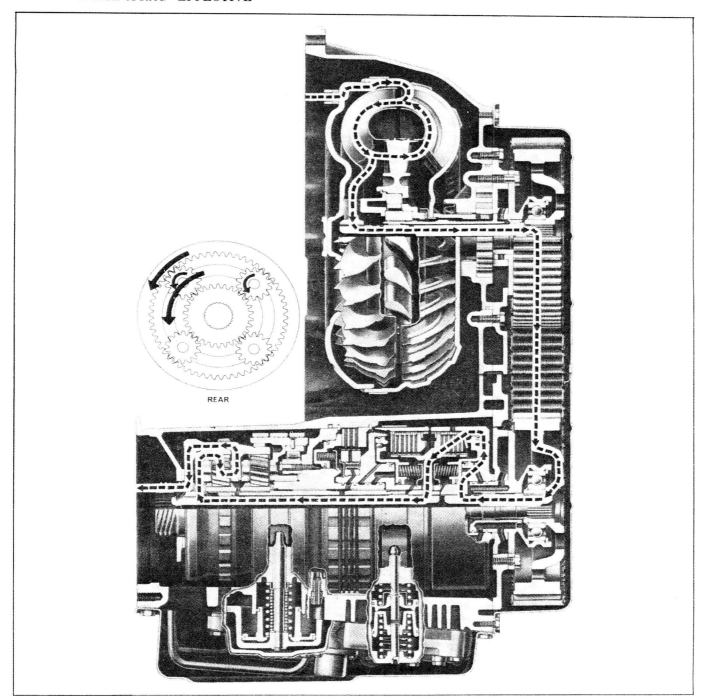

Fig. 7E-3—Drive Range - Second Gear

DRIVE RANGE-THIRD GEAR
(Fig. 7E-4)

FORWARD CLUTCH - APPLIED
ROLLER CLUTCH - INEFFECTIVE

DIRECT CLUTCH - APPLIED
FRONT BAND - RELEASED
REAR BAND - RELEASED

INTERMEDIATE CLUTCH - APPLIED
INTERMEDIATE SPRAG - INEFFECTIVE

In direct drive, engine torque is transmitted to the converter to the drive sprocket, through the link belt, to the driven sprocket and through the forward clutch to the mainshaft and rear internal gear. Because the direct clutch is applied, equal power is also transmitted to the sun gear shaft and the sun gear. Since both the sun gear and internal gears are now turning at the same speed, the planetary gear set is essentially locked and turns as one unit in direct drive, or a ratio of 1:1.

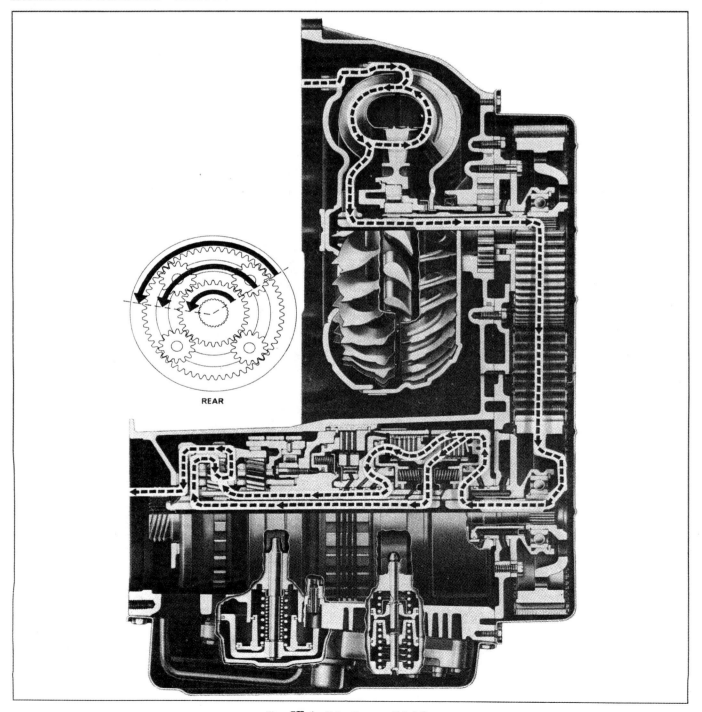

REAR

Fig. 7E-4—Drive Range - Third Gear

SUPER RANGE-SECOND GEAR
(Fig. 7E-5)

FORWARD CLUTCH - APPLIED
ROLLER CLUTCH - INEFFECTIVE

DIRECT CLUTCH - RELEASED
FRONT BAND - APPLIED
REAR BAND - RELEASED

INTERMEDIATE CLUTCH - APPLIED
INTERMEDIATE SPRAG - EFFECTIVE

In second gear, the intermediate clutch is applied to allow the intermediate sprag to hold the sun gear against clockwise rotation. Turbine torque through the forward clutch is now applied through the mainshaft to the rear internal gear in a counterclockwise direction.

Counterclockwise rotation of the rear internal gear turns the rear pinions counterclockwise against the stationary sun gear. This causes the output carrier and output flange to turn counterclockwise in a reduction ratio of approximately 1.5:1.

In second gear, overrun braking is provided by the front band as it holds the sun gear fixed. Without the band applied, the sun gear would overrun the intermediate sprag.

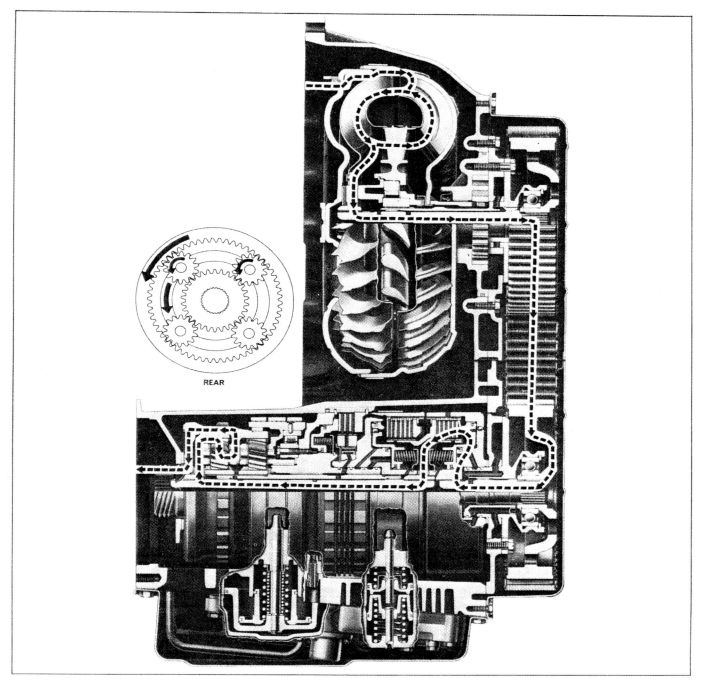

Fig. 7E-5—Super Range - Second Gear

LO RANGE-FIRST GEAR
(Fig. 7E-6)

FORWARD CLUTCH - APPLIED
ROLLER CLUTCH - EFFECTIVE

DIRECT CLUTCH - RELEASED
FRONT BAND - RELEASED
REAR BAND - APPLIED

INTERMEDIATE CLUTCH - RELEASED
INTERMEDIATE SPRAG - INEFFECTIVE

With the selector lever in "L" range, the forward clutch is applied. This delivers turbine torque through the drive sprocket, link belt, and driven sprocket to the mainshaft and turns the rear internal gear in a counterclockwise direction. (Converter torque ratio equals approximately 2:1 at stall.)

Counterclockwise motion of the rear internal gear causes the rear pinions to turn counterclockwise to drive the sun gear clockwise. In turn, the sun gear drives the front pinions counterclockwise, turning the front internal gear, output carrier, and output flange, counterclockwise in a reduction ratio of approximately 2.5:1. The reaction of the front pinions against the front internal gear is taken by the reaction carrier and roller clutch assembly to the transmission case. (Total stall ratio equals approximately 5:1.)

Downhill or overrun braking is provided in "L" range by applying the rear band as this prevents the reaction carrier from overrunning the roller clutch.

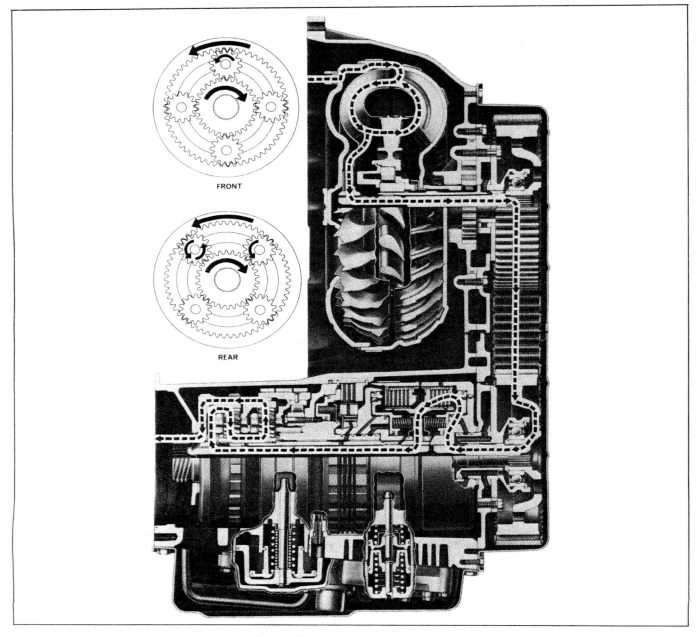

FRONT

REAR

Fig. 7E-6—Low Range - First Gear

REVERSE
(Fig. 7E-7)

FORWARD CLUTCH - RELEASED
LO SPRAG - INEFFECTIVE

DIRECT CLUTCH - APPLIED
FRONT BAND - RELEASED
REAR BAND - APPLIED

INTERMEDIATE CLUTCH - RELEASED
INTERMEDIATE SPRAG - INEFFECTIVE

In reverse, the direct clutch is applied to direct turbine torque, through the drive sprocket, link belt and driven sprocket, to the sun gear shaft and sun gear. The rear band is also applied, holding the reaction carrier.

Counterclockwise torque to the sun gear causes the front pinions and front internal gear to turn clockwise in reduction. The front internal gear is connected directly to the output shaft, thus providing the reverse output gear ratio of approximately 2:1. The reverse torque multiplication at stall (converter and gear ratios) is approximately 4:1.

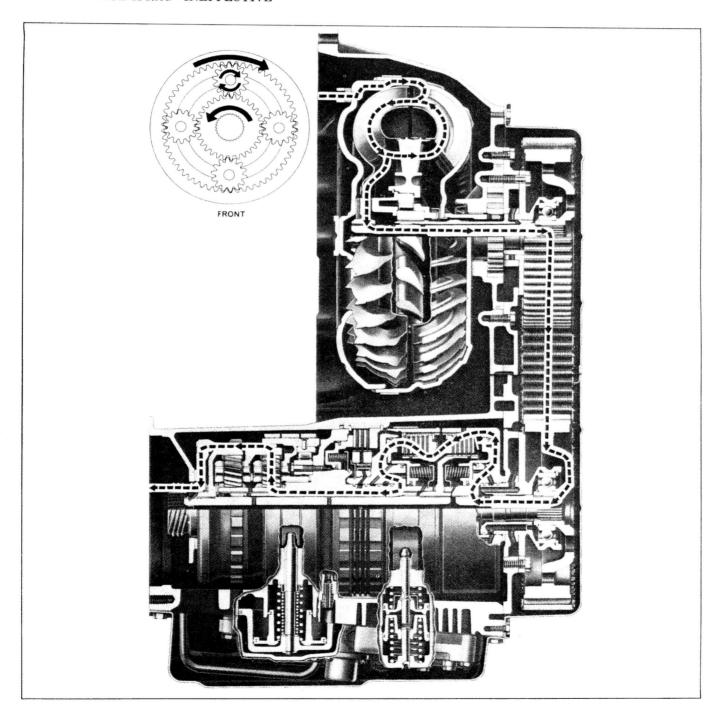

FRONT

Fig. 7E-7—Reverse

OIL FLOW CIRCUITS

The oil flow circuits are similar to the oil flow circuits used in the regular Turbo Hydra-Matic transmission. When tracing oil circuits refer to Figs. 7-14 through 7-21 in the TURBO HYDRA-MATIC TRANSMISSION, Section 7.

OPERATIONS NOT REQUIRING TRANSMISSION REMOVAL

1. Oil cooler fitting replacement or adjustment.
2. Governor assembly service.
3. Vacuum modulator, and valve service.
4. Speedometer driven gear service.
5. Oil level check.
6. Oil pressure check with oil pressure gauge.

UNITS THAT CAN BE SERVICED AFTER REMOVAL OF OIL PAN
(Fig. 7E-8)

1. Oil pan and pan to case gasket.
2. Pressure regulator valve assembly.
3. Valve body assembly.
4. Rear servo and accumulator assembly.
5. Front servo and accumulator assembly.
6. Governor pipes.
7. Detent solenoid.
8. Solenoid connector.
9. Manual linkage.

10. Parking linkage.
11. Valve body to case spacers and gaskets.
12. Check balls (7). See Fig. 7E-9 for proper location.
13. Detent roller and spring assembly.
14. Strainer assembly.

General disassembly and assembly instructions should be followed whenever service is performed with the transmission remaining in the vehicle.

GENERAL SERVICE NOTES

When servicing the transmission, it is recommended that upon disassembly of a unit, all parts should be cleaned and inspected as outlined under CLEANING AND INSPECTION, then the unit should be reassembled before disassembly of other units to avoid confusion and interchanging of parts.

1. Before disassembly of a unit, thoroughly clean the exterior.

2. Disassembly and assembly of the unit and sub assemblies must be made on a clean work bench. As in repairing any hydraulically operated unit, cleanliness is of the utmost importance; therefore, the work bench, tools, and parts must be kept clean at all times.

3. Before installing screws or bolts into aluminum parts, ALWAYS DIP SCREWS OR BOLTS INTO HYDRA-MATIC OIL to prevent screws or bolts from galling the aluminum threads and also to prevent the screws or bolts from seizing.

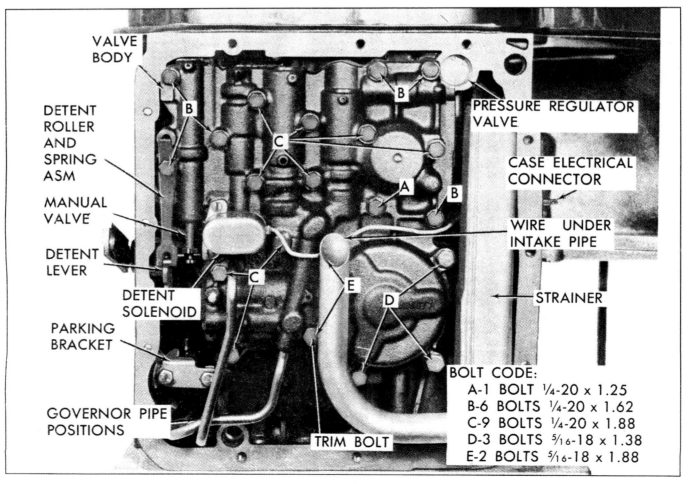

BOLT CODE:
A-1 BOLT ¼-20 x 1.25
B-6 BOLTS ¼-20 x 1.62
C-9 BOLTS ¼-20 x 1.88
D-3 BOLTS ⁵⁄₁₆-18 x 1.38
E-2 BOLTS ⁵⁄₁₆-18 x 1.88

Fig. 7E-8—Oil Pan Removed

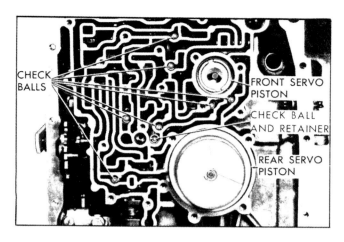

Fig. 7E-9—Location of Check Balls

4. Always use a torque wrench and tighten bolts to the recommended torque specifications when installing bolts into aluminum parts to prevent the possibility of stripping the aluminum threads.

5. If tapped threads in aluminum parts are stripped or damaged, the part can, in most cases, be made serviceable by the careful use of Heli-coils.

6. Seal protecting tools must be used when assembling the units to prevent damage to the seals. Hydra-Matic oil should be applied to all seals before they are assembled into sealed units. The slightest flaw in the sealing surface of the seal can cause an oil leak.

7. All aluminum castings and valve body parts are very susceptible to nicks, burrs and handling damage, so extreme care should be used in handling these parts.

8. The internal snap rings should be expanded and external snap rings compressed if they are to be reused. This will insure proper seating when they are reinstalled into the unit.

9. Replace all "O" rings, gaskets and oil seals that are

removed. Complete overhaul service packages are available for these items.

10. During reassembly of each unit, all internal parts must be lubricated with Hydra-Matic oil.

11. Always refer to the lubrication chart (Fig. 7E-232) for the location of all oil and lubrication holes and passages. Lubrication holes are all shown in the chart.

PARTS CLEANING AND INSPECTION

After complete disassembly of a unit, all metal parts should be washed in a clean solvent and dried with compressed air. All oil passages should be blown out and checked to make sure that they are open and not obstructed. Small passages should be checked with tag wire. All parts should be inspected to determine which parts are to be replaced.

The various inspections of parts are as follows:

1. Inspect linkage and pivot joints for excessive wear.

2. Bearing and thrust surfaces of all parts should be checked for excessive wear or scoring.

3. Check for broken seal rings, damaged ring lands and damaged threads.

4. Inspect seals and "O" rings. (Check these for damage, even though they will be replaced, to determine if they are part of the transmission problem.)

5. Mating surfaces of castings and end plates should be checked for burrs and irregularities. If a good seal is not apparent, burrs or irregularities may be removed by lapping the surface with crocus cloth. The crocus cloth should be held on a flat surface, such as a piece of plate glass.

6. Castings should be checked for cracks and sand holes.

7. Gear teeth should be examined for chipping, scoring, and excessive wear.

8. Valves should be free of burrs, nicks, and chips and the shoulders of the valves must be square. Any burrs or irregularities may be removed by honing. Valves should be free to slide in their respective bores.

9. Inspect composition clutch plates for damaged surfaces and loose facings. If flakes of the facing material can be removed with the thumbnail, the plates should be replaced; however, composition clutch plate discoloration is not an

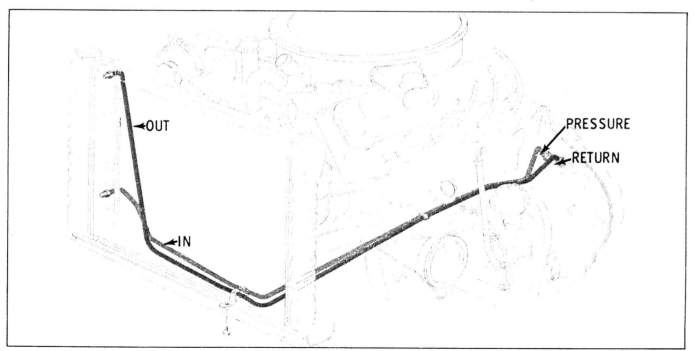

Fig. 7E-10—Oil Cooler Lines

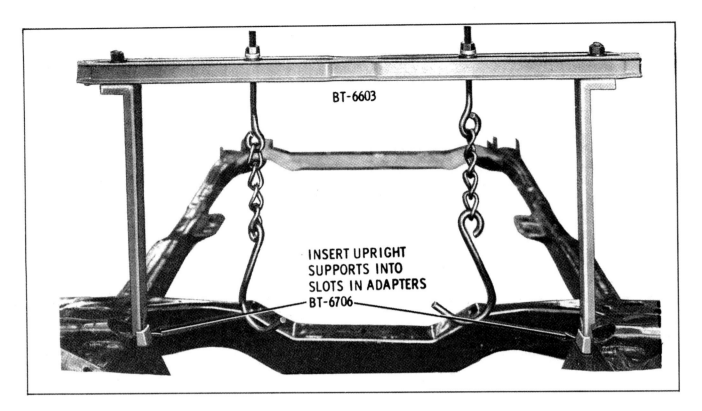

Fig. 7E-11—Installing Support Bars

indication of composition clutch plate failure. Discoloration is natural for these parts.

10. Inspect steel clutch plates for scored or damaged surfaces.

11. Inspect springs for distortion or collapsed coils. Slight wear (bright spots) on the sides of the springs is permissible.

12. When inspecting bushings, fit the mating part into the bushing and observe the amount of looseness. Bushing clearance is excessive if more than .008" exists when checked with a wire feeler gauge.

13. If the transmission shows evidence that foreign material has circulated throughout the transmission or if the oil strainer is dirty, the oil strainer should be discarded and a new one installed upon reassembly of the transmission. (A

Fig. 7E-12—Supporting Engine

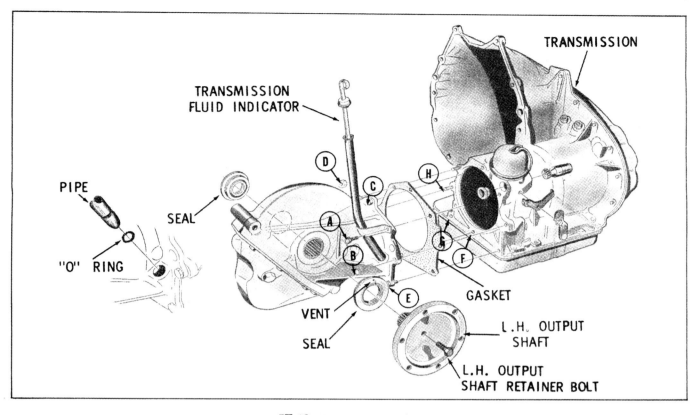

Fig. 7E-13—Transmission Attachment

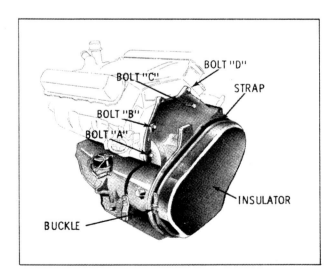

Fig. 7E-14—Transmission to Engine Attachment

NEW STRAINER SHOULD ALWAYS BE INSTALLED FOR A CONVERTER, CLUTCH, OR PUMP FAILURE.)

14. Transmission oil cooler lines should always be flushed and reverse flushed whenever foreign material has circulated throughout the transmission.

15. Always refer to the lubrication chart (Fig. 7E-232) when inspecting the oil passages and holes, for the location of oil passages and lubrication holes.

TRANSMISSION
Remove (less final drive)

1. Disconnect battery.

2. Disconnect oil cooler lines at transmission (Fig. 7E-10) and speedometer cable at governor.

3. Install engine support bar as shown in Figs. 7E-11 and 7E-12.

4. Remove nut "D" and bolts "A", "B" and "C". (Fig. 7E-13) A special wrench such as MAC S-147 must be used on nut "D".

5. Remove bolts "A", "B", "C" and "D". (Fig. 7E-14)

6. Remove flywheel cover plate bolt "A". (Fig. 7E-15)

7. Hoist car.

8. Disconnect starter wiring, then remove starter. (Fig. 7E-15)

9. Remove bolts "B", "C" and "D" from flywheel cover plate. (Fig. 7E-15)

10. Remove flywheel to converter bolt "E". (Fig. 7E-15) Rotate flywheel until all bolts are removed.

11. Disconnect vacuum modulator line and detent wire. (Fig. 7E-16)

12. Install transmission lift. (Fig. 7E-17, 7E-18 and 7E-19)

13. Remove shift linkage.

14. Remove bolts "E", "F", "G" and nut "H". (Fig. 7E-13)

When the last three transmission to final drive bolts are removed, a quantity of oil will be lost.

15. Remove bolts "A" and "B". (Fig. 7E-20)

16. Remove the two upper engine mount bracket to transmission bolts "A" and "B". (Fig. 7E-21)

17. Remove the four bracket to engine mount bolts. (Fig. 7E-21)

18. Slide transmission rearward and down. Engine mount bracket will follow transmission down. Install Converter Holding Tool J-21654 as shown in Fig. 6EB-1.

19. After transmission is removed from car, the link belt cover insulator can be removed or installed. (Fig. 7E-14)

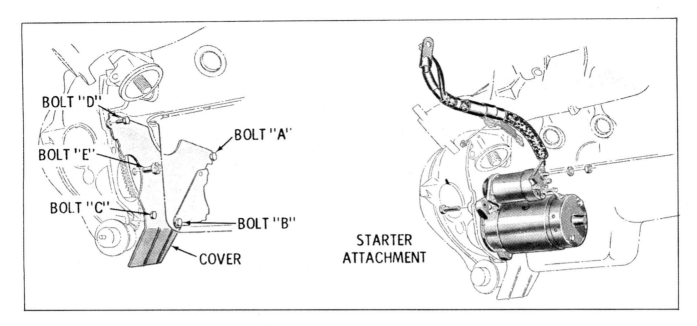

Fig. 7E-15—Starter and Converter Attachment

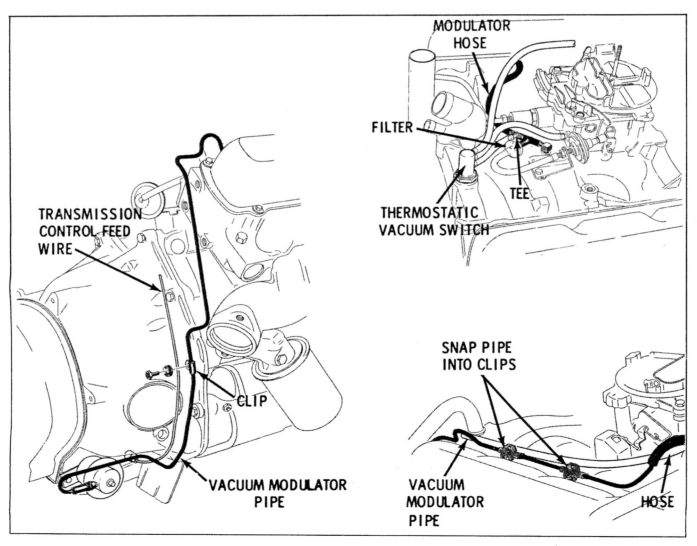

Fig. 7E-16—Modulator Line

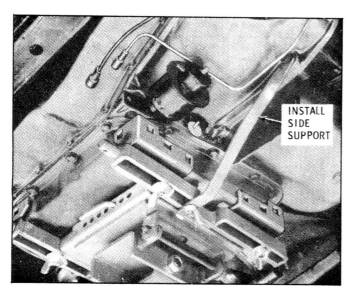

Fig. 7E-17—Transmission Lift in Position

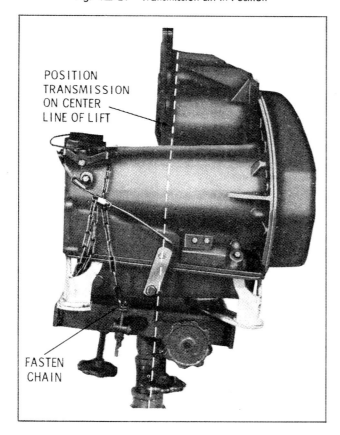

POSITION
TRANSMISSION
ON CENTER
LINE OF LIFT

FASTEN
CHAIN

Fig. 7E-18—Transmission on Lift

Install

When installing the transmission, the motor mount bracket must be positioned loosely on the link belt cover until the transmission is in place; then, reverse removal procedure. Torque bolts as follows:

Before installing the flex plate to converter bolts, make certain that the weld nuts on the converter are flush with the flex plate and the converter rotates freely by hand in this position. Then hand start all

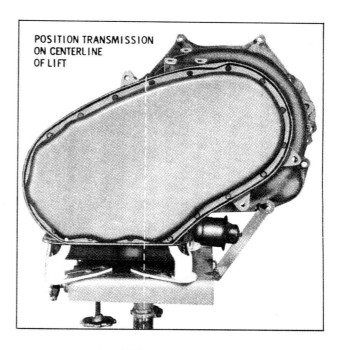

POSITION TRANSMISSION
ON CENTERLINE
OF LIFT

Fig. 7E-19—Transmission on Lift

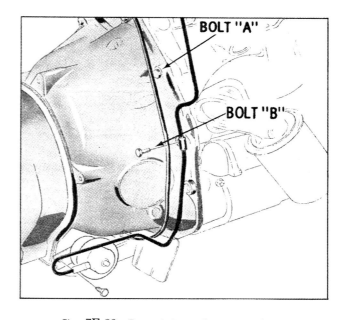

BOLT "A"

BOLT "B"

Fig. 7E-20—Transmission to Engine Attachment

three bolts and tighten finger tight. Torque to specifications. This will insure proper converter alignment.

Engine to Torque Converter Housing	25 ft. lbs.
Engine Bracket to Transmission	55 ft. lbs.
Engine Bracket to Rubber Mount	55 ft. lbs.
Oil Cooler Lines to Transmission	25 ft. lbs.
Final Drive to Transmission Nuts and Bolts	25 ft. lbs.
Torque Converter to Flywheel Bolts	30 ft. lbs.
Flywheel Housing Cover	5 ft. lbs.
Starter to Transmission	30 ft. lbs.

Apply sealer to bolts "E", "F" and "G" (Fig. 7E-13)

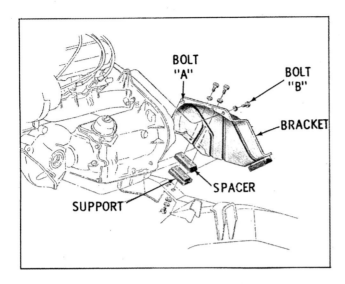

Fig. 7E-21—Engine Mount Attachment

After transmission is installed, check transmission oil level. Refer to PERIODIC MAINTENANCE at the front of this section. Adjust manual control shift linkage.

MINOR SERVICE OPERATIONS

SERVICING THE OIL COOLER

The oil cooler is located in the side tank of the radiator and

its purpose is to cool the oil in the event excessive temperature tends to develop. (Fig. 7E-10)

In a major transmission failure, where particles of metal have been carried with the oil throughout the units of the transmission, it will be necessary to flush out the oil cooler and connecting lines. The oil cooler is a sealed container providing a passage for oil to flow from the inlet to the outlet. Clean solvent can be flushed through the cooler with air pressure. (An engine desludge gun may be used.) The cooler should be back-flushed first through the return line to remove all foreign material possible. Then flush through the inlet line and finish by flushing through the return line. Clean remaining solvent from cooler with compressed air applied to the return line and flush with Hydra-Matic oil.

THROTTLE LINKAGE ADJUSTMENTS
(Refer to ENGINE, Section 6)
MANUAL LEVER ADJUSTMENT

The manual lever adjustment provides proper clearance between the "D" detent in the transmission and the stop for the manual shift lever. The adjustment is made as outlined in Figs. 7E-22 and 7E-23.

TRANSMISSION DISASSEMBLY
CONVERTER, MODULATOR, AND
SPEEDOMETER DRIVE GEAR

Remove

1. With the transmission in cradle or portable jack, remove the torque converter assembly by pulling straight out from the transmission housing.

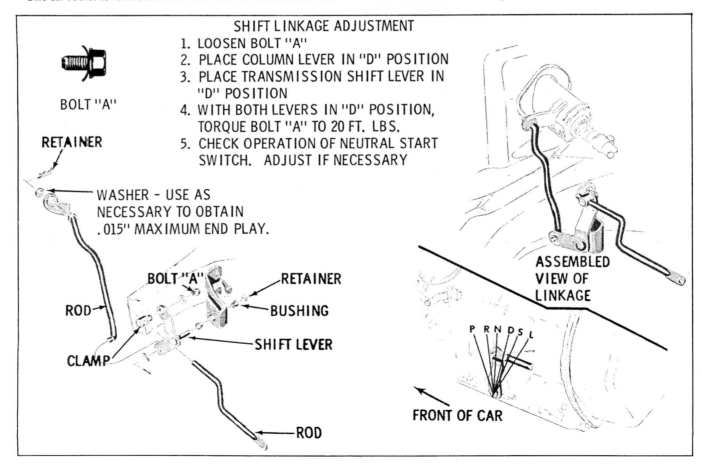

SHIFT LINKAGE ADJUSTMENT
1. LOOSEN BOLT "A"
2. PLACE COLUMN LEVER IN "D" POSITION
3. PLACE TRANSMISSION SHIFT LEVER IN "D" POSITION
4. WITH BOTH LEVERS IN "D" POSITION, TORQUE BOLT "A" TO 20 FT. LBS.
5. CHECK OPERATION OF NEUTRAL START SWITCH. ADJUST IF NECESSARY

BOLT "A"

RETAINER

WASHER - USE AS NECESSARY TO OBTAIN .015" MAXIMUM END PLAY.

ROD

CLAMP

BOLT "A"

RETAINER

BUSHING

SHIFT LEVER

ROD

ASSEMBLED VIEW OF LINKAGE

P R N D S L

FRONT OF CAR

Fig. 7E-22—Column Shift Linkage

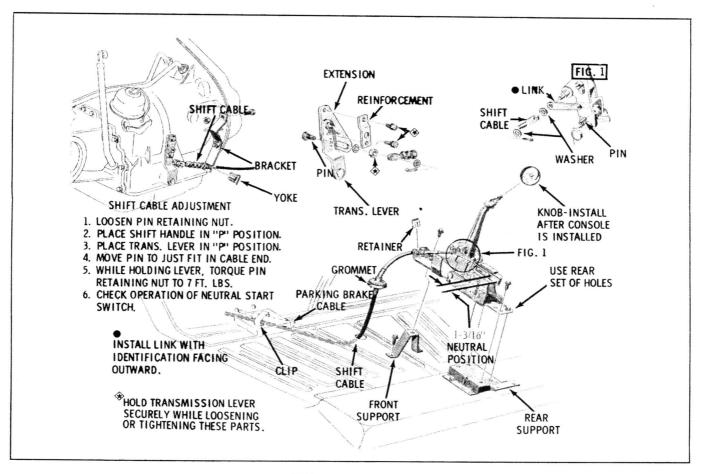

SHIFT CABLE ADJUSTMENT

1. LOOSEN PIN RETAINING NUT.
2. PLACE SHIFT HANDLE IN "P" POSITION.
3. PLACE TRANS. LEVER IN "P" POSITION.
4. MOVE PIN TO JUST FIT IN CABLE END.
5. WHILE HOLDING LEVER, TORQUE PIN RETAINING NUT TO 7 FT. LBS.
6. CHECK OPERATION OF NEUTRAL START SWITCH.

● INSTALL LINK WITH IDENTIFICATION FACING OUTWARD.

⊕ HOLD TRANSMISSION LEVER SECURELY WHILE LOOSENING OR TIGHTENING THESE PARTS.

Fig. 7E-23—Console Shift Cable

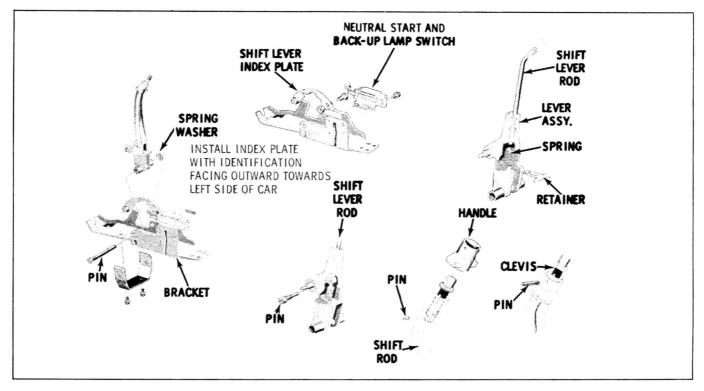

Fig. 7E-24—Console Shift Bracket

Fig. 7E-25—Supporting Bolt Installation

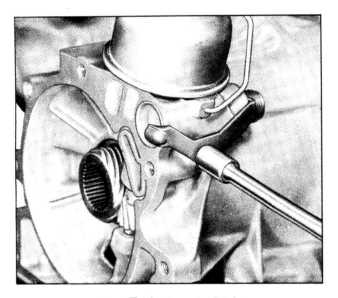

Fig. 7E-26—Removing Retainer

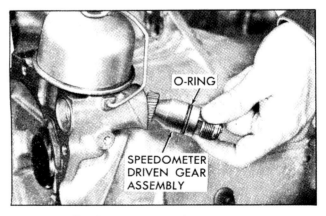

Fig. 7E-27—Removing Speedometer Driven Gear

The torque converter is heavy due to the large amount of oil that it contains.

2. Install two 3/8 x 8 inch bolts into the case to engine mounting face. (Fig. 7E-25)

3. Remove the speedometer driven gear attaching screw and retainer clip. (Fig. 7E-26)

4. Withdraw speedometer driven gear assembly from case

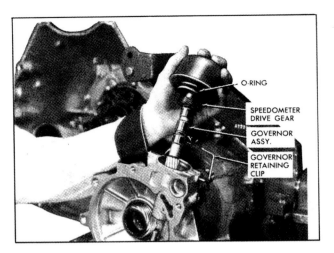

Fig. 7E-28—Removing Governor

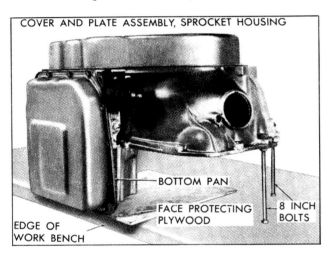

Fig. 7E-29—Transmission on Bench

bore. Remove and discard "O" ring seal. (Fig. 7E-27)

5. Remove the governor attaching clip.

6. Withdraw governor assembly and "O" ring seal from case bore. (Fig. 7E-28)

7. Remove two studs from output end of case and place a piece of plywood under output end of case, place transmission on work bench with bottom pan facing the outside edge of work bench. (Let pan overhang edge of bench.) Stand transmission on the two eight inch bolts and the output flange end of the transmission case. (Fig. 7E-29)

8. Remove vacuum modulator assembly attaching screw and retainer clip. (Fig. 7E-30)

9. Remove vacuum modulator assembly and "O" ring seal from case bore. (Fig. 7E-31)

10. Remove vacuum modulator valve from bushing in case. (Fig. 7E-32)

Modulator bushing may be press fit in case bore and should not be removed with force.

BOTTOM PAN, STRAINER, AND INTAKE PIPE "O" RING SEAL

Removal

1. Remove thirteen bottom pan attaching screws.

2. Remove bottom pan and discard gasket.

3. Remove oil strainer assembly. (Fig. 7E-34)

4. Remove and discard the intake pipe to case "O" ring seal from the oil strainer assembly or from the case counterbore.

Fig. 7E-30—Removing Modulator Attaching Bolt

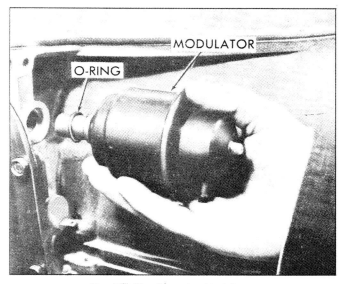

Fig. 7E-31—Removing Modulator

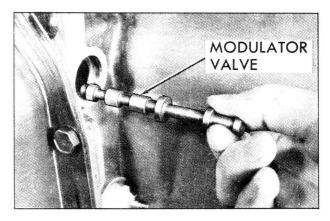

Fig. 7E-32—Removing Modulator Valve

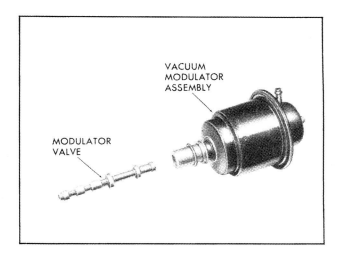

Fig. 7E-33—Modulator and Valve

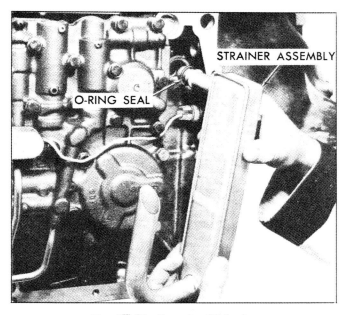

Fig. 7E-34—Removing Oil Strainer

PRESSURE REGULATOR AND BOOST VALVE, CONTROL VALVE ASSEMBLY, GOVERNOR PIPES, DETENT SPRING ASSEMBLY, REAR SERVO, MANUAL AND PARKING LINKAGE, AND CASE CONNECTOR

Removal

1. Compress the pressure boost valve bushing against the pressure regulator spring and remove the retaining snap ring from the case, using J-5403 pliers. (Fig. 7E-35)

2. Remove the pressure boost valve bushing and valve from the case bore. (Fig. 7E-36)

3. Remove the pressure regulator spring from the case bore.

4. Remove pressure regulator valve, spring retainer, and spacer(s) if present, from the case bore.

5. Disconnect detent solenoid connector from case connector. Disconnect detent solenoid wire from inside connector. (Fig. 7E-37)

6. Remove governor feed pipe by pulling straight out. (Fig. 7E-38)

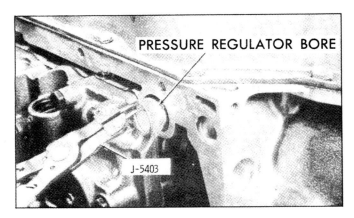

Fig. 7E-35—Removing Retaining Ring

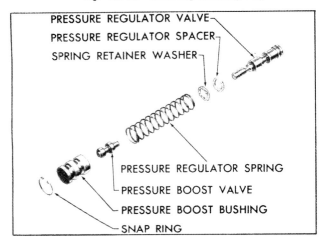

Fig. 7E-36—Pressure Regulator Valve

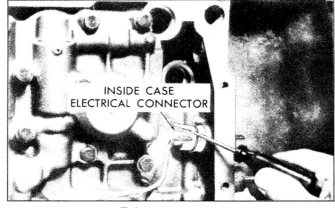

Fig. 7E-37—Removing Connector

7. Remove control valve body to case attaching screws, detent roller spring and assembly. Leave two top bolts in until all other bolts are removed.

Do not remove detent solenoid attaching screws.

8. Remove control valve body assembly, gasket, and remaining governor pipe. (Fig. 7E-39)

Do not allow manual valve to fall out of control valve assembly during removal of control valve assembly.

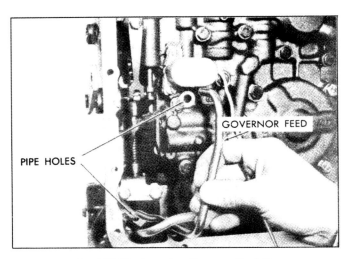

Fig. 7E-38—Removing Governor Feed Pipe

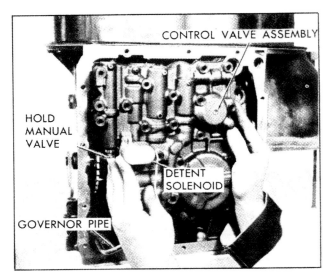

Fig. 7E-39—Removing Control Valve

Fig. 7E-40—Removing Governor Pipe

9. Remove the remaining governor pipe from control valve assembly. (Fig. 7E-40)

10. Remove the control valve assembly spacer plate and gasket. (Fig. 7E-41)

11. Remove the seven check balls from the cored passages in transmission case. (Fig. 7E-42)

The eighth check ball is held in by a retainer and should not be removed unless replacement is required.

Fig. E-41—Removing Gasket and Spacer Plate

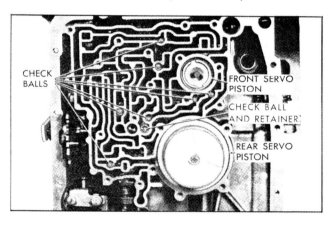

Fig. 7E-42—Check Ball Location

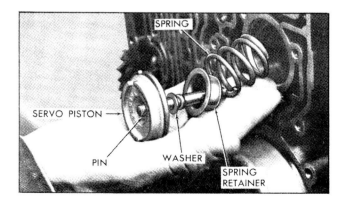

Fig. 7E-43—Removing Front Servo

12. Remove the front servo piston, washer, pin, retainer, and spring from transmission case. (Fig. 7E-43)

13. Remove the rear servo piston assembly from the case. (Fig. 7E-44)

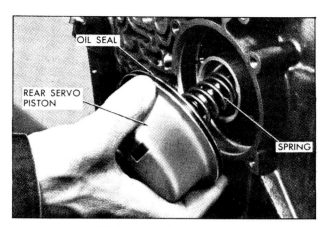

Fig. 7E-44—Removing Rear Servo

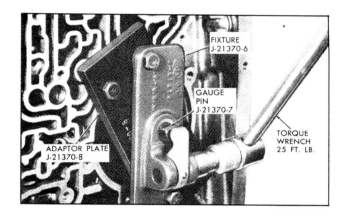

Fig. 7E-45—Checking Band Apply Pin

14. Remove rear servo accumulator spring from case.

15. Make band apply pin selection check. (Fig. 7E-45)

Band Apply Pin Selection

a. Attach Adapter Plate J-21370-8 to case valve body face and torque to 18 ft. lbs. Install fixture Gauge J-21370-6 to J-21370-8 Adapter Plate with two bolts and insert J-21370-7 Gauge Pin. Be sure the pin does not bind when tightening bolts to adapter plate and to case face.

b. Apply 25 ft. lb. torque and note position of step on gauge pin. Below first step requires short pin. Above top step requires long pin, and between steps requires medium length pin. (Fig. 7E-46)

The three selective pins are identified as follows:

PIN IDENTIFICATION	PIN LENGTH
3 Rings	Long
2 Rings	Medium
1 Ring	Short

The identification ring is located near the shoulder end of the pin. Selecting the proper pin length is the equivalent of adjusting the band.

16. If necessary, remove the manual linkage as follows:

a. Loosen the jam nut holding detent lever to manual shaft. (Fig. 7E-47)

b. Remove manual shaft retaining pin from case. Pull straight out. (Fig. 7E-48)

c. Loosen detent lever from machined flats on manual shaft.

STEP LOCATION		PIN IDENT.	SIZE
	TOP STEP OR ABOVE	THREE RINGS	LONG
	THIS AREA	TWO RINGS	MED.
J-21370-7	LOWER STEP OR BELOW	ONE RING	SHORT

Fig. 7E-46—Pin Selection Chart

Fig. 7E-47—Removing Jam Nut

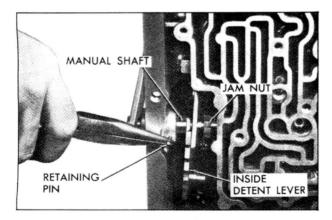

Fig. 7E-48—Removing Retaining Pin

d. Withdraw manual shaft from case bore and remove and discard "O" ring seal from manual shaft. (Fig. 7E-49)

Be careful not to drop jam nut inside case.

e. Remove detent lever, parking brake actuator rod, and jam nut from case.

17. Remove two attaching screws and parking bracket. (Fig. 7E-50)

18. Remove parking pawl shaft retaining pin from case. Pull straight out. (Fig. 7E-51)

19. Remove parking pawl shaft, parking pawl, and return spring from case. (Fig. 7E-52)

20. Remove detent electrical connector sleeve from case. (Fig. 7E-53)

21. Remove and discard "O" ring seal from connector sleeve.

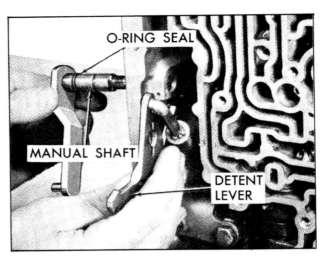

Fig. 7E-49—Removing Manual Shaft and Detent Lever

Fig. 7E-50—Removing Parking Bracket

Fig. 7E-51—Removing Retaing Pin

SPROCKET HOUSING COVER AND PLATE ASSEMBLY, LINK BELT DRIVE AND DRIVEN SPROCKETS

Removal

1. Remove sprocket housing cover attaching bolts.
2. Remove cover and gasket. Discard gasket.

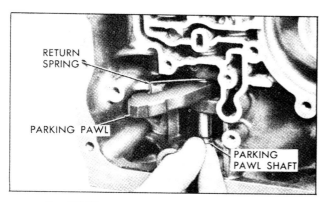

Fig. 7E-52—Removing Parking Pawl, Spring and Shaft

Fig. 7E-55—Removing Sprockets and Link Assembly

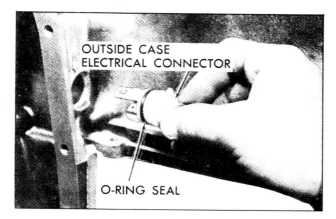

Fig. 7E-53—Removing Electrical Connector

Fig. 7E-56—Removing Tight Sprockets

Fig. 7E-54—Removing Retaining Rings

3. Install J-4646 snap ring pliers into sprocket bearing retaining snap rings located under the drive and driven sprockets, and remove snap rings from retaining grooves in support housing. (Fig. 7E-54)

Do not remove snap rings from beneath the sprockets, leave them in a loose position between the sprockets and the bearing assemblies.

4. Remove drive and driven sprockets, link belt, bearings,

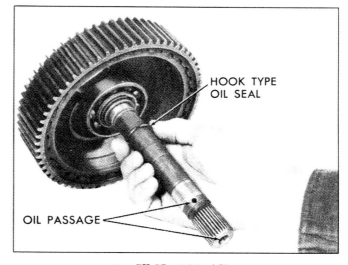

Fig. 7E-57—Oil Seal Rings

and shafts simultaneously by alternately pulling upwards on the drive and driven sprockets until the bearings are out of the drive and driven support housings. (Fig. 7E-55)

If the sprockets are difficult to remove, place a small piece of masonite, or similar material between the sprocket and 1/2 x 9 inch pry bar, and alternately pry upward under each sprocket. Do not pry on the links or the aluminum case. Pry only on the sprockets. (Fig. 7E-56)

5. Remove link belt from drive and driven sprockets.

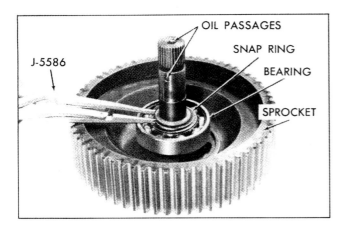

Fig. 7E-58—Removing Retaining Rings

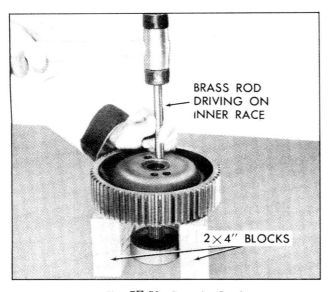

Fig. 7E-59—Removing Bearing

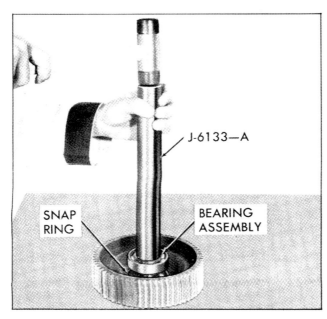

Fig. 7E-60—Installing Bearing

6. Remove the hook type oil seal ring from turbine shaft. (Fig. 7E-57)

7. Inspect drive and driven sprocket bearing assemblies for rough or defective bearings.

Do not remove bearing assemblies from drive and driven sprockets unless they need replacement.

8. If removal of bearing assembly from drive and/or driven sprockets is necessary, proceed as follows:

a. Remove sprocket to bearing assembly retaining snap ring using J-5586, snap ring pliers. (Fig. 7E-58)

b. Mount sprocket, with turbine or input shaft placed in hole in work bench, on two 2" x 4" x 10" pieces of wood.

c. With a hammer and brass rod, drive the inner race, alternately through each of the access openings, until the bearing assembly is removed from the sprocket hub. (Fig. 7E-59)

DRIVE SPROCKET AND TURBINE SHAFT, AND LINK BELT

Inspection

1. Inspect drive sprocket teeth for nicks, burrs, scoring, galling, and excessive wear.

Wear pattern at bottom of teeth is normal.

2. Inspect drive sprocket to ball bearing retaining snap ring for damage.

3. Inspect drive sprocket ball bearing inner race mounting surface for damage.

4. Inspect turbine shaft for open lubrication passages. Run a tag wire through the passages to be sure they are open. See lubrication chart for passage location. (Fig. 7E-232)

5. Inspect spline for damage.

6. Inspect the bushing journals for damage.

7. Inspect the hook type oil seal groove for damage or excessive wear.

8. Inspect the turbine shaft for cracks or distortion.

9. Inspect the link belt for damage or loose links.

Check the guide links. Guide links are the wide outside links on each side of the link belt.

DRIVEN SPROCKET AND INPUT SHAFT

Inspection

1. Inspect driven sprocket teeth for nicks, burrs, scoring, galling, and escessive wear.

Wear pattern at bottom of teeth is normal.

2. Inspect sprocket to ball bearing retaining snap ring for damage.

3. Inspect ball bearing inner race mounting surface for damage.

4. Inspect input shaft for open lubrication holes. Run a tag wire through the holes to be sure they are open. See lubrication chart for location of holes. (Fig. 7E-232)

5. Inspect spline for damage.

6. Inspect bushing journal for damage.

SPROCKET BEARINGS

Install

1. Turn sprocket so that turbine or input shaft is pointing upward.

2. Install new sprocket bearing as follows:

a. Install support snap ring, letter side down, onto shaft.

b. Assemble bearing assembly on turbine or input shaft.

c. Using J-6133-A, drive the bearing assembly onto the

Fig. 7E-61—Checking Front Unit End Play

Fig. 7E-62—Oil Pump Removal

hub of the sprocket until it is resting on the bearing seat of the sprocket. (Fig. 7E-60)

d. Install sprocket to bearing assembly retaining snap ring into groove in sprocket hub.

3. Install hook type oil seal ring on turbine shaft. (Fig. 7E-57)

Turbine and/or input shaft may appear not to be pressed fully into the sprockets. DO NOT attempt pressing shaft into sprocket further as a specific length dimension is held during initial assembly.

FRONT UNIT END PLAY CHECK

1. Make front unit end play check as follows:

a. Install front unit end play checking tool J-22241 into driven sprocket housing so that the soft plastic on the tool can engage the splines in the forward clutch housing. Let the tool bottom on the mainshaft and then withdraw it ap-

proximately 1/16 to 1/8 of an inch and tighten wing nut. (Fig. 7E-61)

b. Remove two of the 5/16" bolts from the driven support housing.

c. Install 5/16" threaded slide hammer bolt with jam nut into one bolt hole in driven support housing.

Do not thread slide hammer bolt deep enough to interfere with forward clutch housing travel.

d. Mount dial indicator on rod and index indicator to register with the forward clutch drum that can be reached through second bolt removed from driven support housing.

e. Push end play tool down to remove slack.

f. Push and hold output flange upward. Place a screwdriver in case opening at parking pawl area and push upward on output carrier.

g. Place another screwdriver between the metal lip of the end play tool and the driven sprocket housing, now push upward on the metal lip of the end play tool and read the resulting end play, which should be between .003" and .024".

The selective washer controlling this end play is the thrust washer located between the driven support housing and the forward clutch housing. If more or less washer thickness is required to bring the end play within specifications, select the proper washer from the chart below.

Thickness	Color
.060" to .064"	Yellow
.071" to .075"	Blue
.082" to .086"	Red
.093" to .097"	Brown
.104" to .108"	Green
.115" to .119"	Black
.126" to .130"	Purple

An oil soaked washer may tend to discolor so that it will be necessary to measure the washer with micrometers to determine its actual thickness.

OIL PUMP

Removal

1. Remove two opposite pump attaching bolts from the drive support housing.

2. Install two 5/16" x 4" guide pins or bolts. (Fig. 7E-62)

3. Remove the remaining pump attaching bolts from the drive support housing.

4. With one hand, hold the under side of the pump, gently tap the guide pin until the pump is removed from the case.

PUMP COVER PLATE AND DRIVE AND DRIVEN SUPPORT HOUSING ASSEMBLIES

Removal

1. Remove the pump cover plate to case attaching screws. Do not remove sprocket support housing bolts at this time.

2. Remove pump cover plate and plate to case face gasket. Discard gasket. (Fig. 7E-63)

3. Remove two hook type oil seal rings from the driven support housing. (Fig. 7E-64)

4. Remove the front unit end play selective thrust washer from the hub of the driven support housing.

Drive and driven support housing assemblies are pressed into and removed with the pump cover plate. Do not remove them unless it is necessary.

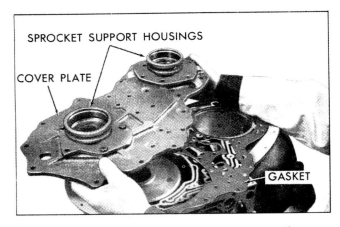

Fig. 7E-63—Removing Support Housings and Cover Plate

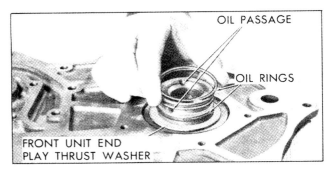

Fig. 7E-64—Removing or Installing Oil Rings and Thrust Washer

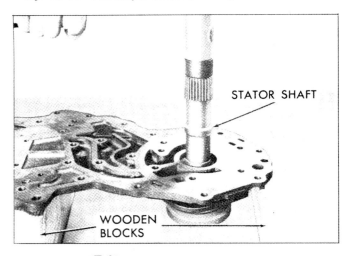

Fig. 7E-65—Removing Drive Sprocket Support

5. If necessary to remove the drive and driven sprocket support housing assemblies, proceed as follows:

a. Remove the remaining sprocket support to pump cover plate attaching bolts.

b. Using a plastic mallet, vigorously strike the stator shaft of the drive sprocket support (Fig. 7E-65) and the hub of the driven sprocket support (Fig. 7E-66) until they are removed from their pump cover plate bores.

When driving the housings out of the pump cover plate avoid damaging or distorting the stator shaft or the ring grooves in the hub of the driven housing.

c. Remove and discard housing to pump cover plate gaskets.

Fig. 7E-66—Removing Driven Sprocket Support

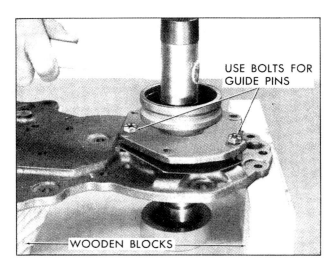

Fig. 7E-67—Installing Drive Sprocket

DRIVE AND DRIVEN SPROCKET

Assembly

Steps 1 through 6 can be omitted if parts were not disassembled.

1. Install drive sprocket support housing to pump cover plate gasket.

2. Install drive sprocket support housing into pump cover plate by using a plastic mallet to seat the housing. Use bolts for guides. (Fig. 7E-67)

3. Install driven sprocket support housing to pump cover plate gasket.

4. Install driven sprocket support housing to pump cover plate attaching bolts for gasket guides.

5. Install driven sprocket support housing into pump cover plate by using a plastic mallet to seat the housing.

6. Install all but two driven support housing to pump cover plate attaching bolts. Torque to 20 ft. lbs.

7. Install proper front unit end play selective thrust washer on the hub of the driven sprocket support housing. Use micrometers to determine the actual thickness of the thrust washer. (Fig. 7E-64)

8. Install two hook type oil seal rings into the grooves in the hub of the driven sprocket support housing.

Fig. 7E-68—Removing Forward Clutch Housing

Fig. 7E-69—Removing Direct Clutch

FORWARD CLUTCH, DIRECT CLUTCH, FRONT BAND ASSEMBLY AND SUN GEAR SHAFT

Removal

1. Remove forward clutch housing assembly, using Tool J-22241. (Fig. 7E-68)

2. Remove forward clutch hub to direct clutch housing thrust washer if it did not come out with the forward clutch housing assembly.

3. Remove direct clutch housing assembly. (Fig. 7E-69)

4. Remove the front band. (Fig. 7E-70)

5. Remove sun gear shaft from gear unit assembly. (Fig. 7E-71)

GEAR UNIT END PLAY CHECK

1. Make rear unit end play check as follows:

a. Install 3/8" bolt for slide hammer into one of the final drive attaching bolt holes. Allow end of case to hang over edge of bench. (Fig. 7E-72)

b. Mount dial indicator on the bolt and index with end of output flange.

c. Move the output flange in and out to read the end play. End play should read .003" to .019". The selective washer controlling this end play is the steel washer having three lugs that is located between the output flange thrust washer and the rear face of the transmission case.

Fig. 7E-70—Removing Front Band

Fig. 7E-71—Removing Sun Gear Shaft

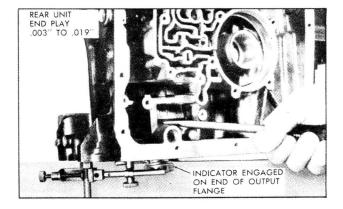

Fig. 7E-72—Checking Rear Unit End Play

If a different washer thickness is required to bring the end play within specifications, it can be selected from the following chart:

Thickness	Notches	or	Numeral
.074" to .078"	None		1
.082" to .086"	1 Tab Side		2
.090" to .094"	2 Tab Side		3
.098" to .102"	1 Tab O.D.		4
.106" to .110"	2 Tabs O.D.		5
.114" to .118"	3 Tabs O.D.		6

Fig. 7E-73—Removing Case Center Support Bolt

CENTER SUPPORT, GEAR UNIT ASSEMBLY, REAR BAND ASSEMBLY, AND REAR UNIT SELECTIVE WASHER

Removal

1. Remove the case center support to case bolt, using a 3/8" 12-point thin wall socket. (Fig. 7E-73)

2. Remove the intermediate clutch backing plate to case snap ring. (Fig. 7E-74)

3. Remove the intermediate clutch backing plate, three composition and three steel clutch plates. (Fig. 7E-75)

4. Remove the center support to case retaining snap ring. (Fig. 7E-76)

5. Install Tool J-21795 with J-6125 slide hammer onto mainshaft. Tool should tighten against shaft. Using the slide hammer as a handle, lift entire support and gear unit assembly from case. (Fig. 7E-77)

Fig. 7E-74—Removing Intermediate Clutch Snap Ring

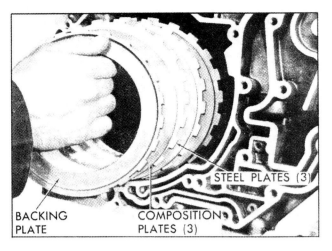

Fig. 7E-75—Removing Backing and Clutch Plates

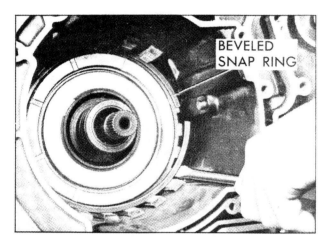

Fig. 7E-76—Removing Case Center Support Snap Ring

Fig. 7E-77—Removing Gear Unit

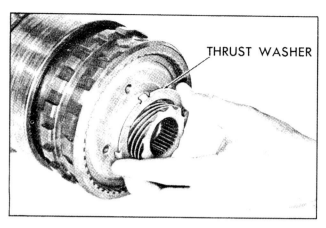

Fig. 7E-78—Removing Thrust Washer

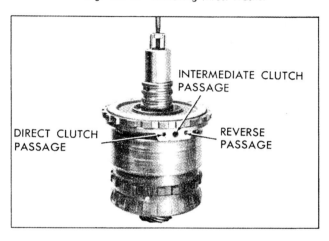

Fig. 7E-79—Gear Unit Positioned on Bench

Fig. 7E-80—Removing Rear Band

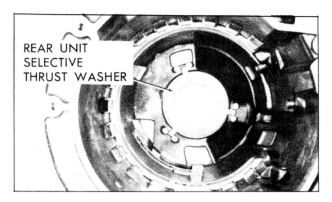

Fig. 7E-81—Removing Selector Washer

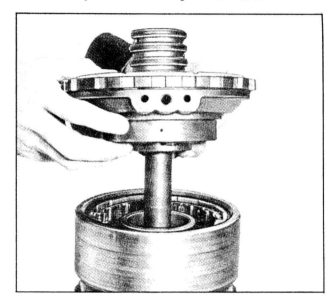

Fig. 7E-82—Removing Center Support

Fig. 7E-83—Removing Thrust Washer

6. Remove the output flange to case thrust washer from the rear of the output flange or inside the case. (Fig. 7E-78)

7. Place the gear unit assembly with output flange facing down on work bench. (Fig. 7E-79)

8. Remove the rear band assembly. (Fig. 7E-80)

9. Remove the rear unit selective washer from the transmission case. (Fig. 7E-81)

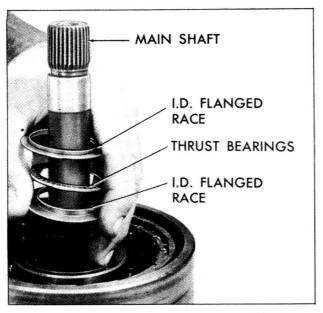

Fig. 7E-84—Removing Sun Gear Races and Bearings

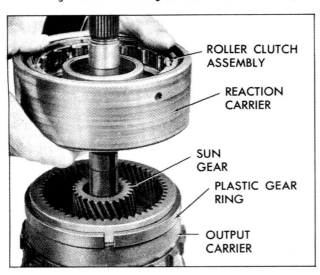

Fig. 7E-85—Removing Reaction Carrier

DISASSEMBLY AND ASSEMBLY OF INDIVIDUAL UNITS

SUPPORT AND GEAR UNIT

Disassembly

1. Remove the case center support assembly. (Fig. 7E-82)
2. Remove the center support to reaction carrier thrust washer. (Fig. 7E-83)
3. Remove the center support to sun gear races and thrust bearing. (Fig. 7E-84)

   One of the races may have been removed with the center support.

4. Remove the reaction carrier and roller clutch assembly. (Fig. 7E-85)
5. Remove roller clutch assembly from reaction carrier. (Fig. 7E-86)
6. Remove front internal gear ring from output carrier assembly. (Fig. 7E-87)

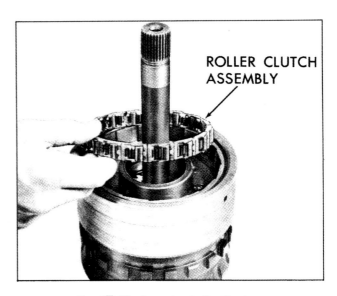

Fig. 7E-86—Removing Roller Clutch

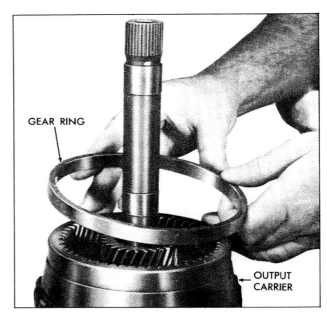

Fig. 7E-87—Removing Front Internal Gear Ring

7. Remove sun gear. (Fig. 7E-88)

8. Remove reaction carrier to output carrier thrust washer. (Fig. 7E-89)

9. Turn assembly over.

10. Remove output flange to output carrier snap ring. (Fig. 7E-90)

11. Remove output flange. (Fig. 7E-91)

12. Remove output flange to rear internal gear thrust bearing and two races. (Fig. 7E-92)

   Do not drop roller thrust bearings.

13. Remove rear internal gear and mainshaft. (Fig. 7E-93)

14. *Remove the rear internal gear to sun gear thrust bearing and two races.* (Fig. 7E-94)

15. If necessary, remove the rear internal gear to mainshaft snap ring to remove mainshaft. (Fig. 7E-95)

Fig. 7E-88—Removing Sun Gear

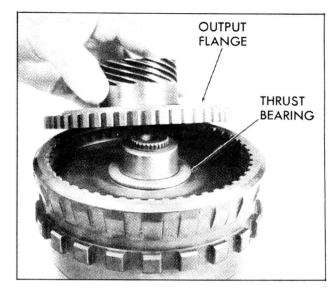

Fig. 7E-91—Removing Output Flange

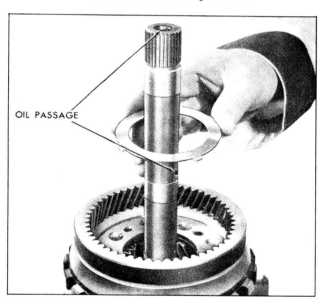

Fig. 7E-89—Removing Output Carrier Thrust Washer

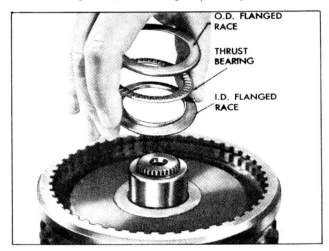

Fig. 7E-92—Removing Thrust Bearing and Races

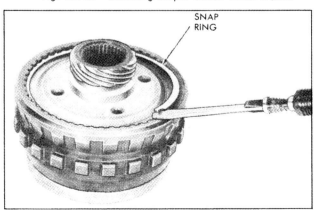

Fig. 7E-90—Removing Output Carrier Snap Ring

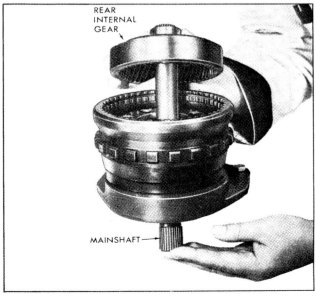

Fig. 7E-93—Removing Rear Internal Gear and Mainshaft

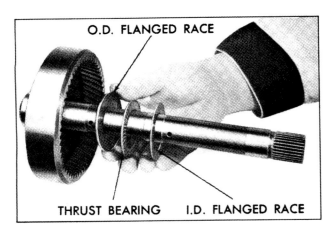

Fig. 7E-94—Removing Thrust Bearing and Races

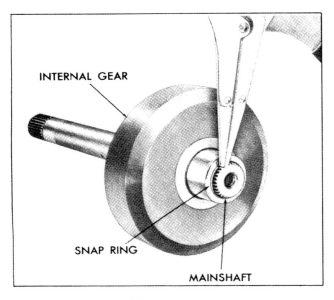

Fig. 7E-95—Removing Snap Ring

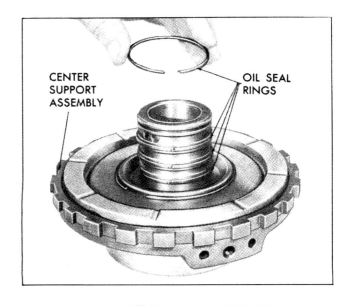

Fig. 7E-96—Removing Oil Seal Rings

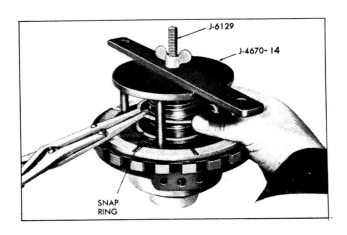

Fig. 7E-97—Removing Snap Ring

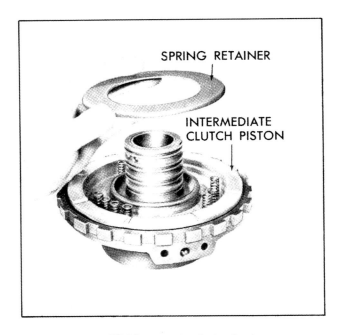

Fig. 7E-98—Removing Spring Retainer

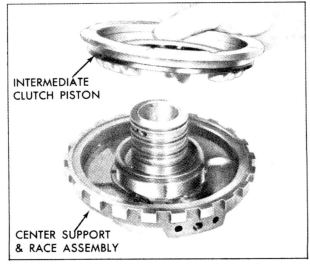

Fig. 7E-99—Removing Intermediate Clutch Piston

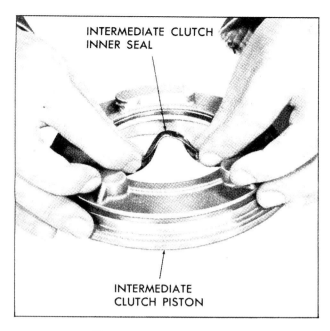

Fig. 7E-100—Removing or Installing Inner Seal

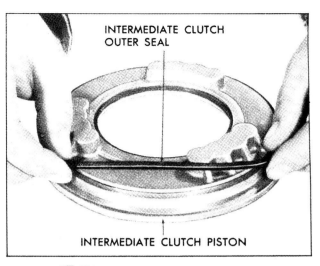

Fig. 7E-101—Removing or Installing Outer Seal

6. Remove and discard the outer piston seal. (Fig. 7E-101)

Do not remove the three screws retaining the roller clutch inner race to the center support.

CASE CENTER SUPPORT

Disassembly

1. Remove four hook type oil seal rings from center support. (Fig. 7E-96)

2. Using clutch compressor or tools J-6129 and J-4670-14, compress the spring retainer and remove snap ring. (Fig. 7E-97)

3. Remove the spring retainer and twelve clutch release springs. (Fig. 7E-98)

4. Remove the intermediate clutch piston. (Fig. 7E-99)

5. Remove and discard the inner piston seal. (Fig. 7E-100)

Inspection

1. Inspect the roller clutch inner race for scratches or indentations. Be sure the lubrication hole is open by running a tag wire through this hole. See lubrication chart (Fig. 7E-232) for location of holes.

2. Inspect the bushing for scoring, wear, or galling.

3. Check oil ring grooves for damage or excessive wear.

4. Air check the oil passages to be sure they are open and are not interconnected. See lubrication chart for location of holes. (Fig. 7E-232)

5. Inspect the piston sealing surfaces for scratches.

6. Inspect the piston seal grooves for nicks and other damage.

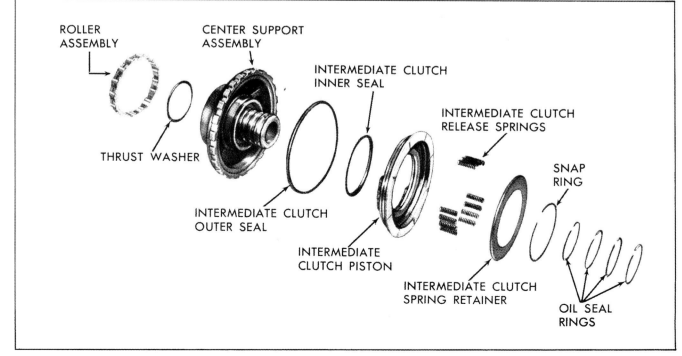

Fig. 7E-102—Center Support Assembly

Fig. 7E-103—Installing Intermediate Clutch Piston

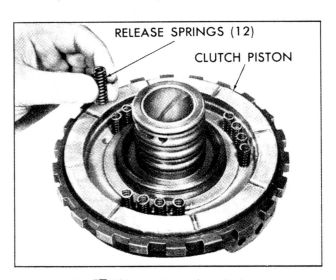

Fig. 7E-104—Installing Release Springs

7. Inspect the piston for cracks or porosity.

8. Inspect the release springs for distortion or collapsed coils.

Assembly (Fig. 7E-102)

1. Install new inner seal on the piston with lip of the seal facing away from the spring pockets. (Fig. 7E-100)

2. Install new outer seal with lip of seal facing away from the spring pockets. (Fig. 7E-101)

Apply Hydra-Matic oil to all seals before installing piston.

3. Install inner seal protector, Tool J-21363, on the center support hub. Install the piston, indexing spring pockets in the piston with cast pockets in center support. (Fig. 7E-103)

Spring pocket recesses in the piston must match cast pocket in center support.

4. Install twelve release springs into the piston. (Fig. 7E-104)

Fig. 7E-105—Air Checking Intermediate Clutch and Piston

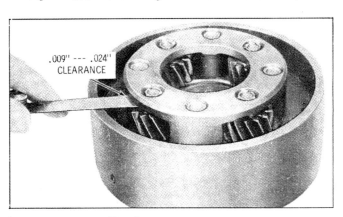

Fig. 7E-106—Checking Pinion End Play

5. Place the spring retainer and snap ring over the springs. (Fig. 7E-98)

6. Using clutch compressor tools J-6129 and J-4670-14, compress the springs and install the snap ring. (Fig. 7E-97)

7. Install four hook type oil rings. (Fig. 7E-96)

8. Air check operation of intermediate clutch and piston. (Fig. 7E-105)

REACTION CARRIER, ROLLER CLUTCH, AND OUTPUT CARRIER

Inspection

1. Inspect band surface on reaction carrier for signs of burning or scoring.

2. Inspect the roller clutch outer race for scoring or wear.

3. Inspect the thrust washer surfaces for signs of scoring or wear.

4. Inspect the bushing for damage. If bushing is damaged, the reaction carrier must be replaced.

5. Inspect the pinions for damage, rough bearings, or excessive tilt.

6. Check pinion end play. Pinion end play should be .009" to .024". (Fig. 7E-106)

7. Inspect the roller clutch for damage.

8. Inspect the roller cage and retaining springs for damage.

9. Inspect the front internal gear in output carrier assembly for damaged teeth.

10. Inspect the output carrier pinions for damage, rough bearings, or excessive tilt.

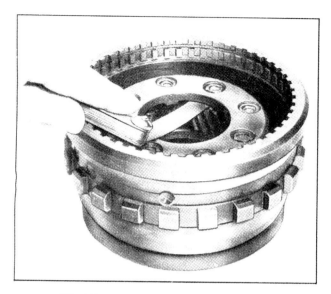

Fig. 7E-107—Checking Output Carrier Pinion End Play

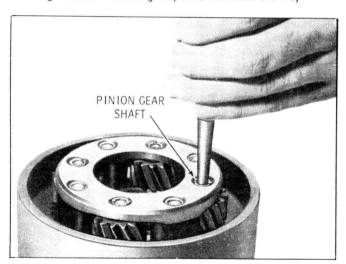

Fig. 7E-108—Removing Pinion Pins

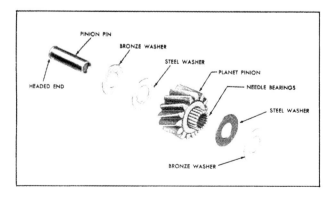

Fig. 7E-109—Planet Pinion Gears

11. Check pinion end play. Pinion end play should be .009" to .024". (Fig. 7E-107)

12. Inspect the parking pawl lugs for cracks or damage.

13. Inspect the output locating splines for damage.

14. Inspect the front internal plastic gear ring for flaking or cracks.

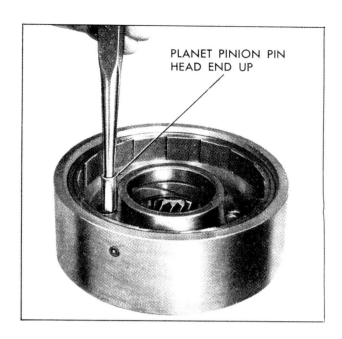

Fig. 7E-110—Installing Pinion Pin

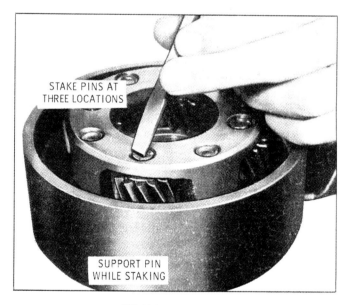

Fig. 7E-111—Staking Pinion Pin

PINION GEARS

Remove and Install

1. Support the carrier assembly on its front face.

2. Using a 1/2" drill, remove the stake marks from the end of the pinion pin, or pins, to be replaced. This will reduce the possibility of cracking the carrier when the pinion pins are pressed out.

Do not allow drill to remove any stock from the carrier as this will weaken the part.

3. Remove the pinions, thrust washers, and roller needle bearings. (Fig. 7E-108)

4. Inspect the pinion pocket thrust faces for burrs and remove if present.

5. Install eighteen needle bearings into each pinion, using petrolatum to hold the bearings in place. Use a pinion pin as a

guide. (Fig. 7E-109)

6. Place a steel and bronze washer on each side of pinion so steel washer is against pinion. Hold in place with petrolatum.

7. Place the pinion assembly in position in the carrier and install a pilot shaft through the rear face of the assembly to hold the parts in place.

8. Drive a new pinion pin into place while rotating pinion from the front. Be sure that the headed end is flush or below the face of the carrier. (Fig. 7E-110)

9. Place a large punch in a bench vise to be used as an anvil while staking the opposite end of the pinion pin in three places. (Fig. 7E-111)

Both ends of the pinion pins must lie below the face of the carrier or interference may occur.

OUTPUT FLANGE

Inspection

1. Inspect the bushing for wear or galling.
2. Inspect the governor drive gear for rough or damaged teeth.
3. Inspect the drive lugs for damage.
4. Inspect lubrication passages.

Rear Internal Gear

1. Inspect the gear teeth for damage or wear.
2. Inspect the splines for damage.
3. Inspect the gear for cracks.
4. Inspect bearing and thrust surfaces for wear or galling.

Sun Gear

1. Inspect the gear teeth for damage or wear.
2. Inspect splines for damage.
3. Be sure oil lubrication hole is open. See lubrication chart (Fig. 7E-232) for location of holes.

Sun Gear Shaft

1. Inspect shaft for cracks or splits.
2. Inspect splines for damage.

3. Inspect bushings for scoring or galling.
4. Inspect the bushing journals for damage.
5. Be sure the oil lubrication holes are open. See lubrication chart (Fig. 7E-232) for location of holes.

Mainshaft

1. Inspect the shaft for cracks or distortion.
2. Inspect the splines for damage.
3. Inspect the bushing journals for damage.
4. Inspect the snap ring groove for damage.
5. Inspect the orificed cup plug pressed into one end of mainshaft. Be sure it is not plugged by running a tag wire through the orifice hole.
6. Inspect for open lubrication passages.

If mainshaft replacement is required, it is necessary to use a shaft with a "V" identification groove on the machined journal at the rear internal gear end of the shaft. Because of a spline change, the current model mainshaft is not interchangeable with past model parts.

GEAR UNIT (Fig. 7E-112)

Assembly

1. Install rear internal gear on end of mainshaft and install snap ring. (Fig. 7E-113)

2. Install the sun gear to internal gear thrust races and bearings against the inner face of the rear internal gear as follows: (Retain with petrolatum). (Fig. 7E-114)

   a. Place the large race against the internal gear with O.D. flange facing rearward or up.

   b. Place the thrust bearing against the race.

   c. Place the small race against the bearing with the inner flange facing into the bearing or down.

3. Install the output carrier over the mainshaft so that the pinions mesh with the rear internal gear. (Fig. 7E-115)

5. Place the above portion of the build-up through hole in bench so that the mainshaft hangs downward.

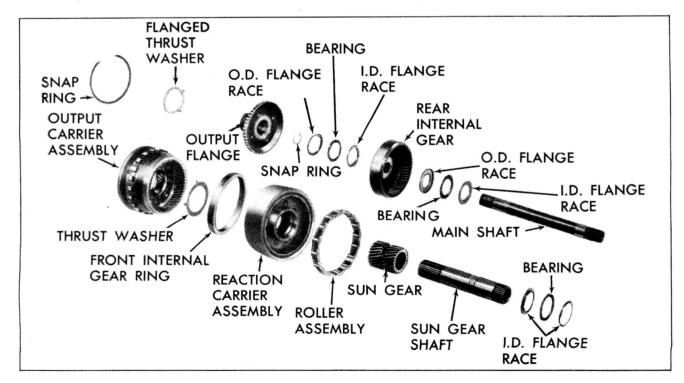

Fig. 7E-112—Gear Unit

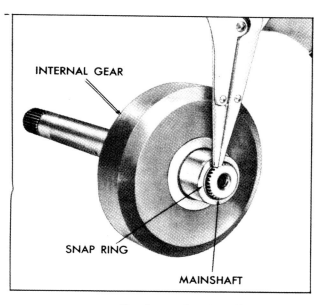

Fig. 7E-113—Installing Snap Ring

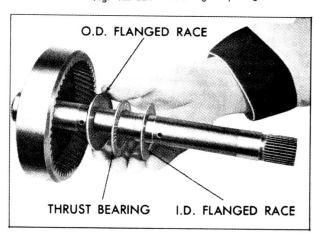

Fig. 7E-114—Installing Thrust Bearing and Races

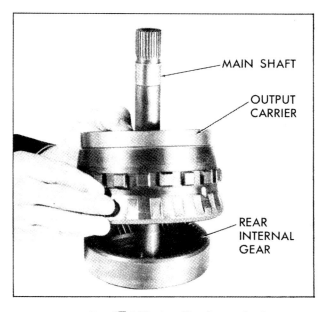

Fig. 7E-115—Installing Output Carrier

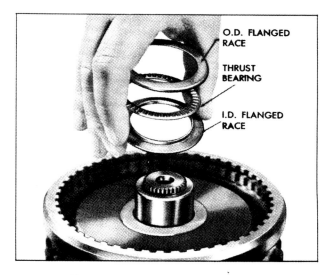

Fig. 7E-116—Installing Thrust Bearing and Races

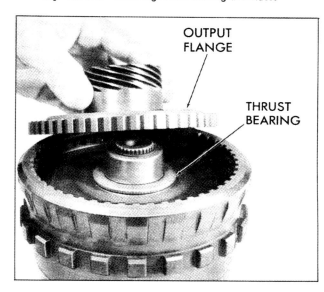

Fig. 7E-117—Installing Output Flange

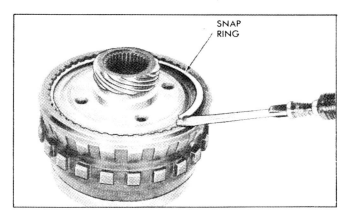

Fig. 7E-118—Installing Snap Ring

6. Install the rear internal gear to output flange thrust races and bearings as follows: (Retain with petrolatum). (Fig. 7E-116)

a. Place the small diameter race against the internal gear

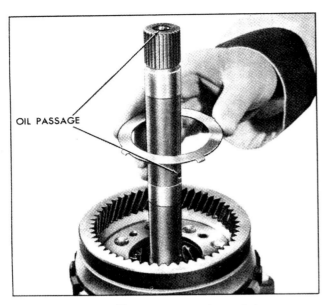

Fig. 7E-119—Installing Thrust Washer

Fig. 7E-121—Installing Gear Ring

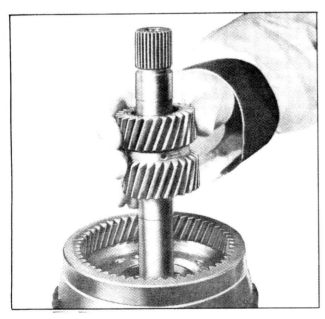

Fig. 7E-120—Installing Sun Gear

Fig. 7E-122—Installing Reaction Carrier

with the center flange facing up.

b. Place the bearing on the race.

c. Place the second race on the bearing with the outer flange cupped over the bearing.

7. Install the output flange into the output carrier assembly. (Fig. 7E-117)

8. Install the output flange to the output carrier snap ring bevel side up. (Fig. 7E-118)

9. Turn assembly over and support so that the output flange faces downward.

10. Lubricate and install the reaction carrier to output carrier plastic thrust washer with the tabs facing down into pockets. (Fig. 7E-119)

11. Install the sun gear with I.D. chamfer end down. (Fig. 7E-120)

12. Install the plastic gear ring over the output carrier. (Fig. 7E-121)

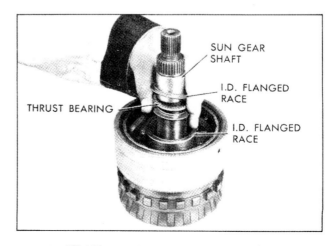

Fig. 7E-123—Installing Sun Gear Thrust Washers

Fig. 7E-124—Installing Thrust Washers

Fig. 7E-126—Installing Center Support

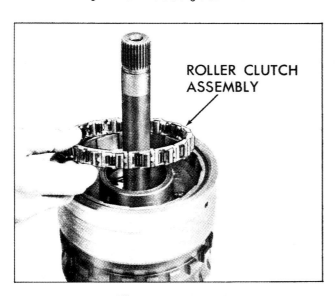

Fig. 7E-125—Installing Roller Clutch

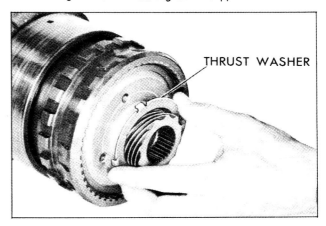

Fig. 7E-127—Installing Thrust Washer

19. Install output flange to case selective thrust washer, tabs in pockets. Retain with petrolatum. (Fig. 7E-127)

INSPECTION
Front and Rear Bands

1. Inspect the lining for cracks, flaking, burning, or looseness.
2. Inspect the bands for cracks or distortion.
3. Inspect the end for damage at the anchor lugs or apply lugs.

Modulator and Valve

1. Inspect the modulator assembly for any signs of bending, distortion, or presence of water or oil.
2. Inspect the "O" ring seal seat for damage.
3. Apply suction to the vacuum tube and check for diaphragm leaks.
4. Inspect the modulator valve for nicks or damage.
5. Inspect case bushing for nicks or scoring.
6. Check freeness of valve operation in case bushing bore.
7. Check modulator bellows, modulator plunger is under pressure (16 lbs.). If bellows are damaged the plunger will have very little pressure.

13. Install the reaction carrier. (Fig. 7E-122)
14. Install sun gear shaft.
15. Install the center support to sun gear thrust races and bearings as follows: (Fig. 7E-123)
 a. Install the large race, center flange up over the sun gear shaft.
 b. Install the thrust bearing against the race.
 c. Install the second race, center flange up.
16. Install the center support to reaction carrier thrust washer into the recess in the center support. Retain with petrolatum. (Fig. 7E-124)
17. Install the roller clutch assembly into reaction carrier. (Fig. 7E-125)
18. Install the case center support into roller clutch assembly. (Fig. 7E-126)

With reaction carrier held, case support should only turn clockwise.

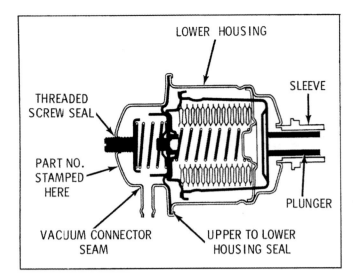

Fig. 7E-128—Vacuum Modulator

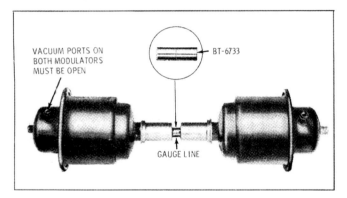

Fig. 7E-129—Checking Vacuum Modulator

VACUUM MODULATOR DIAGNOSIS

Vacuum Diaphragm Check

Insert a pipe cleaner as far as possible into the vacuum connector pipe and check for the presence of transmission fluid. If transmission fluid is found, the modulator should be replaced.

Gasoline or water vapor may settle in the vacuum side of the modulator. If this is found without the presence of oil, proceed to the next check.

Atmospheric Leak Check

1. Apply a liberal coating of soap bubble solution to the vacuum connector pipe seam, the crimped upper to lower housing seam, and the threaded screw seal. (Fig. 7-128)

2. Using a short piece of rubber hose, apply air pressure to the vacuum pipe by blowing into the tube and observing for bubbles. If bubbles appear, replace the modulator.

Do not use any method other than human lung power for applying air pressure, as pressures over 6 psi may damage the modulator.

Bellows Comparison Check

This check is made using an available tool, BT-6733. The gauge compares the load of a known good modulator with a modulator being checked.

1. Install the modulator that is known to be acceptable on either end of the gauge.

2. Install the modulator in question on the opposite end of the gauge. (Fig. 7-129)

3. Holding the modulators in a horizontal position, bring them together under pressure until either modulator sleeve end just touches the line in the center of the gauge. The gap between the opposite modulator sleeve end and the gauge line should be 1/16" or less. If the distance is greater than this amount, the modulator in question should be replaced.

When making the comparison, make sure that both modulators are of the same type. The part numbers are stamped on the dome of the modulator.

Sleeve Alignment Check

Roll the main body of the modulator on a flat surface and observe the sleeve for concentricity to the can. If the sleeve is concentric and the plunger is free, the modulator is acceptable.

If the vacuum modulator assembly passes all of the above checks, it is an acceptable part and should be reused.

Manual and Parking Linkage

1. Inspect the parking actuator rod for cracks, damage, or broken spring retainer lugs.

2. Inspect the actuator spring for damage.

3. Inspect actuator for a free fit on the actuator rod.

4. Inspect the parking pawl for cracks or wear.

5. Inspect the manual shaft for damaged threads, rough oil seal groove or loose lever.

6. Inspect the inside detent lever for cracks or a loose pin.

7. Inspect the parking pawl shaft for damaged retainer grooves, or rough surface.

8. Inspect the parking pawl return spring for deformed coils or ends.

9. Inspect the parking bracket for cracks or wear.

10. Inspect the detent roller and spring assembly.

Case

1. Inspect case assembly for cracks, porosity, or interconnected passages. Air can be blown through passages to determine if they are interconnected. See lubrication chart (Fig. 7E-232) for location of passages.

2. Check for good retention of band anchor pins.

3. Inspect all threaded holes for thread damage.

4. Inspect the intermediate clutch driven plate lugs for damage or brinelling.

5. Inspect the snap ring grooves for damage.

6. Inspect the bore of the governor assembly for scratches or scoring.

7. Inspect the modulator bushing bore for scoring or damage.

8. Inspect the pressure regulator bore for scoring or damage.

Converter

1. Check converter for cracks or broken welds.

2. Check converter hub surfaces for signs of scoring or wear.

3. Check converter for leaks as outlined in Section 7.

REAR SERVO

Disassembly

1. Remove the rear accumulator piston from rear servo piston. (Fig. 7E-130)

2. Remove E-ring retaining rear servo piston to band apply pin. (Fig. 7E-131)

3. Remove rear servo piston and seal from band apply pin.

4. Remove washer, spring and retainer.

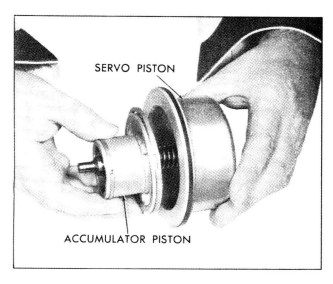

Fig. 7E-130—Removing Accumulator Piston

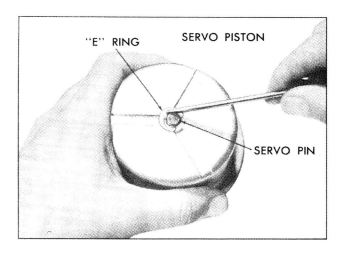

Fig. 7E-131—Removing "E" Ring

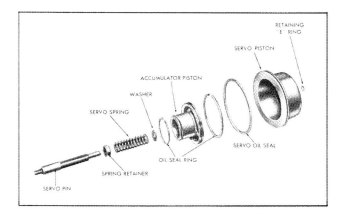

Fig. 7E-132—Rear Servo and Accumulator

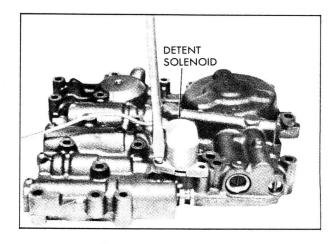

Fig. 7E-133—Removing Detent Solenoid

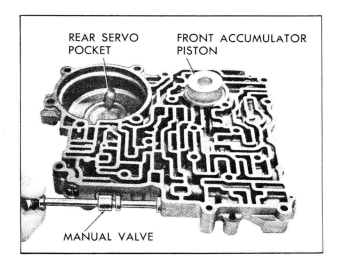

Fig. 7E-134—Removing Manual Valve

Inspection

1. Inspect freeness of accumulator ring in piston.
2. Pick up proper band apply pin determined by band apply pin selection check.
3. Inspect fit of band apply pin in servo piston.
4. Inspect band apply pin and servo piston for scores and cracks.

Assembly

1. Install spring retainer, cup end first, spring and washer on band apply pin. (Fig. 7E-132)
2. Install band apply piston and secure with E-ring. (Fig. 7E-131)
3. If removed, install oil seal ring on servo piston.
4. If removed, install outer and inner oil rings on accumulator piston. Assemble into bore of servo piston.

FRONT SERVO

Inspection

1. Inspect servo pin for damage. Roll pin on a flat surface to determine the straightness of pin.
2. Inspect piston for damaged oil ring groove. Check freeness of ring in groove.
3. Inspect piston for cracks or porosity.
4. Check fit of servo pin in piston.

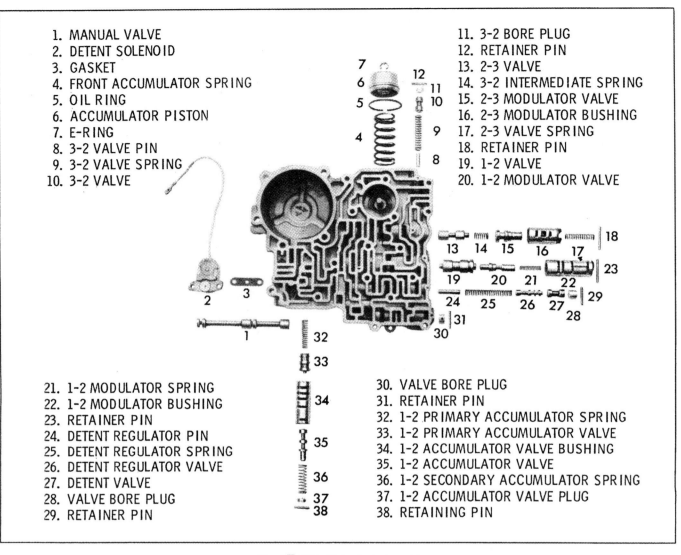

1. MANUAL VALVE
2. DETENT SOLENOID
3. GASKET
4. FRONT ACCUMULATOR SPRING
5. OIL RING
6. ACCUMULATOR PISTON
7. E-RING
8. 3-2 VALVE PIN
9. 3-2 VALVE SPRING
10. 3-2 VALVE

11. 3-2 BORE PLUG
12. RETAINER PIN
13. 2-3 VALVE
14. 3-2 INTERMEDIATE SPRING
15. 2-3 MODULATOR VALVE
16. 2-3 MODULATOR BUSHING
17. 2-3 VALVE SPRING
18. RETAINER PIN
19. 1-2 VALVE
20. 1-2 MODULATOR VALVE

21. 1-2 MODULATOR SPRING
22. 1-2 MODULATOR BUSHING
23. RETAINER PIN
24. DETENT REGULATOR PIN
25. DETENT REGULATOR SPRING
26. DETENT REGULATOR VALVE
27. DETENT VALVE
28. VALVE BORE PLUG
29. RETAINER PIN

30. VALVE BORE PLUG
31. RETAINER PIN
32. 1-2 PRIMARY ACCUMULATOR SPRING
33. 1-2 PRIMARY ACCUMULATOR VALVE
34. 1-2 ACCUMULATOR VALVE BUSHING
35. 1-2 ACCUMULATOR VALVE
36. 1-2 SECONDARY ACCUMULATOR SPRING
37. 1-2 ACCUMULATOR VALVE PLUG
38. RETAINING PIN

Fig. 7E-137—Valve Body Assembly

GOVERNOR ASSEMBLY

All components of the governor assembly, with the exception of the driven gear, are select fit. Each assembly is factory calibrated. The governor, including the driven gear and cover is serviced as a complete assembly.

Governor Inspection

1. Wash all parts in cleaning solvent, air dry and blow out all passages.
2. Inspect governor sleeve for nicks, burrs, scoring or galling.
3. Check governor sleeve for free operation in bore of *transmission case*.
4. Inspect governor valve for nicks, burrs, scoring or galling.
5. Check governor valve for free operation in bore of governor sleeve.
6. Inspect governor driven gear for nicks, burrs, or damage.
7. Check governor driven gear for looseness on governor sleeve.
8. Inspect governor springs for distortion or damage.
9. Check governor weights for free operation in their retainers.

10. Check valve opening at entry and exhaust (.020" minimum).

CONTROL VALVE (Fig. 7E-137)

Disassembly

As each valve train is removed, place the individual valve train in a separate location relative to its position in the valve body. Also, place each part of each valve train in the order that it is removed from the valve bore. None of the valves or springs are interchangeable. Keep them in the proper valve train.

1. Remove two detent solenoid to valve assembly attaching screws. (Fig. 7E-133)
2. Remove detent solenoid and solenoid gasket. Discard gasket.
3. Position valve assembly with lapped face up so that the servo bore and the front accumulator piston are positioned as shown in Fig. 7E-134.
4. Remove manual valve from bore. (Fig. 7E-134)
5. Use a No. 1 easy-out and remove retaining pin and plug from manual bore.

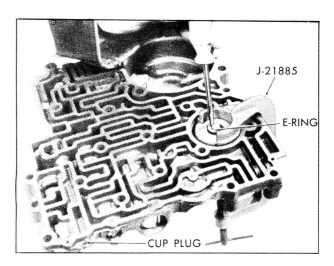

Fig. 7E-135—Removing Front Accumulator Piston

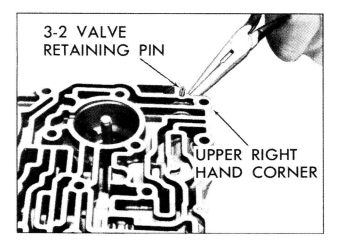

Fig. 7E-136—Removing 3-2 Valve Retaining Pin

6. Install available compressor Tool J-21885 on front accumulator piston and remove retaining E-ring. (Fig. 7E-135)

7. Release Tool J-21885 and remove the tool, the front accumulator piston, and spring from valve assembly.

8. Using a pair of needle nose pliers, compress the bore plug and remove the retaining pin from the 3-2 valve bore located in the extreme upper right hand corner of the valve assembly. (Fig. 7E-136)

9. Remove the bore plug, 3-2 valve and spring from the valve assembly.

10. Remove the retaining pin from the 2-3 valve train bore located directly below and at a right angle to the 3-2 valve.

11. Remove the 2-3 modulator bushing, 2-3 modulator valve and spring, the 3-2 intermediate spring, and the 2-3 valve.

12. Remove the retaining pin from the 1-2 valve bore located directly below the 2-3 valve train bore.

13. Remove the 1-2 modulator valve bushing, 1-2 regulator valve and spring, 1-2 detent valve, and the 1-2 valve.

14. Remove the retaining pin from the detent regulator bore located directly below the 1-2 valve bore.

15. Remove the bore plug, detent valve, detent regulator valve, detent regulator pin and spring.

16. Remove the 1-2 accumulator bushing retaining pin and bore plug from the hole located to the right of the stator valve.

17. Remove 1-2 accumulator valve bushing, 1-2 accumulator valve and secondary spring, 1-2 accumulator primary valve, and spring.

Inspection (Fig. 7E-137)

1. Thoroughly wash and clean valve body in a clean solvent to remove the oil.

2. Inspect valve body for cracked lands in the valve port areas, scratches or porosity in bores, nicks on the machined face, and cracks, scratches, nicks or distortion in the servo bores.

3. Inspect front servo pin for scoring, cracks, and damage to the E-ring groove.

4. Inspect the valves for scoring, cracks, and squareness of corner shoulders.

Valve corners should be sharp and square.

5. Inspect bushings for galling, scratches, or distortion.

6. Check all springs for distortion or collapsed coils.

Assembly (Fig. 7E-137)

1. Install the 1-2 accumulator primary spring in the 1-2 primary valve and install both, spring first, into bore, using a retaining retainer to hold the spring and valve in its operating position until the bushing assembly is installed. Pin goes into first drilled hole in port. (Fig. 7E-138)

2. Install the 1-2 accumulator secondary valve (wide land first) into the 1-2 accumulator bushing.

3. Install the 1-2 accumulator valve bushing into the bore, align the square port on the end of the bushing with the hole for the retaining pin.

4. Install the 1-2 secondary accumulator valve spring and 1-2 accumulator plug into the bushing.

5. Install grooved retaining pin, with the grooves entering the pin hole last, and tap with a hammer until flush with cast surface of the valve body.

6. Install spring, detent regulator pin, detent regulator valve (flat end first), detent valve (flat end first), bore plug, and retaining pin into detent bore. (Compress spring with screwdriver to aid installation of detent valve into the valve body).

7. Install 1-2 valve into 1-2 valve bore, long stem end first.

8. Install 1-2 modulator valve spring, and 1-2 modulator valve into 1-2 modulator valve bushing.

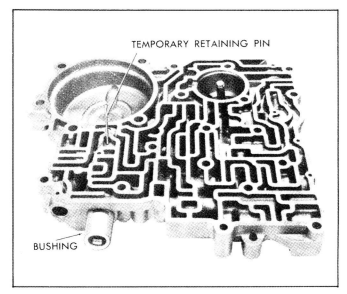

Fig. 7E-138—Temporary Retaining Pin Installation

9. Install 1-2 modulator valve bushing assembly into 1-2 valve bore and install retaining pin into valve body.

10. Install the 2-3 valve (flat end first) into 2-3 bore. Install 3-2 intermediate spring on stem end of 2-3 valve.

11. Install 2-3 modulator valve into 2-3 modulator bushing and install 2-3 modulator bushing (large diameter hole first) into valve body.

12. Install 2-3 valve spring and retaining pin into valve bore.

13. Install 3-2 valve spring, spacer and 3-2 valve (either end first) into 3-2 valve bore.

14. Install valve bore plug and retaining pin into valve body.

15. Using Tool J-21885, install front servo spring, front servo piston, and retaining E-ring into front accumulator piston pocket.

16. Install detent solenoid gasket, detent solenoid, and attaching screws on reverse side of valve body assembly.

17. Check all valve trains to see that they are operating freely by compressing the valves on the springs.

18. Install manual bore plug and retaining pin.

19. Install manual valve into manual bore.

OIL PUMP

Disassembly

1. Mark gears for reassembly and remove drive gear from pump body. (Fig. 7E-139)

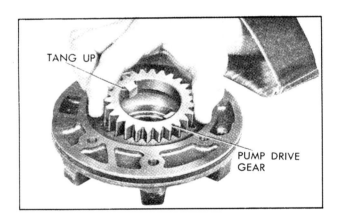

Fig. 7E-139—Removing or Installing Pump Drive Gear

Fig. 7E-140—Removing or Installing Pump Driven Gear

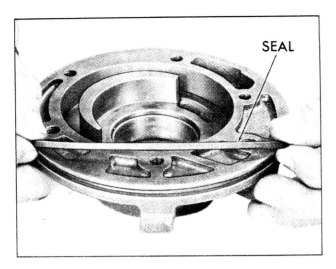

Fig. 7E-141—Removing or Installing Pump to Case Seal

Fig. 7E-142—Checking End Clearance

2. Remove driven gear from pump body. (Fig. 7E-140)

3. Remove and discard pump body to case "O" ring seal. (Fig. 7E-141)

Inspection

1. Using tip of finger, inspect gear pocket and crescent for nicks, burrs, scoring or galling.

2. Inspect drive gear for nicks, burrs, scoring, or galling.

3. Inspect driven gear for nicks, burrs, scoring, or galling.

4. Place pump gears in pump body and check the following gear face to pump face clearances.

   a. Pump body face to gear face can be checked by placing a dial indicator on the J-8619-11 gauge and reading the flatness between the pump face and the pump gears. End clearance should be .0008" to .0015". (Fig. 7E-142)

5. Check face of pump body for nicks, burrs, scoring, or galling.

6. Check pump body face flatness. Overall flatness should be .000" to .002". Use J-8619-11.

7. Inspect bushing for nicks, burrs, scoring, galling, out-of-round, or excessive wear.

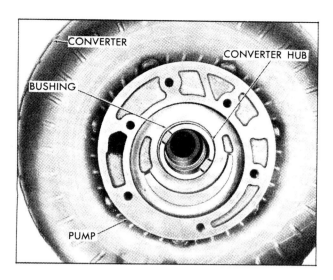

Fig. 7E-143—Checking Bushing Runout

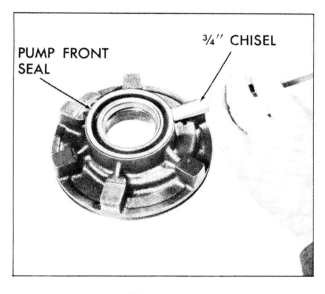

Fig. 7E-144—Removing Front Seal

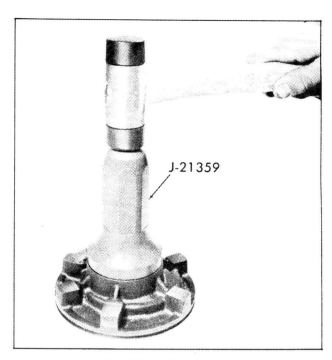

Fig. 7E-145—Installing Front Seal

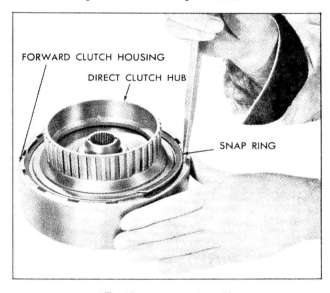

Fig. 7E-146—Removing Snap Ring

a. To check for out-of-round, install pump body on the converter hub and look for eccentricity between pump bushing and converter hub. (Fig. 7E-143)

8. Check for damaged pump cover plate bolt holes.

9. Inspect front seal for damage. If replacement of front seal is necessary, use a standard 3/4" cold chisel and pry front seal from pump body. (Fig. 7E-144)

Assembly

1. If necessary, install a new front seal, using Tool J-21359 to drive the seal in place. Use Sealer No. 1050026 or equivalent on outside of seal before installing into pump. (Fig. 7E-145)

2. Install the driven gear into the pump body. (Fig. 7E-140)

3. Install the drive gear into the pump body with drive tangs up. (Fig. 7E-139)

The drive gear should always be installed with the counterbore down.

4. Install the new pump to case "O" ring seal. (Fig. 7E-141)

FORWARD CLUTCH

Disassembly

1. Place forward clutch on bench. Remove the forward clutch housing to direct clutch hub snap ring. (Fig. 7E-146)

2. Remove the direct clutch hub. (Fig. 7E-147)

3. Remove the forward clutch hub and thrust washers. (Fig. 7E-148)

4. Remove five composition, five steel clutch plates, and one dished steel plate. (Fig. 7E-149)

5. Using J-6129 clutch spring compressor, with Adapters J-4670-14 and J-8765, compress the spring retainer and remove the snap ring. (Fig. 7E-150)

6. Remove the tools, snap ring, spring retainer, and sixteen clutch release springs. (Fig. 7E-151)

7. Remove the forward clutch piston. (Fig. 7E-152)

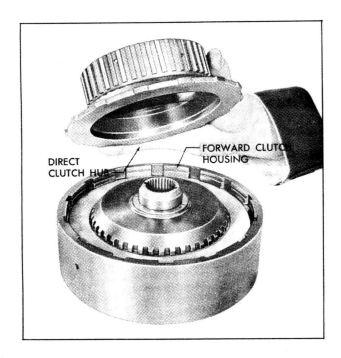

Fig. 7E-147—Removing Direct Clutch Hub

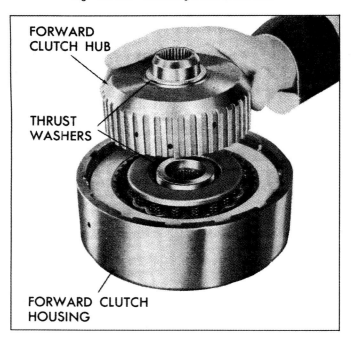

Fig. 7E-148—Removing Forward Clutch Hub and Thrust Washers

8. Remove and discard inner and outer clutch piston seals. (Figs. 7E-153 and 7E-154)

9. Remove and discard the center piston seal from the forward clutch housing. (Fig. 7E-155)

Inspection

1. Inspect the drive and driven clutch plates for signs of burning, scoring, or wear.

2. Inspect the sixteen springs for collapsed coils or signs of distortion.

3. Inspect the clutch hubs for worn splines, thrust faces and open lubrication holes. Run a tag wire through each lu-

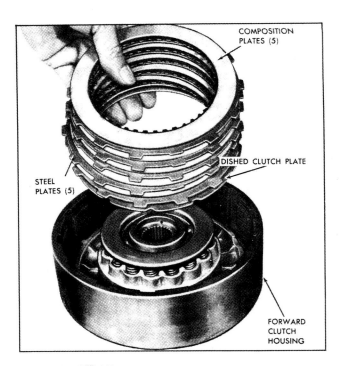

Fig. 7E-149—Removing Forward Clutch Plates

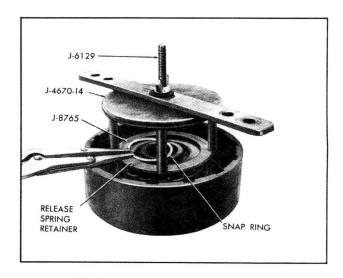

Fig. 7E-150—Removing Forward Clutch Snap Ring

brication hole. See lubrication chart (Fig. 7E-232) for location of holes.

4. Inspect the piston for cracks or excessive porosity on sealing surfaces.

5. Inspect the clutch housing for wear, scoring, open oil passages, and free operation of the ball check. Run a tag wire through lubrication holes. See lubrication chart for location of holes.

Assembly (Fig. 7E-156)

Apply Hydra-Matic oil to all seals before reassembly.

1. Place *new inner and outer seals* on clutch piston, lips away from spring pockets. (Figs. 7E-153 and 7E-154)

Make certain piston has blind hole. Piston with ball check is for direct clutch.

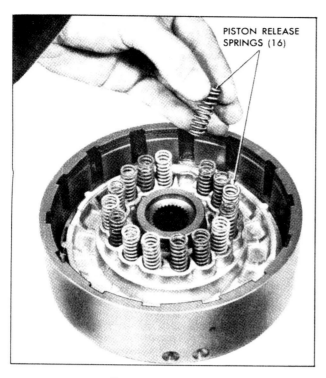

Fig. 7E-151—Removing Release Springs

Fig. 7E-152—Removing Forward Clutch Piston

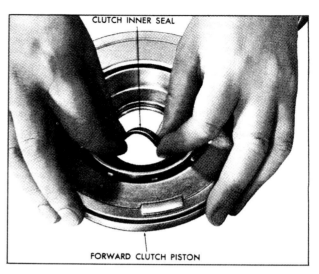

Fig. 7E-153—Removing or Installing Inner Oil Seal

Fig. 7E-154—Removing or Installing Outer Oil Seal

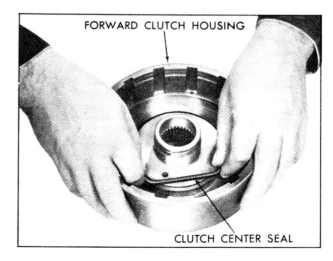

Fig. 7E-155—Removing or Installing Center Oil Seal

2. Place a new center seal on the clutch housing, lip faces up. (Fig. 7E-155)

3. Place seal protector Tool J-21362 over clutch hub. Install outer clutch piston seal protector J-21409 into clutch drum and install piston, rotating the piston on the drum until seated. (Fig. 7E-158)

4. Install sixteen release springs into pockets in piston. (Fig. 7E-159)

5. Place spring retainer and snap ring on springs.

6. Compress springs using clutch compressor Tools J-6129,

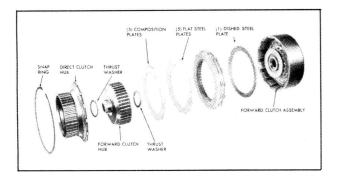

Fig. 7E-156—Forward Clutch Assembly

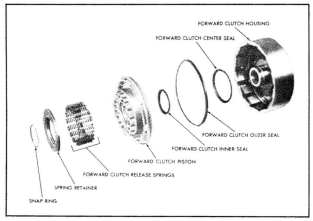

Fig. 7E-157—Forward Clutch Assembly

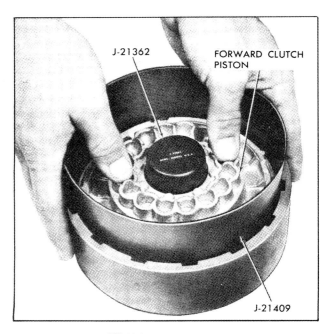

Fig. 7E-158—Installing Forward Clutch

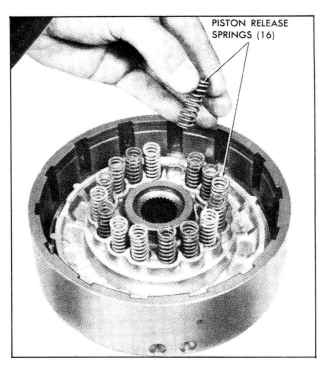

Fig. 7E-159—Installing Piston Release Springs

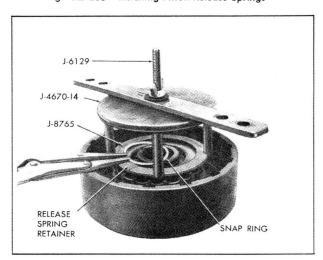

Fig. 7E-160—Installing Snap Ring

J-4670-14, and J-8765 and install snap ring. (Fig. 7E-160)

7. Install the forward clutch hub washers on forward clutch hub. Retain with petrolatum.

The forward clutch hub, identified by a machined groove on the front, or hub side, is NOT interchangeable with past model pre 1968 parts. Due to a

spline change, if replacement of either the forward clutch hub or mainshaft is required, ONLY current model parts must be used. The mainshaft is identified by a "V" groove on the front, or internal gear, end of the shaft.

8. Place forward clutch hub into forward clutch housing. (Fig. 7E-161)

9. Oil and install five composition and five flat steel and one dished steel clutch plate, starting with the dished plate, placed so that the outside diameter contacts the first flat steel plate and then alternating composition and steel. (Fig. 7E-162)

10. *Install the direct clutch hub and retaining snap ring.* (Figs. 7E-163 and 7E-164)

A new direct clutch hub is used in the 1968 models. It is identified by a machined groove on the front face,

Fig. 7E-161—Installing Forward Clutch Hub

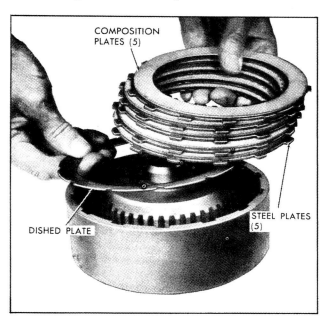

Fig. 7E-162—Installing Forward Clutch Plates

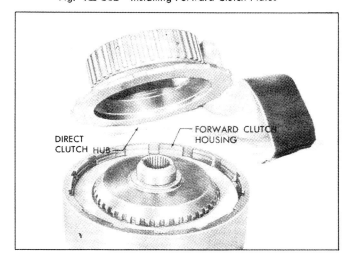

Fig. 7E-163—Installing Direct Clutch Hub

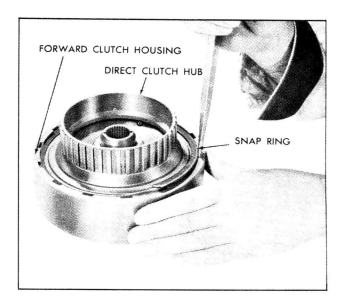

Fig. 7E-164—Installing Snap Ring

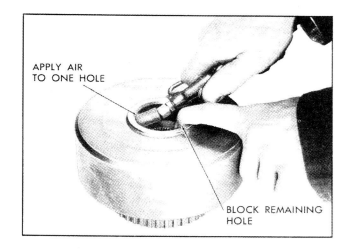

Fig. 7E-165—Air Checking Clutch and Piston

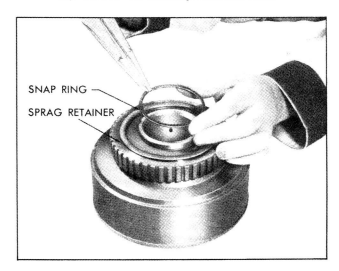

Fig. 7E-166—Removing Snap Ring

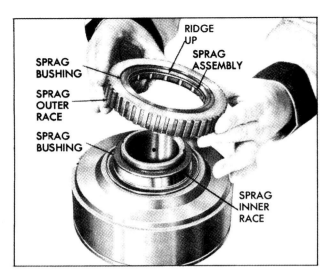

Fig. 7E-167—Removing Sprag, Race and Bushings

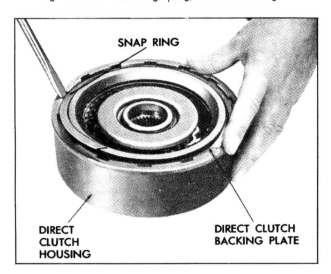

Fig. 7E-168—Removing Snap Ring

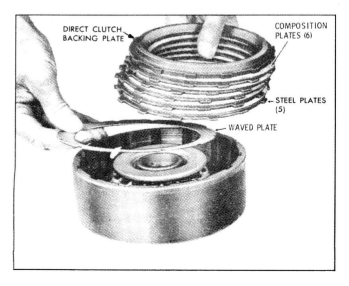

Fig. 7E-169—Removing Clutch Plates

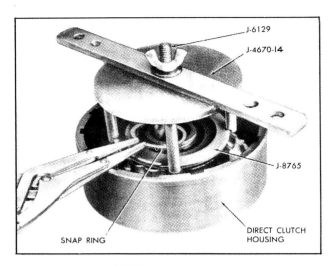

Fig. 7E-170—Removing Snap Ring

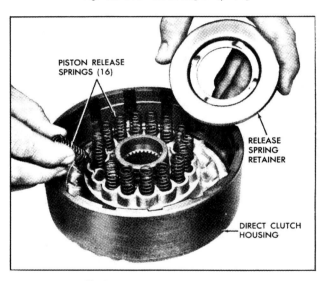

Fig. 7E-171—Removing Piston Release Springs

or long spline side, of the hub. This part change, because of the 6 plate direct clutch assembly, necessitates use of ONLY the 1968 part if replacement is required. Past model parts must NOT be used with the 6 plate direct clutch assembly.

11. Air check clutch and piston operation. (Fig. 7E-165)

DIRECT CLUTCH AND INTERMEDIATE SPRAG

Disassembly

1. Remove sprag retainer snap ring and retainer. (Fig. 7E-166)

2. Remove sprag outer race, bushings, and sprag assembly. (Fig. 7E-167)

3. Turn unit over and remove backing plate to direct clutch housing snap ring. (Fig. 7E-168)

4. Remove direct clutch backing plate, six composition, five steel clutch plates and waved steel plate. (Fig. 7E-169)

5. Using Clutch Compressor Tools J-6129, J-4670-14, and J-8765, compress springs and remove snap ring. (Fig. 7E-170)

6. Remove retainer and sixteen piston release springs. (Fig. 7E-171)

7. Remove the direct clutch piston. (Fig. 7E-172)

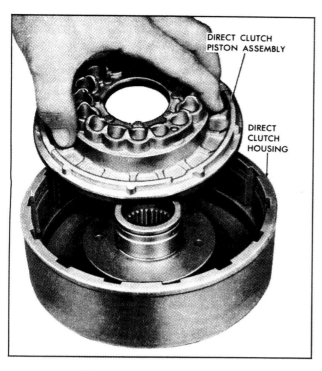

Fig. 7E-172—Removing Direct Clutch Piston

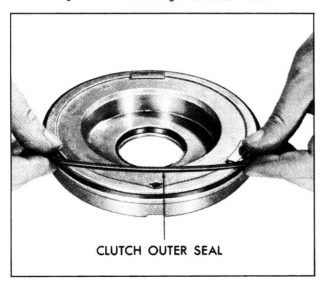

CLUTCH OUTER SEAL

Fig. 7E-173—Removing or Installing Clutch Outer Seal

8. Remove and discard the outer seal from the piston. (Fig. 7E-173)

9. Remove and discard the inner seal from the piston. (Fig. 7E-174)

10. Remove and discard the center piston seal from the direct clutch housing. (Fig. 7E-175)

Inspection

1. Inspect sprag assembly for damage.
2. Inspect sprag bushings for wear or distortion.
3. Inspect the inner and outer races for scratches or wear that can be felt with finger nail.
4. Inspect the clutch housing for cracks, wear, proper opening of oil passages, or wear on clutch plate drive lugs. Probe oil passages with a tag wire to see that hole is open. See oil chart (Fig. 7E-232) for location of oil lubrication passages.

Fig. 7E-174—Removing or Installing Clutch Inner Seal

Fig. 7E-175—Removing or Installing Clutch Center Seal

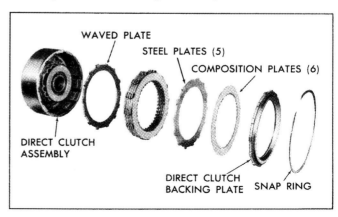

Fig. 7E-176—Direct Clutch Assembly

5. Inspect the drive and driven clutch plates for sign of wear or burning.
6. Inspect the backing plate for scratches or other damage.

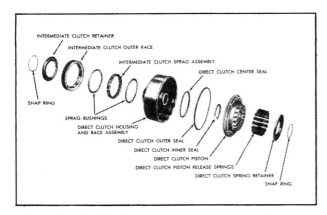

Fig. 7E-177—Direct Clutch Assembly

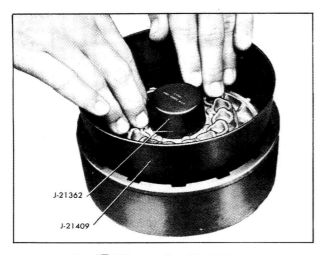

Fig. 7E-178—Installing Clutch Piston

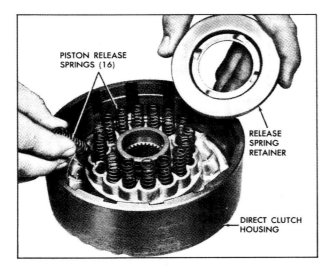

Fig. 7E-179—Installing Release Springs

7. Inspect the clutch piston for cracks, porosity on sealing surfaces, and free operation of the ball check.

Assembly (Figs. 7E-176 and 7E-177)

Apply Hydra-Matic oil to all seals.

1. Install a new inner clutch piston seal on piston with lip

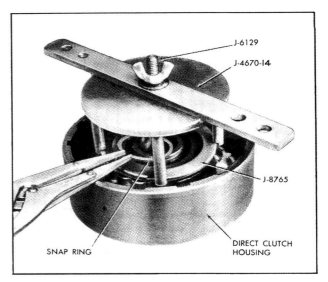

Fig. 7E-180—Installing Snap Ring

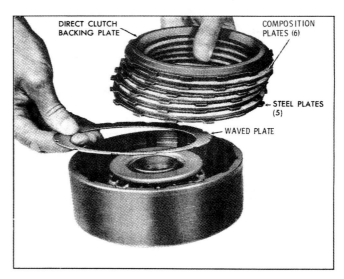

Fig. 7E-181—Installing Clutch Plates

facing away from spring pockets. (Fig. 7E-174)

Make certain piston with ball check is used in direct clutch. Piston with blind hole is used in forward clutch.

2. Install a new outer clutch piston seal with lip facing away from spring pockets. (Fig. 7E-173)

3. Install a new center seal on clutch housing with lip of seal facing up. (Fig. 7E-175)

The direct clutch housing has been changed to accommodate the six plate clutch assembly. Therefore, past model parts are NOT interchangeable with current models.

The six plate housing can be identified by the elimination of the I.D. chamfer on the rear, or clutch plate, end of the housing.

4. Place Seal Protectors, Tool J-21362-Inner, J-21409-Outer, over hub and clutch housing and install clutch piston with a rotating motion. (Fig. 7E-178)

5. Install sixteen springs into the piston. (Fig. 7E-179)

6. Place spring retainer and snap ring on springs.

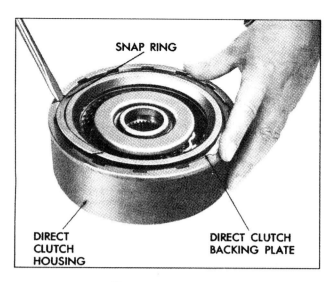

Fig. 7E-182—Installing Snap Ring

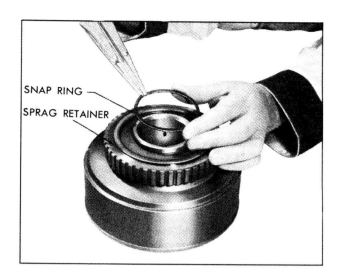

Fig. 7E-185—Installing Sprag Retainer and Snap Ring

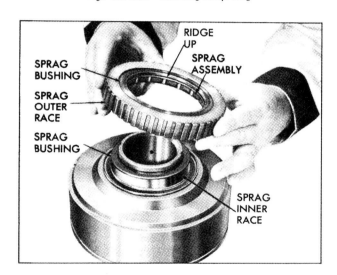

Fig. 7E-183—Installing Sprag

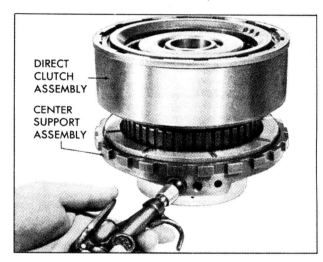

Fig. 7E-186—Air Checking Direct Clutch

7. Using Clutch Compressor Tools J-6129, J-4670-14, and J-8765, install snap ring. (Fig. 7E-180)

8. Oil and install six composition, five flat steel, and one waved steel plate starting with the waved plate and then alternating composition and steel. (Fig. 7E-181)

9. Install the clutch backing plate.

10. Install the backing plate retaining snap ring. (Fig. 7E-182)

11. Turn unit over and install one sprag bushing, cup side up, over inner race.

12. Install sprag assembly into outer race.

13. With ridge or shoulder on inner cage up, start sprag and outer race over inner race with counterclockwise motion. (Fig. 7E-183)

Outer race should turn only counterclockwise. (Fig. 7E-184)

14. Install sprag bushing over sprag, cup side down.

15. Install sprag retainer and snap ring. (Fig. 7E-185)

16. Place direct clutch assembly over center support and air check operation of direct clutch and piston. (Fig. 7E-186)

If air is applied through reverse passage it will escape from the direct clutch passage. This is normal.

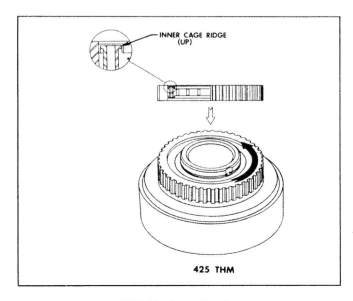

Fig. 7E-184—Sprag Rotation

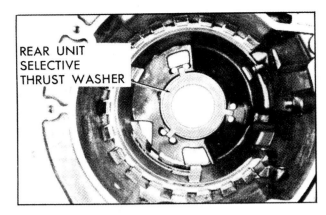

Fig. 7E-187—Installing Rear Unit Thrust Washer

Fig. 7E-188—Installing Rear Band

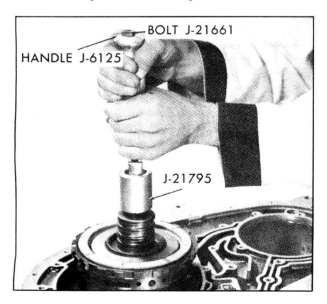

Fig. 7E-189—Installing Gear Unit into Case

ASSEMBLY OF UNITS INTO TRANSMISSION CASE

1. Install the proper rear selective washer (proper washer determined by previous rear end play check) into slots provided inside front of transmission case. (Fig. 7E-187)

Fig. 7E-190—Installing Center Support Snap Ring

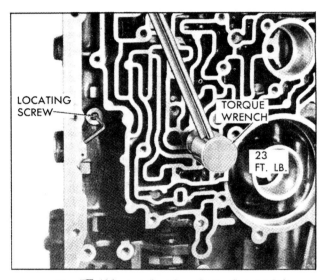

Fig. 7E-191—Installing Case Center Support Bolt

2. Install the rear band assembly so that two lugs index with the two anchor pins. Check band to be sure band ends are seated on lugs by inserting small screwdriver into servo pin hole in case and pushing on band. (Fig. 7E-188)

3. Install the complete gear unit assembly into the case using Tool J-21795 with J-6125 slide hammer. Be sure locating bolt hole in center support lines up with case hole. (Fig. 7E-189)

4. Oil and install center support to case retaining snap ring with the bevel side up. Locate gap adjacent to band anchor pin. Make certain ring is properly seated in case. (Fig. 7E-190)

5. Install and tighten center support locating screw. Torque to 2 ft. lbs.

It may be necessary to shorten dog point end of locating screw by 1/4" to assure proper location of center support.

6. Install case to center support bolt. Torque to 23 ft. lbs. Remove center support locating screw. (Fig. 7E-191)

7. Install three steel and three composition intermediate clutch plates. Start with steel, alternate the plates.

8. Install the intermediate clutch backing plate, ridge up. (Fig. 7E-192)

9. Install the backing plate to case snap ring, locating gap opposite band anchor pin. (Fig. 7E-193)

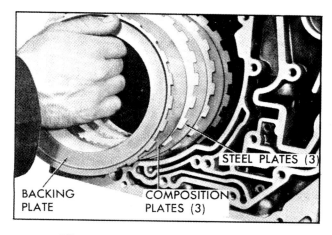

Fig. 7E-192—Installing Backing and Clutch Plates

Fig. 7E-193—Installing Snap Ring

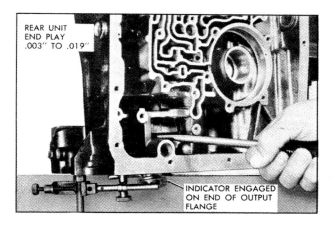

Fig. 7E-194—Checing Rear Unit Ene-Play

10. Check rear end play as follows: (Fig. 7E-194)

a. Install 3/8" bolt into final drive attaching bolt hole. Allow end of transmission to hang over edge of bench.

b. Mount the dial indicator on the bolt and index with the end of the output flange.

c. Move the output flange in and out to read the end play. End play should be from .003" to .019". The selective washer controlling this end play is the steel washer having

three lugs that is located between the thrust washer and the rear face of the transmission case.

If a different washer thickness is required to bring the end play within specification, it can be selected from the following chart:

Thickness	Notches	or	Numeral
.074" to .078"	None		1
.082" to .086"	1 Tab Side		2
.090" to .094"	2 Tab Side		3
.098" to .102"	1 Tab O.D.		4
.106" to .110"	2 Tabs O.D.		5
.114" to .118"	3 Tabs O.D.		6

Fig. 7E-195—Installing Front Band

Fig. 7E-196—Installing Direct Clutch and Sprag

11. If a different selective washer thickness is required it will be necessary to disassemble the transmission back to this washer so that the correct washer can be installed.

12. Install front band with anchor hole placed over the band anchor pin and apply lug facing servo hole. (Fig. 7E-195)

13. Be sure center support oil rings are hooked and centered, then install the direct clutch and intermediate sprag assembly. It will be necessary to twist the housing to allow the sprag outer race to index with the clutch drive plates. The sun gear shaft splines will be flush with housing splines. (Fig. 7E-196)

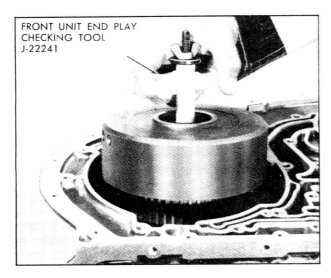

Fig. 7E-197—Installing Forward Clutch

Fig. 7E-198—Installing Pump Cover Plate

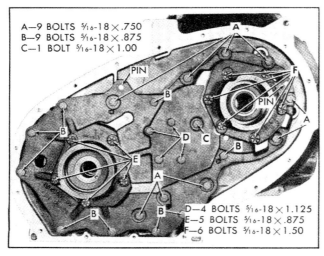

A—9 BOLTS 5/16-18 × .750
B—9 BOLTS 5/16-18 × .875
C—1 BOLT 5/16-18 × 1.00

D—4 BOLTS 5/16-18 × 1.125
E—5 BOLTS 5/16-18 × .875
F—6 BOLTS 5/16-18 × 1.50

Fig. 7E-199—Pump Cover Plate Attaching Screws

Removal of direct clutch drive and driven plates may be helpful.

14. Install the forward clutch hub to direct clutch housing thrust washer on the forward clutch hub. Retain with petrolatum.

15. Install the forward clutch assembly, indexing the di-

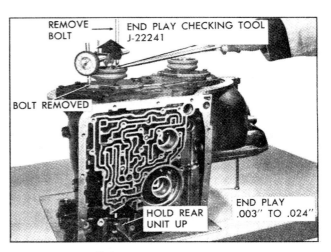

Fig. 7E-200—Checking Front Unit Endplay

rect clutch hub so end of the mainshaft will bottom on end of the forward clutch. If seated it will be approximately flush - 1/4" below pump cover plate face in case. (Fig. 7E-197)

16. Install pump cover plate assembly and gasket. (Fig. 7E-198)

17. Install pump cover plate attaching bolts. Torque bolts to 20 ft. lbs. (Fig. 7E-199)

If the forward clutch housing cannot be rotated (using the driven sprocket as a driver) as the pump cover plate is being pulled into place, the forward or direct clutch housings have not been properly installed to index with all the clutch plates. This condition must be corrected before the pump cover plate is pulled fully into place.

18. Check front unit end play as follows: (Fig. 7E-200)

a. Install a 5/16" threaded slide hammer bolt or J-6126 into bolt hole in pump cover plate. (Install End Play Checking Tool J-22241 into pump cover plate and forward clutch housing.)

b. Mount a dial indicator on the bolt. Index indicator to register with the forward clutch drum that can be reached through second bolt omitted from cover plate.

c. Push End Play Tool J-22241 down to remove slack.

d. Push and hold output flange upward. Place screwdriver in case opening at parking pawl area and push upward on output carrier.

e. Set dial indicator to zero.

f. Pull end play checking tool upward by placing another screwdriver between metal lip of end play tool and the driven sprocket housing.

Read the resulting travel or end play which should be .003" to .024". The selective washer controlling this end play is the washer located between the driven support housing and the forward clutch housing. If more or less washer thickness is required to bring end play within specifications, select the proper washer from the chart below.:

THICKNESS	COLOR
.060 - .064	Yellow
.071 - .075	Blue
.082 - .086	Red
.093 - .097	Brown
.104 - .108	Green
.115 - .119	Black
.126 - .130	Purple

An oil soaked washer may tend to discolor so that it will be necessary to measure the washer for its actual thickness.

19. Install the remaining pump cover plate attaching bolts. Torque bolts to 20 ft. lbs.

INSTALLATION OF FRONT PUMP

1. Mount two 5/16" x 4" guide pins in pump attaching screw holes.

2. Align guide pins with matching holes in pump cover plate and insert bolts into open holes in pump body. (Keep the crescent to the outside of the case.)

3. Tighten bolts, remove guide pins, and insert remaining attaching bolts and tighten to 18 ft. lbs.

LINK BELT, DRIVE AND DRIVEN SPROCKET COVER PLATE AND SPROCKET HOUSING

Assembly

1. Place link belt around the drive and driven sprockets so that the links engage the teeth of the sprockets, colored guide link facing link cover.

2. Simultaneously place link belt, drive and driven sprockets into support housing. (Fig. 7E-201)

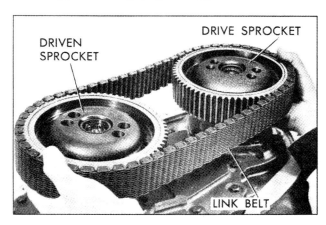

Fig. 7E-201—Removing Sprackets and Link Assembly

Fig. 7E-202—Installing Snap Rings

3. Using a plastic mallet, gently seat the sprocket bearing assemblies into the support housings.

4. Install sprocket assembly to support housing snap rings using J-4646 snap ring pliers. (Fig. 7E-202)

5. Install new case to cover and plate assembly sprocket housing gasket.

6. Install sprocket housing cover and plate assembly and eighteen attaching bolts. Torque bolts to 8 ft. lbs.

One sprocket cover housing attaching bolt is 1/4 inch longer. This bolt must be installed in the tapped hole located directly over the cooler fittings on the transmission case.

PARKING PAWL, BRACKET AND MANUAL LINKAGE (Fig. 7E-203)

Install

1. Install parking pawl (tooth toward the inside of case), pawl return spring and parking pawl shaft into case. (Fig. 7E-204)

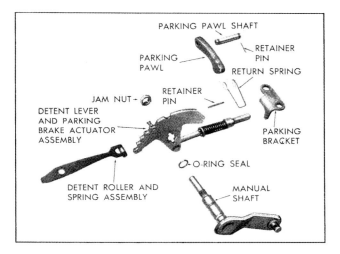

Fig. 7E-203—Manual and Parking Linkage

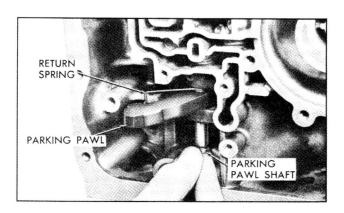

Fig. 7E-204—Installing Parking Pawl Shaft

2. Install the parking pawl shaft retaining pin. (Fig. 7E-205)

3. Install the parking bracket into case (pawl below finger on bracket). Torque the attaching bolts to 18 ft. lbs. (Fig. 7E-206)

4. Install a new manual shaft "O" ring seal on manual shaft.

5. Install the actuator rod plunger under the parking

Fig. 7E-205—Installing Retaining Pin

Fig. 7E-206—Installing Parking Bracket

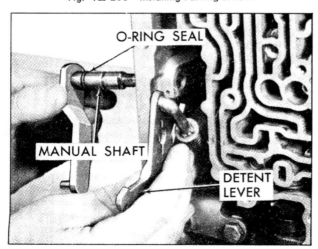

Fig. 7E-207—Installing Manual Shaft

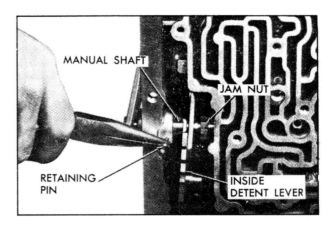

Fig. 7E-208—Installing Retaining Pin

Fig. 7E-209—Installing Locknut

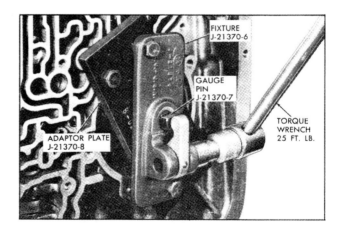

Fig. 7E-210—Checking Band Apply Pin

7. Install manual shaft retaining pin into case. Install the long, smooth end into case first. (Fig. 7E-208)

8. Torque jam nut to 18 ft. lb. (Fig. 7E-206)

REAR SERVO

Install

Before installing the rear servo assembly check band apply pin using Tool J-21370 as follows:

A. Attach the band apply pin selection gauge adaptor plate J-21370-8, J-21370-6 and J-21370-7 to the transmission case with attaching bolts as shown. (Fig. 7E-210)

bracket and over the parking pawl and through hole in detent lever.

6. Install the manual shaft assembly through the case and detent lever. Install the retaining hex-lock nut on the manual shaft. Lever points away from oil pan. (Fig. 7E-207)

STEP LOCATION	PIN IDENT.	SIZE
TOP STEP OR ABOVE	THREE RINGS	LONG
THIS AREA	TWO RINGS	MED.
LOWER STEP OR BELOW	ONE RING	SHORT

J-21370-7

Fig. 7E-211—Pin Selection Chart

Install tool attaching bolts finger tight and check freeness of selective pin. Torque attaching bolts and recheck pin to make certain it does not bind.

B. Apply 25 ft. lb. torque and select proper servo pin to be used from scale on tool.

C. Remove the tool and make note of the proper pin to be used during assembly of the transmission. (Fig. 7E-211)

There are three selective pins identified as follows:

PIN IDENTIFICATION	PIN LENGTH
3 Rings	Long
2 Rings	Medium
1 Ring	Short

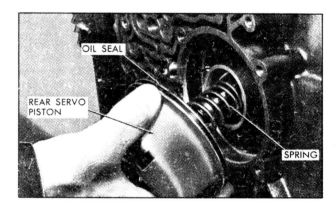

Fig. 7E-212—Installing Rear Servo

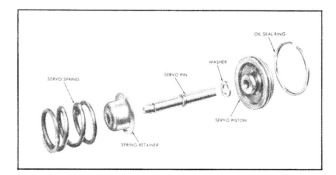

Fig. 7E-213—Front Servo

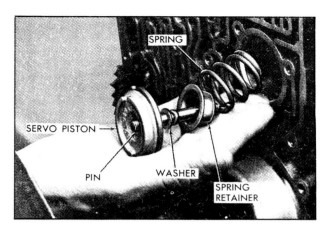

Fig. 7E-214—Install Front Servo

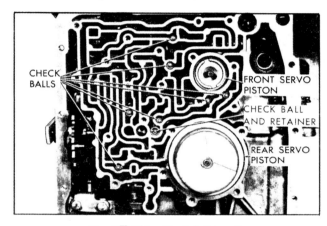

Fig. 7E-215—Check Ball Location

The identification rings are located on the band lug end of the pin. Selecting the proper pin is the equivalent of adjusting the band.

1. Install rear accumulator spring into case.

2. Lubricate and install the rear servo assembly into case. (Fig. 7E-212)

FRONT SERVO, CHECK BALLS, GASKETS, SPACER, AND SOLENOID
Installation

1. Install front servo spring and retainer on front servo pin. (Fig. 7E-213)

2. Install flat washer on front servo pin on end opposite taper.

3. If removed, install oil seal ring on front servo piston. Install piston on apply pin so that part number faces away from spring.

4. Install piston into case so that tapered end of pin is contacting band. (Fig. 7E-214)

5. Check freeness of piston by stroking piston in bore.

6. Install seven check balls into the transmission case pockets. (Use petrolatum to retain balls in case.) (Fig. 7E-215)

7. Install the valve body spacer to case gasket and spacer plate, install guide pins for alignment. (Fig. 7E-216)

Valve body spacer to case gasket should extend approximately 1/8" beyond the spacer plate over the void case channel. (Fig. 7E-217)

If service gaskets are being installed, the valve body spacer to case gasket has an extension which will cover the void case channel.

Fig. 7E-216—Installing Spacer Plate

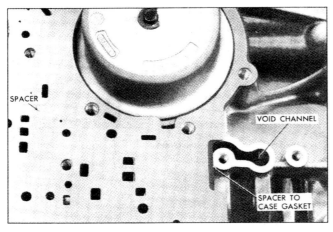

Fig. 7E-217—Valve Body Spacer to Case gasket Identification

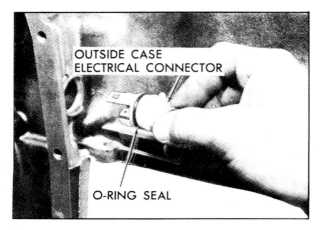

Fig. 7E-218—Installing Connector

8. Install the "O" ring seal on the case solenoid connector.

9. Lubricate and install case connector with lock tabs facing into case, positioning locater tabs up on side of case. (Fig. 7E-218)

Fig. 7E-219—Installing Governor Pipe

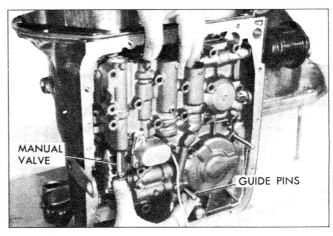

Fig. 7E-220—Installing Control Valve

CONTROL VALVE ASSEMBLY AND GOVERNOR PIPES

Installation

1. Install the control valve assembly to spacer gasket.

2. Install governor screens into case governor pipe holes if removed.

3. Install governor pipe into valve body. (Fig. 7E-219)

4. Install control valve assembly and governor pipe into the transmission. Engage manual valve with detent lever. (Fig. 7E-220)

Be sure manual valve is properly indexed with the pin on the manual detent lever.

5. Install the control valve assembly attaching bolts, and manual detent and roller assembly. (Fig. 7E-221)

6. Torque control valve assembly attaching bolts to 8 ft. lbs.

7. Install governor feed pipe into case and control valve assembly. (Fig. 7E-222)

8. Install detent connector terminal into case electrical connector pushing inward so that detent terminal connections are locked. (Fig. 7E-223)

PRESSURE REGULATOR VALVE

Install (Fig. 7E-224)

1. Install regulator valve, spring retainer, and spacer, if present, into case bore.

2. Install pressure regulator spring into bore.

3. Install pressure boost valve bushing and boost valve into case bore.

4. Compress the pressure boost valve bushing against the

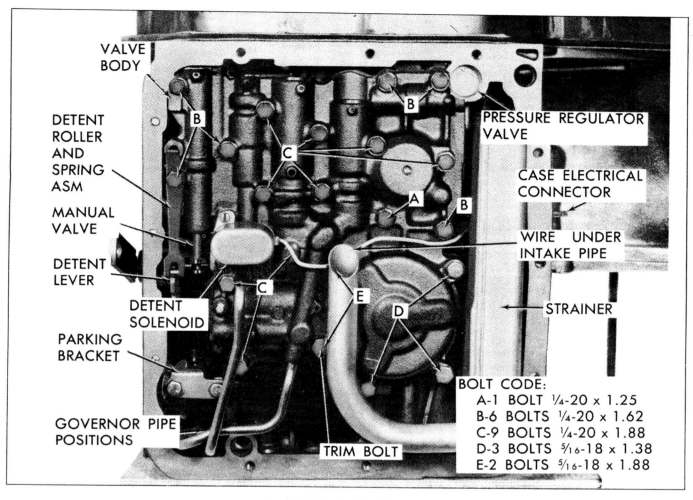

VALVE BODY

DETENT ROLLER AND SPRING ASM

MANUAL VALVE

DETENT LEVER

DETENT SOLENOID

PARKING BRACKET

GOVERNOR PIPE POSITIONS

PRESSURE REGULATOR VALVE

CASE ELECTRICAL CONNECTOR

WIRE UNDER INTAKE PIPE

STRAINER

TRIM BOLT

BOLT CODE:
A-1 BOLT ¼-20 x 1.25
B-6 BOLTS ¼-20 x 1.62
C-9 BOLTS ¼-20 x 1.88
D-3 BOLTS ⁵⁄₁₆-18 x 1.38
E-2 BOLTS ⁵⁄₁₆-18 x 1.88

Fig. 7E-221—Attaching Bolt Location

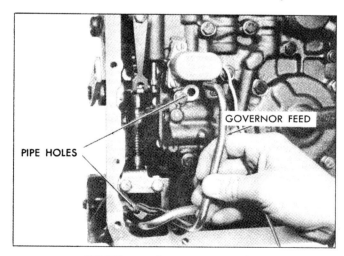

PIPE HOLES

GOVERNOR FEED

Fig. 7E-222—Installing Governor Feed Pipe

pressure regulator spring and install the retaining snap ring into the case, using J-5403 pliers. (Fig. 7E-225)

STRAINER AND INTAKE PIPE

Install

1. Install the case to intake pipe "O" ring seal on strainer and intake pipe assembly. (Fig. 7E-226)

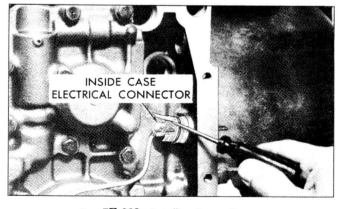

INSIDE CASE ELECTRICAL CONNECTOR

Fig. 7E-223—Installing Detent Connector

2. Install the strainer and intake pipe assembly. (Wire under strainer intake pipe.)

3. Using a new bottom pan gasket, install pan. Torque attaching screws to 10 ft. lbs.

MODULATOR VALVE AND VACUUM MODULATOR

Install

1. Install the modulator valve into the case bushing bore with stem end out.

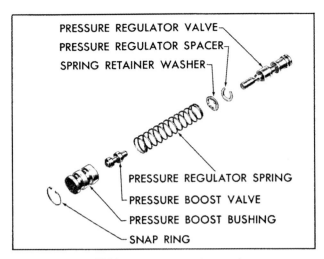

Fig. 7E-224—Pressure Regulator Valve

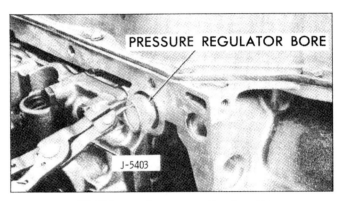

Fig. 7E-225—Installing Pressure Regulator Valve

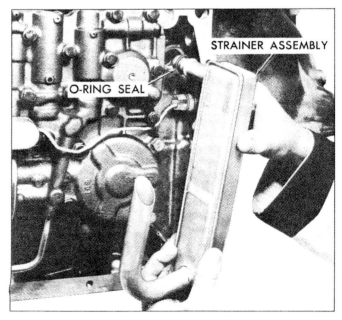

Fig. 7E-226—Installing "O" Ring Seal

2. Install the "O" ring seal on vacuum modulator.

3. Install the vacuum modulator into the case. (Fig. 7E-227)

4. Install the modulator retainer and attaching bolt. Tor-

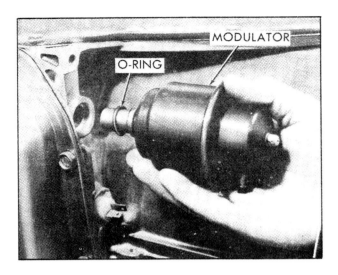

Fig. 7E-227—Installing Vacuum Modulator

Fig. 7E-228—Installing Modulator Retainer Bolt

que bolt to 14 ft. lbs. (Fig. 7E-228)

GOVERNOR

Install

1. Lay the transmission on the oil pan.

2. Position new "O" ring seal on governor assembly then install into the case. (Fig. 7E-229)

3. Attach the governor with the retaining clip.

INSTALL SPEEDOMETER DRIVEN GEAR

1. Install new "O" ring seal on speedometer driven gear assembly.

2. Install speedometer driven gear assembly into transmission. (Fig. 7E-230)

3. Install retainer clip and screw, torque to 3 ft. lbs. (Fig. 7E-231)

INSTALL CONVERTER ASSEMBLY

1. With transmission in cradle or portable jack, install converter into pump, making certain the converter hub slots engage the pump drive gear tangs.

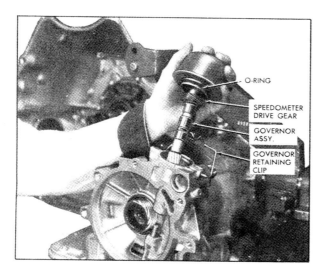

Fig. 7E-229—Installing Governor

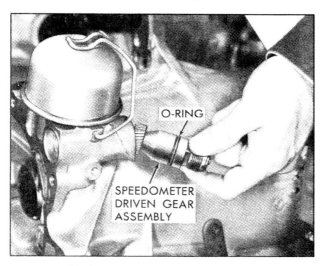

Fig. 7E-230—Installing Speedometer Driven Gear

LUBRICATION CHART (Fig. 7E-232)

The lubrication chart illustrates the lubricating oil flow from the oil pan through the transmission. The chart can be used to assist in location areas of possible oil flow restrictions.

DIAGNOSIS GUIDE

In many of the following diagnosis procedures, it is recommended that air pressure be applied. The purpose of this is to help determine if seal, rings or pistons are stuck, missing or damaged. Therefore, when air is applied, it is important to listen carefully for escaping air and piston action as air is applied to a particular area.

For additional diagnosis information refer to pages 7-77 through 7-81 found in Section 7.

All passages can be located by referring to Fig. 7E-232 through Fig. 7E-237.

NO DRIVE IN "D" RANGE

Possible Causes

A. Low Oil Level
Correct level-check for external leaks or vacuum modulator diaphragm leaking.

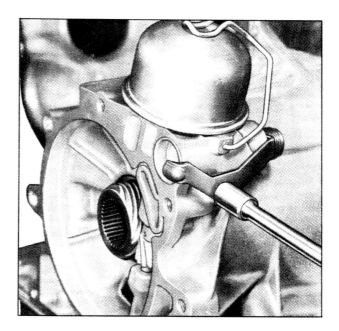

Fig. 7E-231—Installing Retainer Clip

B. Manual Linkage
Maladjusted; correct alignment in manual lever shift quadrant.

C. Low Oil Pressure - Refer to oil pressure chart Fig. 7E-239 and connect oil pressure gauge to transmission.
   1. Strainer Assembly - "O" ring missing or damaged, neck weld leaking, strainer blocked.
   2. Pump Assembly - Pressure regulator stuck or inoperative (located in case); pump drive gear - tangs damaged by converter.
   3. Case - Porosity in intake bore.

D. Control Valve Assembly
Manual valve disconnected from manual lever pin. (Other shift lever positions would also be affected.)

E. Forward Clutch
Forward clutch does not apply - piston cracked; seals missing or damaged (these defects can be checked by removing the valve body and applying air pressure to the drive cavity in the case valve body face. Missing, damaged, or worn oil rings on the driven support housing can also be checked in this manner at the same time because they can also cause the forward clutch not to apply); clutch plates burned.

F. Roller Clutch Assembly
Roller clutch inoperative. Rollers worn, damaged springs, or damaged races. May be checked by placing selector lever in "L" range.

NO DRIVE IN "R" OR SLIPS IN REVERSE

Possible Causes

A. Low Oil Level

B. Manual Linkage

C. Oil Pressure - Refer to Oil Pressure Chart Fig. 7E-239 for specifications.
   1. Vacuum modulator assembly defective.
   2. Vacuum modulator valve sticking.

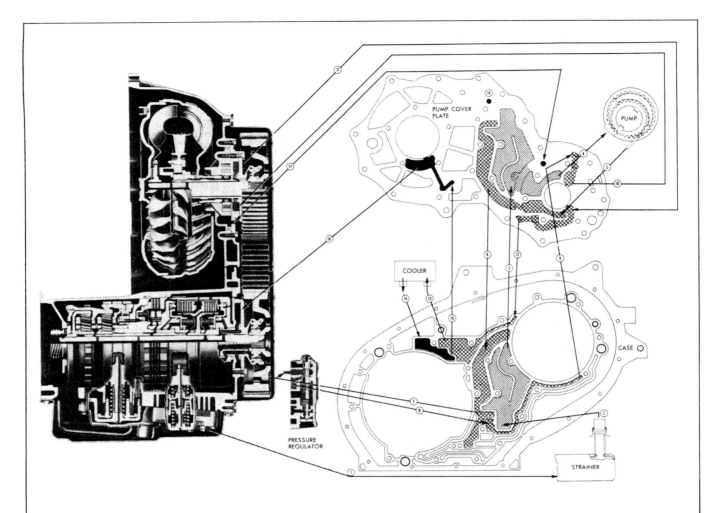

1. OIL FROM SUMP TO STRAINER

2. STRAINER TO CASE PASSAGE

3. CASE PASSAGE TO PUMP COVER PLATE PASSAGE

4. PUMP COVER PLATE PASSAGE TO PUMP

5. PUMP TO PUMP COVER PLATE PASSAGE

6. PUMP COVER PLATE PASSAGE TO CASE PASSAGE

7. CASE PASSAGE TO PRESSURE REGULATOR VALVE

8. PRESSURE REGULATOR VALVE TO CASE PASSAGE

9. CASE PASSAGE TO PUMP COVER PLATE PASSAGE

10. PUMP COVER PLATE PASSAGE TO CONVERTER

11. CONVERTER TO PUMP COVER PLATE PASSAGE

12. PUMP COVER PLATE PASSAGE TO CASE PASSAGE

13. CASE PASSAGE TO COOLER

14. COOLER RETURN TO CASE PASSAGE

15. CASE PASSAGE TO PUMP COVER PLATE PASSAGE

16. PUMP COVER PLATE PASSAGE TO TRANSMISSION POWER TRAIN (ALL INTERNAL LUBRICATION)

NOTE: THE NUMBERS IN THE CROSS SECTION INDICATE THAT THERE ARE ADDITIONAL LUBRICATION HOLES IN THIS AREA THAT ARE NOT SHOWN IN THE CROSS SECTION

17. FRONT SEAL DRAIN BACK HOLE

18. PRESSURE REGULATOR VENT HOLE

Fig. 7E-232—Lubrication Chart

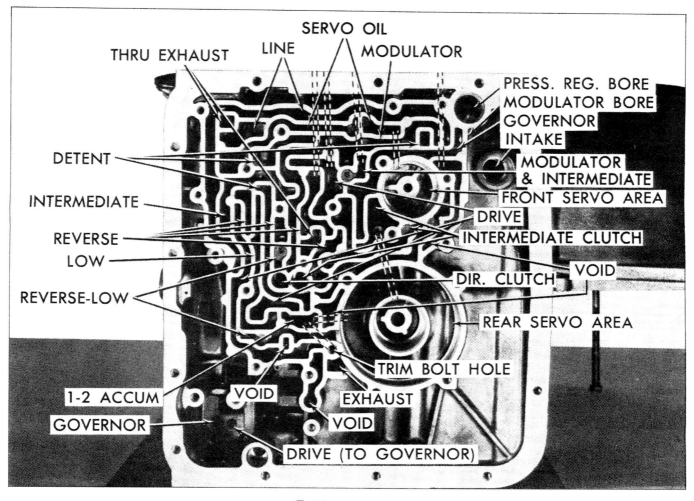

Fig. 7E-233—Case - Oil Passages

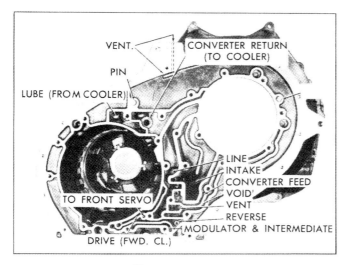

Fig. 7E-234—Oil Passages

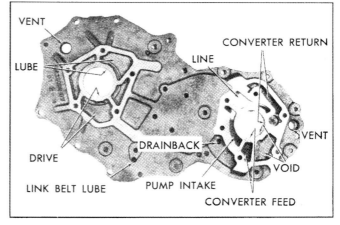

Fig. 7E-235—Oil Passages

3. Restricted strainer, leak at intake pipe, or "O" ring seal.

4. Pump Assembly - Regulator or boost valve sticking.

D. Control Valve Assembly

1. Valve body gaskets - leaking or damaged. (Other mal-

functions may also be indicated.)

2. Low reverse check ball - missing from case (this will cause no overrun braking in low range.)

3. 2-3 valve train stuck open (this will also cause 1-3 up-shifts in drive range.)

4. Reverse feed passage - not drilled - also check case passages. Apply air to reverse passage in case valve body face.

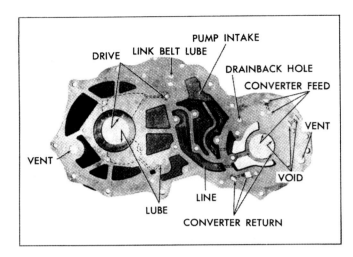

Fig. 7E-236—Oil Passages

E. Rear Servo and Accumulator
1. Servo piston seal ring broken or missing. Apply air pressure to drilled hole in the intermediate clutch passage of the case valve body face to check for piston operation and excessive leakage.
2. Band apply pin too short (this may also cause no overrun braking or slip in overrun braking in low range.)

F. Rear Band
Burned, loose lining, apply pin or anchor pins not engaged, band broken.

G. Direct Clutch
1. Outer seal damaged or missing.
2. Clutch plates burned - may be caused by stuck ball-check in piston.

H. Forward Clutch
Clutch does not release (will also cause drive in Neutral Range).

DRIVE IN NEUTRAL

Possible Causes

A. Manual Linkage - Maladjusted

B. Forward Clutch
Clutch does not release (this condition will also cause No Reverse).

FIRST SPEED ONLY—NO 1-2 SHIFT

Possible Causes
A. Governor Assembly
1. Governor valve *sticking*.
2. Driven gear loose, damaged or worn.
If driven gear shows signs of wear or damage, check output flange drive gear for nicks or rough finish.

B. Control Valve Assembly
1. 1-2 shift valve train stuck closed. Dirt, chips, or damaged valve in 1-2 shift valve train.
2. Governor feed channels blocked, or leaking; pipes out of position.
3. Valve body gaskets - leaking, damaged or incorrectly installed.

C. Case
1. Porosity between oil channels.
2. Governor feed passage blocked, governor bore scored or worn allowing cross pressure leak.

D. Intermediate Clutch
1. Case center support - oil rings missing, broken, defective, Apply air to intermediate clutch passage in case valve body face to check this defect.
2. Clutch piston seals - missing, improperly assembled, cut or damaged. Apply air to the intermediate clutch passage located in case valve body face to check for this defect.

1-2 SHIFT CAN ONLY BE OBTAINED AT FULL THROTTLE

Possible Causes

A. Detent Switch
Sticking or defective - can be detected by pulling electrical connector at transmission and obtaining normal upshifts.

B. Detent Solenoid
1. Loose.
2. Gasket leaking.
3. Sticks open.
4. Electrical wire pinched between cover and casting.

C. Control Valve Assembly
1. Valve body gasket - leaking, damaged or incorrectly installed.
2. Detent valve train stuck - dirt or foreign material.

D. Case Assembly
1. Porosity

FIRST AND SECOND SPEEDS ONLY— NO 2-3 SHIFT

Possible Causes

A. Detent Solenoid
Stuck open (the 2-3 would occur only at very high speeds) may be diagnosed as no 2-3 shift.

B. Detent Switch - Sticking or defective.

C. Control Valve Assembly
1. 2-3 valve train stuck - dirt or foreign material in valve train.
2. Valve body gaskets - leaking, damaged or incorrectly installed.

D. Direct Clutch
1. Case center support - oil rings missing, broken. Apply air to direct clutch passage in case valve body face to check this area.
2. Clutch piston seals - missing, improperly assembled, cut or damaged; piston ball check stuck or missing. Apply air to direct clutch passage in case valve body face to check this condition.

SLIPS IN ALL RANGES

Possible Causes

A. Oil Level Incorrect - check oil level.

B. Oil Pressure Low - *Refer to Oil Pressure Chart Fig. 7E-239 for specifications.*
1. Vacuum modulator defective.
2. Vacuum modulator valve sticking.

3. Oil strainer assembly - plugged or leaks at neck; "O" ring, case to strainer, missing or damaged.

4. Pressure regulator or boost valve sticking.

5. Pump gears damaged or worn, cover plate loose or gasket leaking.

C. Case - Cross channel leaks - porosity.

D. Forward, Intermediate, and Direct Clutches Slipping - composition and steel clutch plates burned. (Burned clutch plates are usually resultant defects; always look for a primary defect that would cause the clutch plates to burn.) Missing feed holes, seals and oil rings, etc., are primary defects.

E. Roller Clutch Assembly - Rollers worn, springs or cage damaged, and worn or damaged races; (operates normally in low and reverse ranges).

SLIPS 1-2 SHIFT

Possible Causes

A. Oil Level Incorrect - Check oil level.

B. Oil Pressure Low - Refer to chart Fig. 7E-239 for pressure specifications.
1. Vacuum modulator assembly - defective.
2. Vacuum modulator valve sticking.
3. Pump pressure regulator valve stuck.

C. Front Servo Accumulator.
1. Piston-cracked or porosity.
2. Oil ring damaged or missing.

D. Control Valve Assembly
1. 1-2 accumulator valve train (may cause a slip-bump shift.)
2. Porosity in valve body or case valve body face.

E. Rear Servo Accumulator - Oil ring missing or damaged; case bore damaged; piston cracked or damaged.

F. Case - Porosity between oil passages. Raised ridge around center support bolt hole-does not allow control valve assembly to seat properly.

G. Intermediate Clutch
1. Piston seals missing, cut, or damaged. Apply air pressure to the intermediate clutch passage in the case valve body face to check.
2. Clutch plates burned. (Burned clutch plates are usually the result of some other defect. Always look for other defects when clutch plates are found burned.)
3. Case Center Support.
   a. Leaks in feed circuits (oil rings damaged or grooves damaged) or excessive leak between tower and bushing.
   b. Center support bolt not seated properly in case.
4. Waved steel plate in intermediate clutch pack - All should be flat.

ROUGH 1-2 SHIFT

Possible Causes

A. Oil Pressure - Refer to Oil Pressure Chart Fig. 7E-239 for specifications.
1. Vacuum modulator - check for loose fittings; restrictions in line; modulator assembly defective.
2. Modulator valve stuck.
3. Pump - regulator boost valve stuck - cover plate loose or gasket leak.

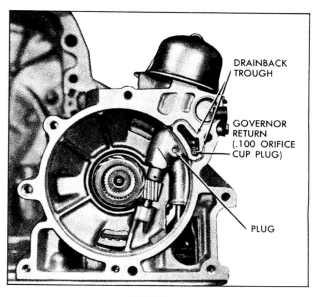

Fig. 7E-237—Oil Passages

B. Control Valve Assembly
1. 1-2 accumulator valve train.
2. Valve body to case bolts loose.
3. Gaskets inverted, off location, or damaged.

C. Case
1. Intermediate clutch passage check ball missing or not sealing.
2. Porosity between channels.

D. Rear Servo Accumulator Assembly
1. Oil rings damaged.
2. Piston stuck. Apply air pressure to the 1-2 accumulator passage in the case valve body face. (You should hear the servo piston move.)
3. Broken or missing spring.
4. Bore scored or damaged.

E. Intermediate clutch
1. Waved steel plate in clutch pack - should all be flat.

SLIPS 2-3 SHIFT

Possible Causes

A. Oil Level - high or low.

B. Oil Pressure Low - Refer to Oil Pressure Chart Fig. 7E-239 for specifications.
1. Modulator assembly defective.
2. Modulator valve sticking.
3. Pump pressure regulator valve or boost valve sticking.

C. Control Valve Assembly
Accumulator piston pin - leak at valve body end.

D. Direct Clutch
1. Piston seals or ball check leaking. Apply air to the direct clutch passage in the case valve body face.
2. Case center support - oil seal rings damaged, excessive leak between tower and bushing. Apply air to the direct clutch passage in the case valve body face. If air comes out the intermediate passage, center support is defective.
3. Extra waved steel plate - should have only one waved plate.

```
                    SHIFT SPEED CHART

   DRIVE RANGE      LIGHT THROTTLE      THRU DETENT
      1-2             6 to 11 mph      35 to 51.5 mph
      2-3           15.5 to 29.5 mph   70 to 85 mph
      3-2           16.5 to 11.5 mph   78 to 61.5 mph
      2-1           10 to 3.5 mph      35 to 17 mph

   LO RANGE

      2-1             51 to 40 mph



        N/V = 38.15 with 3.21:1 axle; 8.85 Tire Size
                Wheel Rev/mile = 713
```

Fig. 7E-238—Shift Speed Chart

ROUGH 2-3 SHIFT

Possible Causes

A. Oil Pressure High - Refer to Oil Pressure Chart Fig. 7E-239 for specifications.
   1. Vacuum modulator assembly defective.
   2. Vacuum modulator valve sticking.
   3. Pump - pressure regulator or boost valve stuck or inoperative.

B. Front Servo Accumulator Assembly
   1. Front accumulator spring missing or broken.
   2. Accumulator piston stuck.

C. Direct Clutch
   1. Extra waved steel plate.

SHIFTS OCCUR AT TOO HIGH OR TOO LOW CAR SPEED

Possible Causes

A. Oil Pressure - Refer to Oil Pressure Chart Fig. 7E-239 for specifications.
   1. Engine vacuum - check at transmission end of modulator pipe.
   2. Vacuum modulator assembly defective.
   3. Modulator valve sticking.
   4. Leak in vacuum line, engine to transmission.
   5. Vacuum modulator line fitting on the carburetor blocked.
   6. Pump - pressure regulator and boost valve train stuck.

B. Governor
   1. Valve stuck or sticking.
   2. Feed holes restricted or leaking; pipes damaged or mispositioned.

C. Detent Solenoid
   1. Stuck open.
   2. Loose on valve body (will cause late shifts).
   3. Feed line screens plugged.

D. Control Valve Assembly
   1. Detent valve train sticking.
   2. 3-2 valve train sticking.
   3. 1-2 shift valve train.
      a. 1-2 regulator valve stuck - will cause 1-2 shift point

to remain the same regardless of throttle opening.
      b. 1-2 detent valve sticking open (will probably cause early 2-3 shift).

E. Spacer Plate Gaskets
   1. Inverted or mispositioned.
   2. Spacer plate orifice holes missing or blocked.
   3. Check balls missing or mislocated.

F. Case
   1. Porosity in channels.
   2. Foreign material blocking channels.

NO PART THROTTLE DOWNSHIFT— (INSTALL PRESSURE GAUGE)

A. Oil pressure - (refer to table for oil pressure specifications)
   1. Vacuum modulator assembly, modulator valve, pressure regulator valve train. (Other malfunctions may also be noticed).

B. Control valve assembly
   1. 3-2 valve stuck, spring missing or broken.

NO DETENT DOWNSHIFTS

Possible Causes

A. Detent Switch
   1. Mispositioned.
   2. Electrical connections loose.

B. Solenoid
   1. Defective.
   2. Electrical connections loose.

C. Control Valve Assembly
   1. Detent valve train stuck.
   2. 3-2 valve stuck - spring missing or broken.

NO ENGINE BRAKING—SUPER RANGE— SECOND SPEED

Possible Causes

A. Front Servo Accumulator Assembly
   1. Servo or accumulator piston rings broken or missing.
   2. Case or valve body bores worn oversize causing excessive leakage.
   3. Servo piston stuck.

B. Front Band
   1. Band worn or burned. (Check for cause).
   2. Band end lugs broken or damaged.
   3. Band lugs not engaged on anchor pins or servo apply pin. (Check for cause).

NO ENGINE BRAKING—LOW RANGE— FIRST SPEED

Possible Causes

A. Control Valve Assembly
Low-reverse check ball missing from case.

B. Rear Servo
   1. Oil seal ring damaged or missing.
   2. Piston damaged or porous causing a leak in apply pressure.
   3. Rear band apply pin short.

RANGE	GEAR	PUMP PRESS.	FORWARD CLUTCH	INTER-MEDIATE CLUTCH	DIRECT CLUTCH	FRONT BAND	REAR BAND
PARK		60-150	OFF	OFF	OFF	OFF	OFF
REV		95-230	OFF	OFF	ON	OFF	ON
NEUT		60-150	OFF	OFF	OFF	OFF	OFF
DRIVE	FIRST	60-150	ON	OFF	OFF	OFF	OFF
	SECOND	60-150	ON	ON	OFF	OFF	OFF
	THIRD	60-150	ON	ON	ON	OFF	OFF
SUPER	FIRST	150	ON	OFF	OFF	OFF	OFF
	SECOND	150	ON	ON	OFF	ON	OFF
LOW	FIRST	150	ON	OFF	OFF	OFF	ON
	SECOND	150	ON	ON	OFF	ON	OFF

Fig. 7E-239—Oil Pressure Chart

C. Rear Band
    1. Band lining worn or burned (check for cause).
    2. Band end lugs broken.
    3. Band ends not engaged on anchor pin or servo apply pin.

Items A, B and C will also cause slip in reverse or No Reverse.

WILL NOT HOLD CAR IN PARK POSITION

Possible Causes

A. Manual Linkage - Maladjusted - external.

B. Internal Linkage
    1. Parking brake lever and actuator rod assembly defective (check for proper actuator spring action).
    2. Parking pawl broken or inoperative.

TRANSMISSION NOISE

Possible Causes

A. Pump Noise
    1. Oil level high or low.
    2. Water in oil.
    3. Driving gear assembled upside down.
    4. Driving or driven gear teeth damaged.
    5. Cavitation due to plugged strainer or damaged "O" ring.

B. Gear Noise - (First Gear Drive Range)
    1. Check pinions in planetary gear set for tooth finish or damage.
    2. Check sun gear and both front and rear internal gears for tooth finish or damage.
    3. Transmission grounded to body.

C. Clutch Noise - During Application
    1. Forward Clutch - (Neutral to drive, park to drive). Check clutch plates.

2. Intermediate Clutch - (1-2 in Super and Drive Range). Check clutch plates.
    3. Direct Clutch - (2-3 shift in drive range and neutral to Reverse, park to reverse). Check clutch plates.

D. Sprocket and Link Belt Noise
    1. Link belt too long. Sounds similar to pop corn popping. (There will be a rough burr along the teeth of the drive sprocket if the link belt is too long). Replace link belt and drive sprocket.
    2. Drive or Driven sprocket teeth damaged.
    3. Engine mounts worn or damaged.

OIL LEAKS

The suspected area should be wiped clean of all oil before inspecting for the source of the leak. Red dye is used in the transmission oil at the assembly plant and will indicate if the oil leak is from the transmission. The use of a "black light '* to identify the oil at the source of the leak is also helpful. Comparing the oil from the leak to that on the engine or transmission dip stick (when viewed by black light) will determine the source of the leak.

Oil leaks around the engine and transmission are generally carried toward the rear of the car by the air stream. For example, a transmission "oil filler tube to case leak" will sometimes appear as a leak at the rear of transmission. In determining the source of an oil leak, it is most helpful to keep the engine running.

Possible Points of Oil Leaks

A. Transmission Oil Pan
    1. Attaching bolts not correctly torqued.
    2. Pan gasket improperly installed or damaged.
    3. Oil pan case mounting face not flat.

B. Cover and Plate Assembly Sprocket Housing Leak
    1. Attaching bolts not correctly torqued.

* A "black light" testing unit such as J-6640 may be obtained from service tool suppliers.

2. Housing to case gasket improperly installed or damaged.

3. Housing to case gasket face not flat.

C. Final Drive to Transmission Leak
   1. Attaching bolts not correctly torqued.
   2. Final drive to transmission gasket improperly installed or damaged.
   3. Mounting surfaces not flat.

D. Case Leaks
   1. Filler pipe "O" ring seal damaged or missing. (Filler pipe is located in the final drive housing).
   2. Mispositioning of filler pipe mounting bracket - loading one side of "O" ring seal.
   3. Modulator assembly "O" ring seal damaged or improperly installed.
   4. Governor cam, "O" ring and bracket damaged or loose.
   5. Manual shaft "O" ring seal damaged or improperly installed.
   6. Line pressure tap plug loose or stripped.
   7. Cooler connectors loose, cracked, or stripped.
   8. Porosity in case.

9. Speedometer driven gear housing "O" ring or lip seal damaged.

E. Front End Leaks
   1. Front seal in pump damaged (check converter neck for nicks, etc., also for pump bushing moved forward).
   2. Garter spring missing or loose on front seal.
   3. Converter weld leaks.
   4. Pump to case "O" ring cut or damaged.
   5. Vent fitting damaged.

F. Oil Comes Out Vent Pipe
   1. Transmission overfilled.
   2. Water in oil.
   3. Cooler lines blocked causing excessive heat.

TOOLS

J-22241 -   Forward Clutch End Play Checking Tool
J-21370-7   Band Apply Selector Pin
J-21370-8   Band Apply Selector Pin Adapter Plate

For usage of additional tools, refer to Figs. 7-256 and 7-257 of the TURBO HYDRA-MATIC TRANSMISSION, Section 7.

TURBO HYDRA-MATIC INFORMATION CHART

For additional specification information refer to Information Chart, Section 7, Page 7-84.

TORQUE CHART

APPLICATION	FT. LBS.
Transmission to Engine Bolts	25
Torque Converter to Flywheel	30
Flywheel Housing Cover	5
Oil Cooler Lines to Radiator and Transmission	25
Final Drive to Transmission	25
Starter Motor to Transmission	25
Solenoid to Valve Body	3
Line Pressure Plug	13
Vacuum Modulator Retainer	18
Valve Body to Case	8
Center Support to Case	23
Manual Shaft to Inside Lever	18
Pump Body to Cover Plate	18
Parking Brake Bracket to Case	18
Oil Pan to Case	12
Sprocket Housing	8
Support Housing to Cover Plate	18
Speedometer Drive Gear Retainer	3

TURBO HYDRA-MATIC BUSHING SERVICE
1966-1968 TORONADO

Bushings are available and can be replaced in the following units. Service bushings do not require reaming.
1. Output Flange
2. Sun Gear Shaft - Front and Rear
3. Case Support
4. Pump Body
5. Stator Shaft 1966 and 1967
6. Stator Shaft 1968

Tools required are J-21465, -1, -3, -5, -6, -15, -16, -17, -19, J-2619, -4, J-8092, J-8647-1. (Fig. 7E-259)

OUTPUT FLANGE BUSHING

With output flange properly supported using Tool J-21465-16, with Slide Hammer J-2619 and Adapter Tool J-2619-4, remove bushing. (Fig. 7E-250)

Using Tool J-21465-1, with Driver Handle J-8092, press or drive replacement bushing into place until tool bottoms. (Fig. 7E-251)

SUN GEAR SHAFT BUSHING - FRONT AND REAR

With sun gear shaft properly supported, using Tool J-21465-15, with Slide Hammer Tool J-2619 and Adapter J-2619-4, remove bushing. (Fig. 7E-252)

Using Tool J-21465-5 with Driver Handle J-8092, press or drive replacement bushing into place until tool bottoms. (Fig. 7E-253)

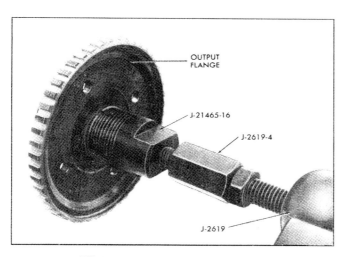

Fig. 7E-250—Output Flange Bushing Removal

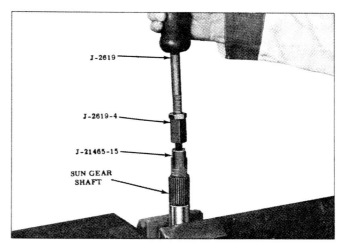

Fig. 7E-252—Sun Gear Shaft Bushing Removal

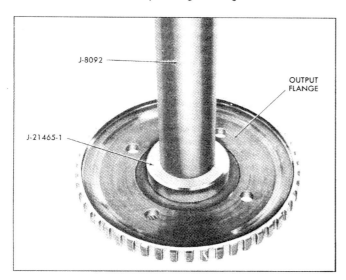

Fig. 7E-251—Output Flange Bushing Installation

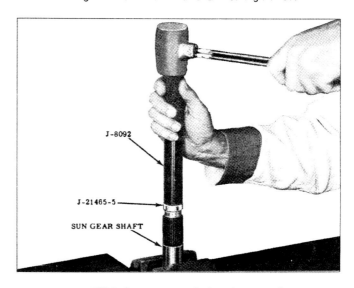

Fig. 7E-253—Sun Gear Shaft Bushing Installation

CASE SUPPORT BUSHING

With case support properly supported on wood blocks, using Tool J-21465-6 with Driver Handle J-8092, remove bushing. (Fig. 7E-254)

Using Tool J-21465-6 with Driver Handle J-8092, press or drive replacement bushing into place, aligning elongated slot in bushing with the drilled hole in the delivery sleeve closest to the piston. Bushing should be .010" below to flush with oil delivery sleeve. (This oil passage port is lubrication to low sprag or roller clutch.) (Fig. 7E-255)

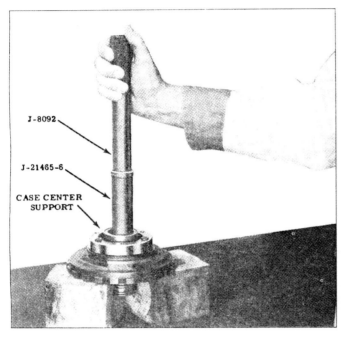

Fig. 7E-254—Case Support Bushing Removal

Fig. 7E-255—Case Support Bushing Installation

PUMP BODY BUSHING

With pump body properly supported and front seal removed, using Tool J-21465-17, with Driver Handle J-8092, remove bushing.

Using Tool J-21465-17, with Driver Handle J-8092, press or drive replacement bushing in place, flush to .010" below the gear pocket face.

Do not allow the bushing to protrude into gear pocket as it will interfere with the rotating gears. Also, use care to prevent damage to the gear pocket face. (Fig. 7E-256)

Fig. 7E-256—Pump Body Bushing Installation

STATOR SHAFT BUSHING - 1966 and 1967

With drive sprocket support and stator shaft properly supported, using Tool J-21465-15 or J-8647-1, with Slide Hammer Tool J-2619 and Adapter Tool J-2619-4, remove bushing.

Using Tool J-21465-19, with Driver Handle J-8092, press or drive replacement bushing into place until tool bottoms.

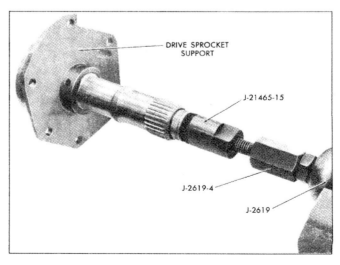

Fig. 7E-257—Stator Shaft Bushing Removal

STATOR SHAFT BUSHING - 1968

With drive sprocket support and stator shaft properly supported, using Tool J-21465-15 or J-8647-1, with Slide Hammer J-2619 and Adapter Tool J-2619-4, remove bushing. (Fig. 7E-257)

Using Tool J-21465-3 with Driver Handle J-8092, press or drive replacement bushing into place until tool bottoms. (Fig. 7E-258)

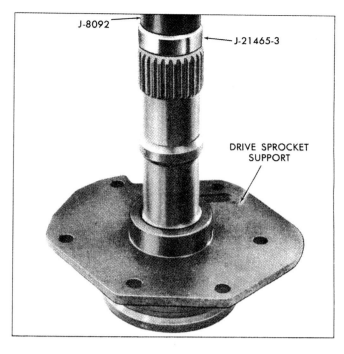

Fig. 7E-258—Stator Shaft Bushing Installation

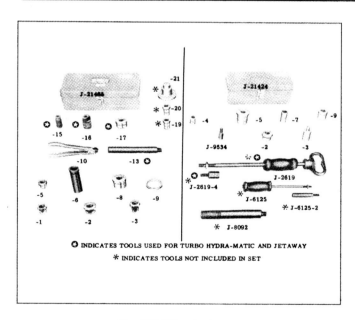

Fig. 7E-259—Tools

J-21424-2	Transmission Case Bushing Installer
J-21424-3	Output Shaft Bushing Installer
J-21424-4	Sun Gear and Flange Bushing Remover and Installer
J-21424-5	Forward Clutch Drum Bushing Remover and Installer
J-21424-7	Stator Shaft Bushing Installer
J-21424-9	Extension Housing Bushing Remover and Installer
J-9534	Output Shaft Bushing Remover
J-2619	Slide Hammer (Large)
J-2619-4	Slide Hammer (Thread Reducer Adapter)
J-6125	Slide Hammer (Small)
J-6125-2	Slide Hammer (Thread Reducer Adapter)
J-8092	Driver Handle (Universal)
J-21465-1	Output Shaft Bushing Installer
J-21465-5	Sun Gear Shaft Bushing Installer
J-21465-6	Case Center Support Bushing Remover and Installer
J-21465-8	Transmission Case Bushing Remover and Installer
J-21465-9	Transmission Case Bushing Installer Adapter Ring
J-21465-10	Transmission Case and Extension Housing Bushing Staking Pliers
J-21465-13	Transmission Case Bushing Extension Handle
J-21465-15	Sun Gear Shaft and Stator Shaft Bushing Remover
J-21465-16	Output Shaft Bushing Remover
J-21465-17	Pump Body Bushing and Extension Housing Bushing Remover and Installer
J-21465-19	Stator Shaft Front Bushing Installer
J-21465-20	Stator Shaft Rear Bushing Installer
J-21465-21	Pump Cover Support

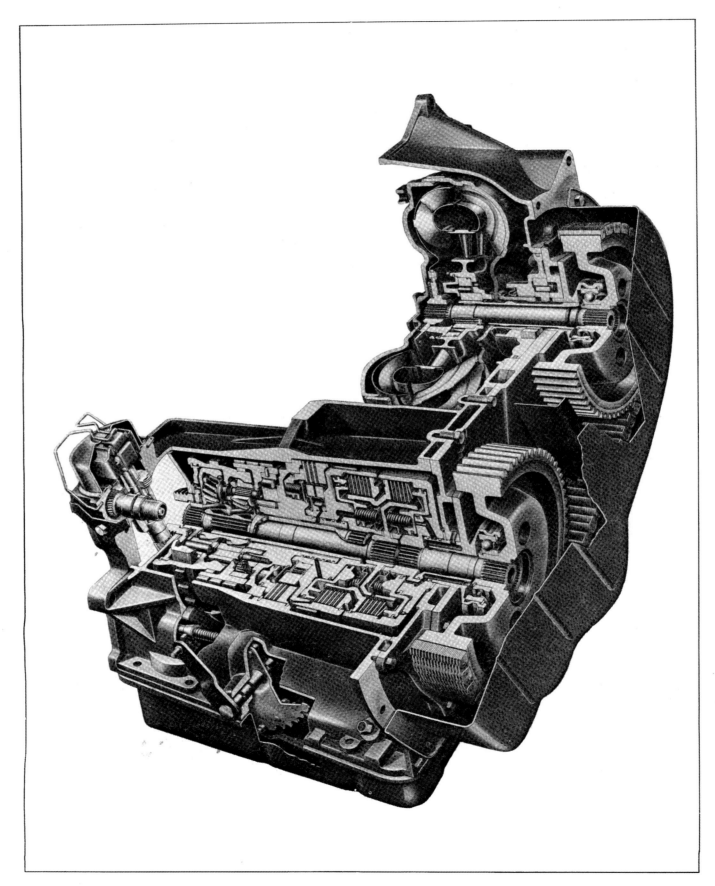

Fig. 7E-260—Toronado Hydra-Matic Transmission Assembly

FUEL TANK AND EXHAUST

CONTENTS OF SECTION 8E

FUEL SYSTEM

DESCRIPTION (Figs. 8E-1 through 8E-3)

The fuel tank used on the Toronado has a capacity of 24 gallons with the fuel filler pipe located behind the license plate. Venting of the fuel tank is provided by two hoses located at the rear of the tank and on the right side of the filler pipe. The hoses are retained by a clip as shown in Fig. 8E-1 and end behind the filler door. A baffle is positioned laterally in the tank to stabilize fuel level and minimize noise.

The gas tank fuel filter is located on the fuel pickup pipe which is part of the tank unit and is not replaceable except by replacing the tank unit. A non-vented gas cap must be used. Use only premium or super premium fuel.

If equipped with air conditioning, a fuel return system is incorporated. The fuel return consists of a pipe clipped to the frame side rail and a hose on each end routed through holes in the frame. The fuel return hose connects to the right front corner of the fuel tank.

The Toronado has a top mounted tank gauge unit. The same gauge is used for air conditioning and non air conditioning equipped cars.

FUEL GAUGE TANK UNIT

Removal

1. Remove fuel tank. (See tank Removal)
2. Remove tank unit retaining cam using Tool J-22554.
3. Remove tank unit from tank.

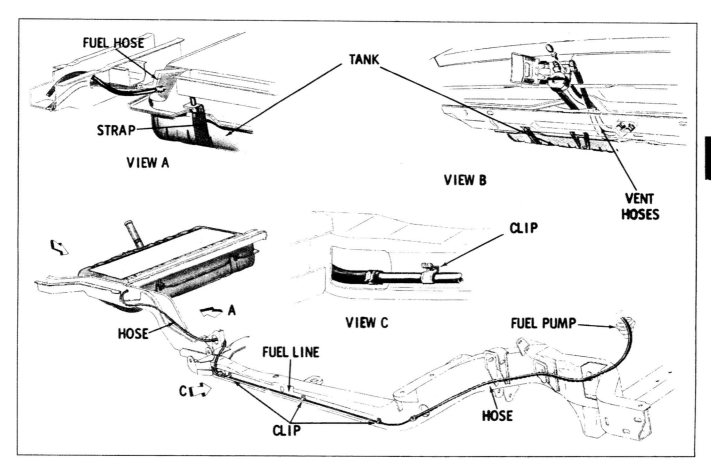

Fig. 8E-1—Fuel System - Toronado

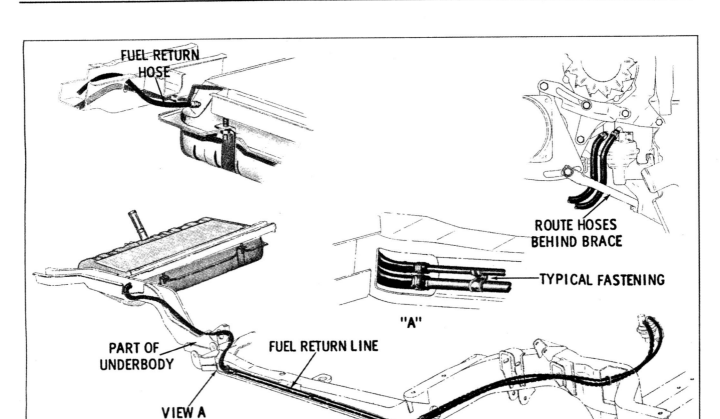

Fig. 8E-2—Fuel Return System - Toronado

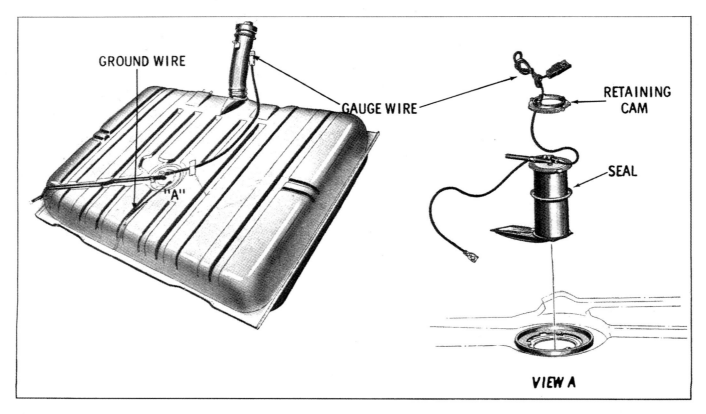

Fig. 8E-3—Tank Unit Installation - Toronado

Installation

1. Position tank unit in tank. (Fig. 8E-3)
2. Install tank unit retaining cam using Tool J-22554.
3. Install fuel tank. (See fuel tank installation)

FUEL TANK

Removal

1. Drain fuel tank.
2. Disconnect tank unit wire from connector in rear compartment.
3. Remove vent hoses from retaining clip. (Fig. 8E-1)

4. Remove ground wire retaining screw from underbody at front of tank.
5. Disconnect fuel hose from tank. (Fig. 8E-2)
6. Support fuel tank and disconnect the two fuel tank retaining straps.
7. Remove tank from car.

Installation

1. Connect tank unit wires. (Fig. 8E-3)
2. Reverse removal procedure.
3. Tighten fuel tank retaining strap nuts to 9 ft. lbs.

EXHAUST SYSTEM (TORONADO)

DESCRIPTION (Figs. 8E-4 AND 8E-5)

Periodic maintenance of the exhaust system is not required; however, if the car is raised for other service, it is advisable to check that the drain holes in the muffler and resonators are in the down position and open to prolong their life.

The muffler supports and the extension insulator brackets are attached to the frame with self-tapping screws. If a screw hole should strip out, it is impossible to use a bolt and nut because of the boxed frame design; therefore, self-tapping hex head 3/8"-16 x 1-1/8" screws should be used.

Annoying rattles and noise vibrations in the exhaust system are usually caused by misalignment of parts.

Aligning the system should be done only when the system is cold, as heat causes the complete system to expand rearward, sometimes as much as 3/4". When servicing any components of the exhaust system, it is important that the exhaust system hang freely in its hangers without binding. If using a single post hoist, it is necessary to use wood blocks to avoid contact between the lift pads and the exhaust system.

For servicing the exhaust manifold heat valve, refer to ENGINE, Section 6.

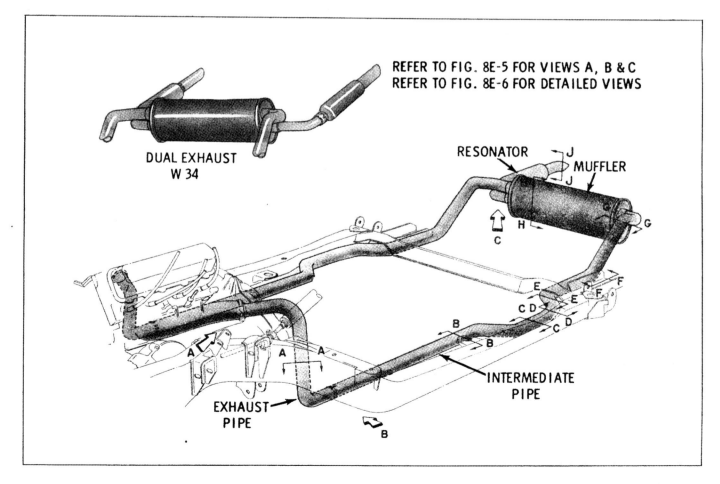

REFER TO FIG. 8E-5 FOR VIEWS A, B & C
REFER TO FIG. 8E-6 FOR DETAILED VIEWS

DUAL EXHAUST W 34

RESONATOR

MUFFLER

EXHAUST PIPE

INTERMEDIATE PIPE

Fig. 8E-4—Exhaust System - Toronado

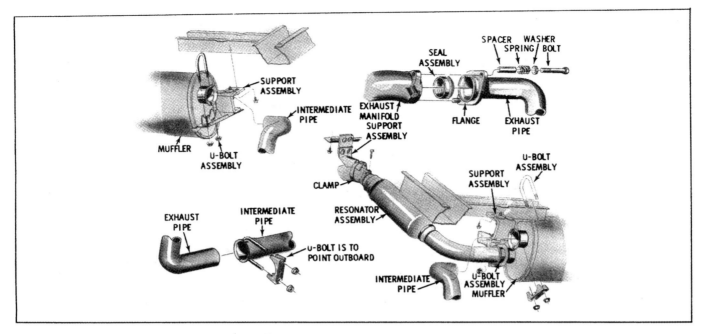

Fig. 8E-5—Exhaust System Connections-Toronado

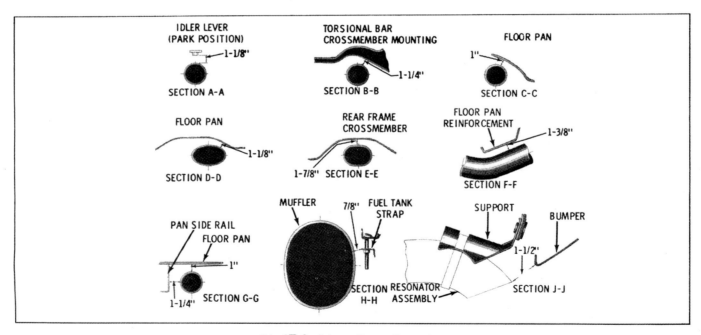

Fig. 8E-6—Exhaust System Connections

TORQUE SPECIFICATIONS

Specified torque is for installation of parts only. Checking of torque during inspection may be 10% below that specified.

APPLICATION	TORQUE
Fuel Tank Attaching Nuts	18 ft. lbs.
Exhaust Extension to Resonator Attaching Screws	18 in. lbs.
Clamp Attaching Nuts	*13 ft. lbs.*
Exhaust Pipe to Exhaust Manifold Attaching Bolts	14 ft. lbs.
Exhaust Extension Insulator to Frame Attaching Screws	13 ft. lbs.
Muffler Support to Frame Attaching Screws	13 ft. lbs.

STEERING

TORONADO

CONTENTS OF SECTION 9E

REPLACEMENT OF STEERING LINKAGE PARTS (Fig. 9E-1)

PITMAN ARM

Removal

1. Loosen the pitman arm nut on the pitman shaft using Tool BT-6704.

2. Remove the flexible coupling bolt at the gear side of the coupling.

3. Disconnect the pitman arm from the relay rod by removing the cotter pin, nut and using Tool J-22292.

4. Remove the three steering gear to frame attaching bolts and raise the steering gear to clear the pitman arm stud from the relay rod and position the steering gear forward enough to allow access to the pitman arm shaft nut.

5. Remove the loosened pitman arm shaft nut and remove the pitman arm using Tool J-5504.

Installation

1. Loosely position the new pitman arm onto the pitman shaft and snug up the pitman arm nut onto the pitman shaft.

Before installing the gear to the frame, lubricate the frame pads where the gear bolts to frame with a light coating of sodium soap fine fiber grease to prevent squeaks between the gear and frame.

2. Slide the gear rearward and index the gear into the flexible coupling and install one gear to frame attaching bolt.

3. Install the pitman arm stud into the relay rod. Install the remaining gear to frame bolts and torque to 70 ft. lbs.

4. Torque the pitman arm shaft nut to 200 ft. lbs. using Adapter BT-6704 with wheels turned to the right. Refer to Torque Adapter Formula.

5. Install the pitman arm stud to relay rod nut and torque to 45 ft. lbs. Install cotter pin.

6. Reset toe in and steering wheel spoke alignment.

IDLER ARM

Removal

1. Disconnect the idler arm from the relay rod using Tool J-22292. (Fig. 9E-3)

2. Remove the idler arm to frame bracket attaching bolt and remove idler arm.

If using a backing wrench on the head of the bolt, be sure to position it in such a manner as to prevent any damage to the radiator core.

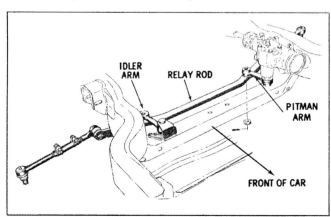

Fig. 9E-1—Steering Linkage

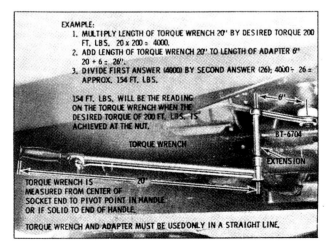

Fig. 9E-2—Torque Wrench with an Adapter Formula

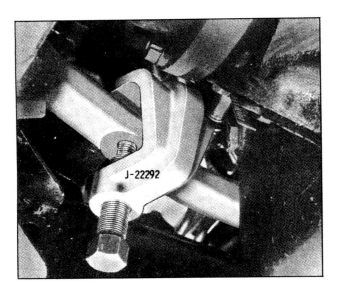

Fig. 9E-3—Disconnecting Relay Joint

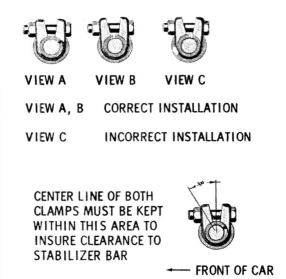

VIEW A   VIEW B   VIEW C

VIEW A, B   CORRECT INSTALLATION

VIEW C   INCORRECT INSTALLATION

CENTER LINE OF BOTH
CLAMPS MUST BE KEPT
WITHIN THIS AREA TO
INSURE CLEARANCE TO
STABILIZER BAR

← FRONT OF CAR

Fig. 9E-4—Tie-Rod Clamp Positioning

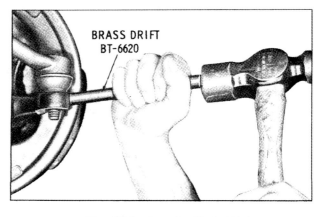

BRASS DRIFT
BT-6620

Fig. 9E-5—Removing Tie-Rod End

1. Install idler arm to frame and torque nut to 95 ft. lbs.
2. Reconnect the idler arm to the relay rod and torque nut to 45 ft. lbs. Install a new cotter pin.
3. Reset toe in and steering wheel spoke alignment.

TORQUE ADAPTER FORMULA (Fig. 9E-2)

When using a torque wrench with an adapter the reading on the torque wrench will not reflect the actual torque of the bolt because of the extra length of the combined torque wrench and adapter. To obtain the correct torque reading in these cases, use the following formula:

1. Multiply the length of the torque wrench by the number of pounds of the desired torque.
2. Add the length of the torque wrench to the length of the adapter.
3. Divide the first answer by the second answer. The result will be the corrected torque reading.

For example, if you have a 20" torque wrench and a 6" torque adapter and the specified torque is 200 ft. lbs., you would use the above formula as follows:

1. Multiply length of torque wrench (20") by the desired torque, 200 ft. lbs. 20 x 200 = 4000.
2. Add length of torque wrench (20") to length of adapter (6") 20 + 6 = 26.
3. Divide first answer (4000) by second answer (26) 4000 ÷ 26 = 154.

154 ft. lbs. will be the reading on the torque wrench when the desired torque of 200 ft. lbs. is achieved at the bolt.

TIE RODS

Remove and Install

Whenever the tie rod end is assembled to the tie rod and prior to assembling the tie rod end to the steering knuckle, make certain that an equal number of the tie rod and tie rod end threads are exposed at each end of the tie rod sleeve. Tie rod adjuster sleeve clamps must be kept within 30° of the vertical center line to insure clearance to stabilizer bar. (Fig. 9E-4)

Tie rod end joint to knuckle may be removed as shown in Fig. 9E-5. On installation torque to 45 ft. lbs.

STEERING GEAR

ADJUSTMENT (On Car)

OVER-CENTER ADJUSTMENT

The over-center adjustment is the only power steering gear adjustment which can be made on the car; however, in order to make this adjustment, it is also necessary to check the combined ball and thrust bearing pre-load.

1. Remove pitman arm from relay rod using Tool J-22292.
2. Loosen the pitman shaft adjusting screw locknut and thread the adjusting screw out to the limit of its travel through the pitman shaft side cover.
3. Disconnect the horn wire at the relay, then remove the horn button or ornament from the steering wheel.
4. Count the number of turns of the steering wheel through its full travel to locate the steering wheel at its center of travel.
5. Check the combined ball and thrust bearing pre-load with an inch-pound torque wrench on the steering shaft nut by rotating through the center of travel. Note the highest reading.
6. Tighten the pitman shaft adjusting screw until the torque wrench reads 4 to 8 in. lbs. higher than the previous reading on the steering shaft. The total over-center pre-load should not exceed 16 in. lbs.
7. While holding the pitman shaft adjusting screw, tighten the locknut and recheck the adjustment.

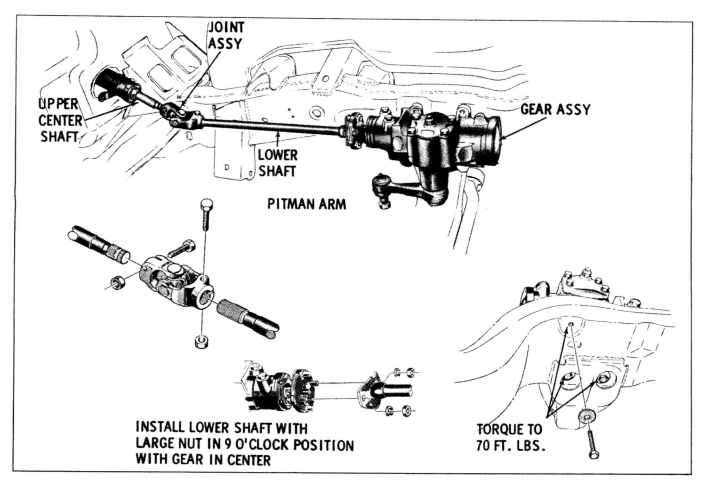

Fig. 9E-6—Steering Gear and Shaft Installation

8. Install the horn button or ornament and connect the horn wire. Connect the pitman arm to the relay rod. Torque pitman arm nut to 45 ft. lbs.

STEERING GEAR (Fig. 9E-6)

Removal and Installation

1. Remove the coupling flange hub bolt.

2. Disconnect the hoses from the pump and cap the pump and hose fittings.

> **On cars equipped with a cooler assembly disconnect the return hose at the inlet pipe of the cooler assembly.**

3. Hoist the car.

4. Remove the pitman arm from the relay rod using Tool J-22292.

5. Remove the three bolts attaching the gear to the frame side rail, permit the lower shaft to slide free of the coupling flange, then remove the gear with the hoses attached.

Before installing the steering gear, apply a sodium soap fine fiber grease to the gear mounting pads to prevent squeaks between the gear housing and the frame. Make certain there is a minimum of .040" clearance between coupling hub and steering gear upper seal. Install the coupling flange hub bolt and torque to 18 ft. lbs. Before tightening the steering gear to frame bolts, shift the steering gear as necessary to place it in the same plane as the steering shaft so that the flexible coupling is not distorted. Tighten the steering gear to frame bolts to 70 ft. lbs. Install pitman arm to relay rod. Tor-

que nut to 45 ft. lbs. Install cotter pin.

After the hoses are connected to the pump, add power steering fluid as necessary to bring the fluid level to the full mark. Run engine at idle for 30 seconds, then run at fast idle for one minute before turning steering wheel. With the engine running, turn the steering wheel through its full travel two or three times to bleed air from the system. Recheck the oil level and add oil if necessary.

COOLER ASSEMBLY

Removal

1. Remove vacuum reserve tank. (Fig. 9E-7)

2. Remove three attaching screws, cooler to L.H. Filler Plate and lower radiator support. (Fig. 9E-8)

3. Remove return hoses from cooler pipes and cap return hoses.

4. Remove cooler assembly through L.H. filler plate opening.

Installation

1. Install cooler assembly through L.H. filler plate opening and install three attaching screws to L.H. filler plate and lower radiator support. (Fig. 9E-8)

2. Remove protective caps and install return hoses to cooler pipes using new clamps.

3. Fill pump reservoir with fluid No. 1050017 or equivalent and start engine. Add additional fluid as needed to retain fluid level at the full mark.

4. Check for leaks. Repair as necessary.

5. Stop engine.

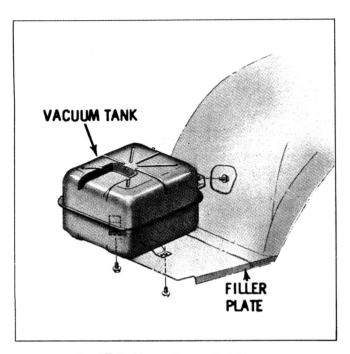

Fig. 9E-7—Vacuum Reserve Tank Mounting

6. Install vacuum reserve tank. (Fig. 9E-7)

POWER STEERING PUMP

Removal

1. Loosen power steering pump pulley nut. Do not loosen belt tension as tension will aid in holding pulley.

2. Remove power steering pump belt.

On A.C. equipped cars, generator belt will have to be loosened first.

3. Remove pump pulley nut and pulley.

4. Remove nuts "A", "B" and screw "C", then remove bolt and nut "D". (Fig. 9E-9)

5. Move pump away from engine and disconnect hoses from pump. Plug the hoses so that no impurities will contaminate fluid. Cap the pump fittings.

Installation

To install, reverse removal procedures.

Torque - Nuts "A" and "D" and screw "C" to 20 ft. lbs.
Nut "B" to 30 ft. lbs. Pump pulley nut to 60 ft. lbs.

Fill reservoir with fluid No. 1050017 or equivalent, then bleed pump by turning pulley counterclockwise until air bubbles cease to appear. Refill reservoir to proper level. Adjust pump belt as outlined under PUMP BELT ADJUSTMENTS, Section 9.

STEERING WHEEL (Figs. 9E-10 and 9E-11)

Removal

1. Pry emblem up to disengage locking tang.

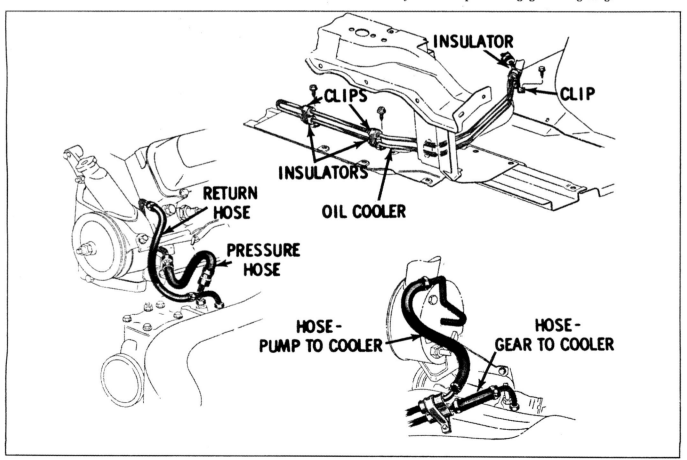

Fig. 9E-8—Power Steering Pump and Cooler Hose Routing

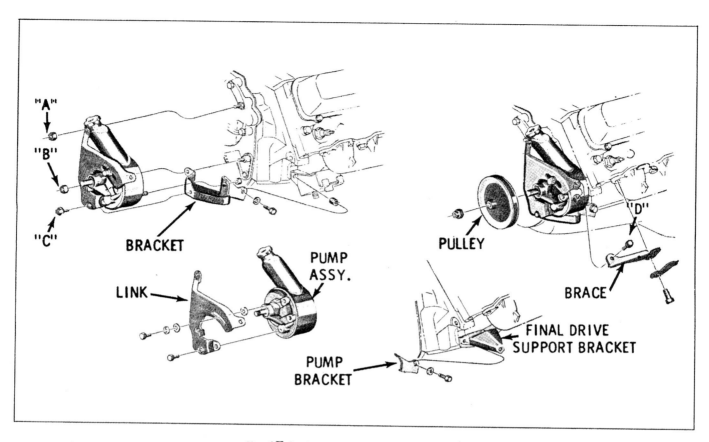

Fig. 9E-9—Power Steering Bracket Mountings

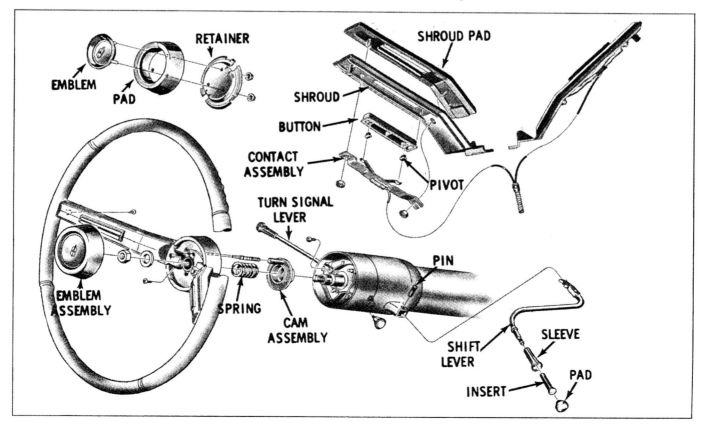

Fig. 9E-10—Deluxe Steering Wheel

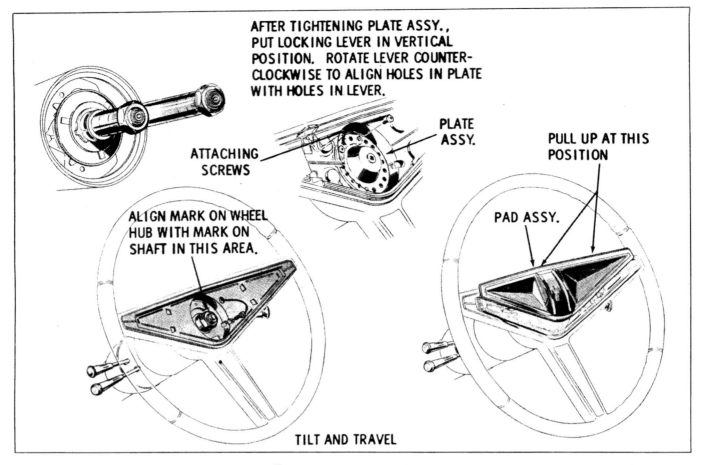

Fig. 9E-11—Tilt and Travel Steering Wheel

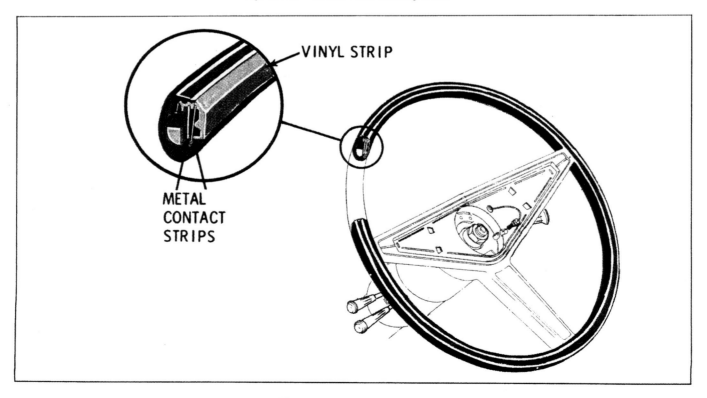

Fig. 9E-12—Horn Contact - Tilt and Travel

2. Remove steering wheel attaching nut and washer, then using a puller such as BT-61-9, remove the steering wheel from the steering shaft. Remove puller from steering wheel.

Installation

1. With the marks on the steering wheel and steering shaft aligned, install the wheel, flat washer and nut.

When mark on steering wheel hub and shaft are lined up, wheel spokes should be horizontal as car is driven straight ahead.

If spokes are not horizontal, it will be necessary to adjust the tie rod ends until steering wheel assumes its proper position. When a new steering gear is installed, it may be necessary to adjust steering wheel spoke alignment even though spoke alignment had been correct for the old gear.

2. Torque the nut to 35 ft. lbs.
3. Align tangs of emblem with contact hole in wheel assembly. Push in to lock.

HORN CONTACT

The horn contact for deluxe wheel is installed as shown in Fig. 9E-10.

The horn contact on the tilt and travel wheel is not serviced. (Fig. 9E-12)

STEERING COLUMN (Fig. 9E-13)

Removal

1. Disconnect negative battery cable.
2. Remove steering wheel.
    Deluxe-Refer to Steering Wheel-Section 9E.
    Tilt and Travel-Refer to Steering Wheel-Section 9.
3. Disconnect shift levers from lower end of column.
4. Place daub of paint on steering shaft at slot in joint assembly and then remove bolt from joint assembly.
5. Disconnect turn signal and cornering light wiring con-nectors.
6. Disconnect neutral start and back-up wiring connec-tors.
7. Remove shift indicator needle.
8. Remove bolts from inner and outer covers at floor pan (Fig. 9E-13)
9. Remove four bolts "Z" from clamp assy. (Fig. 9E-13)
10. Remove nut "C" (Fig. 9E-13)
11. Remove nuts "A" and "B" (Fig. 9E-13) Remove clamp assy. and wedge.
12. Carefully lift steering column from inside of car.

All elements of energy absorbing steering columns are sensitive to damage and MUST BE HANDLED WITH CARE.

13. Install column in vise using holding fixture J-22573.

Installation

1. Remove column from holding fixture and carefully position through toe-pan. With the aid of a helper at lower end of column, align paint mark on joint assy. onto shaft from gear. Attach bolt loosely. Torque to 80 ft. lbs.
2. Loosely attach clamp assy. to support with wedge and install nuts "A" and "B" (Fig. 9E-13) loosely.
3. Install 4 bolts "Z" to bracket. Torque to 15 ft. lbs.
4. With the aid of a helper, align flex coupling and torque nuts "A" and "B" to 20 ft. lbs.
5. Position wedge rearward until finger tight and install nut "C" and torque to 20 ft. lbs.
6. Install toe pan screws ("1") and torque to 4 ft. lbs. (Fig. 9E-13)
7. Install toe pan clamp screws ("2") and torque to 4 ft. lbs.
8. Install remaining toe pan screws ("3") and torque to 4 ft. lbs.
9. Connect neutral start and back-up wiring connector.

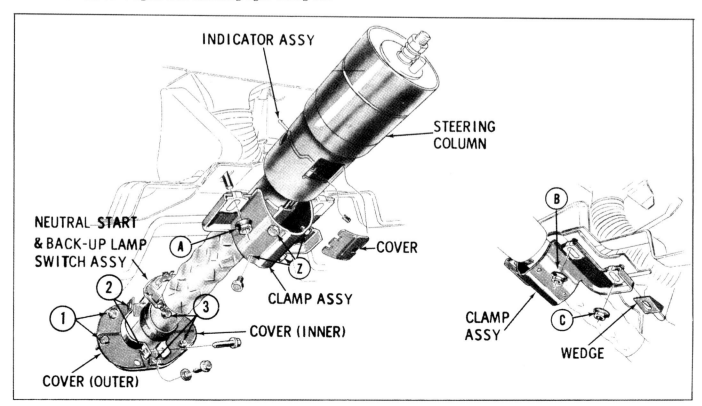

Fig. 9E-13—Steering Column

10. Connect turn signal and cornering light wiring connectors.

11. Install shift indicator needle.

12. Connect shift levers at lower end of column.

13. If neutral start and or back-up switch was removed, refer to Section 9A, Fig. 9A-105 for adjustment procedures.

14. Install steering wheel. Torque nut to 35 ft. lbs.

15. Connect negative battery cable.

TORQUE SPECIFICATIONS

APPLICATION	FT. LBS.
Pitman Shaft Nut	200
Pitman Arm to Relay Rod Nut	45 Min.
Idler Arm to Relay Rod Nut	45
Idler Arm to Bracket Nuts	95
Tie-Rod End to Knuckle Nut	45
Companion Flange Nuts	18
Steering Gear to Frame Bolts	70
Steering Wheel Nut	35
Lower Center Shaft to Joint Bolt	60
Lower Shaft to Joint Bolt	60

WHEELS AND TIRES

TORONADO

CONTENTS OF SECTION 10E

GENERAL DESCRIPTION

The factory installed tires are engineered specifically for the Toronado. These tires are designed to operate satisfactorily with loads up to and including the full rated load capacity, when inflated to the recommended pressures.

Correct tire pressures and driving technique have an important influence on tire life. Heavy cornering, excessively rapid acceleration, and unnecessary sharp braking increase tire wear. When replacement is necessary, the original equipment type tire should be used.

MAINTENANCE RECOMMENDATIONS

Tire Rotation

To equalize wear it is recommended that the four road tires be rotated at least every 6,000 miles as shown in Fig. 10E-1. It is not necessary to rotate the spare.

Tire Inflation

Recommended inflation pressure is 24 lbs. front and 22 lbs. rear when tires are cool. When the car is driven a few miles, tires warm up causing pressure increase. If pressures are checked when tires are warm, they may be up to 6 lbs. higher. Tires should be properly inflated, and inflation pressures checked regularly, including the spare tire.

Spare Tire Storage

The spare tire, jack assembly and wrench are stored as shown in Fig. 10E-2.

Tire Size

The standard tire size for Toronado with or without air conditioning is 8.85 x 15. A 235R15 radial ply is available as an option.

TIRE AND WHEEL RUNOUT

Inflate tires to recommended pressure. Tires should be checked immediately after car has been driven to avoid false readings due to the tendency of tires to take a temporary "set" after standing for a period of time.

Wheels and tires can be checked for runout at points indicated and should not exceed the following limits. (Fig. 10E-3)

Tire and Wheel Assembly	- Radial - Lateral	.060" .085"
Wheel	- Radial - Lateral	.035" .045"

TIRE INFORMATION

The factory installed tires are selected to provide the best all around tire performance for normal operation. They are also designed to operate satisfactorily with loads up to and including the full rated load capacity when inflated to the recommended pressure.

The over-all tire wear is about the same as on rear wheel drive cars of comparable weight. However, correct tire pressures and driving technique have an important influence on tire life. Heavy cornering, excessively rapid acceleration, and unnecessary sharp braking increase tire wear. When replacement is necessary, the original equipment type tire should be used.

TIRE ROTATION

As on any vehicle, traction can be adversely affected by lack of tire tread, so worn tires should be replaced before the tread is completely gone.

Factory installed tires incorporate built-in tread wear indicators to assist in determining when the tires have been worn to the point of needing replacement. These indicators are molded into the bottom of the thread grooves and will appear as 1/2-inch wide bands when the tire tread depth becomes 1/16th of an inch. When the indicators appear in two or more adjacent grooves, tire replacement due to tread wear is recommended.

So that tires are exposed to equal and balanced wear, it is recommended that the four road tires be rotated at least every 6,000 miles, in accordance with the Fig. 10E-1. It is not necessary to rotate the spare. Torque wheel nuts to 115 ft. lbs.

INFLATION PRESSURES

To insure the proper tire inflation follow the recommendations in the tire inflation pressures table. Keep tires properly

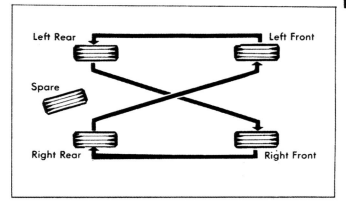

Fig. 10E-1—Tire Rotation

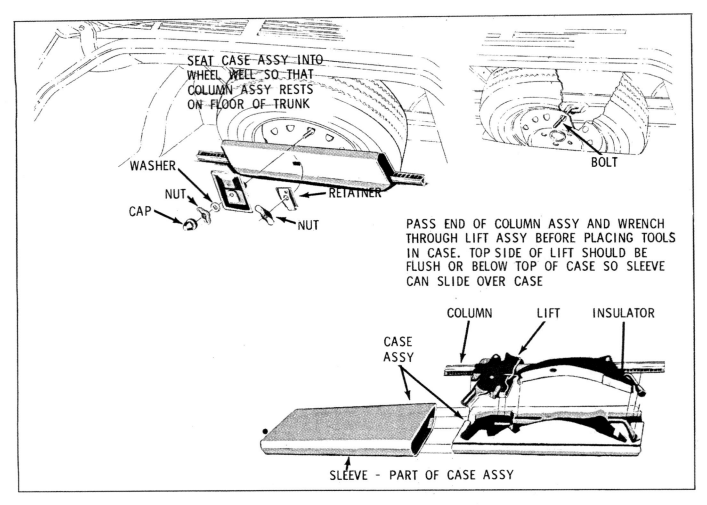

SEAT CASE ASSY INTO WHEEL WELL SO THAT COLUMN ASSY RESTS ON FLOOR OF TRUNK

WASHER

NUT

CAP

RETAINER

NUT

BOLT

PASS END OF COLUMN ASSY AND WRENCH THROUGH LIFT ASSY BEFORE PLACING TOOLS IN CASE. TOP SIDE OF LIFT SHOULD BE FLUSH OR BELOW TOP OF CASE SO SLEEVE CAN SLIDE OVER CASE

COLUMN   LIFT   INSULATOR

CASE ASSY

SLEEVE - PART OF CASE ASSY

Fig. 10E-2—Spare Tire and Jack Storage

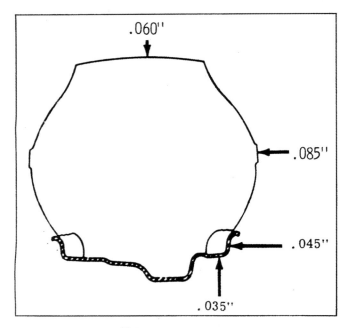

.060"

.085"

.045"

.035"

Fig. 10E-3—Tire and Wheel Runout

inflated, and check inflation pressures periodically. This will insure the best tire life and riding comfort, over the full range of driving conditions.

RECOMMENDED COOL TIRE INFLATION PRESSURES - POUNDS PER SQUARE INCH			
		* Normal Inflation All Loads	
SERIES	TIRE PLY	Front	Rear
Toronado	2 (4-Ply Rating) & Radial Ply	24 Lbs.	22 Lbs.

*When the car is driven a few miles, tires warm up causing pressure increase. If tire pressures are checked when tires are warm they may be up to 6 pounds higher than the pressures *shown on the chart.*

For continuous high speed operation (over 75 mph) increase tire pressure (cool) 4 pounds over the above recommended inflation pressures up to a maximum of 32 psi for 4 ply rating tires.

Over inflation at light loads will have an adverse effect on the car ride and tire tread wear pattern. Under inflation will promote heat and abnormal wear.

VEHICLE LOAD CAPACITY AND DISTRIBUTION

Full load capacity is:		
SERIES	1100 Lbs. Total:	3 Passengers Front Seat
		3 Passengers Rear Seat
Toronado		200 Pounds Luggage
When towing trailers, the allowable passenger and cargo load must be reduced by an amount equivalent to the trailer tongue load on the trailer hitch.		

FRONT WHEEL BALANCING

Balancing front wheels on the Toronado using on-car balancing equipment and using engine power to spin the wheels requires the following:
1. Set parking brake.
2. Block opposite wheel being balanced.

Do not exceed a speedometer reading of 35 mph while spinning the wheel.

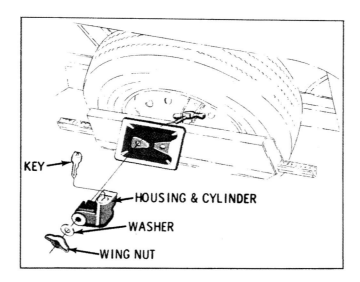

KEY

HOUSING & CYLINDER

WASHER

WING NUT

Fig. 10E-4—Spare Wheel Lock

CHASSIS SHEET METAL
TORONADO

CONTENTS OF SECTION 11E

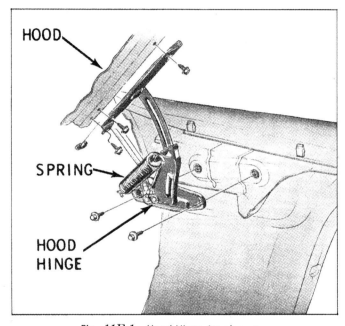

Fig. 11E-1—Hood Hinge Attachment

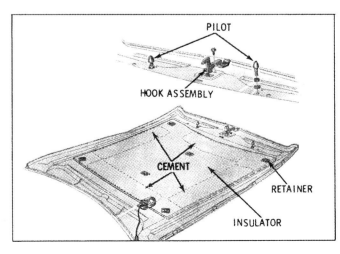

Fig. 11E-2—Hood Insulator

HOOD ASSEMBLY

Removal and Installation

Prior to removal of the hood, it is suggested that adjoining areas be covered to prevent damage.

With the hood supported, scribe the hinge position on the hood reinforcement and remove the two hinge to hood screws from each hinge. (Fig. 11E-1)

When installing hood, position the hood to the scribed lines, torque screws to 25 ft. lbs. The hinge is provided with elongated holes for alignment and if necessary, shift hood to properly align. If necessary to install a new hood insulator, refer to Fig. 11E-2.

HOOD HINGE SPRING

Removal and Installation

To remove the spring from the hood hinge, raise hood approximately 12" and place Tool BT-6813 over the spring. (Fig. 11E-3) Raise hood and the spring will unhook. Block hood in this position and remove spring.

Fig. 11E-3—Hinge Spring Tool in Position

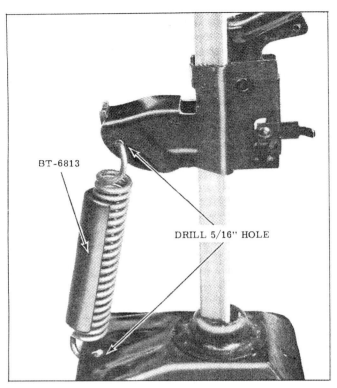

Fig. 11E-4—Installing Hinge Spring Tool

When installing a new spring, stretch the spring (Fig. 11E-4) and place Tool BT-6813 over the spring. Position spring (with tool in place) on hinge. Lower hood slightly to expand spring, then remove tool.

HOOD HINGE

Removal and Installation (With Spring Removed)

Place protective covers on fender at hinge area. Mark the hinge outline on fender and hood to facilitate alignment. (Fig. 11E-1) Support the hood at front and rear and remove the two hinge-to-hood screws, then remove the hinge-to-fender screws.

Using the scribe marks as a guide, install the hinge screws and torque to 25 ft. lbs. Check hood alignment after hinge installation. The hinge is provided with elongated holes for alignment and if necessary, shift hood to properly align.

HOOD LATCH ASSEMBLY (Fig. 11E-5)

The hood latch assembly is bolted to the radiator support assembly. Four bolts retaining the latch assembly to the radiator support are accessible from the top side. Remove the clip from rod. Remove attaching bolts and remove latch assembly through opening between top of front bumper and radiator support. The bolt holes are oversize for alignment purposes. The assembly should be lubricated periodically with lubriplate. Torque screws to 20 ft. lbs.

RADIATOR SUPPORT ASSEMBLY (Fig. 11E-5)

The radiator support assembly is a welded assembly and will be serviced as a complete assembly.

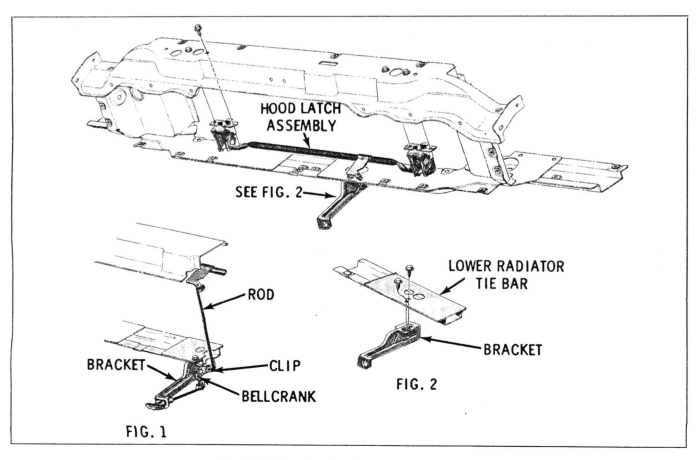

Fig. 11E-5—Hood Latch and Radiator Support Assembly

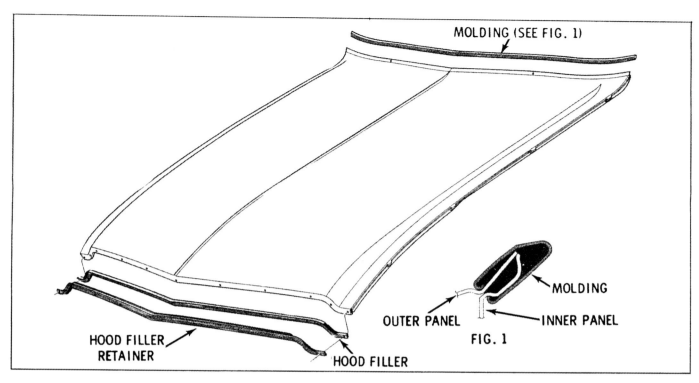

Fig. 11E-6—Hood Moldings

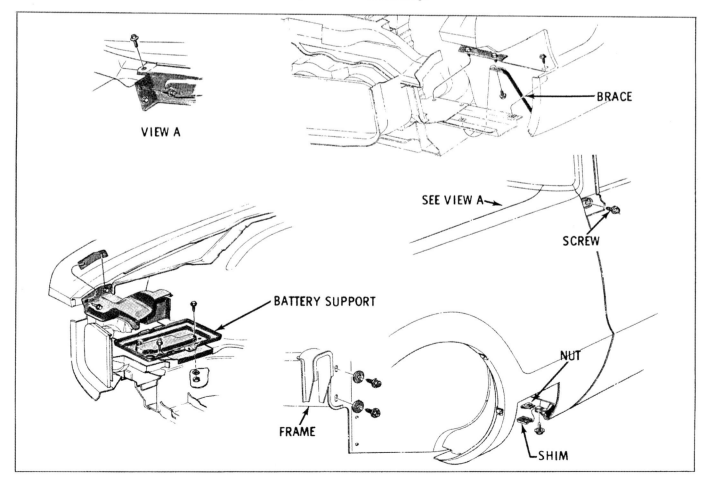

Fig. 11E-7—Fender Installation

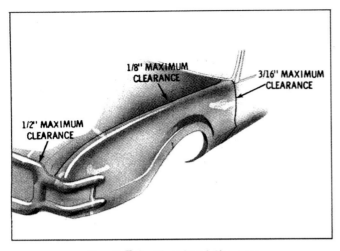

Fig. 11E-8—Sheet Metal Clearance

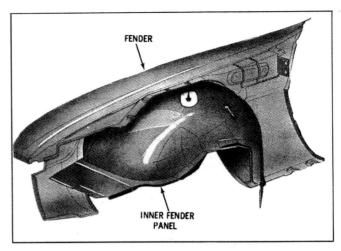

Fig. 11E-9—Fender Filler Plate Attachment

FENDER ASSEMBLY

Removal

1. Remove bumper (refer to Bumper Section).
2. Remove the screws indicated in Fig. 11E-7.
3. Remove the 4 screws at valance panel.
4. Remove two attaching bolts from lower fender brace.
5. Remove hood hinge to fender attaching screws and support hood.
6. For right fender, if equipped with antenna, it will be necessary to:
   a. Loosen plastic nut and remove mast assembly.
   b. Remove the lead-in assembly mounting nut, upper spacer and gasket.
   c. Push the lead-in assembly down through the fender and body.

It will be necessary to remove battery (right side) and vacuum tank and headlamp remote control valve. (left side).

7. Along inner fender flange, remove five screws securing fender filler to fender. (Fig. 11E-9)
8. Remove wheel opening molding.
9. Along edge of wheel opening, remove six screws securing fender filler to fender. (Fig. 11E-10)

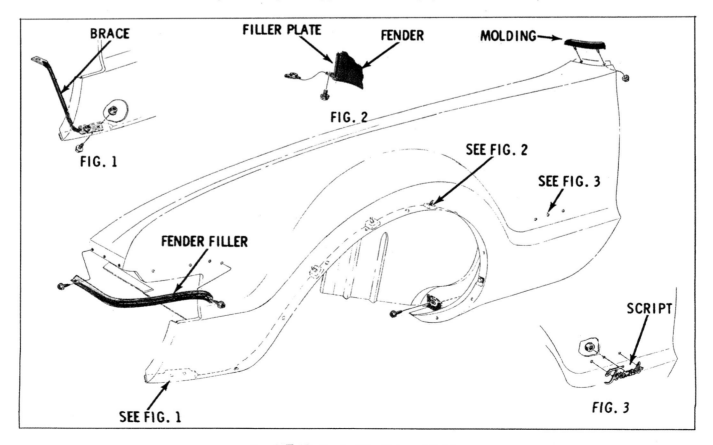

Fig. 11E-10—Fender Filler Plate and Moldings

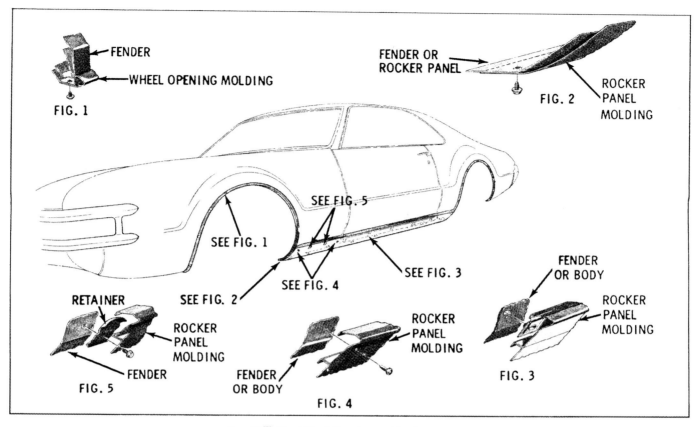

Fig. 11E-11—Wheel Opening and Rocker Moldings

10. Remove rocker panel molding.
11. Remove fender.

Installation

To install the fender, reverse the removal procedure. Refer to ACCESSORIES Section for antenna installation. The fender attaching bolt holes are elongated to permit adjust-

ment and, in addition, there are shims available to be used at proper locations. Shim locations are used to obtain alignment of the fender to the door. (Fig. 11E-8)

When installing a fender, tighten the attaching bolts just enough to permit shifting as required. After proper alignment is obtained, tighten all attaching screws and bolts. Torque

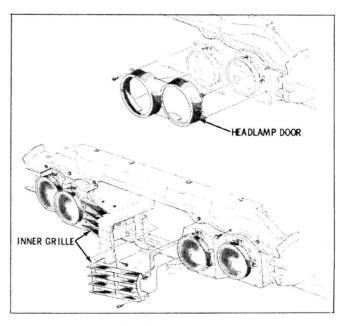

Fig. 11E-12—Headlamp Actuator Door

Fig. 11E-13—Headlamp Assembly

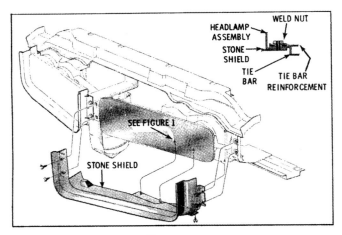

Fig. 11E-14—Stone Shield

fender-to-body bolts to 25 ft. lbs. Torque remaining screws to 20 ft. lbs. Refer to Bumper Section for bumper alignment.

FILLER PLATE (Fig. 11E-9 and 11E-10)

Removal

1. Raise car, support on floor stands, remove wheel assembly.
2. Remove fender as outlined.
3. If side being serviced has battery support attached, remove battery support.
4. For left side, remove windshield washer jar and power steering line bracket.
5. Disengage wiring harness clips from filler plate.

6. For right side, disconnect wiring from horn relay junction block, buzzer assembly and disconnect ground wire.
7. Remove filler plate to radiator support bolt.
8. Remove filler plate to frame bolts.
9. Remove filler plate.

If equipped with comfortron for right side, remove range relay. If equipped with U.H.V. ignition system, remove amplifier. Torque all attaching screws to 20 ft. lbs.

To install, reverse removal procedure.

MOLDINGS

Fender moldings, script, and rocker panel moldings:

To remove moldings and script refer to Figs. 11E-10 and 11E-11.

Brush a thick application of sealer over studs and nuts of moldings and scripts after assembly.

HEADLAMP ACTUATOR DOOR
Remove and Replace (Fig. 11-12)

1. On left side, remove three attaching bolts on vacuum tank. Slide vacuum tank over and remove bolt and nut from outer end of door. On right side, it will be necessary to remove battery.
2. Remove retainer from actuator pin and disconnect pin from actuator door.
3. Remove two screws from end of inner grille.
4. Remove nut from inner end of actuator door.
5. Open actuator door to full open position and remove actuator door.

To install, reverse removal procedure.

When installing actuator door, tape bushing to brackets to prevent loss of bushing during assembly.

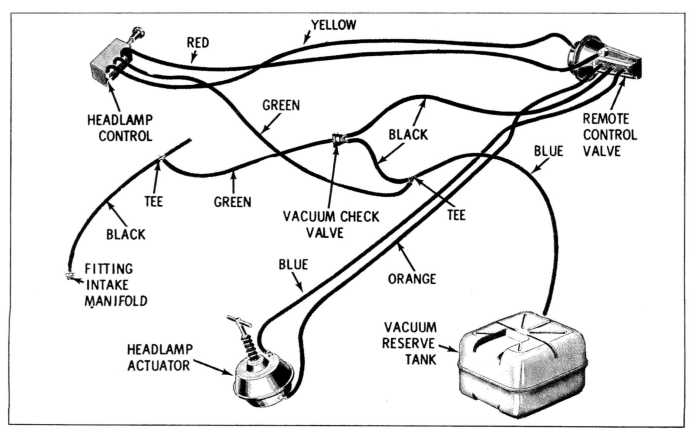

Fig. 11E-15—Headlamp Vacuum Hose Routing (Except W-34)

HEADLAMP ASSEMBLY

Removal (Fig. 11E-13 and 11E-14)

Open headlamp grille assembly and remove headlamp door and inner grille. Close headlamp grille assembly and disconnect headlamp wire connection. Remove the three upper attaching bolts. Remove the three lower attaching bolts (two are removed through opening in front bumper and one is removed from the rear of the bumper).

Slide headlamp assembly to center of car and remove through opening between upper bumper and upper radiator support.

To install reverse removal procedure.

TORONADO VACUUM OPERATED HEADLAMPS

OPERATION EXCEPT W-34 (Fig. 11E-15)

Engine operation will create a reserve supply of vacuum in the reserve tank. Vacuum will also be directed through the green hose to the center port of the headlamp control and to the center port of the remote control valve through the black hose.

With the light switch in the off position, vacuum is connected to the "OFF" port of the switch through the yellow hose to the "OFF" side of the remote control valve diaphragm. With the remote control valve in the "OFF" position, the vacuum source at the center port of the valve is connected to the "CLOSE" side of the actuator through the orange hose. The vacuum holds the actuator shaft down to keep the headlamp grilles in the closed position.

When the headlamp switch is pulled out, to turn on the lights, vacuum to the yellow hose is cut off at the switch and the "ON" port is connected to the source vacuum. This vacuum through the red hose causes the remote control diaphragm to move the valve to the "ON" position. Movement of the valve cuts off vacuum to the "OFF" port opening it to atmosphere and connects the "ON" port to vacuum. Since this port is connected to the "OPEN" side of the actuator by the blue hose, the diaphragm moves up causing the shaft to rise and open the headlamp grilles by means of the connecting levers.

In the event of a vacuum failure, the grilles may be raised manually by lifting upward on the lower edge of both grilles at the same time and holding both units in the full "UP" position for a moment to allow the catch to lock them in the "UP" position until the vacuum operation can be restored.

If the grilles do not raise and there is no vacuum failure or loss of vacuum, it will be necessary to disconnect the vacuum hose at the vacuum tank before manually lifting the grilles.

OPERATION (W-34 Only Fig. 11E-15A)

Toronados equipped with the W-34 option use a thermostatic vacuum switch in the vacuum operated headlamp system. The purpose of this switch is to open the headlamp grilles when engine coolant reaches 220°F which allows more air to pass through the radiator. The thermostatic vacuum switch is located in the left side of the radiator.

Vacuum for the entire system is provided from the intake manifold through a vacuum hose to a green hose that leads to a check valve. The vacuum splits at the check valve through

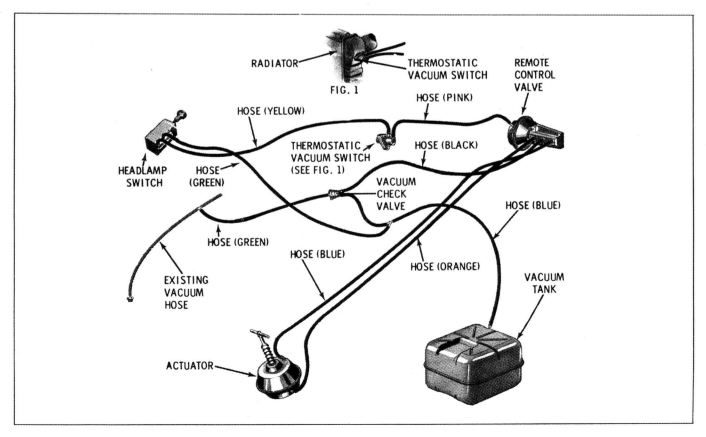

Fig. 11E-15A—Headlamp Vacuum Hose Routing (W-34 Only)

a black hose to the remote control valve. The other branch from the check valve leads to a tee through another black hose. At the tee a blue hose connects to the vacuum reserve tank and a green hose to the headlamp switch.

With the headlamp switch in the "off" position, vacuum is directed through the headlamp switch through the yellow hose to the thermostatic vacuum switch. With the engine coolant below 220°F., vacuum is directed through the thermostatic vacuum switch and through the pink hose to the closed side of the remote control valve diaphragm. With the remote control valve in the closed position, the vacuum source at the center port of the valve is connected to the closed side of the actuator through the orange hose. Vacuum holds the actuator shaft down to keep the headlamp grilles in the closed position.

With the headlamp switch in the "on" position, vacuum is cut off at the headlamp switch, depleting the vacuum in the yellow hose, thermostatic vacuum switch, pink hose and to the closed side of the remote control valve. Spring pressure inside the remote control valve moves the valve to the open position. With the remote control valve in the open position, the vacuum source at the center port of the valve is connected to the open side of the actuator through the blue hose. Vacuum holds the actuator shaft up to keep the headlamp grilles in the up position.

THERMOSTATIC VACUUM SWITCH (Fig. 11E-15A)

When the engine coolant temperature is below 220°F., the thermostatic vacuum switch is open. With the thermostatic vacuum switch open, the vacuum operated headlamp system operates in the normal way.

When the engine coolant temperature is above 220°F., the thermostatic vacuum switch closes, vacuum no longer holds the remote control valve in the closed position. Spring tension moves the valve to the open position and vacuum is directed to the actuator to the open side of the diaphragm. This moves the grilles up to allow more air for cooling to pass through the radiator. The headlamps will not come on.

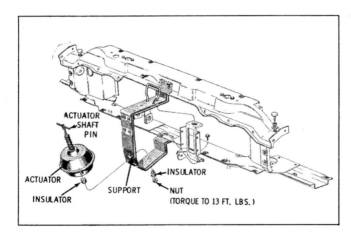

Fig. 11E-16—Headlamp Actuator Removal

HEADLAMP VACUUM ACTUATOR ASSEMBLY

Remove (Figs. 11-16 and 11-17)

1. Remove retaining clips from actuator shaft pin.
2. Disconnect actuator shaft pin from actuator door arms.
3. Remove lower radiator deflector.
4. Remove vertical center brace.
5. Remove the actuator attaching nut and insulator. Disconnect vacuum hoses from actuator.
6. Remove two bolts from actuator support to lower support.
7. Pull down on actuator support only far enough to remove actuator from the right side of actuator support.

Upper insulator may come off at this time. Note position of insulator for assembly.

8. Remove the center bolt from the valance panel and pull down on valance panel only enough to remove actuator assembly from car.

Installation

For installation, reverse removal procedure.

Torque actuator attaching nut to 13 ft. lb. and make sure actuator is free to move in lower insulator after tightening attaching nut.

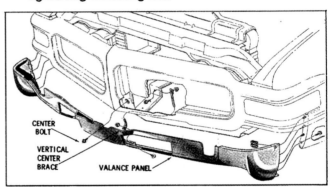

Fig. 11E-17—Valance Panel and Vertical Brace

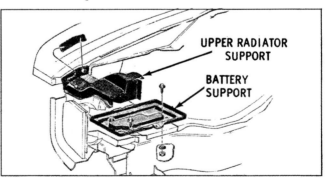

Fig. 11E-18—Battery Support

CHASSIS ELECTRICAL, INSTRUMENTS AND WIPERS

TORONADO

CONTENTS OF SECTION 12E

ITEMS LISTED IN THE TABLE OF CONTENTS ARE FOR TORONADO. FOR SERVICE PROCEDURES AND RECOMMENDATIONS NOT LISTED, REFER TO SECTION 12, 31-86 SERIES.

CHASSIS ELECTRICAL

BATTERY (ENERGIZER)

Refer to Section 12 for periodic maintenance and test procedure.

WIRING CIRCUIT

A combination junction and fuse block is mounted on the cowl under the instrument panel. Each wire from the fuse panel is color coded to simplify servicing. (Fig. 12E-1)

The wiring harness installation under the instrument panel is shown in Figs. 12E-2 and 12E-3.

The wiring harness installation in the engine compartment is shown in Figs. 12E-4, 12E-5 and 12E-7.

The fuse block, fuse size and location are shown in Fig. 12E-8.

CAPACITOR DISCHARGE IGNITION SYSTEM

Service procedure for the C. D. Ignition System used on the Toronado is the same as the procedure listed for the 31-86 Series. The only difference is in removal of the amplifier assembly.

Removal C. D. Amplifier (Fig. 12E-6)
1. Disconnect negative battery cable.
2. Disconnect the following leads from the amplifier harness assembly.
   A. Tachometer Pickup
   B. Harness Ground
   C. + and - Coil Wires
   D. Distributor Connector
   E. Connectors at Fuse Panel
   F. Connector at Junction Block
3. Remove vacuum tank.
4. Remove three retaining nuts from amplifier assembly and remove amplifier.

To install, reverse removal procedure.

CHARGING CIRCUIT (Fig. 12E-9)

The charging circuit consists of a battery, Delcotron generator, regulator and generator warning light. Cars without air conditioning are equipped with a 42 amp. generator. Cars with factory installed air conditioning are equipped with a 55 amp. generator.

TEMPERATURE GAUGES (Fig. 12E-5)

The Toronado is equipped with both a HOT light and STOP ENGINE light mounted in the instrument panel. The HOT light has an amber lens and is electrically controlled by the engine temperature switch in the intake manifold. The STOP ENGINE light has a red lens and flashing bulb and is electrically controlled by a temperature switch mounted in the head bolt between No. 5 and No. 7 cylinder.

HORNS

The horns are mounted as shown in Fig. 12E-10. Horns can be removed from the under side of car between bumper and lower tie bar.

LICENSE LAMP ASSEMBLY

In order to change either the lamp or the lens, it will be necessary to remove the license lamp assembly from the bumper. (Fig. 12E-11)

HYDRAULIC BRAKE SWITCH TESTING

For service procedures on this switch, refer to Periodic Service Chart in General Information Section.

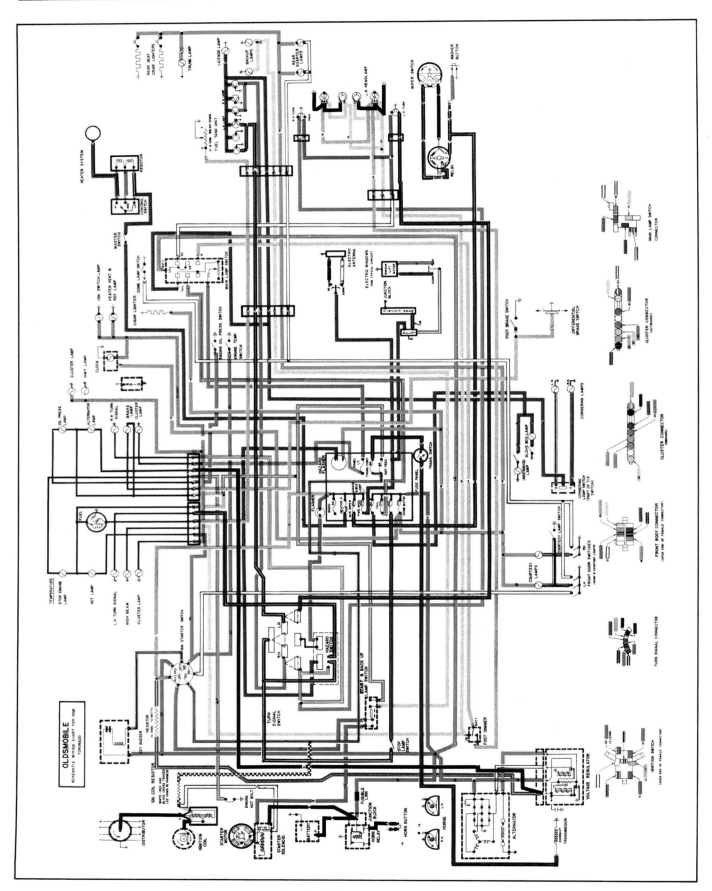

Fig. 12E-1—Wiring Diagram

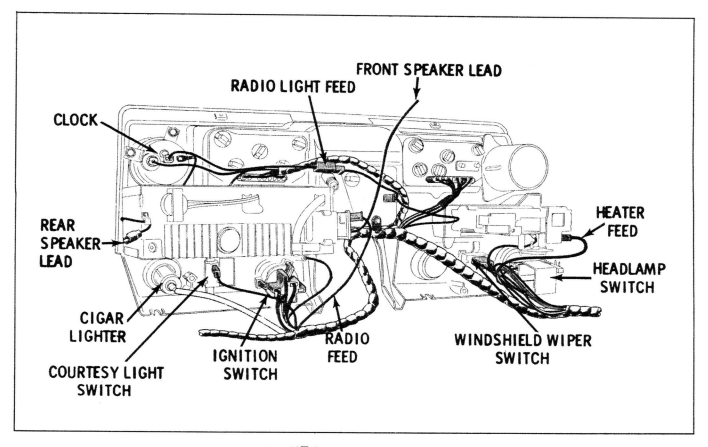

Fig. 12E-2—Instrument Panel Wiring

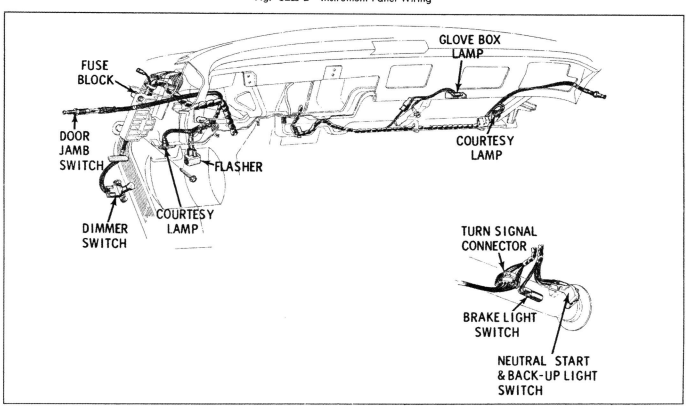

Fig. 12E-3—Instrument Panel Wiring Harness

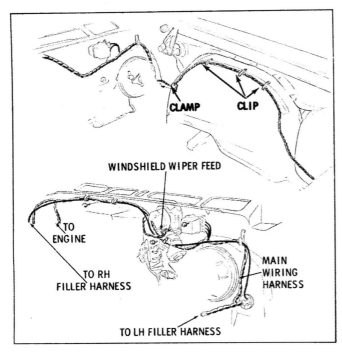

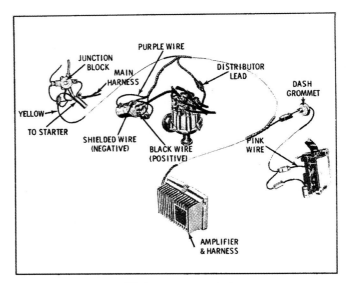

Fig. 12E-6—C.D. Pictorial Diagram

Fig. 12E-4—Chassis Wiring Harness

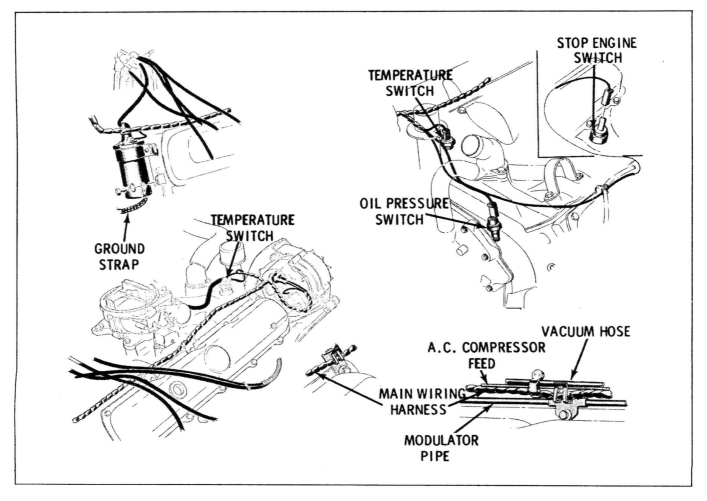

Fig. 12E-5—Engine Wiring

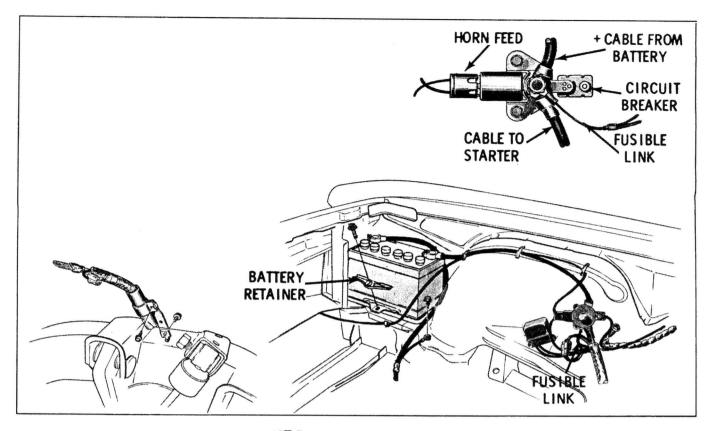

Fig. 12E-7—Battery and Cable Installation

TORONADO HORN RELAY-BUZZER (ANTI-THEFT KEY WARNING SYSTEM)

DESCRIPTION

The horn relay-buzzer operates when the driver's door is opened to remind the driver that the ignition key has been left in the ignition switch.

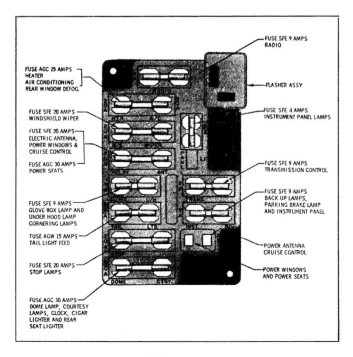

Fig. 12E-8—Fuse Block

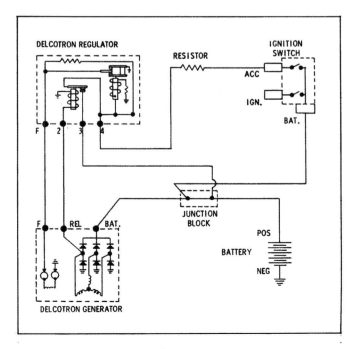

Fig. 12E-9—Charging Circuit

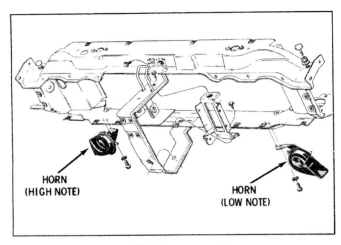

Fig. 12E-10—Horn Installation

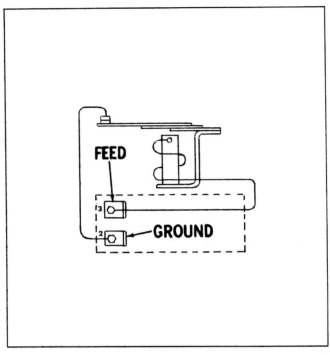

Fig. 12E-12—Buzzer Diagram

BUZZER OPERATION (Fig. 12E-12)

With the key in the off position and fully inserted into the ignition switch, the No. 2 terminal on buzzer is connected to ground through the door switch when the driver's door is opened. Current then flows from the battery, energizing the coil, then through the buzzer contacts, the ignition switch and door switch to ground. The energized coil causes the buzzer contacts to open, which de-energizes the coil, and the buzzer contacts then reclose. This cycle then repeats many times per second to give the buzzing sound. Closing the door, or removing the key will stop the buzzing action.

BUZZER CHECK

1. Make sure the key is fully inserted into the ignition switch and in the "off" position.

2. Open the driver's door, and observe the dome lamp.

3. If both the dome lamp and buzzer fail to operate, check the door switch for defects.

4. If the dome lamp is on, but the buzzer fails to operate, remove the buzzer from its mounting.

5. Connect a jumper lead from the No. 2 terminal to ground.

6. If the buzzer operates, check the ignition switch wiring and ignition switch.

7. If the buzzer does not operate, connect a voltmeter from No. 3 terminal to ground.

8. If the reading is zero, the circuit is open between this point and the battery.

9. If a voltage reading is obtained, replace the buzzer.

The No. 1 terminal on the buzzer is not used.

TAIL LAMP AND LENS (Fig. 12E-11)

REMOVE AND INSTALL (LENS OR BULB)

1. Remove the two lens retaining screws.

2. Remove the lens and gasket.

3. Bulbs may be removed if necessary.

To install, reverse removal procedure.

REMOVE AND INSTALL (LAMP ASSEMBLY)

1. Lift up rear compartment trim and disconnect wiring.

2. Remove bolts and lower rear bumper. Refer to REAR BUMPER REMOVAL, Section 14E.

3. Remove five retaining bolts from lamp assembly and remove lamp.

To install, reverse removal procedure.

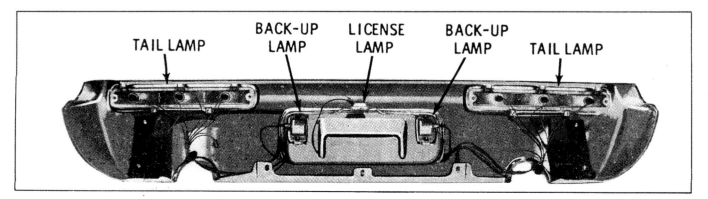

Fig. 12E-11—Tail Lamp and License Lamp

1968 LAMP USAGE
TORONADO

BULB NO.	USAGE
194	Speedometer, Odometer and Shift Indicator
194	High Beam Indicator
194	Fuel, Temperature, Ammeter and Oil Gauge
194	Turn Signal Indicator
194	Brake Warning Lamps
194	Generator Warning
194	Engine Temperature Indicator-Hot (Amber Lens)
168	Oil Pressure Warning
1895	Heater, Ventilation & Air Conditioning Control
1895	Console Compartment
1895	HMT Shift Indicator - Console Only
257	Stop Engine Warning
1445	Ignition Switch
1445	Cruise Control
1816	Electric Clock
1893	Radio Dial
631	Underhood
631	Trunk
90	Courtesy
97	Courtesy Light-Console
68	Front Seat Back
212	Rear Quarter Lamps
212	Door Lamps
212	Glove Box and Map

EXTERNAL LAMPS

BULB NO.	USAGE
97	License
1157A	Parking & Turn Signal
1157	Tail and Stop
97A	Side Marker-Front
194	Side Marker-Rear
1156	Back-Up
1195	Cornering Lamp
L-4001	Headlamp-Upper Beam
L-4002	Headlamp-Upper & Lower Beam

FUSE SPECIFICATION AND LOCATION

APPLICATION	NAME OF FUSE CIRCUIT ON FUSE BLOCK	FUSE TYPE AND AMPERES
Heater . . . . Air Conditioning . . . . Rear Window Defogger	HTR-A/C	AGC 25
Windshield Wiper	W/S Wiper	SFE 20
Electric Antenna . . . . Power Windows & Cruise Control	RELAY ANT	SFE 20
Power Seats	RELAY ANT	AGC 30
Glove Box Lamp . . . . Underhood Lamp	GL BX U/H	SFE 9
Tail Lamp Feed . . . . Cornering Lamps . . . . Side Marker Lamps	TAIL LTS	AGW 15
Stop Lamps	STOP	SFE 20
Dome Lamp, Courtesy . . . . Lamps, Clock, Cigar . . . . Lighter and Rear . . . . Seat Lighter	DOME CTSY	AGC 30
Radio	RADIO	SFE 9
Panel Lamps	PANEL LT	SFE 4
Transmission Control	TRANS	SFE 9
Back-Up Lamps . . . . Parking Brake Lamp and Instrument Panel .	INST B/U	SFE 9

The following circuits either employ circuit breakers or have fuses located as indicated.

APPLICATION	TYPE	LOCATION
Head Lamps	Circuit Breaker	In light switch
Electric Seat and/or Window Motor	Circuit Breaker	On horn relay junction
Directional Signal Flasher	3 Lamp-Yellow Cover	In clip behind instrument panel
Air Conditioner	In-Line Fuse 30 amp	In wire between junction block and high blower relay
Hazard Warning Flasher	2-8 Lamp-Green Cover	In fuse block

INSTRUMENT PANEL

TORONADO

CONTENTS OF SECTION 12EA

CONTROL PANEL (Fig. 12EA-1)

Removal

1. Disconnect negative battery cable.
2. If equipped with cruise control, disconnect control cable at regulator.
3. Disconnect speedometer cable at transmission.
4. Remove screws from R.H. lower pad assembly and filler. (Fig. 12EA-2)
5. Remove nuts "A", "B" and "C" as shown in Fig. 12EA-3 and retain wedge for use when installing.
6. If equipped with tilt and travel, tilt down to lowest position and let steering wheel rest on seat cushion. With a standard column, use a 4" x 4" block of wood between steering wheel and seat. This will help to prevent accidental disconnecting of hoses and wiring when tilting control panel out to perform service repairs.
7. Loosen bolt "A" and "B" approximately 1/4". (Fig. 12EA-2)
8. Disconnect radio lead-in.
9. Remove screws "C" and "D" (Fig. 12EA-2) and tilt control panel outward from the top.
10. Disconnect the following electrical connectors:
    a. All printed circuit multiple connectors.
    b. Radio.
    c. Clock.
    d. Ignition switch.
    e. Lighter.
    f. Headlight switch.
    g. Wiper and washer switch.
    h. Accessory switches.

11. Disconnect L.H. air outlet hose.
12. Remove the 3 attaching bolts from A/C or heater control and remove from control panel without disconnecting hoses or wiring.
13. Remove bolts "A" and "B" (Fig. 12EA-2) and remove control panel.
14. To install, reverse removal procedures. For steering column attachment refer to Section 9EA.

SERVICING INDIVIDUAL UNITS

RADIO

Removal (Fig. 12EA-5)

1. Disconnect control knobs and nuts from front of dash.
2. Remove control panel. Refer to CONTROL PANEL, Items 1 through 9.
3. Disconnect radio feed wire.
4. Disconnect dial lamp.
5. Remove attaching nut from support to radio.
6. Remove radio from rear of control panel.

CLOCK

Removal (Fig. 12EA-6)

1. Remove control panel. Refer to CONTROL PANEL, Items 1 through 9.
2. Disconnect clock feed and lamp.
3. Remove three attaching bolts.

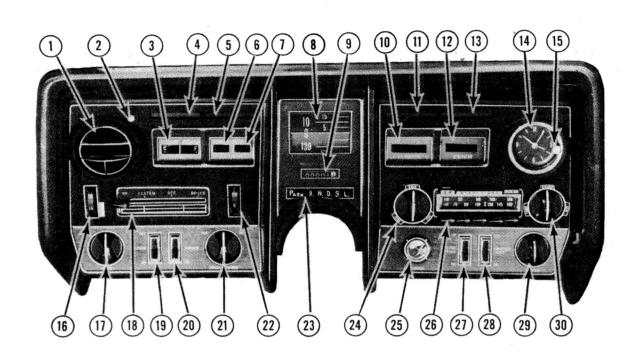

1. OUTLET L.H.
2. OUTLET KNOB L.H.
3. FUEL GAUGE
4. L.H. DIRECTIONAL INDICATOR
5. HIGH BEAM INDICATOR
6. HOT TEMPERATURE INDICATOR
7. "STOP ENGINE" WARNING LIGHT
8. SPEEDOMETER
9. ODOMETER
10. OIL PRESSURE INDICATOR
11. BRAKE WARNING LIGHT
12. CHARGING SYSTEM INDICATOR
13. R.H. DIRECTIONAL INDICATOR
14. CLOCK
15. CLOCK SETTING KNOB

16. TEMPERATURE DIAL
17. LIGHT SWITCH
18. HEATER OR A/C CONTROL
19. WINDSHIELD WIPER SWITCH
20. WINDSHIELD WASHER SWITCH
21. CRUISE CONTROL SWITCH
22. CRUISE CONTROL SPEED SELECTOR
23. TRANSMISSION INDICATOR
24. RADIO VOLUME AND TONE CONTROL
25. IGNITION SWITCH
26. RADIO
27. ELECTRIC ANTENNA SWITCH
28. COURTESY LIGHT SWITCH
29. CIGAR LIGHTER
30. MANUAL STATION SELECTOR

Fig. 12EA-1—Control Panel

4. Remove clock from rear of control panel.

IGNITION SWITCH (Fig. 12EA-7)

Removal

1. Disconnect negative battery cable.
2. Turn switch to ACC. position.
3. Insert a paper clip into the small hole in the front side of the switch, while turning the key counterclockwise the lock will pop out.

4. Remove the escutcheon using Tool BT-6817-1.
5. Remove switch from back side of control panel and remove wiring connector.

WINDSHIELD WIPER AND WASHER SWITCH (Fig. 12EA-7)

Removal

1. Disconnect negative battery cable.
2. Disconnect wiring at switch.

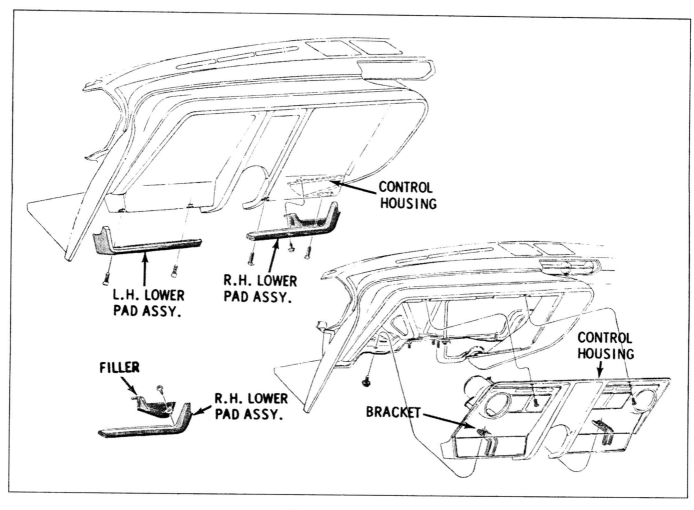

Fig. 12EA-2—Control Panel Attachment

3. Remove attaching bolts and remove from rear of control panel.

HEADLAMP SWITCH (Fig. 12EA-7)

Removal

1. Disconnect negative battery cable.
2. Remove knob by first pulling knob out to the HEAD-LIGHT position, then depress the spring loaded button on switch body and pull knob out of switch assembly.
3. Remove escutcheon nut using Tool BT-6817-2.
4. Remove headlamp switch from rear of control panel.
5. Disconnect wiring and vacuum hoses.
Carefully disconnect vacuum hoses and note the color coding of each.

CRUISE CONTROL SWITCH (Fig. 12EA-8)

Removal

1. Disconnect negative battery cable.
2. Remove knob and using Tool BT-6817-2 remove escutcheon.
3. Remove switch from rear of control panel.
4. Disconnect wiring harness at connector.
5. Remove switch.

ACCESSORY SWITCHES (Fig. 12EA-7)

Removal

1. Disconnect negative battery cable.
2. Disconnect wiring at switches.
3. Remove attaching bolts.

CIGAR LIGHTER (Fig. 12EA-7)

Removal

1. Disconnect negative battery cable.
2. Disconnect feed wire from lighter.
3. Unscrew retainer from rear of control panel while holding lighter case and escutcheon.
4. Remove case and escutcheon from front of control panel.

HEATER AND/OR A/C CONTROL ASSEMBLY (Fig. 12EA-9)

Removal

1. Remove control panel, refer to CONTROL PANEL, Items 1 through 9.
2. Disconnect wiring connectors.
3. Disconnect vacuum hoses.
4. Remove three attaching bolts and remove control assembly.

SPEEDOMETER CABLE

Removal

1. Remove control panel, Steps 1 through 9.

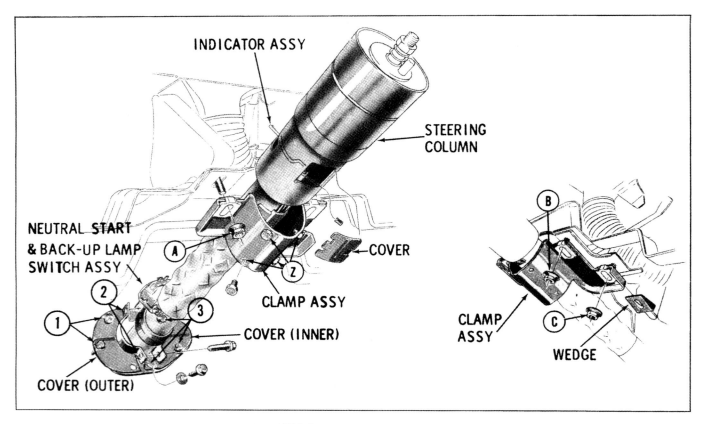

Fig. 12EA-3—Steering Column Attachment

2. Disconnect cable at speedometer.
3. Remove cable.

SPEEDOMETER

Removal

1. Remove control panel. Refer to CONTROL PANEL, Items 1 through 9.
2. Disconnect printed circuit connectors.
3. Remove radio. Refer to Radio Removal.
4. Remove eight attaching screws, cover to cluster.

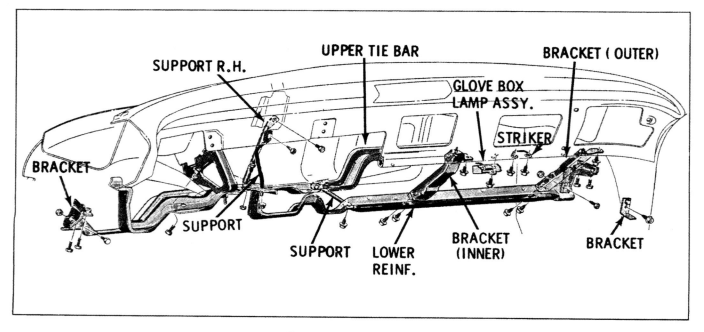

Fig. 12EA-4—Instrument Panel Supports

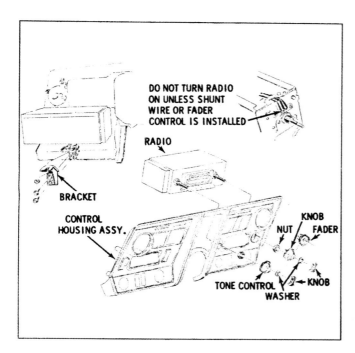

Fig. 12EA-5—Radio Mounting

5. Remove four attaching bolts, cover to speedometer head.

OUTLET L.H. (Fig. 12EA-6)

Removal

1. Remove control panel. Refer to CONTROL PANEL, Items 1 through 9.
2. Remove shut off knob from front of panel.
3. Remove three attaching bolts.

CRUISE CONTROL DIAL ASSEMBLY (Fig. 12EA-10)

Removal

1. Remove control panel. Refer to CONTROL PANEL, Items 1 through 9.
2. Disconnect dial lamp.
3. Remove two attaching bolts.

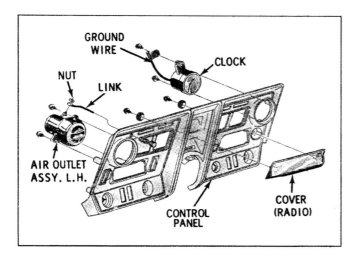

Fig. 12EA-6—Clock Mounting

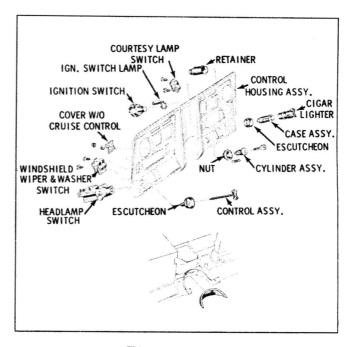

Fig. 12EA-7—Switch Attachments

4. Remove dial assembly from rear of control panel.

OIL AND GENERATOR PRINTED CIRCUIT

Removal

1. Remove control panel. Refer to CONTROL PANEL, Items 1 through 9.
2. Disconnect wiring connectors.
3. Remove four screws, printed circuit to control housing.
4. Remove lamp sockets.
5. Printed circuit can be replaced at this time.

FUEL GAUGE AND PRINTED CIRCUIT

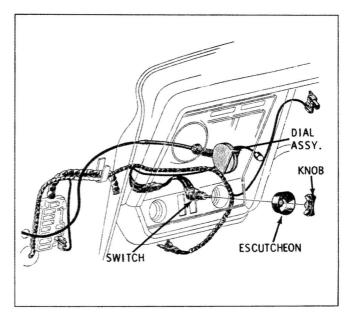

Fig. 12EA-8—Cruise Control Switch

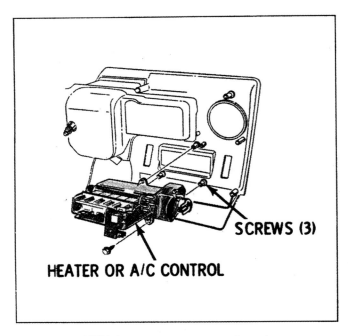

Fig. 12EA-9—Heater or A.C. Control Attachment

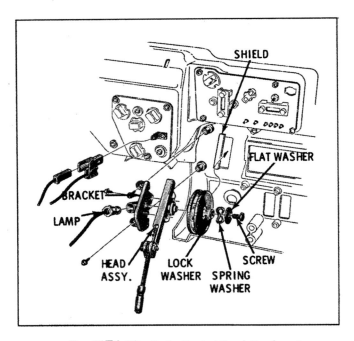

Fig. 12EA-10—Cruise Control Head Attachment

Removal

1. Remove control panel. Refer to CONTROL PANEL, Items 1 through 9.

2. Disconnect wiring harness connector.

3. Remove four attaching bolts (printed circuit to control housing) and remove assembly.

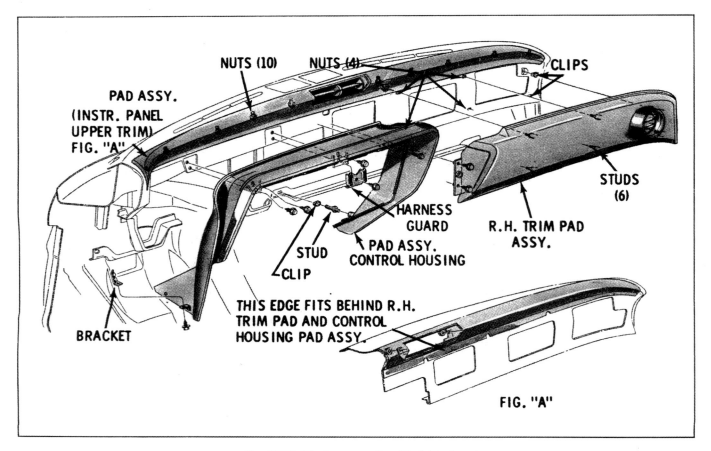

Fig. 12EA-11—Instrument Panel Pad Attachment

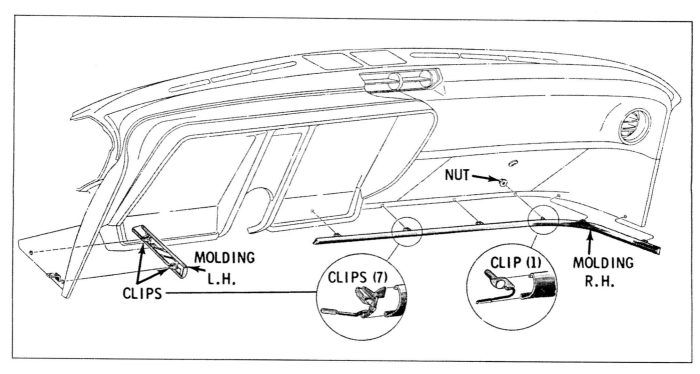

Fig. 12EA-12—Molding Attachment

4. Fuel gauge: Remove three nuts and remove gauge.

5. Printed circuit: Remove fuel gauge and lamps to replace.

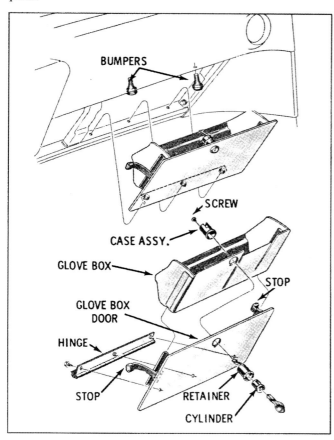

Fig. 12EA-13—Glove Box Attachment

PRINTED CIRCUIT—SPEEDOMETER LAMPS

Removal

1. Remove control panel. Refer to CONTROL PANEL, Items 1 through 9.

2. Disconnect wiring connector.

3. Remove lamp sockets.

4. Remove three attaching bolts and remove printed circuit.

APPLIQUE PANELS—L.H. AND R.H.

Removal

L.H. applique panel can be replaced without removing any of the controls, by lifting edge of applique panel and peeling panel from control panel.

R.H. applique panel will require removing the escutcheon from the ignition switch and then removing applique as described for L.H. applique.

PAD ASSEMBLY—CONTROL HOUSING (Fig. 12EA-11)

Removal

1. Remove control panel. Refer to CONTROL PANEL REMOVAL, Steps 1 through 9.

2. Remove the (7) attaching screws (pad to instrument panel).

3. Pulling pad assembly at lower R.H. corner will pull stud from clip and pad assembly can be removed.

PAD ASSEMBLY R.H. (Fig. 12EA-11)

Removal

1. Remove pad assembly—control housing and glove box. Refer to PAD ASSEMBLY—CONTROL HOUSING and GLOVE BOX REMOVAL.

2. Disconnect R.H. vent outlet hose.

3. Remove two screws and four nuts and remove pad. Extreme R.H. attaching studs will pull out of clips.

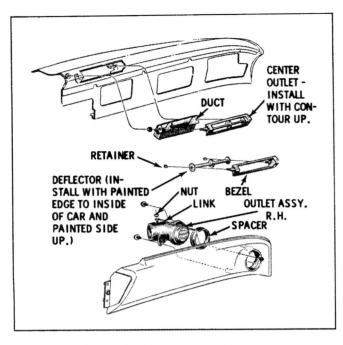

Fig. 12EA-14—Center and R.H. Outlets

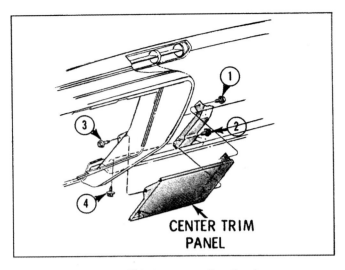

Fig. 12EA-15—Center Trim Panel

PAD ASSEMBLY—INSTRUMENT PANEL UPPER TRIM (Fig. 12EA-11)

Removal

1. Remove pad assembly R.H., Refer to PAD ASSEMBLY R.H. REMOVAL.

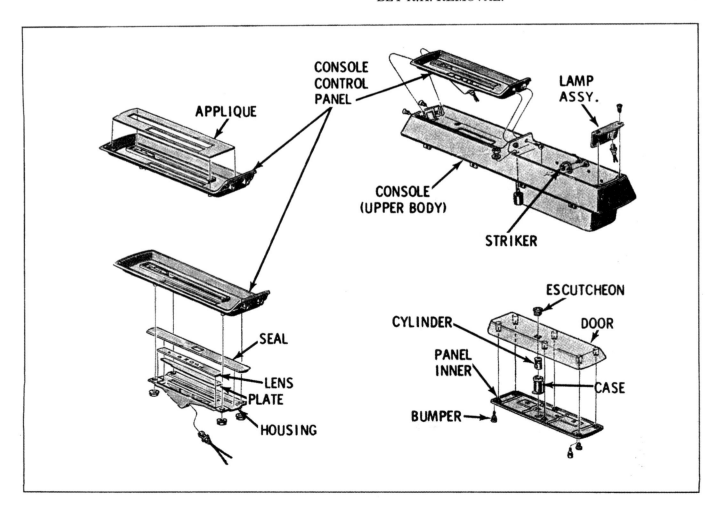

Fig. 12EA-16—Console Attachment

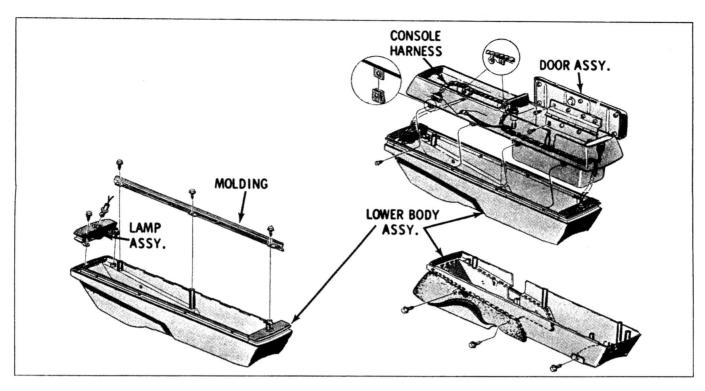

Fig. 12EA-17—Console Attachment

2. Remove the ten attaching nuts as shown in Fig. 12EA-11.

3. Remove pad assembly.

MOLDING—LOWER L.H. (Fig. 12EA-12)

Removal

By carefully prying, molding clips will unsnap and molding can be removed.

MOLDING—LOWER R.H. (Fig. 12EA-12)

Removal

Remove nut from clip bolt as shown in Fig. 12EA-12 and carefully pry molding at clips and remove.

GLOVE BOX (Fig. 12EA-13)

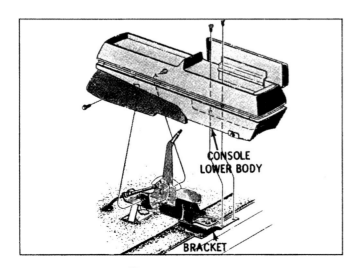

Fig. 12EA-18—Console Attachment

Removal

1. Remove glove box lock assembly.
2. Pull up on glove box to remove.

GLOVE BOX DOOR (Fig. 12EA-13)

Removal

1. Remove glove box.
2. Remove three attaching screws, hinge to glove box door.

OUTLET R.H. (Fig. 12EA-14)

Removal

1. Remove knob from shut off control rod.
2. Remove glove box. Refer to GLOVE BOX, REMOVAL.
3. Remove hose from outlet.
4. Remove three attaching screws and remove from rear of R.H. trim pad assembly.

CENTER OUTLET

Removal

1. Remove pad assembly (Instrument Panel Upper Trim). Refer to PAD ASSEMBLY (Instrument Panel Upper Trim).
2. Remove nuts from center outlet and remove from front of instrument panel.

CENTER TRIM PANEL (Fig. 12EA-15)

Removal

1. Open glove box and remove screw No. 1.
2. Remove screws 2, 3 and 4 from behind dash.
3. Remove panel from front of dash.

CONSOLE (Figs. 12EA-16-17-18)

For console attachment, refer to Figs. 12EA-16-17-18.

WINDSHIELD WIPER SYSTEM
TORONADO

DESCRIPTION (Figs. 12EB-1 and 12EB-2)

The wiper system used on the Toronado consists of the transmission assembly and a round two-speed depressed park motor, very similar to that used on 54 through 86 Series. For servicing the gear and motor section, refer to Section 12B, ROUND MOTOR.

The motor has two external leads with an external over-all measurement of 4-1/2" long. The motor has a gray colored drive gear with a gear ratio of 51:1. The motor crankarm is identified by the letter G.

A windshield washer system is used on all motors and the servicing of the pump is covered in Section 12B. Refer to Fig. 12EB-3 for hose routing and nozzle fastening.

For additional specifications, refer to Section 12B, ROUND MOTOR.

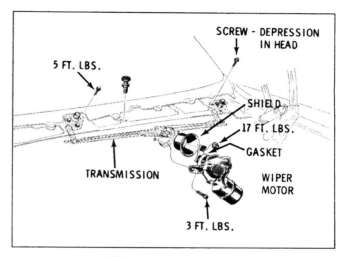

Fig. 12EB-1—Wiper Motor Attachment

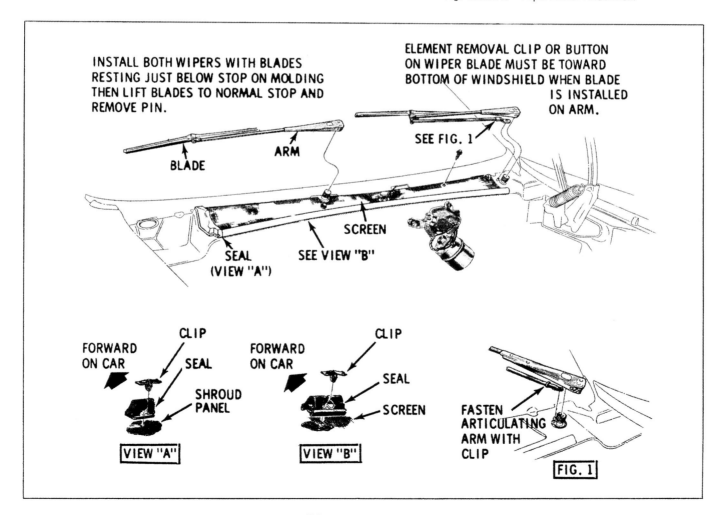

Fig. 12EB-2—Wiper Blade Adjustment

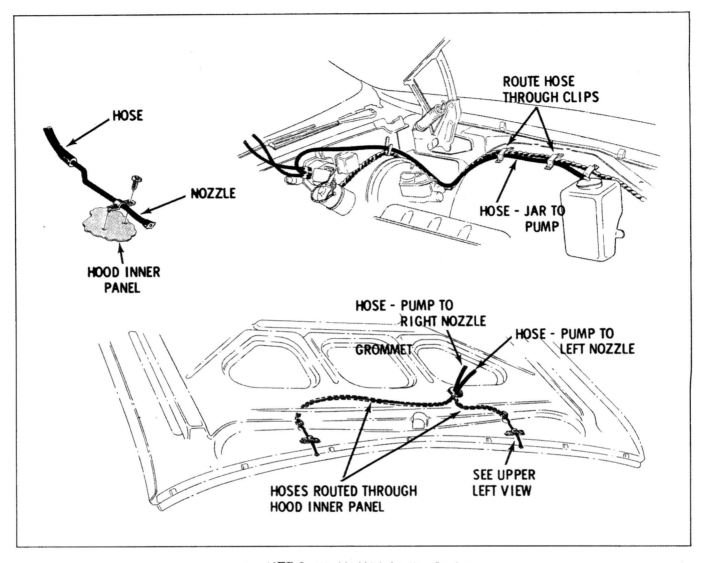

Fig. 12EB-3—Windshield Washer Hose Routing

RADIATOR AND GRILLE

ITEMS LISTED IN THE TABLE OF CONTENTS ARE DIFFERENT FOR TORO-NADO SERIES. FOR SERVICE PROCEDURES AND RECOMMENDATIONS NOT LISTED, REFER TO SECTION 13, 31-86 SERIES.

CONTENTS OF SECTION 13E

MAINTENANCE RECOMMENDATIONS

For maintenance recommendations, refer to Section 6K, ENGINE COOLING SYSTEM. For cooling system capacities, refer to Section 0, GENERAL INFORMATION AND PERIODIC MAINTENANCE.

RADIATOR (Figs. 13E-1 and 13E-2)

Removal

1. Drain radiator.
2. Remove upper radiator baffle. Detach the fan shroud and slide back over fan.

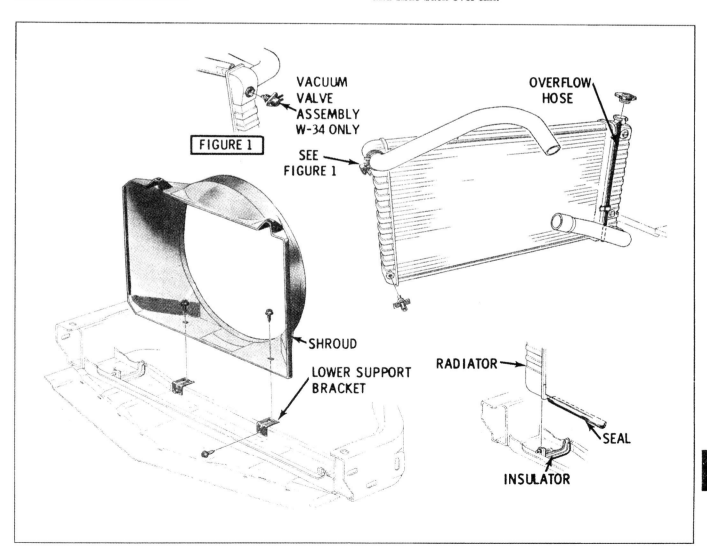

Fig. 13E-1—Radiator, Overflow Hose and Fan Shroud

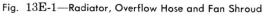

3. Disconnect upper and lower radiator hose and overflow hose.

4. Disconnect and cap automatic transmission cooler lines.

5. Lift radiator upward to disengage from lower supports and remove from car.

Installation

1. Install radiator in lower support being sure seals are correctly positioned.

2. Connect automatic transmission cooler lines, upper and lower radiator hoses and overflow hose.

3. Install fan shroud and upper radiator baffle.

4. Fill radiator using existing coolant or new coolant as recommended in GENERAL INFORMATION, Section 0.

GRILLE ASSEMBLY (Figs. 13E-3 and 13E-4)

Grille Removal

1. Remove nuts holding grille to grille plate.

2. Remove nuts holding script and name plate to grille.

Grille Installation

1. Install script and name plate to grille.

2. Install grille to grille plate.

Grille Plate Removal

1. Remove vacuum hose at vacuum tank and raise grille assembly to open position.

2. Remove retainer ring and lever from actuator.

3. Remove nut and bushing from center pivot bolt.

4. Loosen and slide rearward, battery or vacuum tank, to gain access to outer pivot nut and bushing.

Grille Plate Installation

1. Tape bushings to grille plate.

2. Install grille plate into position and install outer pivot bolt and nut.

3. Raise grille and install inner pivot nut.

4. Install lever and retaining ring.

5. Connect vacuum hose at vacuum tank.

6. Reposition and install either the vacuum tank or battery.

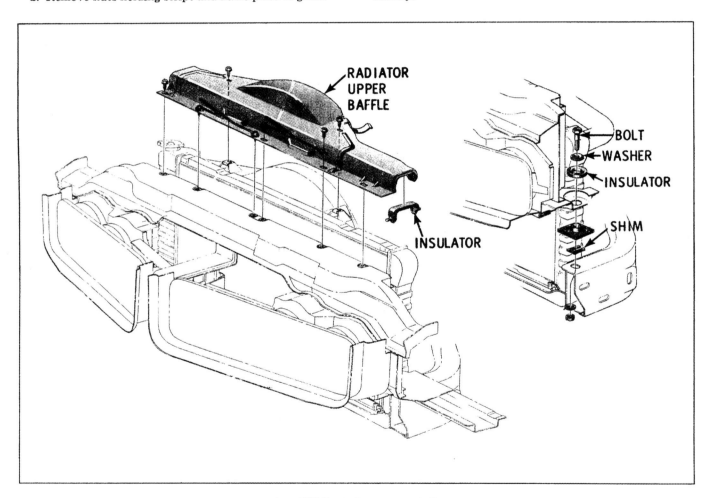

Fig. 13E-2—Radiator Upper Baffle

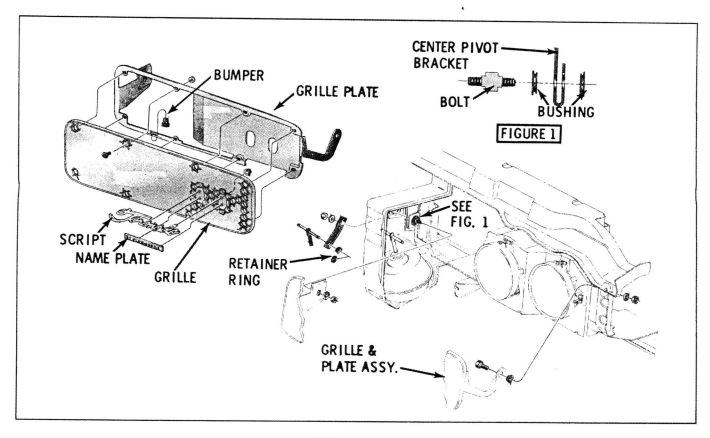

Fig. 13E-3—Grille Assembly

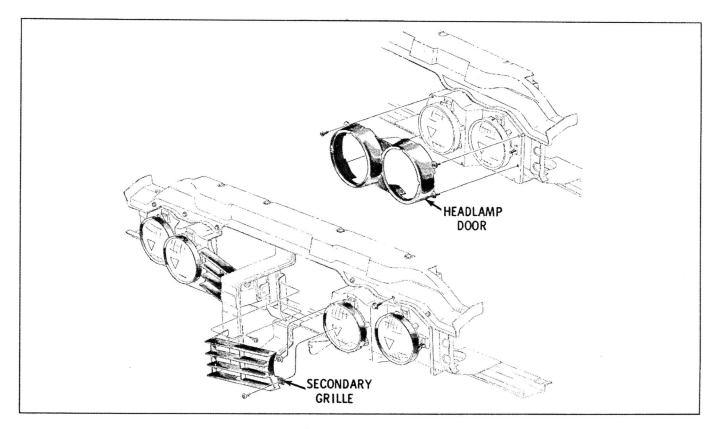

Fig. 13E-4—Secondary Grille Assembly

BUMPERS

TORONADO

CONTENTS OF SECTION 14E

FRONT BUMPER (Fig. 14E-1)

Removal

1. Disconnect both lamp assembly wiring.
2. Loosen outer brace to frame attaching bolt.
3. Remove bolt from brace at center of bumper.
4. Remove the 4 bracket to bumper attaching bolts and remove bumper

To install, reverse removal procedures. Align bumper horizontally and bumper to fender clearance should be the same on both ends. The braces are elongated for alignment purposes. Torque as indicated under **TORQUE SPECIFICATIONS**.

REAR BUMPER (Fig. 14E-2)

Removal

1. From under car, remove bracket to frame attaching bolts. Note number of shims used.

2. Remove bumper to center brace attaching bolt.
3. From inside of trunk, disconnect wiring to back-up lamps, tail lamps and license lamp.
4. Lift rear compartment trim to gain access to bracket attaching bolts and remove bolts, then remove bumper assembly.

To install, reverse the removal procedures. Bumper alignment is obtained by using shims as shown on Fig. 14E-2.

BACK-UP LAMP ASSEMBLY

Either back-up lamp assembly can be removed from the bumper through the opening at the license plate bracket.

TAIL LAMP ASSEMBLY

Removal

1. Disconnect tail lamp wiring.
2. Remove bracket to frame bolt. (Inside rear compartment).
3. Remove bracket to frame bolt. (From under car).

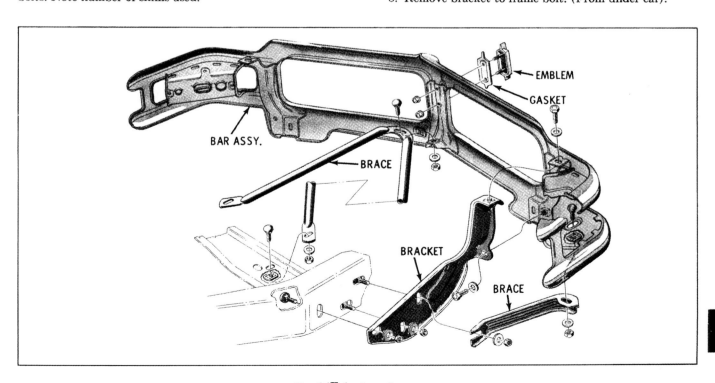

Fig. 14E-1—Front Bumper

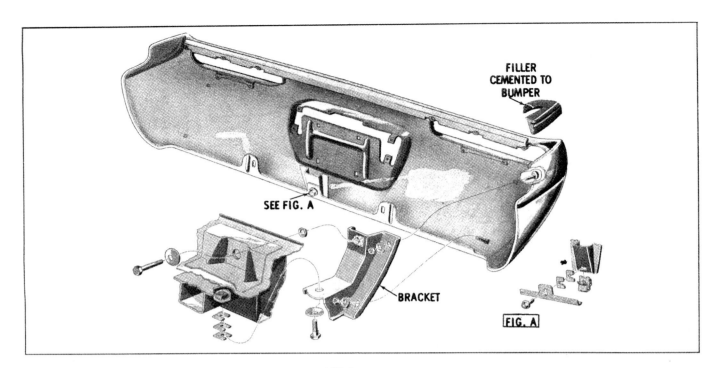

Fig. 14E-2—Rear Bumper

4. Remove the center brace to bumper attaching bolt.

5. Carefully pull bumper end rearward until tail lamp assembly attaching nuts can be removed.

To install, reverse removal procedure.

TAIL, BACK-UP AND LICENSE LENS OR BULBS

All lens or bulbs can be removed from rear of bumper by removing the attaching bolts.

PARK, TURN AND MARKER LAMP ASSEMBLY (FRONT)

Removal

1. For R.H. remove battery. For L.H. remove vacuum reserve tank.

2. Remove attaching bolts and remove lamp assembly from front of bumper.

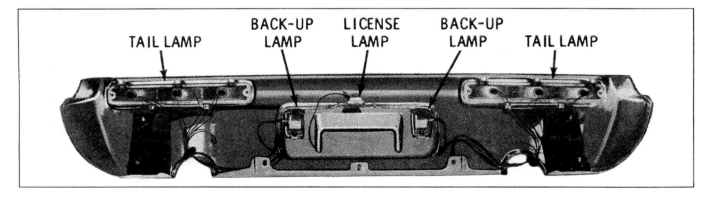

Fig. 14E-3—Rear Bumper Lamp Mountings

TORQUE SPECIFICATIONS

APPLICATION	FT. LBS.
FRONT BUMPER	
Center Brace to Bumper Nut	45
Center Brace to Frame Nuts	45
Bracket to Bumper Nuts	45
Bracket to Frame Nuts	70
Outer Brace to Bumper Nut	45
REAR BUMPER	
Bracket to Frame Bolts	60
Bracket to Bumper Nuts	25
Brace to Bumper Bolt	18

ACCESSORIES

TORONADO

CONTENTS OF SECTION 15E

Fig. 15E-1—Deluxe Radio

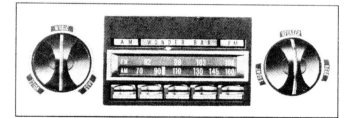

Fig. 15E-2—AM-FM Wonder Bar

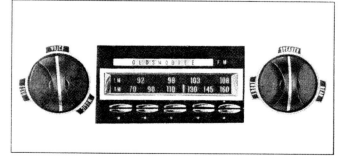

Fig. 15E-3—AM-FM Stereo

RADIO (Figs. 15E-1, 15E-2 and 15E-3)

Radio service procedures not listed in this section can be found in Section 15.

Remove and Install (Fig. 15E-4)

1. Disconnect negative battery cable.
2. Remove right hand filler to control housing pad assembly.
3. Remove shift indicator needle.
4. Remove steering column attaching nuts and lower bracket.
5. Disconnect speedometer cable at transmission.
6. Remove attaching nuts from cluster lower brackets, leaving brackets attached to the instrument panel.
7. Remove two upper instrument panel screws and lay cluster assembly on steering column.

A protective covering must be used to protect steering column.

8. Remove radio knobs, washers or rear seat speaker control.
9. Remove radio attaching nuts and escutcheons.
10. Disconnect all wiring and antenna lead-in.
11. Remove lower radio support bracket attaching nut.
12. Remove radio from instrument panel.
To install, reverse the removal procedure.

STEREO ADAPTER REMOVAL

Refer to Fig. 15E-5 when performing the following.

1. Disconnect negative battery cable.
2. Disconnect cables to rear seat speaker and to receiver assembly.
3. Remove two retaining screws and remove adapter assembly.
To install reverse removal procedure.

The Stereo Receiver and Adapter have identical serial numbers and the units must be kept together for service and installation.

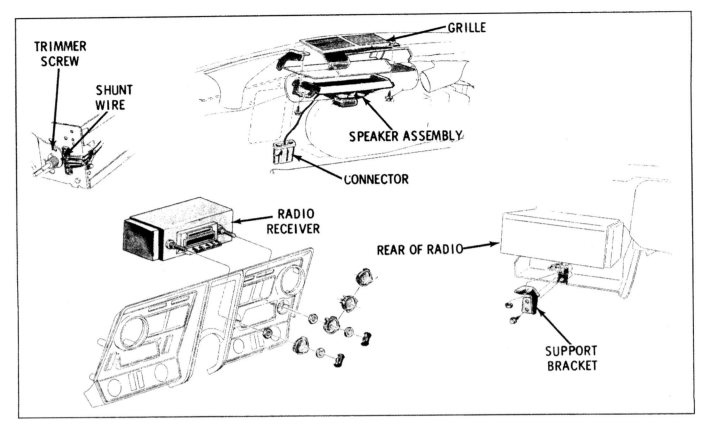

Fig. 15E-4—Radio and Speaker Installation

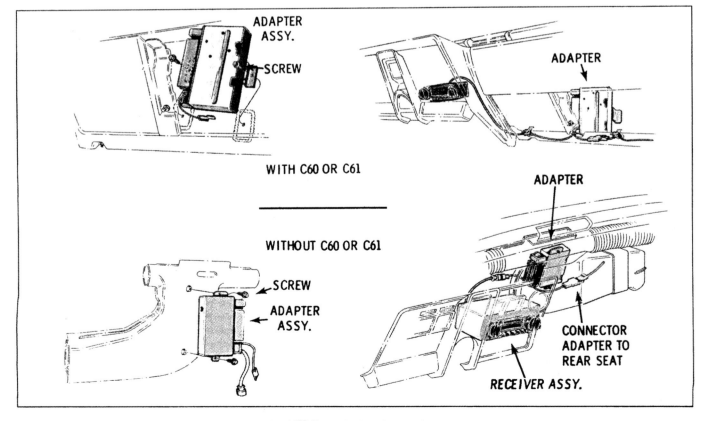

Fig. 15E-5—Radio Installation - Stereo

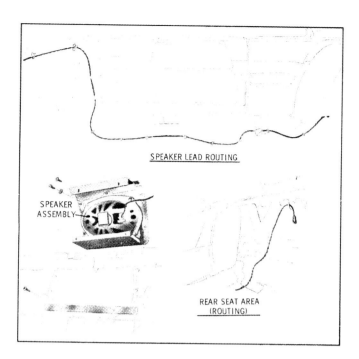

Fig. 15E-6—Rear Seat Speaker Installation

RADIO DIAL LAMP

The radio lamp plugs into the top side of the receiver. It is not necessary to remove the receiver to replace the bulb.

TRIMMER ADJUSTMENT (Fig. 15E-4)

1. Extend antenna to approximately 31 inches.

   AM-FM radio must be set on the AM band.

2. Remove the manual tuning knob and escutcheon or rear seat speaker fader control, if so equipped.
3. If car is equipped with a rear seat speaker, insert a shunt wire as shown in Fig. 15E-4.

   Do not turn on radio unless shunt wire is installed.

4. Turn the volume control full on and tune the receiver to a weak station at approximately 1400 kilocycles.
5. With a small screwdriver, adjust the antenna trimmer until loudest signal is received.
6. Turn off radio. Remove shunt wire, if equipped with a rear seat speaker.

FRONT SPEAKER REMOVAL (Fig. 15E-4)

1. Disconnect battery, remove glove box and remove stereo tape player if equipped.
2. If non A.C., remove right trim panel and disconnect lower instrument panel reinforcement to the right corner of control housing. Loosen control panel and lay cluster assemblies on steering column as outlined in Radio R and R. Remove heater outlet, ventilator air duct adapter, and duct.
4. Remove right hand defroster duct and hose (A.C. only).
5. Disconnect lead from receiver and remove two speaker attaching screws and remove speaker.

TAPE PLAYER—STEREO

For test procedures refer to Section 15.

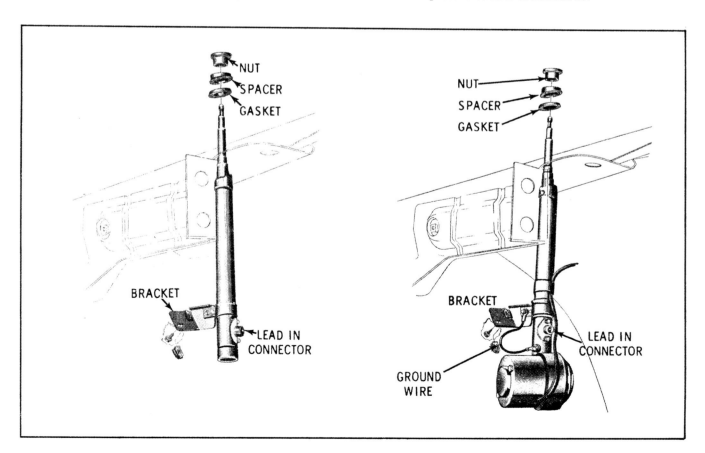

Fig. 15E-7—Antenna Installation

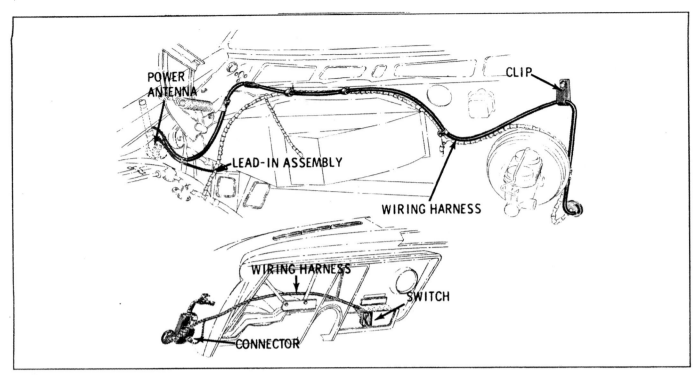

Fig. 15E-8—Power Antenna Lead In Routing

TAPE PLAYER REMOVAL

Refer to Figs. 15E-9, 15E-10 when performing the following steps.)

1. Disconnect negative battery cable.

2. Remove four attaching screws and remove player assembly.

3. Disconnect all wiring at connectors.

To install, reverse removal procedure.

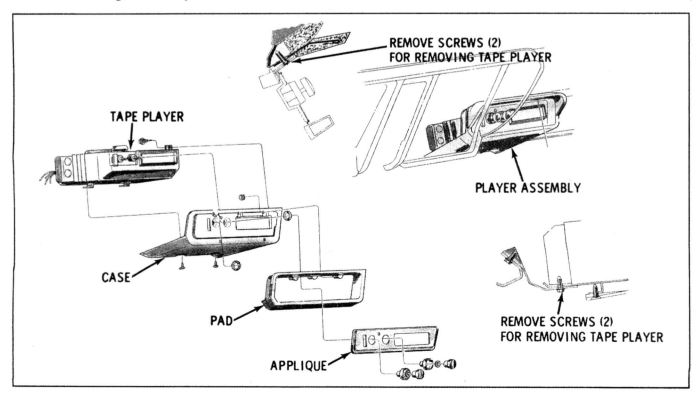

Fig. 15E-9—Stereo Tape Player Installation

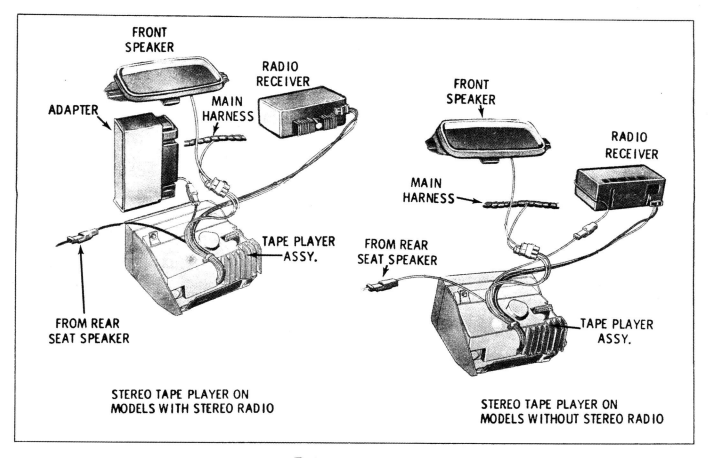

Fig. 15E-10—Stereo Tape Player Wiring

CRUISE CONTROL

For service procedures not listed in this section, refer to Section 15.

DESCRIPTION

The automatic lock-in Cruise Control is a driver-operated speed regulation device that may be used either as a speed reminder or as an automatic speed control for any car speed between 25 mph and 85 mph.

The major components of the automatic lock-in Cruise Control are: the regulator assembly mounted in the engine compartment and the selector control assembly, located on the lower left side of the instrument panel.

The regulator is driven by a flexible drive cable from the transmission. The drive cable also drives the speedometer cable that runs from the regulator to the speedometer. The selector control assembly is connected to the regulator by means of a bowden cable. A rod connects the regulator to the accelerator and carburetor throttle rod.

The selector control assembly is shown in Fig. 15E-11. Speed settings are secured by use of a calibrated thumb wheel. The selector dial is numbered with speed markings from 30 mph to 80 mph, in increments of 5 mph. The numbers on the dial are illuminated for night driving. The switch located below selector dial turns the unit on and off, and activates the unit for automatic control.

When the switch is in the OFF position, the unit has no effect at any car speed. Once the switch has been moved to the ON position, the unit is on and accelerator back pressure will be felt as a warning at the speed the selector dial is set for. Depressing the pushbutton momentarily activates an auto-

matic relay switch in the regulator indicating the unit is set for automatic control. Once the unit is set for automatic control, the unit will lock in automatically, whenever back pressure is felt on the accelerator pedal at the speed the selector dial is set for.

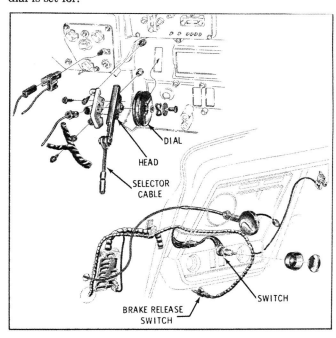

Fig. 15E-11—Speed Selector Control

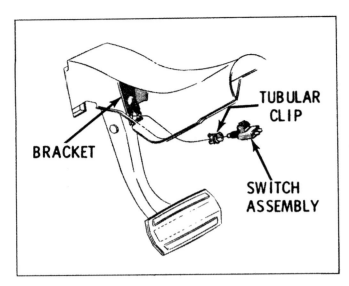

Fig. 15E-11A—Brake Release Switch

The complete electrical circuit for the Cruise Control is shown in Fig. 15E-12. A reversible electric motor in the regulator actuates the rod between the regulator and the carburetor. Motor feed points for forward and reverse energizing of the motor are closed and opened by a governor, under control of a governor spring that is compressed or relaxed to calibrated positions, corresponding to selected speeds by the bowden cable leading to the selector control.

SPEED SELECTOR CONTROL AND/OR CABLE REMOVAL AND INSTALLATION (Fig. 15E-11)

1. Disconnect battery.
2. Remove retainer spring and pull bowden cable to remove from regulator.
3. Attach a five-foot piece of wire or heavy string to disconnected end of control cable. If necessary, rotate selector dial to low speed position to facilitate attachment of wire.

Attaching the wire or string to end of control cable will insure cable being routed properly when selector control assembly is reinstalled.

4. Remove steering column attaching nuts and lower bracket.
5. Remove shift indicator needle.
6. Disconnect speedometer cable at transmission.
7. Remove attaching nuts from cluster lower brackets, leaving brackets attached to the instrument panel.
8. Remove two upper instrument panel screws and lay cluster assembly on steering column.

A protective covering must be used to protect steering column.

9. Remove two screws attaching control to instrument panel and remove control assembly and cable.

Refer to "Cable Adjustment" (Section 15) and reverse removal procedure.

BRAKE RELEASE SWITCH ADJUSTMENT (Fig. 15E-11A)

1. Insert switch into tubular clip until switch body seats on tubular clip.

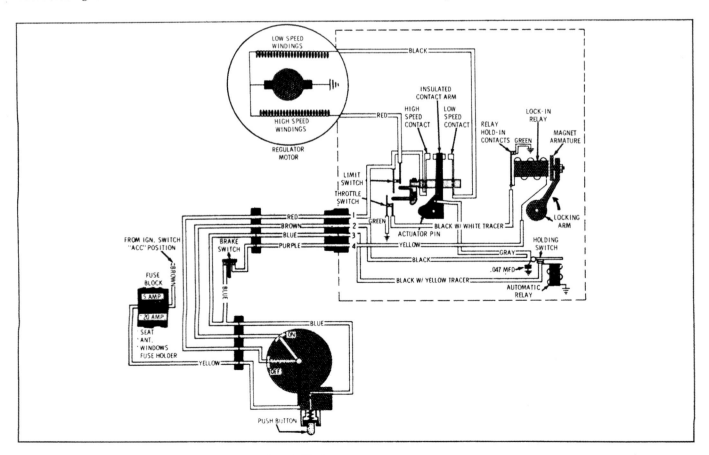

Fig. 15E-12—Cruise Control Schematic

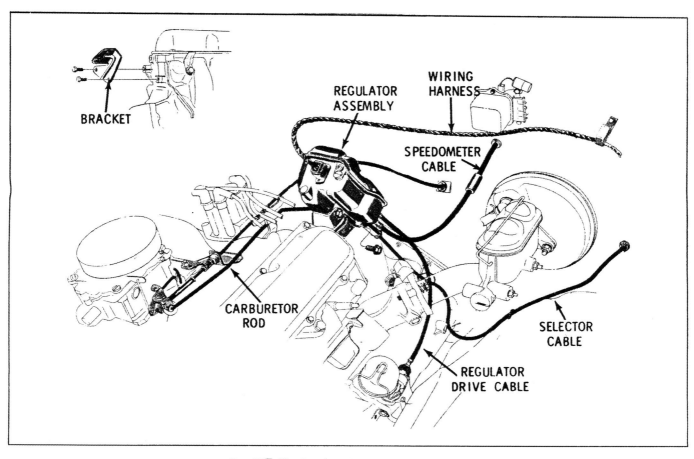

Fig. 15E-13—Regulator Mounting - Cable Routing

2. Pull brake pedal rearward against internal pedal stop. Switch will be moved in tubular clip providing proper adjustment.

REGULATOR (Fig. 15E-13)

Removal

Whenever a regulator is removed, the car can be driven with the speedometer operating by removing the regulator cables from the speedometer and installing a standard speedometer cable and housing assembly.

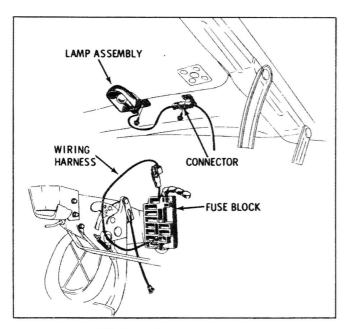

Fig. 15E-14—Under Hood Lamp Installation

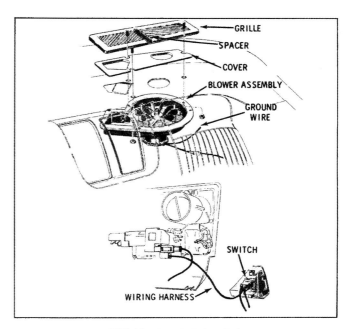

Fig. 15E-15—Rear Window Defogger

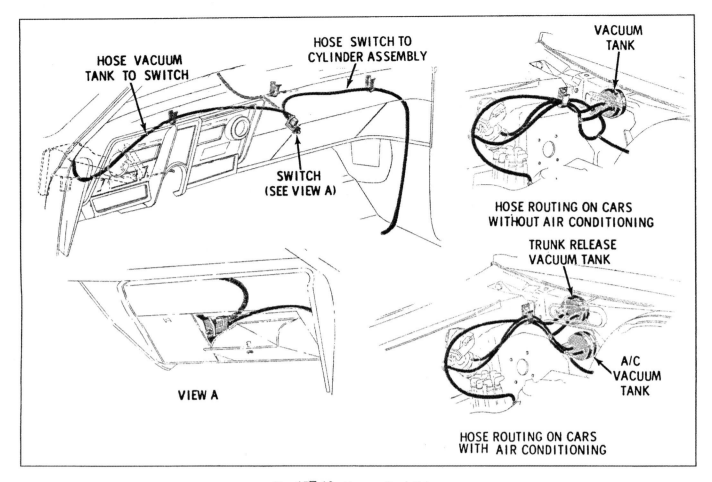

Fig. 15E-16—Vacuum Trunk Release

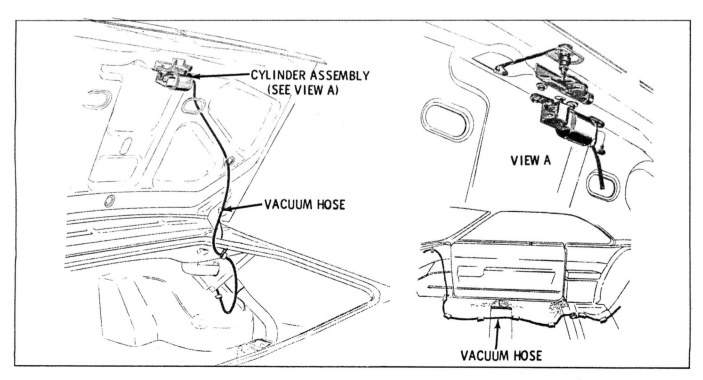

Fig. 15E-17—Vacuum Trunk Release

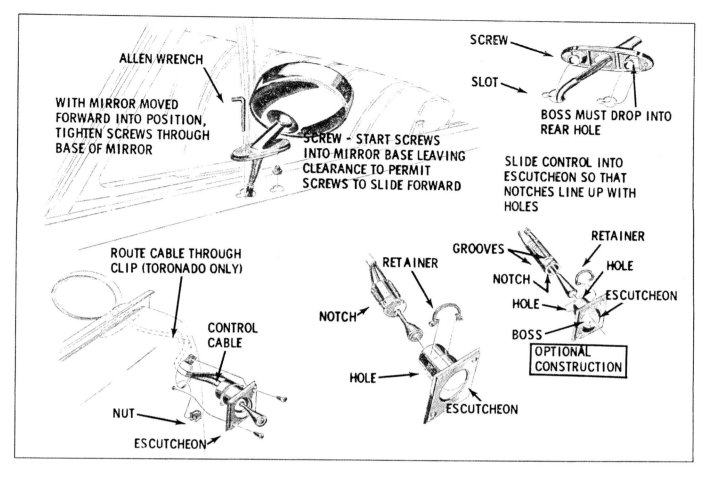

Fig. 15E-18—Remote Control Mirror

1. Disconnect multiple electrical connector at regulator.
2. Disconnect drive cable and speedometer cable at regulator.
3. Remove retainer spring and pull bowden cable to remove from regulator.
4. Disconnect accelerator rod at exterior arm on regulator.
5. Remove two bolts securing regulator to mounting bracket and remove regulator, leaving mounting bracket attached to the engine.

Installation

1. Position regulator on mounting bracket and secure to bracket with two bolts.
2. Connect accelerator rod to exterior arm.
3. Push bowden cable into dust shield and secure with retainer spring.
4. Rotate selector dial to low speed stop to secure control cable into adjusting coupling.

This step must be performed or unit will control in "ON" position or lock in "AUTO." position at low speed, regardless of selected setting.

5. Connect drive cable and speedometer cable to regulator.
6. Connect multiple electrical connector at regulator.

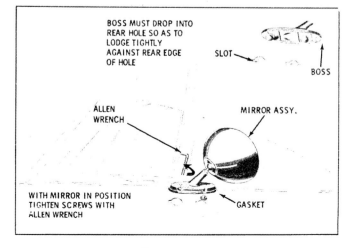

Fig. 15E-19—Outside Mirror

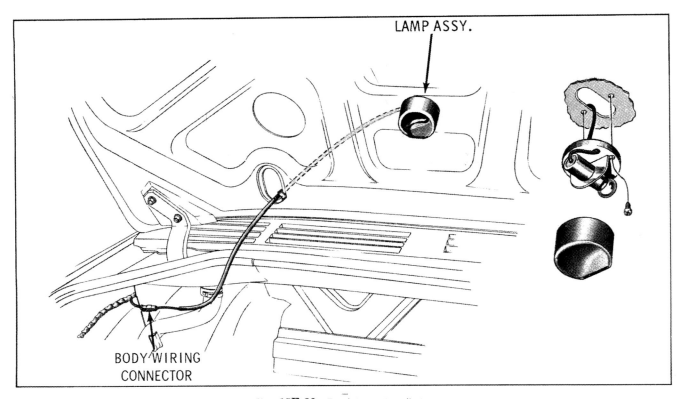

Fig. 15E-20—Trunk Lamp Installation

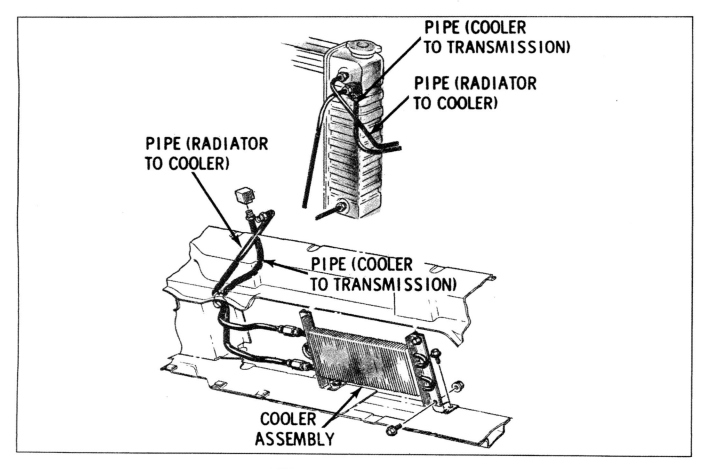

Fig. 15E-21—Transmission Oil Auxiliary Cooler

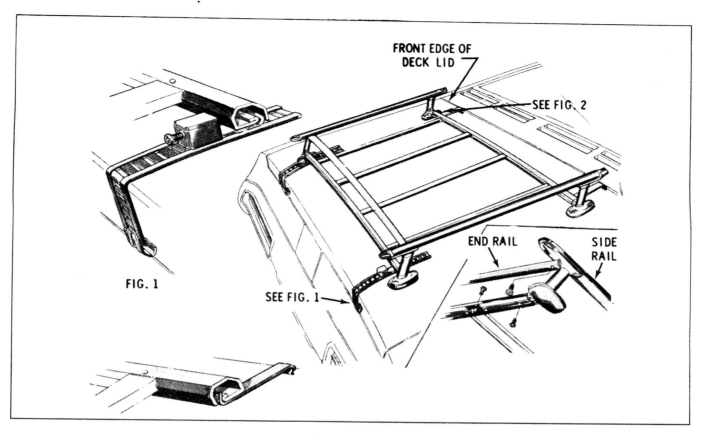

Fig. 15E-22—Luggage Carrier

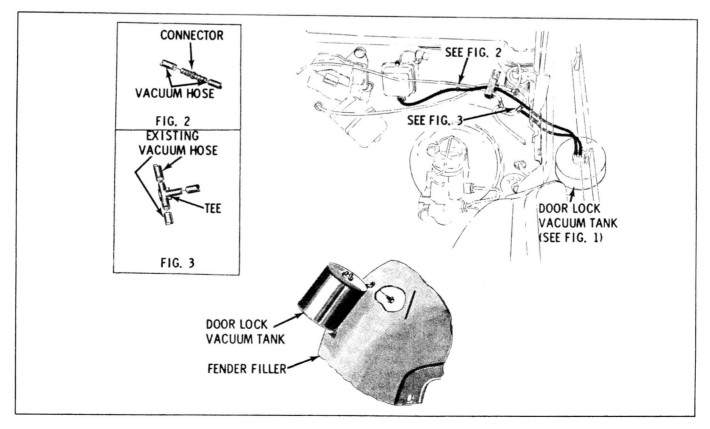

Fig. 15E-23—Vacuum Door Lock Hose Routing

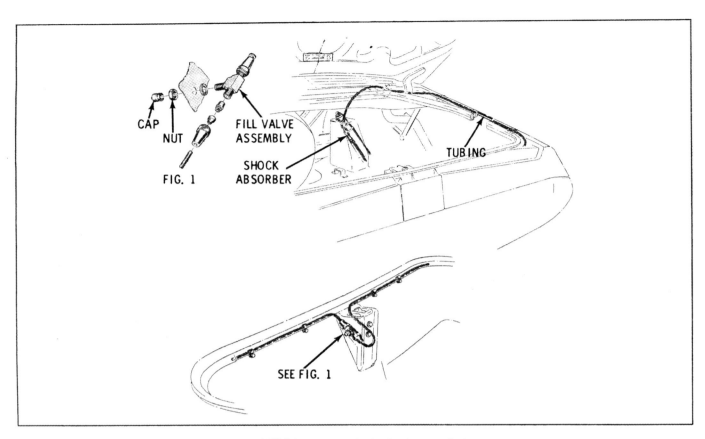

Fig. 15E-24—Superlift Shock Absorber Installation

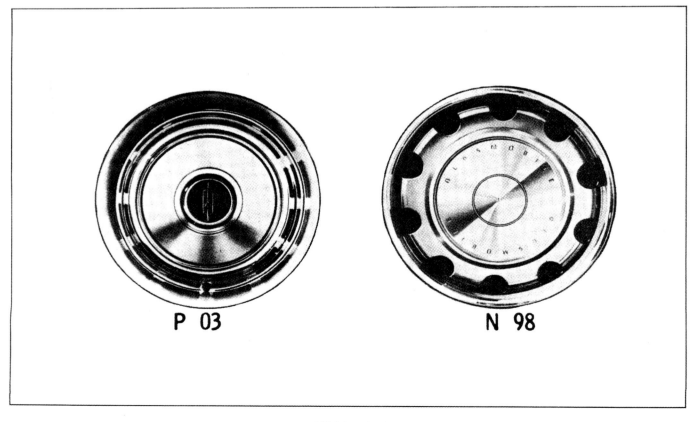

Fig. 15E-25—Wheel Discs